AF505824

Contested State Identities and Regional Security in the Euro-Mediterranean Area

Contested State Identities and Regional Security in the Euro-Mediterranean Area

Raffaella A. Del Sarto

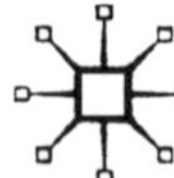

CONTESTED STATE IDENTITIES AND REGIONAL SECURITY IN THE EURO-MEDITERRANEAN AREA
© Raffaella A. Del Sarto, 2006.

First published in 2006 by
PALGRAVE MACMILLAN™
175 Fifth Avenue, New York, N.Y. 10010 and
Houndmills, Basingstoke, Hampshire, England RG21 6XS
Companies and representatives throughout the world.

PALGRAVE MACMILLAN is the global academic imprint of the Palgrave Macmillan division of St. Martin's Press, LLC and of Palgrave Macmillan Ltd. Macmillan® is a registered trademark in the United States, United Kingdom and other countries. Palgrave is a registered trademark in the European Union and other countries.

ISBN-13: 978–1–4039–7063–3
ISBN-10: 1–4039–7063–7

Library of Congress Cataloging-in-Publication Data

Del Sarto, Raffaella A.
    Contested state identities and regional security in the Euro-
  Mediterranean Area / Raffaella A. Del Sarto.
       p. cm.
    Includes bibliographical references and index.
    ISBN 1–4039–7063–7
     1. European Union countries—Relations—Mediterranean Region.
  2. Mediterranean Region—Relations—European Union countries.
  3. European Union—Mediterranean Region. 4. National
  security—Mediterranean Region. 5. Political stability—Israel.
  6. Israel—Politics and government—1993– 7. Political stability—Egypt.
  8. Egypt—Politics and government—1981– 9. Political stability—Morocco.
  10. Morocco—Politics and government—1999– I. Title.

JZ1570.A545D45 2006
355′.03301822—dc22   2005054531

A catalogue record for this book is available from the British Library.

Design by Newgen Imaging Systems (P) Ltd., Chennai, India.

First edition: July 2006

10 9 8 7 6 5 4 3 2 1

Printed in the United States of America.

To Nadir

Contents

Acknowledgments   ix

Abbreviations and Acronyms   xi

Introduction   1

Part I   The Argument and Its Setting

1. Region-Building and Contested State Identities   9

2. Theoretical Framework   29

3. Historical Background and Regional Perspective   55

Part II   Case Studies

4. Israel   87

5. Egypt   131

6. Morocco   177

Conclusion   221

Notes   235

Referenes   247

Index   273

Acknowledgments

Above all, this research has benefited from the support of my two former Ph.D. supervisors, Emanuel Adler and Alfred Tovias. Always constructive and encouraging, Emanuel's suggestions immensely contributed to the sharpening of my arguments, and thanks to him, I rediscovered the fascination of IR theory. In spite of his numerous commitments, he always found the time for providing exceptionally valuable feedbacks on my draft chapters as well as for stimulating discussions on world politics. Alfred was always extremely supportive in both academic and practical matters, in spite of our disagreements on a number of political issues. My research benefited immeasurably from his in-depth knowledge of Euro-Mediterranean relations, his down-to-earth criticism, his attention to details, and our sometimes very Mediterranean style of discussing current political events. It is difficult to find the right words to thank both Alfred and Emanuel for their extraordinary level of academic and personal support throughout the years.

I am also especially grateful to Richard Gillespie and Joel Peters for their highly valuable comments on what was then my doctoral thesis and their consistent encouragement. During 2000–2002, my research benefited from a doctoral grant of the Leonard Davis Institute for International Relations at the Hebrew University of Jerusalem, to which I would like to express my gratitude. In the process of substantially revising the original manuscript in 2005, I am very grateful to the Robert Schuman Centre of the European University Institute in Florence for providing a unique working environment.

The preparation of this book substantially benefited from a large number of (mostly informal) discussions with government officials, academics, NGO activists, journalists, and businesspeople across the Euro-Mediterranean area. I would like to thank them for their patience and highly valuable insights. For many fruitful discussions over the years, I would also like to thank my colleagues and friends working on Euro-Mediterranean issues, academics and practitioners alike. Thanks to all those who care about the people of the Mediterranean/Middle East, although, as we all know, dealing with the politics of this area is sometimes exasperating. My friends and colleagues Federica Bicchi and Tobias Schumacher deserve a very special "thank you" for the ongoing exchange of ideas, as well as for their amity.

On the personal side of things, I am very thankful to my family for their support and for always being there for me. I would also like to thank Sharon Lev and Sabaï Ramedhan-Levi (and Ari) for their fantastic friendship, particularly during the difficult times of the *Intifada* in Israel/Palestine. Also, I am grateful to Susan Vahabzadeh, Conny Blum, and Armin Schmittfull for being great friends during so many years. Finally, I am immensely grateful to Nadir ("the rare one" indeed) for being there all the way. He provided crucial emotional and logistical back-up and succeeded in making me laugh even at times when that was the last thing I felt like doing.

Abbreviations and Acronyms

ACRS	Working Group on Arms Control and Regional Security
AKP	*Adalet ve Kalkinma Partisi*, Justice and Development Party—Turkey
ASEAN	Association of Southeast Asian Nations
ASU	Arab Socialist Union—Egypt
CAP	Common Agricultural Policy
CEDEJ	Centre d'Études et de Documentation Économique, Juridique et Sociale, Cairo
CFSP	Common Foreign and Security Policy (of the EU)
Commission	Commission of the European Communities (also European Commission)
CSCE	Conference on Security and Co-operation in Europe
CSCM	Conference on Security and Co-operation in the Mediterranean
EC	European Community (or European Communities)
EFTA	European Free Trade Area
EIB	European Investment Bank
EMP	Euro-Mediterranean Partnership
ENP	European Neighbourhood Policy
EP	European Parliament
ESDP	European Security and Defence Policy
EU	European Union
EuroMeSCo	Euro-Mediterranean Study Commission (EMP network of strategic studies institutes)
FEMISE	Forum Euro-Mediterranéen des Instituts Economiques (EMP network of economic research institutes)
FIS	*Front Islamique du Salut*, Islamic Salvation Front—Algeria

GMP	Global Mediterranean Policy
IBDR	International Bank for Development and Reconstruction
IMF	International Monetary Fund
IR	International Relations (as an academic discipline)
MAP	Mediterranean Action Plan
MDS	*Mouvement Démocratique Social*—Morocco
MEDA	*Mesures d'accompagnement* (financial instrument of the EMP)
MENA	Middle East and North Africa
MNP	*Mouvement National Populaire*—Morocco
NAFTA	North American Free Trade Area
NATO	North Atlantic Treaty Organization
NDP	National Democratic Party—Egypt
NGO	Nongovernmental organization
NPT	Non-Proliferation Treaty
NRP	National Religious Party (Mafdal)—Israel
OAS	Organization of African States
OPEC	Organization of Petroleum Exporting Countries
OSCE	Organization for Security and Co-operation in Europe
PA	Palestinian Authority
PJD	*Parti de la Justice et du Développement, al-hizb al-'adala wa at-tanmia*—Morocco
PKK	*Partiya Karkerên Kurdistan*, Kurdistan Workers Party
PLO	Palestine Liberation Organization
PND	Parti National Démocratique—Morocco
Polisario Front	*Frente Popular de Liberación de Saguía al Hamra y Río de Oro*, Popular Front for the Liberation of Saguía al-Hamra and Río de Oro—Western Sahara
RNI	*Rassemblement National des Indépendants*—Morocco
Tagammu'	*Al-hizb at-tagammu' al-watani at-taqaddumi al-wahdi*, National-Progressive Unionist Party—Egypt
UC	*Union Constitutionnelle*—Morocco
UJT	United Torah Judaism (ultra-orthodox party list)—Israel
UMA	*Union du Maghreb Arabe*, Arab Maghreb Union
UN	United Nations
UNDP	United Nations Development Programme

UNEP	United Nations Environment Programme
UNFP	*Union Nationale des Forces Populaires*—Morocco
UNODC	United Nations Office on Drugs and Crime
USFP	*Union Socialiste des Forces Populaires*—Morocco
WEU	West European Union
WMD	Weapons of mass destruction

Introduction

Explanations of the lamentable status of Mediterranean regional security generally tend to focus on the fate of Arab–Israeli peacemaking. This study aims at highlighting a different aspect, namely the negative impact of unsettled state identities on the emergence of regional security schemes in the Mediterranean area. More specifically, the case under consideration is the Euro-Mediterranean Partnership (EMP) initiative of the European Union (EU), which was launched in November 1995 in Barcelona. During the first years of its existence, the EMP relied on a region-building approach to regional security, thus implying the promotion of common interests and common regional themes. However, implicitly or explicitly the EMP's region-building approach was bound to affect the self-definition of states, the type of regional relations, and the preferred concept of regional order. By focusing on the case studies of Egypt, Israel, and Morocco, this study argues that domestic conflicts over state identities put a strain on the ability of states to consistently engage in Euro-Mediterranean region-building and to develop a strategy toward regional security. Thus, this analysis attracts the attention to *domestic constraints* to regional security on a Euro-Mediterranean basis.

With the start of the Middle East peace process in the early 1990s, the Mediterranean witnessed a dramatic increase in diplomatic activity aimed at promoting stability and security. The EMP (or Barcelona Process), then comprising the 15 EU member states and 12 "southern" parties, was certainly the most encompassing policy initiative addressing Mediterranean security. However, this initiative did not seek to tackle security problems in the conventional way. Indeed, the EMP did not exclusively focus on the military aspects of security, it did not solely involve governments and the military, and neither was it aimed against a common enemy, as is often the case in "classical" security schemes. Rather, the primary aim of the Barcelona Process was to promote extensive regional cooperation in a large number of different issue areas by involving various sectors of state and society. Moreover, the initiative emphasized the importance of common interests, common problems, and shared regional features in an alleged Euro-Mediterranean region. While the EMP can be seen as an original experiment of constructing a *security region*, it could not rely on any blueprints or instruction manuals. Indeed, the few cases that may qualify as successful security regions, such as the EU itself, NATO, or ASEAN, cannot be separated from the specific historical conditions under which they emerged. In addition, these cases greatly differ from each other in their purpose, rationale, institutional framework, and degree of integration.

The success of the EMP's region-building approach depended on whether the participating states would be willing and able of truly becoming part of the region under construction. In order to do so, they would have to alter their self-definition, type of regional relations, and the concept of regional order. Thus, the EMP's region-building approach had an implicit, yet significant impact on the *identity of states*. Yet, most states in the southern Mediterranean are facing domestic problems related to their political identity and the core values that characterize the state. Indeed, most Arab countries face the well-known tension between pan-Arab and statist identities, while they are simultaneously challenged by political Islam, a growing presence of religion in general, and "Western" values of modernization. Similarly, Turkey and Israel have witnessed internal conflicts regarding the primacy of secular versus religious, modern versus traditional, and "Western" versus "Middle Eastern" values. An unspecified "Mediterranean identity" is latently present in all these countries, albeit with a rather marginal political significance. In addition, most states in the Mediterranean must deal with the problem of ethnic and religious minorities, while they are also affected by processes of economic and cultural globalization. In short, most of these countries find themselves in a continuous and often difficult search for their identity. In view of these constraints, the question is, then, whether these states are capable of altering their self-definition in order to become part of a "new" Euro-Mediterranean region.

Seeking to answer this question necessitates an analysis of both regional and domestic politics across the Mediterranean. Moreover, the altered prospects of peace and regional security since the launching of the Barcelona Process must be considered. Indeed, during much of the 1990s, multilateralism and collective security were the signs of the times, particularly in the Mediterranean and Middle East

(Walt 1991; Karsh and Sayigh 1994; Maoz 1997). At the same time, there was an increasing preoccupation with alternative approaches to security in the study of International Relations (IR). Influenced by the unpredicted and surprisingly peaceful end of the cold war, IR had started to depart from its traditional focus on "hard security" issues, strategic conditions, and military strength and to give greater importance to domestic factors, culture, and identities. The EU's attempts to forge a Euro-Mediterranean region as an alternative approach to security corresponded to this particular historical context and general ideational development. Less than a decade later, however, the prospects of Euro-Mediterranean region-building dramatically deteriorated. The second Palestinian *Intifada*, or uprising, erupted at the end of September 2000, the Middle East peace process collapsed, and in the aftermath of the terrorist attacks on New York and Washington in September 2001, Samuel Huntington's division of the world into allegedly clashing civilizations gained currency (Huntington 1996). Differentiated considerations of complex phenomena in world politics threaten to give way to black-and-white thinking patterns, in which there are *evil states* that form an axis (Bush 2002), in which the "West" is contrasted to Islam, and the latter becomes a synonym for terrorism. Indeed, these simplifying thinking patterns translate into statements on the "superiority of the Western civilization," as Italian prime minister Silvio Berlusconi propagated (*Corriere della Sera* September 27, 2001), and into calls for launching a *crusade* against (Islamist) terrorism, to mention the ill-fortunate first reaction of U.S. president George W. Bush (*New York Times* September 17, 2001: 2). Animosity against Muslims has currently taken hold of the "West," including EU states, where it is often linked to the issue of immigration. States with predominantly Muslim populations have reacted with consternation to these developments. At the same time, the persistence of violence on the Israeli-Palestinian track, including Palestinian suicide bombings and harsh Israeli policies vis-à-vis the Palestinians, led to the reemergence of the "old" Arab-Israeli fault-line. Israel's military superiority and the perceived tolerance of its policies by the "West" have further strengthened anti-Western sentiments in many Arab Mediterranean states, and the U.S.-led invasion of Iraq in 2003 has partly fueled such sentiments even further. The EU's regional security initiative has undoubtedly suffered from all these developments. But they have also overshadowed any alternative explanation for the difficulties of the EMP. However, the domestic identity constraints to Euro-Mediterranean security, which stand at the center of this study, were present well before the collapse of the Middle East peace process and the events of 9/11. In fact, the EMP lagged far behind the expectations and witnessed repeated setbacks ever since it was launched. In spite of the initial interest of the participating parties, most EMP partners lacked a coherent strategy toward Euro-Mediterranean regional security, in the event that there was any strategy at all.

With the EU launching the European Neighbourhood Policy in 2003–2004 in the context of the EU's latest round of enlargement, Euro-Mediterranean relations have entered a new phase. Although the Barcelona Process is formally still in place, the Neighbourhood Policy departs from the EMP's original region-building approach by proposing a differentiated and bilaterally oriented policy (Del Sarto and Schumacher 2005). Hence, given the altered regional and global parameters of Euro-Mediterranean relations, the core time-span of this investigation encompasses the first seven years of the EMP, that is, from November 1995 until the end of 2002. Thus, the end date of our investigation is set roughly two years after the outbreak of the second *Intifada* and one year after the events of 9/11.

This book, which consists of two main parts, is structured along the following lines: The first part, which comprises three chapters, elaborates on the link between contested state identities and regional security in the Euro-Mediterranean area from a theoretical, historical, and regional perspective. Thus, by focusing on the specific features of the EMP initiative and its implications for state identity, the first chapter develops the argument and its underlying assumptions, while the second chapter takes the reader to the theoretical underpinnings of regional security and region-building, state identity, domestic conflicts over state identity, and foreign policy. Starting in the early 1990s, the third chapter provides a brief historical background to the EMP, and it also discusses Euro-Mediterranean relations and domestic politics in the southern Mediterranean from a broad regional perspective. The second part of this book moves to the detailed and empirical examination of three case studies, namely Israel, Egypt, and Morocco. Each of the three empirical chapters makes three moves: It first explores the emergence of the portrayed identity of the respective state, along with the salience of alternative (and possibly incompatible) identity preferences of different domestic groups. This part of the discussion considers developments since political independence as far as Egypt and Morocco are concerned, and since the founding of the state in the case of Israel. Second, we discuss the state's position toward, and engagement in, Euro-Mediterranean region-building. Finally, the EMP's attempted identity manipulations are assessed in light of the domestic identity fault-lines and constraints.

The Mediterranean counts as the "the cradle of civilization" and as the origin of cultures in antiquity. The long and eventful history of the Mediterranean area has witnessed periods of fertile cultural exchange, but also of foreign domination, conflicts, and wars. Undoubtedly, ethnic and cultural diversity has characterized the Mediterranean area since the dawn of history, much in contrast to other areas such as northern Europe. Until the present, pronounced political, cultural, and socioeconomic heterogeneity along with conflicts within and among states are probably the most prominent features of the Mediterranean and Middle East. However, as in former times, the Mediterranean still lies at the crossroads between East and West, North and South. And in view of international developments of the last years, the importance of the Mediterranean is most likely to increase. The combination of these factors offers a challenging background to an inquiry into the identity dimension of foreign policy and regional security. As this book argues, contested state identities cannot be ignored in explaining the meager achievements of regional security schemes in general, and the EMP in particular—quite independently of worsening global and regional conditions. Thus, while contributing to a better understanding of Mediterranean politics, this research sheds light on contested identities as a crucial, but often overlooked, factor in the study of international relations.

Part I

The Argument and Its Setting

1

Region-Building and Contested State Identities

In its original design, the Euro-Mediterranean Partnership that was launched at the Barcelona Conference in November 1995 was an unusual, and quite ambitious, policy initiative. Initially comprising the then-15 EU member states and 12 partners from the southern Mediterranean,[1] the declared aim of the EMP was to turn the Mediterranean into an area of peace, stability, and prosperity (Barcelona Declaration 1995). With it, the main concern of the EMP was *security*.

As the EMP celebrated its tenth anniversary in November 2005, the balance sheet was not particularly positive. The eruption of the second *Intifada* in late September 2000 and the subsequent collapse of the peace process paralyzed the EMP's regional dimension during much of the last five years. And the frequent invocation of a "clash of civilizations" in the aftermath of 9/11, as well as the changed perceptions related to it, did not improve the prospects of Euro-Mediterranean regional security either. Although the EMP is formally still in place, its original design has witnessed significant modifications in the framework of the EU's Neighbourhood Policy, launched in 2003–2004 (Del Sarto and Schumacher 2005). However, the original EMP encountered serious difficulties almost since its beginning. Why is this so? Why was the EMP not able to take off, but rather witnessed repeated setbacks and stalemates ever since it was launched?

Although a number of explanations are possible, this book directs attention to domestic politics in the EMP partners, and in particular to the high incidence of domestic fragmentation in the southern Mediterranean. Since this fragmentation also revolves around the preferred political identity of the state, this book will link the latter to the ability, or inability, of EMP partners to engage in a regional security project on a Euro-Mediterranean basis. Thus, the main argument explored in this book is that domestically contested identities of EMP partners negatively affect their ability to engage in Euro-Mediterranean regional security. This argument, however, is only conceivable if we take the particular nature of the original EMP into account, including the challenges it posed to state identity. Hence, this chapter makes a double move: It first explores the region-building approach that the EMP embodied and subsequently provides an overview of the problems related to state identities in the EMP partners. An integration of the findings helps to shed light on how the link between Euro-Mediterranean regional security and contested state identities in the southern Mediterranean can be conceptualized.

The EMP's Approach to Mediterranean Security

Although the European Community (EC), and later European Union, has a long history of seeking to develop a coherent approach toward the Mediterranean (Grilli 1993; Lister 1997), previous efforts had remained interlocked with the cold war and the Arab–Israeli conflict. The end of the cold war, along with beginning of the Madrid peace process in 1991, seemed to provide the adequate conditions for seeking to address Mediterranean security in a regional and multilateral framework (Commission 1992, 1993). Thus, in 1994, the EU Commission recommended to strengthen the EU's Mediterranean policy and proposed the establishment of a Euro-Mediterranean Partnership, which took up the three-basket structure of the Conference on Security and Co-operation in Europe (CSCE) (Commission 1994, 1995a). At the same time, the EMP sought to reproduce the EU's own success story of regional security and prosperity based on an ongoing economic and political integration process. Yet in the case of the EMP, the EU's efforts targeted an area that is *external* to it. The somewhat experimental character of the EMP deserves a discussion of the EMP's incentives, tools, objectives, and underlying logic.

Incentives, Objectives, and Tools

What motivated the EU to launch the EMP? What were its main objectives and how are they reflected in the EMP's design? Due to the geographic proximity, the EU considers the Mediterranean as a "priority area of strategic importance." While acknowledging various areas of "Euro-Mediterranean interdependence, notably environment, energy, migration, trade and investment" (European Council 1994), the EU's incentives for launching the Barcelona Process were undoubtedly pragmatic and self-interested.

Indeed, the EU sought to address perceived security threats deriving from a lack of economic development in its southern periphery which comprised rising Islamist fundamentalism,[2] combined with illegal immigration into the EU (Aliboni et al. 1996). In fact, already after the end of the cold war and the demise of Communism, "Islam" became a dominating threat perception in the "West," often reflecting traditional and distorted images of the Orient (Said 1995).[3] Given the presence of an already important immigrant population from the southern Mediterranean in most EU countries, along with rising xenophobia in Europe, EU governments consider the issue of immigration as particularly important. Moreover, the EU defined drug trafficking, the proliferation of weapons of mass destruction (WMD), and ecological hazards in or around the Mediterranean Sea as security issues. Finally, securing the EU's oil and gas supply from the southern Mediterranean and its hinterland, for which regional stability is crucial, was and has remained a key strategic consideration of the EU.

The EU's economic interests also played an important role. The aim of establishing a Euro-Mediterranean free-trade area in industrial goods must clearly be seen in the context of the pressures exerted by economic globalization and the emergence of large trading blocs such as the North American Free Trade Area (NAFTA). Thus, the EMP's free-trade agreements also aim at increasing EU exports while enabling the transfer of production sites to the southern periphery, where labor and production costs are much lower than in Europe. Certainly, this rationale may well go to the detriment of the Mediterranean partners (Tovias 1997) and turn them into "satellite economies of Europe" (Joffé 1996: 197). Yet EU officials tend to stress that, independent of the EU's economic benefits, in the era of economic globalization southern Mediterranean countries will have to liberalize their economies at any rate—with or without the EMP (Patten 1999a).

In view of these considerations, the EMP defined three main objectives: First, the "creation of an area of peace and stability based on the principles of human rights and democracy," second, the "creation of an area of shared prosperity" through the gradual establishment of a free-trade area, and third, the "improvement of mutual understanding among the peoples of the region and the development of a flourishing civil society" (Commission 2000b: 7). To this end, the EMP stipulated a structured process of Euro-Mediterranean cooperation in three "baskets": First, cooperation in political and security matters; second, economics and finance; and, third, cooperation in social and cultural affairs. Euro-Mediterranean cooperation on these issues was to comprise both a bilateral and a regional dimension.

In the first basket, the EMP established a regular political dialogue for the promotion of peace, security, and stability, based on the principles of international law. These include respect for human rights, nonintervention in internal affairs, respect for the territorial integrity of states, and peaceful settlement of disputes. Furthermore, the dialogue was meant to foster cooperation in the prevention of and fight against terrorism, organized crime, and drug abuse. It also aimed at promoting WMD nonproliferation regimes, arms control and disarmament, along with confidence-building measures (Barcelona Declaration 1995).

In the second "basket," the stipulated free-trade area in industrial goods set the year 2010 as target date, based on bilateral agreements between the EU and single EMP partners in a first step, and free-trade agreements among the EMP partners in a second. Furthermore, cooperation in the areas of investments, environment protection, natural-resource management, energy policies, and scientific research was to be enhanced. The EU committed itself to financially support the stipulated reform process in the EMP partner states from the EU budget, economic assistance of individual EU members, and loans of the European Investment Bank (EIB).

Finally, the basket on social and cultural affairs was intended to promote the understanding between the peoples of the Euro-Mediterranean area based on dialogue and respect between cultures and religions. This basket also includes the development of human resources, health and sustainable development, job creation, the reduction of migratory pressures, and the common fight against illegal immigration, racism, and xenophobia (Barcelona Declaration 1995). The three-basket structure of the EMP already points to a *region-building approach* to security (Neumann 1994) that is characterized by a number of specific features, as the next section discusses.

A Region-Building Approach to Euro-Mediterranean Security

Although the Barcelona Declaration (1995) also mentions military security,[4] the reference to economic development, political dialogue, and cooperation in social affairs shows that Euro-Mediterranean security is defined in much broader terms. With it, the EMP reflects a traditionally more *European* approach to security (Müller 1993). But why and to what extent did the original EMP display a region-building approach? Four aspects, elaborated below, as worth considering here.

First, unlike Europe's Mediterranean policy hitherto, which was mainly bilateral, the original EMP displayed an explicit regional and multilateral design. Although the EC/EU traditionally labeled its southern periphery as "the Mediterranean," the idea of a *Mediterranean region* is far from being self-evident. Describing a geographical reality, we would not necessarily find the term in a dictionary of political regions. But instead of spending time on debating on whether a Mediterranean region exists or not, the EU simply treated it as axiomatic from the outset (Commission 1994, 1995a, 2000a, 2000b; Bin 1996; FMES et al. 1997). Thus, the main assumption seemed to be that, at the end of the day, it is not relevant whether a Mediterranean region really exists: what matters is that people believe that it does. With it, the social, cultural, and political construction of the Mediterranean was central to the EMP.

Second (allegedly) shared values, interests, and identities played a prominent role within the EU's regional approach. Not surprisingly, the seminal work of Fernand Braudel (1972) on the Mediterranean world in the age of Philip II, stipulating the coherence of the Mediterranean, was repeatedly quoted in EMP documents. Similarly, there were recurrent references to "unifying" images of the Mediterranean, such as the "cradle of civilization," the "birthplace of three monotheistic religions," or the "area of cross-cultural fertilization" (Bin 1996; FMES et al. 1997). This process somewhat reminds us of an attempt of creating a security community characterized by shared values among its members (Deutsch et al. 1957; Adler and Barnett 1998). However, the EMP was never about expanding the EU—which qualifies as a security community—to include the Mediterranean partners. Indeed, it did not envisage EU membership for the EMP partners. Thus, as a weaker version of security community, we may define the aim of the EMP as the creation of a *security region*. In a security region, common values and identity themes, on which the indivisibility of security rests, may not be as deeply anchored and institutionalized as in a security community. Pragmatic considerations and common interests may thus play a greater role. However, a security region still presupposes that a group of states believes that its members inhabit the same geographical space within a given regional order, in which the security of its members is indivisible. For this reason, security regions must rely on common values that underscore the region's uniqueness and provide some sort of "we-feeling."[5] However, in order to become truly part of such a region, the participating states must alter the way they define themselves. With it, the EMP sought to reshape the concept of regional order prevailing in the EMP partner states, while altering the patterns of regional relations—which include relations between former or present adversaries as well as relations to the EU. Thus, the EMP at least inexplicitly implied the *manipulation of the identity of states.*

The third key element of the region-building approach is the involvement of various state and nonstate actors, along with the importance attached to civil society. In this vein, the Barcelona Declaration (1995) explicitly calls upon the participants to "strengthen and/or introduce the necessary instruments of decentralized co-operation to encourage exchanges between those active in development within the framework of national laws." Similarly, the "improvement of the mutual understanding among the peoples of the region and the development of an active civil society" is defined as a key priority of the partnership (Commission 2000: 4). Thus, an active civil society is viewed as indispensable for the emergence of a common regional agenda. This reasoning explains why the EMP subsumed cooperation in such "exotic" areas as education, culture, and social affairs under the headline of security.

Finally, the EU's approach to Mediterranean security was based on a long-term vision. In this vein, the EU stated that the "ultimate benefit of the efforts undertaken within the framework of the Barcelona process will not be visible until some time in the future" (Commission 2000a: 16). This perspective was certainly realistic, mainly because the concept of security varies considerably from state to state across the Mediterranean (Perthes 1996; Guazzone 1996; Said Aly 1996), and given that interstate and intrastate conflicts are an persistent feature of the region. Particularly with regard to the Arab–Israeli conflict, the EU stated that "the Euro-Mediterranean initiative is not intended to replace other activities and initiatives undertaken in the interest of peace, stability and development of the region, but . . . will contribute to their success" (Barcelona Declaration 1995). Thus, while treating the Barcelona Process as a future-oriented meta-project, the EU could relate to persisting conflicts in the region as if they were short-term events at a "lower" level. In this vein, the EU stressed that the EMP was meant to prepare the ground for peacemaking, but that it would acquire its particular importance *after* a comprehensive Middle East peace agreement will be reached (European Council 2000).

Thus, the EU's region-building approach to Mediterranean security as reflected in the EMP implied the restructuring of internal political processes as well as the establishment of a permanent dialogue. But within this approach, security also relies on civil society and is finally about the emergence of common interests, values, and identifications. With it, the EMP *sought to redefine the concept of security*. At the same time, the logic of the Barcelona Process also reflected the EU's particular way of exerting influence in world politics, as the next section argues.

EU Normative Power and the EMP

The EU has often been termed a "civilian power" in international politics (Duchêne 1973). This concept describes the exertion of influence through nonmilitary means—mainly economic diplomacy—and the importance attached to the spreading of democratic values. The notion of "civilian power" also came to comprise a reluctance to use military force in world politics, unless it is viewed as a last resort for achieving humanitarian objectives, along with the conviction that dialogue, consensus, and international law shall regulate international relations. In this context, the EU's international role has also been termed postnationalist, implying the tendency to disconnect the state from the nation (Waever 1996). While these observations do not necessarily apply to single EU member states, the EU's "civilian power" is obviously also related to the lack of military power under a common EU command. Yet the EU succeeded in turning this "flaw" into an asset, and the civilian-power narrative became central to the EU's self-perception (Nicolaidis and Howse 2002).[6] Certainly, the emergence of this self-image may also be linked to Europe's traditional reliance on the United States in matters of international security, as Kagan (2003) argued. Nevertheless, there is an EU-specific set of values that defines both the EU and its external relations, which, with some exaggeration, may be termed a Kantian-type of culture (Adler and Crawford 2006).

In fact, the values promoted by the EU on the international stage reflect the core themes of how the EU *defines itself*. This is the basis of the argument of Ian Manners (2002) on "normative power Europe." The relationship between EU identity and its policies has been high-lighted in different cases and contexts (Waever 1996; Wintle 1996; Merlingen et al. 2001). Exporting EU values is also central to the EU's security policy, since the "EU as civilian power achieves security by instilling expectations and dispositions in near-abroad states, to the effect that the adoption of EU norms and values will gain them inclusion into the ranks of the EU" (Adler and Crawford 2006: 10).

The region-building approach of the EMP corroborates the normative-power argument, since the liberal set of values that underpins the EMP mirrors the EU's core values. Thus, the EU's defining principles of human rights, the rule of law, and democracy are interchangeable with those of the EMP, identified as "partnership, dialogue and consensus, not majority voting" by a senior EU official (Di Cara 2001). Similarly, the EMP promotes inclusion and cooperation as a basis for regional peace and stability, which very much correspond to Europe's own experience. Certainly, in view of the political realities in the Middle East and Mediterranean, seeking to export the European model to this area seemed out of touch with reality. This narrative is explicable, however, by keeping in mind that the EMP reproduced the EU's own historical experience, which is central to both Europe's self-definition (Waever 1996) and its exertion of normative power.

With the launching of the EMP—and at least until the EU adopted the European Neighbourhood Policy in 2003–2004—the EU's normative power exercise vis-à-vis its southern periphery became attached to the Mediterranean theme. This theme came to comprise the regional dimension of the EMP as well as the EU's positions on different political issues in the region, such as the peace process or human-rights practices. Thus, in spite of the formal separation between the Middle East peace process and the EMP (Barcelona Declaration 1995), it is illustrating that the EU's declarations on the Middle East peace process are regularly published in the EU's electronic EMP publications, such as *Euromed Report* or *Euromed Special Feature*.[7] Chris Patten, former EU commissioner for external relations, also blurred the distinction between the different issue areas when he stated, "Let me turn now to the other pressing challenges to Europe's Mediterranean policy: the Middle East peace process" (Patten 2000).

Moreover, the region-building logic imposed itself on the EU's *bilateral* relations with the single EMP partners, which predated the Barcelona Process by far. In this vein, the bilateral and multilateral tracks of the EMP were institutionally linked to each other through MEDA (*Measures d'accompagnement*), the main financial instrument of the EMP.[8] Similarly, free-trade agreements, on which bilateral negotiations had started long *before* the launching of the partnership, were a posteriori linked to the EMP and termed "Euro-Mediterranean Association Agreements," as in the case of Tunisia, Israel, and

Morocco.[9] Moreover, high-level visits of EU officials to single states in the region were regularly depicted as EMP events. In this vein, the visit of former EU Commission President Romano Prodi to various EMP partners in January 2001 was put under the EMP headline, although Prodi mainly discussed strictly bilateral issues, such as trade relations, human rights, or, as in the case of Algeria, the EU's contribution to political stability (*Euromed Special Feature* January 29, 2001, February 21, 2001). The EU clearly expressed its propagated order of priorities by stating that within its Mediterranean policy "[m]ultilateralism is now as common as, *and even prevalent over*, traditional bilateral approaches" (Commission 2000b: 15; italics added). But how does the EU's vision for the Mediterranean compare to reality? The next section turns its attention to this question.

Vision and Reality

Certainly, the Barcelona Process has shown a remarkable degree of continuity thus far. There have been regular conferences and informal meetings of the EMP foreign ministers, along with regular sectoral ministerial meetings under the different chapters of the EMP, and seminars involving government officials, policy advisers, and academics. Different networks, such as among research institutes (such as the Euro-Mediterranean Study Commission, or EuroMeSCo), chambers of commerce, and industrial federations have been established. Training seminars for Euro-Mediterranean diplomats are being financed through the EMP. A continuous political dialogue and various decentralized projects have been established (Aliboni and Said Aly 2000). And the establishment of a project on the prevention and mitigation of natural and man-made disasters, in which all the EMP partners take part, counts as one of the most important projects in the realm of confidence-building measures.

Despite the initially scarce attention paid to the third basket of the Barcelona Process, it produced some interesting initiatives, such as the projects on the common cultural heritage, youth exchange programs, initiatives in the audio-visual area, and various other civil society projects. Resulting from the greater importance given to intercultural dialogue after 9/11, the so-called Anna Lindh Euro-Mediterranean Foundation for the Dialogue between Cultures, located in Alexandria, Egypt, was established in 2004. In the economic realm, most southern EMP partners have signed a bilateral free-trade agreement with the EU by now—Syria being the last EMP partner to have concluded negotiations in 2004.[10] As for the financial assistance through the MEDA program, €3,435 million of the allocated €4,422 million was transferred between 1995 and 1999; MEDA II, which covers the period between 2000 and 2006, is endowed with €5,350 million. Loans from the EIB reached € 4,808 million between 1995 and 1999, and for the period 2000 to 2007 the EIB has a mandate of € 6,400 million, plus € 1 million in own resources.[11]

As the EMP enters into the second decade of its existence, the overall evaluation of its achievements greatly depends on how one measures success or failure, but it is clear that the EMP did not live up to the high expectations it had initially raised. For instance, there has been a notable lack of progress on "hard security" issues, such as arms control and WMD nonproliferation regimes (Selim 2000; Heller 2000; Biscop 2003). The EU has also been relatively weak in promoting democratization and improving human-rights conditions in most EMP partners (Jünemann 2001; Commission 2000b: 5). The overall economic rationale of the EMP, along with the relatively meager financial support for the modernization process it prescribes, also remains problematic (Tovias 1997; Kienle 1998b). In this context, the EU's protectionism regarding trade in agricultural products has repeatedly been criticized (Tovias 2006). Additional flaws comprise the slow pace of the negotiations and ratification process of Euro-Mediterranean agreements, the reluctance of some EMP partners to accelerate the pace of economic transition, the persistent low volume of South–South trade, and rather limited EU investments in the region (Commission 2000b: 5). Admitting that the "spirit of Barcelona" had been fading away over the years, the EU Commission repeatedly called for reinvigorating the partnership. In this vein, the EU's Common Strategy on the Mediterranean, adopted at the 2000 EU summit in Feira, stressed the necessity to adopt more concrete measures as well as a stricter follow-up of the EMP (Jünemann 2001).

However, a number of important regional and global developments also impacted on the EMP over the years. To begin with, the EMP was launched in the general euphoria that accompanied the signing of the Oslo II accords between Israel and the Palestine Liberation Organization (PLO), which had taken place only two months earlier.[12] Yet from 1996 on, the Oslo peace process recurrently entered stalemates, and collapsed at the end of 2000. Rather unsurprisingly, it turned out that the fate of the Middle East peace process affected the progress of the EMP. Second, 9/11 and subsequent terrorist attacks in Europe and other parts of the world most dramatically evidenced the seriousness of international terrorism of an Islamist matrix. Yet the sudden fame of the oversimplifying thesis on the "clash of civilizations" of Samuel Huntington (1996), the rise of anti-Muslim sentiments in the "West," and repeated statements equating Islam with terrorism were certainly not helpful to Euro–Mediterranean relations. Moreover, after 9/11 the EU became even more lenient regarding human-rights violations in some of the EMP partner states for the sake of combating terrorism. Finally, with the 2004 EU enlargement, 10 new member states entered the EU, including Malta and Cyprus, two former EMP partners. In December 2004, the EU also set a date for the start of accession negotiations with Turkey. Without Turkey, however, the remaining EMP partners will consist of eight—and if the current EMP "observer" Libya should fully join the EMP, nine—Arab states and Israel. In the current state of affairs, this is certainly not a good recipe for enhancing regional cooperation. More important, however, the EU's newly developed Neighbourhood Policy (Commission 2003, 2004), which resulted from EU enlargement, relies on an explicitly bilateral and differentiated approach toward the EU's eastern and southern neighbors. Thus, it overrides the regional logic of the EMP (Del Sarto and Schumacher 2005).

A number of additional conflicts between and within states in the area also impacted on the Barcelona Process. The civil war in Algeria following the aborted 1991 elections is but one case in point. In general, many Arab states witnessed domestic conflicts, often related to the rise of Islamist opposition movements. Relations between Morocco and Algeria have remained difficult. During much of the 1990s, relations between Turkey and Greece remained tense, and the conflict over Cyprus has not been settled yet. Neither have EU–Turkish relations been easy over the years, given that the EU repeatedly postponed the decision on Turkey's EU membership. And while Turkey and Syria repeatedly clashed over the Kurdish issue in the late 1990s, Ankara entered a strategic relationship with Israel from 1996 on, to the dismay of Arab states (Gresh 1998). Syria and Turkey, on the other hand, signed two military cooperation agreements in June 2002, much to the displeasure of Israel (*BBC Monitoring Middle East* June 10, 2002). Moreover, while Spain and Morocco repeatedly argued over fisheries and immigration, in July 2002 both sides almost clashed militarily over the small and uninhabited Parsley/Laila islet. Outside of the EMP framework, but still around the Mediterranean, the 1990s also witnessed conflicts between Greece and Macedonia,

Libya and its neighbors, and, most prominently, the countries of former Yugoslavia.

Thus, in the light of a number of regional and global developments, along with recurring conflicts and altering patterns of alignments in the last decade, there was no development toward the recognition of common interests or values in the Euro-Mediterranean area. In the following sections, this observation is further elaborated.

Seeking to Explain Setback

In the early 1990s, the conditions for peace in the Middle East and, with it, for Euro-Mediterranean security, seemed more than promising. What explains, then, the deteriorating prospects toward the end of the same decade? Is it really a matter of altered conditions, or are there additional factors which may explain this outcome?

Common Explanations

In the literature, the most common explanations of the EMP's difficulties point to the unresolved Arab–Israeli conflict (Aliboni and Said Aly 2000; Biscop 2003). Another set of explanations revolves around potentially contradicting "logics" within the EMP (Solingen 2003). Thus, stability and economic liberalization may contradict each other, since economic reforms may actually cause instability, at least in the short term (Tovias 1997). Wide-ranging *political* reforms may also be incompatible with stability, the events in Algeria being the best example. Similarly, the EMP's implicit assumption that economic liberalization will eventually lead to democratization remains questionable (Solingen 2003; Bicchi et al. 2004). And security and democratization may contradict each other, particularly in the context of fighting terrorism in the post–9/11 era (Haddadi 2006). A third group of explanations points to cultural diversity and the power of history. According to this argument, Europe underestimates the colonial experience of the South (Said Aly 1996; Guazzone 1996), while failing to understand the complex political realities in the region. Fourth, a more optimistic explanation points to the time factor. In view of the pronounced diversity in the region and the proneness for conflict within and among states, a Euro-Mediterranean region cannot be expected to emerge overnight. Finally, some analysts dismiss the value of cooperative, or "soft," approaches for inducing change in the Mediterranean and Middle East altogether (Heller 2004).

The last point raises the question of viable alternatives. Indeed, the "balance-of-power" approach of the cold war did not succeed in preventing conflicts and wars in the region. Similarly, bilateral development cooperation characterizing Euro-Mediterranean relations in the previous decades was rather unsuccessful. And military means may not enhance regional stability and security either, as the current situation in Iraq demonstrates. On the other hand, the region-building logic of the EMP was remarkably successful in other areas. The European integration process after World War II and the CSCE experience serve as examples here. The fact that the recently launched "Greater Middle East Initiative" of the U.S. administration takes up the EMP logic also shows that the latter is not that absurd after all. Certainly, some of the explanations for the setbacks of the EMP are plausible to a certain extent, particularly their combination. Some questions, however, remain unexplained, such as the oscillating nature of Euro-Mediterranean relations in general, and the failure of *any* regional initiative thus far, be it the Arab Maghreb Union (UMA), the multilateral track of the Madrid peace process, or the EMP.

In fact, while the EU adopted a regional strategy toward its southern periphery, the EMP partners did not develop a Mediterranean policy of their own. Thus, EU officials repeatedly regretted that the EMP partners lacked a "national strategy" vis-à-vis the Mediterranean (Di Cara 2001), and the Euro-Mediterranean Parliamentary Forum (2001) reached the same conclusions. However, the states of the southern Mediterranean have actually a long history of belonging to the same grouping in international relations, as discussed further below. The failure of the EMP partners of developing a Mediterranean strategy may have different reasons. One is certainly the persistence of conflicts and unstable regional relations. Indeed, it is difficult to develop a consistent strategy if the political situation in the region repeatedly witnesses dramatic changes, as during the last decade. But a state's failure to respond to a regional and multilateral policy logic may also have domestic reasons. Thus, it is possible that the promotion of common values and regional identity themes in the framework of the EMP's region-building approach encounters domestic resistance in some states. In a similar vein, regional security on a Euro-Mediterranean basis may not be compatible with the propagated core values of single states. It is even conceivable that recurring interstate conflicts in the region and the difficulties to engage in regional security schemes are two expressions of the same disease, which originates at the *domestic* level. The next paragraphs briefly explore key domestic issues and political patterns in the southern Mediterranean.

Domestic Fragmentation in the Southern Mediterranean

While the nation-state is a relatively recent invention in the Mediterranean and Middle East (Luciani 1990; Lewis 1998), many societies in the region are characterized by a high degree of cultural, ethnic, and religious heterogeneity (Kliot 1989; Roque 1997). In most states, the religious–secular fault-line has deepened, and there are different challenges to state authority and prevailing identity themes.

As for Arab Mediterranean states, political leaders have been employing different strategies to counter the strengthening of Islamism, ranging from co-option to plain repression (Chartouny-Dubarry 2000). The Islamist challenge certainly exploits political and economic discontent against the background of worsened economic conditions, which also eroded the legitimacy of the providential Arab state (Sadiki 2000; Dawisha 1988a: 282–283; Ibrahim 1998). Particularly in times of economic and political troubles, the Islamist discourse seems appealing, since it offers certainties in assigning guilt for crises, thus blaming the "corrupt and infidel elites" and their attachment to the "unbelieving West." Fouad Ajami (1999) has suggested that the Islamist phenomenon actually reflects the ideological bankruptcy of pan-Arab and socialist ideologies against the backdrop of reality. The Islamist challenge also implies an internal conflict about the interpretation of Islam (Said 1995: 333; Roberson 1998; Al-Ashmawy 1989) and its place in public life. Thus, the phenomenon entails a much wider domestic fragmentation on intrinsic values, and finally the identity of the state. But secular opposition movements are also challenging state authority, and with it, traditional identity themes.

In spite of their different political systems, Israel and Turkey share a similar experience in this regard. In Turkey, the rise of Islamist-conservative parties, such as the Welfare Party in the 1990s, and presently the AKP (Justice and Development Party), raises questions about Turkey's political identity (Ergil 2000). In Israel, the persistent struggle between religious orthodoxy and secular democracy entails a deep conflict about political culture and predominant values (Kimmerling 1998).

Over the last decades, several developments seem to have exacerbated the domestic divisions. Thus, processes of modernization and globalization have led to the erosion of traditional social structures and identity themes in most states of the Mediterranean and Middle East. As for Arab states, the durability of which had somewhat surprised many scholars at the end of the 1980s (Dawisha and Zartmann 1988), the decline of pan-Arabism and the "triumph of the state" (Sela 1998: 350) may well have reduced one source of friction. But worsening economic conditions constitute new challenges to state authority. Moreover, the rise of Islamist movements entails an additional source of friction, especially for those states that entered military alliances with the "West," or adopted a moderate stance toward Israel. While the Palestine problem had a strong unifying effect on fragmented Arab societies, the advent of the Arab–Israeli peace process additionally generated new divisions and questioned the legitimacy of Arab rulers (Ajami 1992, 1999). In fact, making peace with Israel contradicts a number of unifying myths that are deeply rooted within Arab societies—not because they are intrinsic to Arab or Islamic "culture," but because their leaders promoted these myths for instrumental reasons over several decades.

Yet in Israel too, the beginning of the peace process brought a number of inherent contradictions to the fore. Recognizing the Palestinian right of national self-determination and the legitimacy of Palestinian territorial claims potentially undermines the moral justification provided by Israel's identity for its own territorial claims (Weissbrod 1997). Turkey, on the other hand, has witnessed an increasing protest of its ethnic minorities since the end of the cold war, such as the Kurds and the Shi'ite Alawi. With the erosion of the myth of national unity, a rising prominence of Islam, and economic liberalization, modern Turkey started to depart from its political foundations of nationalism, secularism, and statism (Kasaba and Bozdoğan 2000). In the quest for a replacement, modern Turkey is deeply divided on which way to choose.

To sum up, ethnic divisions, rising religious forces, political and economic discontent, and societal fragmentation around the southern Mediterranean entail domestic conflicts about the political design of the state. Over the last decades, several internal and external developments have exacerbated the societal fragmentation and contributed to the erosion of the unifying identity themes. It is against this background that we might understand the difficulties of EMP partners to engage in regional politics, which entail the promotion of themes and values that they allegedly share with their neighbors.

An Alternative Explanation

The EU's promotion of regionalism and multilateralism on a Euro-Mediterranean basis did not have much impact on the foreign policy of most southern EMP participants. Considering the EMP's rationale of promoting common interests, values, and regional identity themes, the question of how the lack of a regional strategy of southern EMP states relates to the high incidence of societal fragmentation becomes crucial.

A number of scholars highlighted the impact of domestic politics on foreign-policy making (Putnam 1988; Moravcsik 1997). This argument has been widened by the proposition that national identity is strongly related to foreign policy as well as relations among states (Bloom 1990; Campbell 1992; Kienle 1995; Barnett 1999). Others have argued that "culture matters" in international relations (Katzenstein 1996b). Yet our discussion so far pointed to the importance of domestic conflicts about the political identity of states and their repercussion on foreign-policy making, particularly with regard to Euro-Mediterranean regional security.

Contested State Identities and
Regional Security: The Argument

Drawing attention to the identity dimension of foreign policy—identity referring here to the political identity of states—we argue that the lack of progress in Euro-Mediterranean region-building cannot sufficiently be explained without paying attention to state identities that are contested at the domestic level. The main argument is that the unsettled identity of a state puts a strain on the consistent evolution of regional security relations on a Euro-Mediterranean basis. Region-building necessitates a reconsideration of how a state defines itself and its place in the regional and international arena, and how it relates to other states. These questions, however, cannot be clearly answered as long as the political design of the state is contested at the domestic level. Inconsistent relations among the EMP partners, problematic relations with "Europe and the West," along with a lack of strategy toward Euro-Mediterranean region-building, would be a result of the deeply contested identity of these states. To put it simply, a state cannot consistently define who its enemies and its friends are, to which region it belongs, and, therefore, what the priorities of its foreign policy are, as long as it does not know what, or "who," it is. This argument is particularly salient as far as region-building initiatives, such as the EMP, are concerned, precisely because they necessitate the emergence of common interests, values, shared beliefs, and regional identity themes. Hence, engaging in the creation of a security region necessitates the reshaping of state identity, and this may also require a choice of one concept of identity over others.

There is no doubt that many EMP partners share a number of "Mediterranean" features, which are often part of their cultural and literary traditions in one way or the other. But in all states, the Mediterranean option may potentially exclude more powerful identity preferences. At the same time, political leaders may be forced to promote strong "unifying" themes that are based on more "traditional" loyalties in order to keep potential domestic conflicts under control. This may explain why even under favorable global conditions in the post–cold war era, southern EMP partners were not able to consistently develop a Mediterranean policy, let alone a Mediterranean identity. By linking the inability to form regions to domestic identity conflicts, the setbacks and oscillating prospects of the Barcelona Process become intelligible. Hence, the domestic struggle over state identity will be treated as an independent variable that affects the ability to consistently engage in Mediterranean region-building, treated here as the dependent variable.

What are the inherent assumptions of this argument? As elaborated further in the next chapter, one set of assumptions regards the relationship between (contested) state identities and foreign policy in general terms: First, states tend to adopt a specific political identity in their relations to other states, which is reflected in their foreign policy. In this vein, it makes a difference in terms of foreign policy whether a state portrays itself as, say, a "liberal democracy," a "world power," an "Asian tiger," or a "guardian of Islam." Second, different identity preferences of domestic groups may entail different preferences regarding the type of foreign relations and regional order. Hence, religious fundamentalists (of whatever denomination) may have a quite different vision of international relations and regional order than secularist or liberal forces. Third, states that are characterized by strong societal fragmentation may use foreign policy as a tool for legitimizing state authority and/or increasing societal cohesion (Buzan 1991). This pattern has repeatedly been observed with respect to Arab states, often implying rather unpredictable foreign-policy actions (Dawisha 1988b). Finally, political elites of highly fragmented societies may be forced to use strong unifying symbols to ensure their political legitimacy. These symbols, however, are most likely to be based on the motive of collective (or "national") exclusivity and distinctiveness, and may thus contradict the engagement in multilateral ventures.

These assumptions have a number of theoretical implications as far as social identities and foreign-policy analysis is concerned: First, states do not possess intrinsic or unchangeable identities. Rather, identities of states are social phenomena; the formation and reshaping of state identities are continuous social processes. Second, the shaping of state identities is not only a social, but also a highly political, process. Indeed, state identities may be manipulated and exploited by political elites for instrumental reasons, such as justifying state authority or specific policies. Third, although they can be manipulated, identities are "real." They influence the definition of "self," "other," regional order, and, in general, the perception of reality. In this vein, a state's self-perception affects the definition of foreign-policy interests, which are not fixed and primordial, but rather socially constructed in function of a state's identity (Wendt 1994). Finally, this research assumes the relevance of domestic factors for explaining foreign-policy outcome.

Testing the Argument

In line with our argument, we expect that southern EMP partners with a strongly contested identity will be characterized by an inconsistent strategy toward Euro-Mediterranean region-building, or a lack of strategy altogether. Conversely, states with a low degree of identity contestation are considered more likely to develop a strategy toward regional security on a Euro-Mediterranean basis. This hypothesis, however, deserves some fine-tuning. Indeed, domestic identity conflicts may vary in nature and intensity across states, and they may not pose a foreign-policy problem in all cases, or regarding every foreign-policy issue. Thus, there are a number of intervening factors and variables, such as the degree of social polarization, and the type of state–society relations, which are explored more systematically in the next chapter.

But how does the causal link between contested state identities and Euro-Mediterranean regional security manifest itself *in practice*? The frequent reassessment of relations to the Euro-Mediterranean neighbors—in spite of material factors remaining the same—certainly points to a state's difficulties in developing a coherent regional strategy, or a lack thereof. And while we may expect different, and contradicting, interpretations of the objectives of the EMP, the Mediterranean identity theme, along with references to common interests or values on a Euro-Mediterranean basis, will be notably absent in the official discourse.

In order to test our argument, we will provide a historical and regional perspective by discussing Euro-Mediterranean relations over the last decades and further elaborating on domestic developments in the southern Mediterranean. The three case studies that are analyzed in detail, namely Israel, Egypt, and Morocco, were chosen precisely because they differ from each other in many respects. Thus, at prima facie these states maintained different positions toward Euro-Mediterranean regional security and the EU as its main promoter. They are characterized by different political systems and state–society relations. And the political identity of these states seems to be unsettled to various degrees. A final consideration appertains to the general importance given to the Arab–Israeli fault-line in Mediterranean and Middle Eastern politics. While Israel is obviously central to it, it may be relevant that Egypt is a significant player in the wider Arab–Israeli conflict, while Morocco is situated at its periphery. A comparison of the findings in the three cases, thus, allows us to assess the relevance of our argument and its assumptions and to identify relevant intervening variables.

Thus, testing our argument in the three case studies entails the analysis of the predominant identity discourse and the domestic challenges, the exploration of each country's relations to its Euro-Mediterranean neighbors, and the subsequent investigation of the possible impact of domestic identity conflicts on foreign-policy making in general, and Euro-Mediterranean regional security in particular. Of course, assessing alternative domestic- and foreign-policy preferences, including those of the political opposition, is a tricky business in authoritarian states. For this reason, we also explore domestic trends that may indicate whether alternative identity preferences are present and relevant. Besides an extensive review of the academic literature, our empirical research consults official and semi-official documents on foreign policy and state identity. Interviews with government officials and experts support this investigation. As noted in the introduction, the time frame of this study is limited to the first seven years of the EMP, thus avoiding obvious explanations linked to the collapse of the peace process and 9/11. However, this book also considers developments that took place afterwards if they are relevant for the subject under consideration. As far as Euro-Mediterranean relations are concerned, the background provided by this book starts after the end of the cold war. For every case study, a short history of state identity is provided. For Egypt and Morocco, the starting point of this investigation is the aftermath of national independence, and for Israel, the establishment of the state.

This book does certainly not claim that the discrepancy between vision and reality of the Barcelona Process can be explained in terms of identity alone. Politics in general, and international relations in particular, do not follow mono-causal explanations. The (temporary?) collapse of the Middle East peace process, the events of 9/11, and factors appertaining to the EU itself certainly had a negative impact on the prospects of Euro-Mediterranean regional security. This research seeks to show, however, that unsettled state identities are a significant and independent factor that must be considered for explaining the difficulties of the EMP in particular, and of regional security initiatives in general. By approaching international relations from an alternative perspective, this book supports the argument that foreign-policy interests "are defined by actors who respond to cultural factors" (Katzenstein 1996a: 2). Yet going beyond this affirmation, the research also evidences the relevance of *domestic factors* for the study of world politics, while opening up the "black box" of state identities. As we have touched upon a wide range of theoretical issues, the next chapter elaborates on the theoretical underpinnings of our argument.

2

Theoretical Framework

This chapter focuses on the theoretical premises of the argument that contested state identities negatively affect a state's ability to engage with Euro-Mediterranean regional security. This discussion of the theoretical framework will start with a review of different schools of thought within the theory of IR. As this discussion touches upon questions of reality, truth, and knowledge, these issues will briefly be addressed in a second step. Subsequently, we theoretically elaborate on how identities, and in particular state identities, can be studied, while conceptualizing the impact of *contested* state identities on foreign-policy interests, and consequently, outcome.

Interests and Identities in IR

The focus on contested state identities as a possible explanation of the difficulties of the EMP has led us to the questioning of the very nature of foreign-policy interests. Certainly, the argument of this book does not lie within the range of approaches that have been dominating IR during most of its relatively young existence as an academic discipline. In fact, since IR's theoretical preoccupation with foreign and security policy developed around the cold war, the realist school traditionally stood at the center (Nye and Lynn-Jones 1988; Walt 1991). As it is well known, realism defines "interests" in terms of military capabilities, deterrence strategies, and power politics. In spite of repeated calls for broadening the definition of security and interests from the mid-1980s onwards (Ullman 1983; Buzan 1983), the rationalist and systemic view prevailed in IR theory. With it, the predominant assumption is that a state's foreign policy and security interests are exogenous and a priori given, an assumption that is discussed—and challenged—in the following sections.

Traditional Approaches: Realism, Neo-Realism, and Neo-Liberalism

The starting points of realism and neo-realism are the anarchical nature of the international system, nation-states as principal actors within it, and the rational behavior of states in their pursuit of power. Under these conditions, conflicts and wars are viewed as inevitable. Thus, the balance of power, or, better, *the balancing of power*, becomes the central mechanism of international relations (Morgenthau 1967; Carr 1964). The classical realists, however, can be criticized for not having defined the key concepts of "power" and "interest" in a consistent way, if at all. Thus, Hans Morgenthau (1967: 9, 122–144) asserted that the determining elements of power include material resources, the ability to influence the behavior of other states, domestic structures, state–society relations, as well as "the political and cultural environment" of foreign-policy making. While the assertion that both material resources and the possibility to exert influence define power is somewhat tautological (Keohane 1986a: 11), realist theory remains notably vague regarding the question of what state interests are and how they may change.

Giving absolute priority to the systemic level, neo-realism is much clearer on this point. In his influential reformulation of realist theory, Kenneth Waltz (1979) even insists that IR must focus solely on systemic factors in order to meet the conditions of theory.[1] According to Waltz, international anarchy and the position of the state within the system determine an actor's national interests, which merely reflect material capabilities and strategic circumstances (Waltz 1979: 18, 65; Gilpin 1981). Changing foreign-policy interests, then, must be a result of an altered distribution of capabilities or changed strategic conditions. Yet this point is certainly contestable. To give an example, the cold war did not end because of altered systemic conditions, but as a result of profound domestic changes *within* the former Soviet Union. As Robert Keohane (1986b: 182) correctly argues, neo-realism's "efforts to define the national interest on a priori basis . . . or to use the concept for prediction and explanation, have been unsuccessful." Applied to the Euro-Mediterranean case, neo-realism may offer an explanation for the launching of both the Arab–Israeli peace process and the EMP by pointing to the end of the cold war as an altered systemic condition. For the recurrent political stalemate and the EMP's lack of success, however, realism and neo-realism have no plausible explanation, since the strategic conditions did not notably change during the 1990s. Neither do they succeed in explaining altering patterns of

Euro–Mediterranean relations, including the reluctance of EMP partners to engage in the creation of a security region.

As is well known, institutional neo-liberalism was intended to challenge neo-realism's dominant position in IR theory, along with the strictly systemic view of world politics. However, neo-liberalism eventually adopted the same premises as the latter: The state is viewed as unitary actor in an anarchical system which, in turn, determines state behavior, and states act in a self-interested and rational way (Keohane 1986a). What distinguishes neo-liberal theory from neo-realism, however, is the former's emphasis on the role of international institutions. Thus, according to neo-liberalism, "cooperation can under some conditions develop on the basis of complementary interests," and "institutions, broadly defined, affect the patterns of cooperation that emerges" (Keohane 1984: 9). In other words, neo-liberalism still considers conflict as inherent in the international system, but, unlike neo-realists, not as inevitable. Moreover, unlike neo-realism, neo-liberal regime theory implicitly assumes the relevance of norms for foreign-policy behavior. However, neo-liberal scholars tend to treat these "explicit or implicit principles, norms, rules" on which international regimes are based, and "around which actors' expectation converge in given areas of international relations" (Krasner 1982: 186), as exogenous factors that reflect a state's preexisting foreign-policy interests (Krasner 1993).

Thus, neo-liberal scholars did not succeed in correcting the deficiencies of realism and neo-realism discussed above. As a result, neo-liberalism cannot reasonably explain the inconsistent evolution of Euro-Mediterranean relations in the event that material realities remain unchanged. In our case, neo-liberalism's focus on institutionalized cooperation among states is not relevant either, since the inconsistent evolution of Euro-Mediterranean relations seems to precisely prevent the emergence of such a cooperation.

The Challengers: Liberal Theory and Constructivism

A paradigmatic alternative to the systemic view of IR is Andrew Moravcsik's reformulation of liberal IR theory (Moravcsik 1997). This approach stipulates that societal groups, and their ability to promote their interests, determine a state's foreign-policy behavior. Liberal theory is based on three core assumptions: First, individuals and private groups are the most important actors in international politics. They act rationally in their pursuit of welfare under constraints imposed by material scarcity, divergent values, and inequality in their societal influence. Second, states are not actors, but institutions representing the interests of the dominant domestic groups, termed *state preferences*. A priori, a state's preferences are independent of the interests of other states, but the latter may impose certain constraints on a state's realization of its preferences. The configuration of state preferences determines state behavior in the international arena (Moravcsik 1997: 516–520). Thus, liberal theory directly challenges Waltz's claim that it "is not possible to understand world politics simply by looking inside of states" (Waltz 1979: 65) by suggesting that, on the contrary, *looking inside of states* leads to the only valid explanation of world politics. Thus, liberal theory provides an explanation for variation in a state's foreign policy "while holding power and information constant" (Moravcsik 1997: 537). Unlike traditional IR approaches, the liberal school of thought explains foreign policy as a function of the domestic context, and it focuses on how domestic conflicts over preferences, not international anarchy, impose policy outcomes.

Applied to the Euro-Mediterranean case, liberal theory would explain foreign-policy variation in terms of domestic conflicts over preferences and changing coalitions in power. Moreover, the so-called ideational variant of liberal theory proposes that "disjunctures between borders and identity are important determinants of international conflict and cooperation" (Moravcsik 1997: 526). This point seems also interesting for explaining prospects and failures of the EMP.

However, there are several objections to liberal IR theory. First, by exclusively concentrating on domestic politics, liberal theory goes to the other extreme by ignoring the state-level in the analysis. This move is a problematic oversimplification, since domestic and international politics intersect at the state-level (Putnam 1988). Here, various feedback processes take place, and additional information, interests, and pressures, such as of political elites, intelligence services, or the international community, may intervene. Second, the rationality assumption, which liberal theory shares with realism and neo-liberalism, remains questionable. In fact, by referring to the relationship between national identity and territorial borders in explaining cooperation and conflict, liberal theory implicitly corrupts its own rationality assumption, as it unintentionally points to a possible incompatibility of identities and rationality. Finally, liberal theory does not answer the question of why some states are characterized by domestic struggle over preferences that may impact on foreign policy, while others are not.

Constructivist approaches represent a further challenge to traditional IR theory. Like liberal theory, constructivism defies the systemic perspective of world politics, along with the assumption that state interests are a priori given (Wendt 1992; Adler 1997b). But unlike liberal theory, constructivism also challenges the rationality assumption by viewing actors as responding to social norms and values. Although constructivist approaches do not ignore material determinants of foreign policy, they however regard them as acquiring meaning through the social dimension (Onuf 1989: 40; Adler 1997a: 255). Alexander Wendt (1995: 73) clarifies this point in a marked example: "500 British nuclear weapons are less threatening to the United States than 5 North Korean nuclear weapons, because the British are friends of the United States and the North Koreans are not."

An innovation of constructivist approaches is the focus on the relationship between interests and state identity (Wendt 1994; Neumann 1996; Berger 1996). Gaining important insights from the research on "security communities" (Deutsch et al. 1957; Adler 1997a; Adler and Barnett 1998), constructivist approaches suggest that social norms, values, and beliefs shape the self-understanding of the state, that is, its identity. In turn, a state's identity affects the perception of other states, and with it, of national interests. Thus, constructivist scholars equally defy the claim of traditional IR theory that states possess a priori given and stable identities, conversely arguing that state identities are socially constructed, and can therefore change. Studies of national identity (Anderson 1991; Haas 1993) confirm this perspective.

With regard to the EMP, a constructivist approach would lend itself to focus on unsettled state identities that frequently witness processes of reshaping and reconstruction. Given the wide-spread phenomenon of domestic fragmentation in the southern Mediterranean, this proposition is certainly worth considering. However, it touches upon a theoretical problem. Constructivist scholarship tends to treat state identity as a unitary concept as soon as it is applied to empirical case studies. While Wendt (1999) openly defends what has been termed "systemic" constructivism (Price and Reus-Smit 1998: 268–269; Ruggie 1998: 881), the implicit state-centric perspective of much constructivist scholarship excludes consideration of domestic conflicts over state identity, which may impact on foreign-policy making. Indeed, diametrically opposed domestic preferences regarding the identity of the state may considerably narrow-down a government's space of maneuver in foreign policy. Moreover, since external threats generally contribute to the reproduction and reconstruction of a state's identity (Buzan et al. 1998: 120; Campbell 1992), governments might use an external threat to give a sense of unity to a deeply divided population—even if political realities change. Thus, in its unitary version, the concept of state identity in constructivist theory is of limited value.

Culture, Identity, and the "Third Debate"—Second Edition

The revolutionary changes that marked world politics in the late 1980s prompted a renewed preoccupation with cultural factors in IR from the 1990s onwards (Goldstein and Keohane 1993b; Katzenstein 1996b; Lapid and Kratochwil 1996). Since mainstream IR theory was unprepared for either the end of the cold war or the resurrection of ethnic conflicts—and even failed to explain them in the aftermath—IR scholars were inevitably forced to question their predominant analytical categories. The new "burst of critical scrutiny in the IR discipline" (Lapid 1996: 4) also affected the concept of security, which similarly witnessed the "intrusion" of culture and identity (Katzenstein 1996b; Bush and Keyman 1997; Goldgeier 1997; Adler and Barnett 1998). The rethinking of culture characterized realism and neo-liberalism (Goldstein and Keohane 1993a; Krasner 1993; Buzan et al. 1998) as well as the postmodernist, feminist, and constructivist challengers (Campbell 1992; Tickner 1996; Wendt 1994). Combined with the general rise of constructivist approaches, this trend also directed attention to meta-theoretical questions. Indeed, how compatible is the study of culture and identities with rationalist and positivist approaches that had dominated IR hitherto? How can these phenomena be studied, and what does it imply for our understanding of science? In a way, the preoccupation with this set of questions echoed the so-called Third Debate of the 1980s (Lapid 1989), which was sparked by critical theory and its questioning of the validity of positivism[2] in the social sciences (Walker 1988; Hoffman 1991; Linklater 1990, 1992).[3] On these issues, constructivist approaches adopted similar positions as critical theory (Price and Reus-Smit 1998).

Indeed, in ontological terms, that is, regarding the question of what the world is made of, both constructivism and critical theory challenge the existence of purely utility-rationalist actors. Moreover, both approaches are at least critical of the assumption that the real world exists independently of the human mind (Hoffman 1991; Adler 1997b; Ruggie 1998). In epistemological terms, that is, regarding the question of "how reality can be known," both constructivist and critical scholarship question the validity of law-like generalizations in the social sciences. To quote John Ruggie (1989: 880, footnote 138): "How many cases have there been of nuclear bipolarity? Or of any other kind, for that matter? How many hegemons have there been 'like' the United States in the twentieth century, or Britain in the nineteenth?"

Over the last decade, there has been an increase of systematic accounts of what may be called post-positivist social science (Searle 1995; Wendt 1999; Adler 1997b; Ruggie 1998; Kubálková et al. 1998b), along with a growing body of empirical research. Yet the diversity regarding meta-theoretical starting points within IR persists until the present. Thus, considering the subject of the present book, which position does it adopt? It is to these questions that we shall now turn our attention to.

Reality, Truth, and Knowledge: Contested Foundations

The questions of what the world is made of and how we can know about it have been preoccupying philosophers since centuries. Yet for IR, these questions are more than relevant. Indeed, we cannot study international politics "without making powerful assumptions about what kind of things are to be found in international life, how they are related, and how they can be known" (Wendt 1995: 5). All IR theories make these assumptions, at least implicitly. Yet alternative, and partic-ularly post-positivist, approaches are often accused of not *scientifically* proving their arguments. This is even more the case if such "esoteric" phenomena as culture and identities are the subject of scientific inquiry. For this reason—and since important issues such as causality are at stake—we briefly clear the meta-theoretical foundations of this book.

The World Out There

What is the world like? What are its main components, and how do they relate to each other? Besides being interesting questions per se, assumptions about "what is" fulfill a specific task within science. In fact, ontology is preoccupied with the question of what the world must be like for science to be possible (Bhaskar 1975: 23; Quine 1963: 16–17).

The broadest agreement can probably be reached on the assumption that the world consists of material objects, which may be observable or not. In addition, most would probably agree on the existence of "ideational" facts, such as norms, ideas, practices, customs, and beliefs.

Laws and legislation, political ideologies, religions, the concept of sovereignty, property rights, and citizenship are examples of these "ideational" phenomena. In contrast to material objects, their existence is very much dependent on society. Thus, if we assume that these "ideational" facts are real, their "being real" somewhat differs from that of material objects. Indeed, while a mountain may exist independently of people believing that it does, social facts do not. As John Searle (1995: 31–32) has put it: "Part of being a cocktail party is being thought to be a cocktail party; part of being a war is being thought to be a war." The key mechanisms through which these "facts" become reality are *social institutionalization* and *intersubjective agreement* (Berger and Luckmann 1966). Indeed, a cocktail party would not be a cocktail party, and a war would not be a war, if only *one* individual—or only a few, for that matter—thought of the event in question as being a cocktail party, or a war. These examples, as well as of other social practices such as getting married, or stopping at a red traffic-light, also show that human behavior acquires a meaning only because of the preexistence of society. At the same time, people reproduce society and may transform it. Thus, society "is both the ever-present *condition* . . . and the continually reproduced *outcome* of human agency" (Bhaskar 1979: 43, original italics).

But how do material and "ideational" facts relate to each other? And which role does the human mind play in this context? The present book adopts the position that "brute" material facts may well exist independently of both social phenomena and of the mind of their observers. Thus, there is a commitment to scientific realism, which stipulates that the (material) world exists independently of our minds and of our knowledge of them (Blackburn 1994: 320; Manicas 1998). However, even this commitment, which in the current IR literature often serves as justification for a proper scientific stance, needs some fine-tuning. The reason is that processes of interpretation are also relevant when it comes to material factors. Indeed, material objects acquire a meaning through social convention and institutionalization; their *social significance* is dependent on the human mind. To give an example, our current economic thinking and way of life presupposes the scarcity of resources. But according to anthropological literature, traditional societies of gatherers and hunters—then and now—firmly believe that there is an abundance of natural resources and food. And yet they are referring to the *same physical world*.

Thus, scientific realism serves as an ontological reference point, which makes experimentation, and finally science, intelligible (Bhaskar 1975).

However, the moment we accept the assumption that "*the manner in which the material world shapes and is shaped by human action and interaction depends on dynamic normative and epistemic interpretations of the material world*" (Adler 1997b: 322, original italics), we depart from the commitment to scientific realism in its absolute version. Thus, we accept what has been termed "*internal* realism" (Putnam 1995: 172, original italics), which still differs from the anti-realist claim that things do *not* exist independently of our minds (Blackburn 1994: 319–320).

Affirming that social facts exist as "real-world" phenomena, the meaning of which, however, is dependent on social conventions has two important implications. First, it entails that social phenomena are not eternal and globally valid, but dependent on time and place. Second, collectively accepted interpretations of the material world—which include norms, beliefs, and identities—affect human behavior. They may be compared to lenses through which we see events and situations, and they direct human action, mostly unconsciously. For this reason, the assumption that "rational" human behavior is purely utility-oriented must be rejected.

How Can We Know?

The minimalist version of scientific realism has important epistemological consequences. If the social world is based on social conventions, meaning and interpretation become our main concerns. But in this case, how can we know anything to be true? And if our minds take part in the process of interpretation, how is knowledge in the social sciences possible?

For theorists who accept the maximalist version of scientific realism—Realism with a capital R, as Putnam (1995: 172) termed it—these questions are quite easy to answer. Indeed, the assumption that the real world exists independently of human thinking permits a clear distinction between subject and object. This leads to the propositions that some of our beliefs are correct descriptions of reality, even if they may be incomplete, and that we possess the appropriate scientific tools to verify that (at least) some of our observations of the world are objectively true (Blackburn 1994: 320). This position lends itself to espouse a positivist approach to science.[4] In this vein, social phenomena can be studied like natural objects; observation leads to objective knowledge; and law-like generalizations are the basis of explanations and predictions (Hollis 1994: 49).[5] In the study of IR, most neo-realist and neo-liberal scholars at least implicitly subscribe to this approach to science.

Clear-cut propositions about scientific knowledge and "truth" are far more complicated for social scientists who defend an intersubjective ontology, as most constructivist and critical scholars do.[6] Refraining from a neat distinction between subject and object somewhat contradicts any approach "which applies scientific method to human affairs conceived as belonging to a natural order open to objective inquiry," as Martin Hollis (1994: 49) characterizes positivism in the social sciences. Indeed, an intersubjective ontology implies that the study of cultural and social phenomena cannot be purely "objective," as it necessarily rests on *meanings* of reality. These meanings are dependent on "value ideas" through which we observe the social world in specific times and places (Weber 1922). Thus, the human mind, or, better, *collective human minds*, plays a crucial role in deciding what counts as scientific knowledge (Quine 1963: 42). To put it differently, as much as communication is a social process of making sense of the world, so is knowledge. Certainly, this affirmation is particularly tricky for the social sciences, as they are part of their own field of inquiry. Indeed, the social sciences are "*internal* with respect to their subject matter in a way in which the natural sciences are not" (Bhaskar 1979: 59).

Thus, seeking to attain absolute "truth"—Truth with a capital T—must be rejected as a certainly desirable, but unrealistic, goal. This does not mean that the whole scientific enterprise is to be dismissed altogether. But the approach toward science necessitates a greater modesty and pragmatism. In this vein, it is possible to call observations or theories "true"—with a lowercase t—by taking previous experiences, commonly accepted theories, the cultural context, and language into account, as they provide the background conditions of intelligibility. Thus, things are true "*just in so far as they help us to get into satisfactory relation with other parts of our experience*" (James 1995: 58, original italics). Within this approach to science, reason plays an important role, as it substantially decides about the validity of a given explanation (Adler 1997b: 329). Thus, the assessment of truth follows rigorous definitions and theoretical constructs.

These propositions have a number of additional implications. First, refuting the possibility of objective observation implies that the social world, and human behavior within it, must be understood "from within" (Hollis 1994: 151). Thus, interpretative strategies are the adequate tool for seeking to explain the meaning of behavior. Max Weber's concept of *verstehen* (understanding) very much depicts this approach to the social sciences (Weber 1922: 503–512). Second, "understanding from within" implies a departure from generalizing, or deductive, explanations that are widely associated with positivist science. Indeed, law-like generalizations will not help us to understand the meaning of actions within a specific cultural context. Moreover, the registration of causal laws presupposes a closed system, but in the social sciences, the objects of scientific inquiry can only manifest themselves in *open systems* without control conditions. Hence, while theories in the social sciences cannot be predictive, but exclusively explanatory, only *particularizing* strategies can explain the social world (Bhaskar 1979: 27 ff.; Hollis and Smith 1992: 50 ff.). The aim of these strategies is not to show that a specific situation "A" occurred due to circumstance "B," because all "B" cause "A," but rather to explain why a specific outcome is *so and not otherwise* (Weber 1972: 11–12). Finally, in the social sciences, *reasons for action*—which may result from utilitarian considerations, social norms, or identities—are accepted as *causes*. Indeed, the aim is to explain what people think they are doing and what their actions mean in a specific sociocultural context (Weber 1922: 503).

To sum up, the approach to truth and knowledge adopted here is based on the philosophical school of pragmatism (Goodman 1995) and critical realism (Bhaskar 1975, 1979; Archer et al. 1998).[7] It asserts that scientific knowledge in the social sciences consists of temporarily valid and partial descriptions of "reality." Since social science is preoccupied with intersubjective meanings and social relations within open systems, theories can only be nonpredictive and explanatory, while they are "*necessarily* incomplete" (Bhaskar 1979: 62, original italics). True statements about the social world are based on logically and empirically plausible interpretations of why specific outcomes occurred the way they did and not otherwise—or alternatively, why specific outcomes did *not* occur although they were the most utility-rational, and thus logically expected. After this excursion into metaphysics and the review of IR literature in the previous section, we now outline the theoretical framework of this book.

A Liberal-Constructivist Approach

For studying the suggested link between contested state identities and regional security we propose a constructivist-oriented framework of analysis, which however incorporates one premise of liberal IR theory. This theoretical approach has a number of theoretical and methodological implications, as discussed in the following sections. The outline of our theoretical framework ends with a brief definition of the key concept of state identity.

A Constructivist Framework ...

Considering its particular set of ontological and epistemological premises, a constructivist theoretical framework is almost imperative for the study of contested state identities and their impact on regional security. Indeed, since state identities are undoubtedly based on inter-subjective understandings, assuming a neat distinction between subject and object is pointless. The study of political identities also notably differs from assessing the international distribution of power. While the latter permits a positivist epistemology—weapons and resources can "objectively" be counted or measured—the study of identities necessitates a post-positivist approach.

Certainly, studying different case studies, as in this research, permits to single out specific factors that are crucial in all cases. Yet in view of our argument, the type of explanation cannot consist of generalizing strategies and deductive models that characterize classical positivism. This book adopts a particularizing strategy instead. Yet, seeking to understand "from within" also implies that we must refrain from any judgment on whether a specific identity concept is "rational" in the sense of expected benefits, or whether this or that interpretation of the EMP is "real." Rather, the aim is to explore "what the actor thinks he or she is doing" in his or her social context. This also implies the attempt to understand the core values, which, according to the actor, are indispensable for the definition of his or her collective. It goes without saying that this exercise becomes meaningless by stipulating that actors are "rational" in purely utilitarian terms.

In addition, the extensive work on security communities (Adler 1997a; Adler and Barnett 1998) within constructivist scholarship provides the appropriate theoretical tools for understanding why the formation of security regions necessitates the emergence of shared regional identity themes. Thus, a constructivist framework also permits to consider the EMP's region-building efforts as potential *manipulations* of the identity of the participating states.

To sum up, a constructivist approach permits to treat contested state identities as the independent variable, and a state's ability to engage in Euro-Mediterranean regional security as the dependent variable, while it also accounts for *change*. Similarly, foreign-policy interests are not considered as given and unchangeable, and actors are not conceived as purely utility-rational, but rather as responding to social norms and identities. Finally, in accordance with a constructivist framework, this book does not present general true statements about the world, but rather an empirically informed interpretation of a specific outcome, that is, the meager achievements in Euro-Mediterranean regional security, which is dependent on time and place.

... and the Liberal Premise

As briefly noted above, a constructivist approach to the study of contested state identities is nevertheless problematic. Although most constructivist scholars intend to problematize social identities, most empirical studies conducted in this spirit tend to treat state identity as a *unitary* concept. And while single case studies have focused on the *transformation* of state identity and its effect on foreign policy (Berger 1996), the impact of highly *contested* state identities on foreign policy has so far been overlooked.

Our exploration of contested state identities and their impact on regional security, however, must start by considering domestic preferences. Therefore, it presumes a bottom-up approach. But what are the methodological implications for such a move? To begin with, a broadening of the unitary concept of state identity as employed in most constructivist literature is required. If we assume that domestic divisions on the preferred political design of the state may affect foreign policy, the "commitment to states as units of analysis, and to the importance of systemic or 'third image' theorizing" (Wendt 1995: 72) must be modified. While treating the domestic level as *analytically prior*, the constructivist framework of analysis will thus borrow one of the basic assumptions of liberal theory, that is, the attention given to domestic politics and preferences.[8] Thus, our theoretical approach may well be termed *liberal-constructivist*.

Second, adopting a liberal-constructivist approach to the study of state identities and regional security has implications for the level of analysis. In practical terms, it becomes necessary to repeatedly shift from the state level to the domestic level of analysis and back. For instance, exploring a state's foreign-policy identity involves the state level. Yet the consideration of domestic preferences as far as state identity, relations to other states, and regional order are concerned must be carried out at the domestic level. And assessing the strategy of governments toward the EMP once more requires a shift to the state level. However, only a combination of the findings obtained at both levels of analysis permits to assess whether and how domestic conflicts over state identity impact on a government's policy toward regional security on a Euro-Mediterranean basis. Thus, while repeatedly shifting from one level of analysis to the other, we propose a reintegration of both levels for explaining outcome, thus broadly following the conceptualization of Kowert and Legro (1996: 487–488). In this context, it is worth reminding that the choice of one level of analysis is a purely theoretical exercise the aim of which is to "slice," and thus simplify, a complex reality. We now provide a brief definition of the abstract concept of state identity, which has admittedly been treated as self-evident so far.

State Identity: A Definition

Identity is an abstract notion that is difficult to employ. This is reflected in the over-abundant number of viable definitions in the literature, which are partly conflicting. Similarly, in spite of some attempts to conceptualize *state identity* (Wendt 1999; Kowert and Legro 1996), there are no concise definitions of this concept in the IR literature.

In the present book, the term *identity* will exclusively refer to *social* (or *collective*) *identities*, defined as regulative accounts of actors themselves and of their relationships to others.[9] Since identities are formed, maintained, or modified over time through relations with significant others, identities are a profoundly social phenomenon (Berger and Luckmann 1966: 173 ff.). As their most basic function, social identities set boundaries between "we" and "other." For this reason, they are necessarily based on symbols, myths, and cultural and historical narratives, which give them a meaning, provide internal cohesion, and succeed in mobilizing the solidarity of the majority of the collective. Social identities are not a priori given, but rather a product of social construction, a "cultural artefact of a particular kind" (Anderson 1991: 4).

The term *state identity* refers to the state as a collective. It entails both the construction of statehood and nationhood and refers to the political self-image that a state adopts in the international arena—such as "democratic," "regional leader," or "superpower." This image is shaped by the political, legal, and economic system, but also by national, religious, geographical, and historical narratives. Powerful domestic groups may thus shape, and manipulate, the identity of a state. Moreover, state identities are influenced by relations to other states as well as by historic events and (sometimes changing) norms of the international environment. Since states relate to other international actors through their self-image (Bush and Keyman 1997: 318–319), state identities influence the definition of foreign-policy interests.

There is, however, much more to say on the concept of state identity, its features and the role it plays in both domestic and international politics. The exploration of these questions necessitates a conceptualization of the dynamics of social identities in general, and the subsequent application of these findings to the concept of state identity.

State Identity, Its Functions, and Its Domestic Contestation

What are the political functions of state identities? Under which conditions may state identities become the subject of domestic struggles? And how does it impact on foreign policy in general and regional security schemes in particular? We start this exploration by considering a number of important insights on collective identities of the disciplines of social psychology and inter-group sociology.

Collective Identities and Social Interaction

An individual's quest for social identity corresponds to a basic psychological *need*. Since the mind exerts a pressure to classify perceptions, shared identifications reduce uncertainty, give a sense of "belonging," and help to structure and simplify a complex social world. However, processes of identification are not necessarily irreversible. Although individuals are born into a specific cultural and social background, there still is a relatively wide margin to choose between identities, and consciously change parts of it (Tamir 1999).

The key ingredient of identities is the reference to an "other." In fact, the tracing of boundaries between "self" and "other" is an *essential* and continuous element of identity formation (Durkheim 1964: 115–122). Within this process, several feedback mechanisms between "self" and "other" take place. Although some sort of personal identity is prior to interaction, people tend to internalize the attitude of the "other" toward the "self." This process has been termed "reflective appraisal," since "actors come to see themselves as a reflection of how they think Others see or 'appraise' them" (Wendt 1999: 327). Not every "other," however, will have the same effect on identity formation. The literature refers here to a "significant other," defined as those who are able to trigger processes of identity formation and reshaping. Wendt (1999: 331–332) suggests that power and dependency relations determine the significance of "the other." But in fact, any other who potentially threatens the positive identification of the "self" may count as a "significant other."

Identification processes do not follow black-and-white patterns. They are much more ambiguous than that. Anne Norton (1988: 45) argues that in addition to the "self" and "other," there is a third category, which she calls "simultaneously other and like." Moreover, identification processes require language, which "articulates systems of sociopolitical order and serves as the instrument for placing individuals within those systems" (Norton 1988: 46). In this vein, language is the medium for defining, reassessing, and potentially changing, the key categories of social identities. Any social identity, ranging from identification with the own family, neighborhood, city, or high school, up to a specific sexual, religious, ethnic, or national identity is based on these psychological needs and patterns.

Although individual behavior somewhat differs from group behavior (Hogg and Abrams 1988), the key mechanisms of individual identification processes are similar to those of *collective* identity formation. Interestingly, it has been demonstrated that social interaction almost automatically forges patterns of collective identifications among complete strangers (Sherif 1966). Moreover, the arbitrary division of individuals into two distinct groups is sufficient to generate intergroup discrimination and competition (Hogg and Abrams 1988; Tajfel 1982). Emile Durkheim (1964) observed that social cohesion within a group first necessitates the establishment of a boundary vis-à-vis other groups. Thus, delineating the "out-group" is not the *result* of social integration within the "in-group," but rather its necessary *precondition*.

In-group and out-group perceptions tend to be biased. This bias entails the conviction that the others are different from the own collective, while there is a deeply grounded belief to be "better than them." Thus, members of social groups create and maintain a positively defined difference from other groups, and together they will "preserve, defend and enhance their common identity" (Bloom 1990: 26). In this context, inter-group conflicts play an important role, as they tend to increase the solidarity within a group. However, any given identity is constituted in relation to a specific situation or subject (Linklater 1990). Thus, groups that compete with each other in a specific situation may be part of a common collective in other circumstances. For instance, supporters of two local soccer teams may be adversaries while their respective teams play against each other. Yet the fans of both teams will share a "we-feeling" when their *national* team plays against the team of another state. Collective identities, thus, are not only multiple, but also relational.

Thus, social interaction is the source of collective identities, and it is crucial in all inter-group processes (Berger and Luckmann 1966). Indeed, the integrating motives of any collective identity are the result of intersubjective meanings, which emerge and are maintained through communication and language (Norton 1988). In this context, Muzafer Sherif (1966) noted that collective identities are generally based on a common enemy, a common problem, common interests, or common values. But as much as these motives may "objectively" exist, they may also be distorted, or even freely invented (Anderson 1991). Thus, social communication also opens the way for the (intentional or unintentional) manipulation of the identity discourse by influential members of the collective (Bloom 1990; Norton 1988).

Moreover, communication is essential for the process of reflective appraisal between different collectives referred to above. But social interaction between hostile collectives does not necessarily lead to increased animosity. In fact, social learning (Adler 1991) may produce some sort of rapprochement, and even the emergence of shared values, provided that the patterns of inter-group relations change first. As Sherif (1966: 25) noted, it "is exceedingly difficult to change attitudes when inter-group relationships remain the same." Changed patterns of inter-group relations may thus give rise to altered perceptions, but this will only succeed if the other side takes up the new role and changes its attitude accordingly (Wendt 1999: 328). It should be stressed here that the image of a significant out-group is an intrinsic part of the conception of the in-group. For this reason, changed attitudes and behavior toward a former "enemy" necessarily demand a *redefinition of the identity of the own collective.* Applying these observations to states helps us to shed light on the political functions of state identity and its underlying mechanisms.

State Identities Between "Nations" and International Politics

State identities provide unifying motives to the citizens of specific states, while they also lend a state a distinct international role. Hence, state identity constitutes the link between national identity and international politics. State identities are undoubtedly a *political phenomenon.* In this context, Peter Katzenstein (1996a: 6) noted that the "process of constructing nation- and statehood typically is explicitly political and pits conflicting actors against each other."

Collective identities referring to states were born in Europe with the emergence of the modern nation-state, against the backdrop of the Enlightenment and the novel idea of national self-determination. The respective "nations," however, did not exist until then; they needed to be created.[10] Thus, in many cases, such as France, states forged the respective "nations" (Anderson 1991; Llobera 1993). Conflicts and wars with other political entities often reinforced the rise of national identities, which, in the European context, were typically based on an alleged cultural homogeneity and a stipulated congruity between nation and territory. In the developing world, national identities emerged much later, usually in the context of decolonization. Here, state identity was often propped upon existing patterns of social identifications, such as those based on ethnicity, religion, or kinship. But as in Europe, national identities often emerged in the context of conflicts with other states—most prominently the former colonial power.

Thus, national identities were useful for triggering mass mobilization and increasing social cohesion (Bloom 1990: 83). But there is more to this. In fact, national identities became the most important criterion for legitimate government. In Europe, for instance, a territorially defined national identity provided legitimacy to *secular* states after the dismissal of religiously defined state sovereignty (Ruggie 1993). And until the present, state authority and national sovereignty depend on the positive identification of citizens with the state (Norton 1988: 47; Haas 1993). Put differently, the state must be perceived "as being involved in a common endeavor in relation to an external threat; or [as acting] beneficently towards its citizens" (Bloom 1990: 75). This legitimizing function is double-fold, as it refers both to the population and the international environment. Indeed, the international recognition of a state very much depends on the assumption that the state represents "the nation." Thus, without identity, there can hardly be state authority, political legitimacy, or national sovereignty, and without them, no state would be able to survive.

The identification process of a population with the state follows the patterns of positive in-group identification and out-group discrimination described above (Goldgeier 1997: 143). Hence, state identities must employ powerful motives, which, however, are often the result of rather arbitrary choices. Identity themes will also be rather ambiguous, as they potentially need to provide social cohesion to an often heterogeneous population. Moreover, as much as social communication is crucial for maintaining the integrating force of state identity, it also permits manipulations by the political elites. However, at any given time, the options for identity manipulation are limited by the stipulated boundaries of acceptable behavior (Norton 1988: 48). In this context, Sherif (1966: 87) notes that "in order to be a 'leader' [of a group] . . . an individual must be responsible to pursue the goals of his group within the prevailing bounds for acceptable means. If he transgresses these limits, someone—sooner or later—will expose him as a traitor."

How are these issues related to foreign policy? In fact, the adoption of a specific role in relation to other states is central to international relations. Thus, Wendt (1999: 21) suggests that the "daily life of international politics is an on-going process of states taking identities in relation to Others, casting them into corresponding counter-identities, and playing out the result." More pointedly, David Campbell (1992) explains U.S. foreign policy exclusively in terms of identity politics. Although this perspective may be too narrow, foreign policy corresponds to social interaction between states as collectives. Thus, foreign policy is the medium through which the boundaries to other states are delineated. In this vein, foreign policy will not only reflect a stipulated state identity, but potentially contribute to the strengthening of identity, as a number of authors have argued (Barnett 1996; Berger 1996; Kienle 1995; Dagi 1993). At the same time, state identity makes some foreign-policy actions more legitimate and intelligible than others (Barnett 1999: 10)—both vis-à-vis the population and the international community.

In this context, issues of national security are particularly important. Arnold Wolfers's definition of security stresses that "[s]ecurity, in any objective sense, measures the absence of threats to acquired values, in a subjective sense, the absence of fear that such values will be attacked" (Wolfers 1962: 150). Hence, any reference to a potential threat to national security is an extremely powerful theme. At the same time, presenting someone or something as an existential threat to national security probably provides the strongest legitimization of foreign-policy action—both internally and externally. Indeed, the "securitization" of an issue means to "transfer [it] to the agenda of panic politics" (Buzan et al. 1998: 34). This move also justifies the violation of political and administrative rules and procedures that otherwise have to be respected.

Thus, although identity perceptions are undoubtedly "real," the construction of state identity is *instrumental* and has precise political functions. As figure 2.1 illustrates, these functions can be summarized as follows: First, state identity increases internal cohesion through the delineation of cognitive boundaries to other states. Second, it legitimizes state authority internally, and sovereignty externally. Third, it provides legitimacy to foreign-policy action, both domestically and internationally. Thus, patterns of enmity or amity on the international stage will reflect, and be constructed in relation to, the political identity of the state and its citizens. The next section conceptualizes the factors

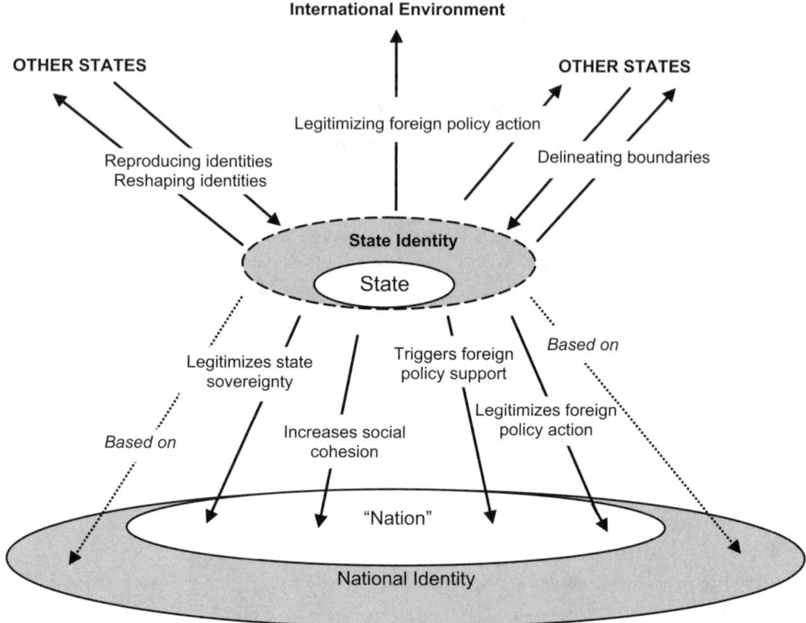

Figure 2.1   Functions of state identity.

that may trigger, or alternatively alleviate, domestic conflicts over state identity, and explores the conditions that determine the impact of contested state identities on foreign policy.

Contested State Identities: Intervening Variables

Domestic groups may have quite different preferences regarding the core values of their state. Since the international environment is not a stable parameter either, state identities may continuously be exposed to internal struggle, transformation, and change. Moreover, as state identities must be vague enough to comprise various sub-identities, different interpretations of state identity prevailing in any given society may be inherently contradicting. Nevertheless, conflicting interpretations of state identity may stand side by side as long as there is *no need to choose* between them. Thus, domestic conflicts over state identity are likely to arise whenever different interpretations of state identity are no longer compatible because they call for different action, that is, policy. Thus, we may understand domestic struggle over state identity as a competition between domestic groups in trying to impose their respective interpretation in view of specific policy choices.

However, there are several factors and developments that may trigger, or exacerbate, domestic identity conflicts. At the domestic level, these include for instance demographic change, altered patterns of political representation, a change of territorial borders, and altered socio-economic patterns (Barnett 1999: 10). In addition, a change of leadership may prompt the deepening of domestic fault-lines, as a new leader may strengthen the political representation of one particular group (Gross-Stein 1999). Similarly, an extreme attempt to manipulate state identity by a political leader may be a triggering factor, since, as noted above, the manipulation of state identity may only be gradual and must respect certain limits. Other "triggering" factors may occur at the international level. Thus, any new situation that is no longer compatible with the self-image of a state, and that erodes the defining themes of the latter, may prompt domestic conflicts over state identity. These situations may include the dismissal of a former "enemy" (or emerging patterns of cooperation with the latter), or increasing ideological differences with a former "friend." Similarly, the transnational diffusion of certain norms could generate such a situation (Finnemore 1996). In this context, the virulence of domestic conflicts will somewhat depend on the degree of unexpectedness and extent of international change, along with the degree of disjuncture between state identity and the new environment.

The "triggering" factors and developments will often cut across domestic and international politics, or have repercussions at both levels. However, comparable developments may affect states in a different way. In one state, for instance, they may provoke fervent domestic conflicts, while they may prompt a rather *peaceful transformation* of identity in another state.[11] Certainly, identity conflicts may eventually lead to a transformation of state identity, as much as any crisis is a potentially powerful source of change. Thus, domestic conflicts over state identity may also be interpreted as the attempt to preserve a given state identity in the face of new challenges, as cultures and identities always tend to self-preservation.

But which factors determine whether, under comparable "negative" conditions, domestic identity conflicts will be more or less fervent? We may think of a number of such indicators. First, while the degree of religious or ethnic heterogeneity within a given state may not necessarily be significant, the compatibility of different identity preferences will be more relevant. However, this is also dependent on the distribution of the mutually exclusive preferences. Indeed, if the identity preference of a small minority is incompatible with that of the majority, the outcome will be relatively insignificant. But if a society is divided into two or three almost equal groups that maintain incompatible preferences, the struggle will be more fervent. Second, domestic identity conflicts will be more salient in the absence of a "talented" political leadership that succeeds in aptly manipulating the identity discourse. To put it more sarcastically, the significance of domestic conflicts will depend on the ability of political leaders to "invent" new common problems, interests, values, or threats. Alternatively, emphasizing positively defined difference vis-à-vis other states may be helpful. Third, the promotion of overarching identity themes, for example at the regional level, may be a powerful tool for reducing domestic identity tensions, as Brigid Laffan (1996) has argued in the context of the EU. Fourth, any real situation of threat (such as that caused by military tensions, attacks, or ecological disasters) may exert a unifying pressure on society. Finally, while a common enemy may only be temporarily "effective" to overcome internal tensions, institutionalized cooperation toward what has been termed "super-ordinate" common goals is one of the most efficient ways of reducing inter-group conflict (Sherif 1966; Hogg and Abrams 1988). The variables that may trigger, or conversely alleviate, domestic identity conflicts will be relatively insignificant if considered separately. Only the assessment of the *interplay* of the various factors in a specific time and place will shed light on the question of why and when identity conflicts are more or less pronounced. In other words, the various factors discussed so far may be mutually reinforcing, although they may neutralize each other in other cases.

Contested Identities, Foreign Policy, and Regional Security

Our final step consists in conceptualizing the impact of contested state identities on regional security. When and under which conditions do domestic conflicts over state identity affect a state's foreign policy in general, and its policy toward regional security schemes in particular?

To begin with, not every domestic fault-line in terms of identity will be equally relevant for the realm of foreign policy, and not every domestic identity divide will bear the same importance for all foreign-policy areas. For this reason, it is first necessary to assess whether domestic identity divides touch upon the question of how to relate to specific other states or issue areas. Indeed, some foreign-policy actions may bring the incompatibility of domestic identity preferences to the fore, while others may not. Thus, specific foreign-policy decisions may entail a need to *choose* between different preferences, which could previously stand side by side. Conversely, if the different domestic preferences show a fair degree of compatibility even under new international circumstances (and in light of specific foreign-policy decisions), a rather peaceful transformation of state identity is possible.

If a specific foreign-policy issue touches upon a domestic fault-line in terms of state identity, we may expect an inconsistent and contradictory foreign-policy discourse and behavior. However, this will also depend on the type of political system and state–society relations. Thus, in a democratic state, a given domestic polarization will be reflected at the legislative or the decision-making level. Thus, in democratic states, contested state identities will be not only be more *visible*, but also more *politically significant*. Indeed, a government may find it extremely difficult to implement a foreign-policy course that potentially contradicts the identity preference of important domestic groups. Conversely, domestically contested identities may have a weaker impact on foreign policy in authoritarian states. This also implies that domestic conflicts over state identity may be less visible in authoritarian regimes, although they may exist.

Confronted with domestic fragmentation, governments (or leaders) may adopt a stronger stance toward a former adversary, or promote integrating themes that underline the in-group/out-group bias. These efforts may also be supported by specific foreign-policy actions. In fact, "the opportunity is always present for a government to deliberately use foreign policy as a method of mobilizing the mass national public sentiment away from internal political dissension, and achieving political integration," as William Bloom (1990: 82) has put it. Alternatively, in the face of controversial foreign-policy decisions that touch upon domestic identity fault-lines, political leaders may adopt a strategy of inertia and postpone crucial decisions. This strategy may not be particularly wise, but, at least in the short term, it may alleviate domestic divisions. The different factors and developments that may trigger, or alternatively alleviate, the impact of contested identities on foreign policy are depicted in figure 2.2.

Finally, in view of domestic identity conflicts, attempts to engage in the creation of a security region may be a particularly difficult undertaking, particularly if it involves former (or present) adversaries. Indeed, in view of contested state identities, political leaders may be

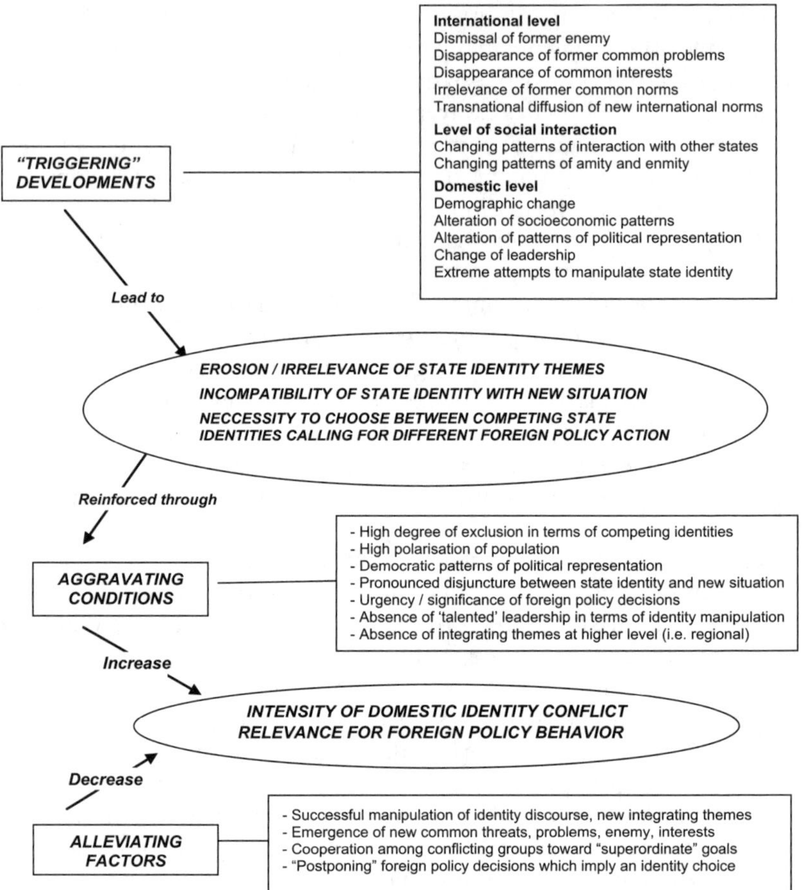

Figure 2.2   Interplay between triggering developments, aggravating conditions, and alleviating factors influencing the intensity of domestic conflicts over state identity and their relevance for foreign-policy behavior.

forced to promote "exclusive" identity themes and to emphasize the in-group/out-group bias. This potentially contradicts the promotion of values and identity themes that a state allegedly shares with the other regional neighbors—the necessary ingredient of regional security schemes. The in-group/out-group bias may thus undermine efforts to search for a common ground with the neighbors in the region. For this reason, regional initiatives are likely to fail until the internal conflicts over state identity have not been soothed.

Summary

The review of IR theory has shown that traditional approaches cannot provide the theoretical tools for studying the subject under discussion, as they consider foreign-policy interests as given. At the same time, traditional IR approaches tend not to pay attention to the identity of states, let alone the relations between identities and interests. Thus, region-building as an alternative approach to regional security and its identity implications can hardly be studied with a traditional IR approach. Constructivist approaches, on the other hand, allow the study of these phenomena and their interrelation, as they start from different meta-theoretical premises. While arguing in favor of the *social* character of international relations, these approaches depart from the strictly positivist foundations of classical IR theory, including the clear distinction between subject and object, the aim of reaching statements of absolute and timeless truth, and the generalizing model of explanation and prediction.

However, in order to explore the impact of *domestic* identity conflicts on a state's ability to engage in Euro-Mediterranean region-building, the constructivist-oriented framework is expanded to include one of the premises of liberal IR theory, namely the importance given to domestic factors. In methodological terms, this proposition is relevant for the level-of-analysis problem. This book proposes to consider both the domestic and the state level, and to subsequently integrate the findings obtained at both levels.

Based on the findings of sociology and social psychology, we have applied the key functions and dynamics of collective identities to states. State identity has been defined as the self-image that a state adopts on the international stage—which is based on a portrayed national identity. Thus, taking the state as the collective of its citizens as a reference point, state identities increase societal cohesion through the formation of boundaries to other states, while they legitimize foreign-policy action, state authority, and the existence of states (representing distinctive "nations") in the international arena. In a similar vein, it is possible to transfer the conditions under which collective identities are formed, strengthened, and modified to the realm of state identity. Social interaction and communication among groups thus correspond to foreign policy and relations among states.

Finally, the discussion of the conditions under which a state's identity may become contested at the domestic level and influence foreign-policy making has shown that different preconditions and factors may be relevant. It is assumed that their interplay will determine outcome in practice. Indeed, the degree of societal polarization, the type of state–society relations and political representation may greatly vary from state to state, and the same can be said about international developments that may trigger, or alleviate, domestic identity conflicts. In accordance with the epistemological premises of this book, we thus argue in favor of adopting a particularizing strategy for explaining causes and outcome in international relations.

3

Historical Background and Regional Perspective

This chapter puts the Euro-Mediterranean Partnership in a historical context while providing a regional perspective on the suggested link between contested state identities and Euro-Mediterranean regional security. Thus, we first discuss previous policy initiatives addressing Mediterranean security and subsequently provide an overview of Euro–Mediterranean relations since the early 1990s. In this context, the response of major states in the southern Mediterranean to the EU's region-building logic since the launching of the EMP is explored. Finally, this chapter gives an overview of domestic developments in the Mediterranean/Middle East by keeping possible foreign-policy implications in mind.

Background of the EMP

The preoccupation of the "West" with Mediterranean security has quite a long history. At the same time, the EMP was the continuation of the EC/EU's Mediterranean policy of the previous decades, as discussed in the following sections. In this context, it should be noted that the EU, and before that the EC, is far from being a unitary actor in world politics—although it maintains a foreign policy (Regelsberger et al. 1997; Tonra and Christiansen 2004; Carlsnaes et al. 2004). In the framework of this book, however, the complex institutional mechanisms of EU foreign-policy making, and the difficulties related to it, will not be considered.

The "West" and the Mediterranean during the Cold War

The interest of the "West" in Mediterranean security dates back to the beginning of the cold war. NATO, for instance, viewed the Mediterranean as a strategic unit and considered it as Europe's southern flank, which had to be defended from the Soviet threat as much as Western Europe itself. The CSCE also recognized the Mediterranean's relevance for European security. In the 1975 Helsinki Final Act, the CSCE members committed themselves to expand the dialogue "to include all the states in the Mediterranean, with the purpose of contributing to peace, reducing armed forces in the region, and widening the scope of co-operation" (quoted after Fenech 1997: 171). Some states, such as Italy, had also proposed to expand CSCE membership to non-European Mediterranean countries. Although the superpowers rejected this proposition, CSCE members and Mediterranean countries established informal diplomatic contacts. From 1978 on, an official Mediterranean forum within the CSCE was created, leading to a regular Mediterranean security dialogue of the CSCE, and later the OSCE (Organization for Security and Co-operation in Europe) (UNIDIR 1995). The Barcelona Convention of 1976 established an additional diplomatic forum dealing with nonmilitary aspects of Mediterranean security under the United Nations Environment Programme (UNEP) and the Mediterranean Action Plan (MAP). Signed by all the Mediterranean states and the members of what was then the EC, UNEP/MAP monitors the ecological status of the Mediterranean Sea and its environment (Haas 1989; Spiteri 1994).

The EC showed an interest in the Mediterranean since the very beginning of the European integration process. Article 237 of the 1957 Treaty of Rome referred to the possibility of future membership of south European Mediterranean countries, such as Spain and Greece, but Article 131 of the Rome Treaty also specifically addressed "non-European countries which have special relations" with the EC founding members. With this provision, the EC had Morocco and Tunisia in mind, which had just reached political independence from France and Spain (unlike Algeria, which then was still part of France). A separate "Joint Declaration of Intent" communicated the aim of the newly established EC to soon negotiate an economic association with Morocco and Tunisia, as well as with Libya (Grilli 1993: 183).

During the 1960s and the early 1970s, the EC concluded various bilateral trade agreements with Mediterranean countries. This first phase of the EC's Mediterranean policy consisted of partly arbitrary ad hoc responses to local trade problems, and reflected different economic and political interests of the EC members vis-à-vis Mediterranean countries.[1] Following wide criticism of the rather incoherent approach, the EC adopted its "Global Mediterranean Policy" (GMP) in 1972. Although "global" may not have been the most appropriate label, the new approach nevertheless sought to address the Mediterranean more systematically. Moreover, the EC acknowledged the importance of economic development in the Mediterranean, from which the EC would also benefit. Since trade provisions alone were not viewed as sufficient for achieving this aim, the following round of agreements signed with Mediterranean countries included financial five-year protocols as well as provisions covering cooperation in social matters (Grilli 1993, 185; Lister 1997, 84–87; Tovias 1977).[2]

The GMP certainly aimed at increasing the EC's influence through the distribution of trade privileges to countries that were trade dependent on the EC. But, as Alfred Tovias (1996) argues, the EC sought to increase its influence in areas in which the trade dependence was high and the involvement of the superpowers low. Thus, European Free Trade Area (EFTA) countries and the former colonies in Africa, the Caribbean, and the Pacific clearly enjoyed a higher priority than the Mediterranean. Moreover, the GMP was certainly a regional approach, but it was not multilateral. In addition, the low importance attached to the area resulted in rather limited trade preferences and comparatively modest financial assistance. Nevertheless, with the adoption of the GMP, the EC started addressing the *stability* of the Mediterranean. By declaring that the aim of the cooperation was "the establishment and maintenance of peace, stability and progress in the region" (European Council 1973), the EC adopted the idea that trade, financial assistance, and cooperation in other areas would foster economic growth and stability. Considering the EC's proximity to the Mediterranean—which back then still included several southern European states—the aim of achieving stability and economic progress can clearly be read as a *security concern* of the EC.

The outbreak of the 1973 Yom Kippur/October War between Israel and bordering Arab states, the oil crisis affecting Europe, as well as cold-war politics, restricted a consistent implementation of the EC's policy. In the aftermath of the 1973 war, the EC nevertheless introduced a new tool in its relations with the Mediterranean, or parts of it, namely that of political dialogue. This was reflected in the opening of the Euro–Arab Dialogue in 1975.[3] But several developments stood in the way of the EC's efforts to coherently address the Mediterranean region. First, the late 1970s and early 1980s witnessed a number of altered regional alignments in the Middle East following the change of regime in Iran, the Camp David peace agreement between Egypt and Israel, the Soviet invasion of Afghanistan, and the outbreak of the Iran–Iraq war. Although Ghassam Salamé (1994a: 242) suggests that the failure of the GMP "was caused less by Europe than by the complexities and feuds in the Middle East," developments within the EC itself were also significant. The creation of the EC's single market and the admission of first Greece, and subsequently Spain and Portugal into the EC in 1981 and 1986 respectively further widened the gap between Europe and its southern periphery. The EC's southern enlargement certainly succeeded in stabilizing the *northern shore* of the Mediterranean. But it widened the socioeconomic gap between the two shores. Indeed, the EC's southern enlargement increased the self-sufficiency of the EC in typically Mediterranean agricultural products, such as olive oil, fresh vegetables, and citrus fruits, thus reducing the trade preferences of Maghreb and Mashreq countries in exporting these goods to the EC. Moreover, Portugal's textile industry stood in direct competition with that of Egypt and Tunisia.

The countries in the Maghreb and Mashreq thus experienced a further economic marginalization (Edwards and Philippart 1997; Tovias 1996; Joffé 1996; White 2001). Since by the mid-1990s, Maghreb and Mashreq countries—with the exception of Israel—had experienced the largest decline in real per capita income of any developing region, along with a widening trade deficit, a thorough revision of the EC's policy seemed necessary. Thus, in November 1989, the EC Commission proposed the "Redirected Mediterranean Policy," which the EC formally adopted one year later (Commission 1990). In this context, the EC explicitly stated that, due to its proximity "the stability and prosperity of the Mediterranean region are essential to the stability and prosperity of the Community," and that "in a wider sense, the security of the Community is at stake" (Commission 1990). While identifying mass immigration into the EC, religious fundamentalism, WMD proliferation, drug trafficking, and ecological hazards in or around the Mediterranean Sea as security threats, the Renovated Mediterranean Policy put a new emphasis on economic reforms in Mediterranean countries. In addition, it provided financial support for cross-border projects and increased development aid and EIB loans—yet without improving the trade conditions of the Mediterranean partners (Tovias 1996). In addition, the new approach stressed the importance of political dialogue with the southern neighbors.

Mediterranean Politics after the Cold War

As long as the cold war prevailed, Western Europe was mainly preoccupied with a possible superpower confrontation, which as worst-case scenario foresaw a nuclear war on European soil. The quite sudden dissipation of the cold war led to a thorough reassessment of the EC/EU's external relations. At the same time, once the veil of the cold war was lifted, the problems in the Mediterranean periphery seemed even more severe. But immediately after the end of the cold war, German unification and the political transformation in Central and Eastern Europe attracted the EC's main attention, temporarily leaving the Mediterranean aside. However, this development prompted the EC's Mediterranean countries to seek to counterbalance the EC's preoccupation with the east and put the Mediterranean back onto the EC's agenda.

In this vein, during a meeting in the temporarily revitalized Euro–Arab Dialogue in December 1989, former Italian foreign minister Gianni De Michelis proposed to expand the spirit of Helsinki to the Mediterranean, and the governments of Italy and Spain officially proposed the establishment of a Conference on Security and Co-operation in the Mediterranean (CSCM) at the CSCE opening speeches in September 1990. France, which initially criticized the initiative as inadequate for such a vast area as the Mediterranean, supported a smaller framework of cooperation. This proposal developed first into the so-called 4 + 5 Dialogue comprising Spain, France, Italy, and Portugal as European parties, and Algeria, Morocco, Tunisia, Libya, and Mauritania as their western Mediterranean counterparts. With the addition of Malta on the European side, the dialogue subsequently became the "5 + 5 Dialogue." Later on revising its position, France signed with Italy, Spain, and Portugal a joint document on the CSCM, published in January 1991. Although the initiative never formally materialized, the idea of addressing Mediterranean security through an overall strategy of cooperation and partnership was reiterated in several initiatives that were to follow.

But the end of the cold war also resulted in altered patterns of global and regional politics. The military and political constellation of actors in the 1991 Gulf War was the most visible case in point, since most Arab countries, including Syria and Egypt, aligned with the U.S.-led coalition against the fellow Arab country Iraq. At the end of the same year, the Madrid peace process started (Peters 1996). With the election of the late Itzhak Rabin as Israeli prime minister in 1992 and the beginning of the Oslo peace process between Israel and the Palestinians, the patterns of Middle East politics seemed to have changed in a profound and irreversible manner. Hence, an encompassing regional approach toward the Mediterranean seemed possible.

Several international actors sought to seize the opportunity. The West European Union (WEU) launched a Mediterranean dialogue in June 1992, and NATO followed at the end of 1994. The Inter-Parliamentary Union started to implement CSCM conferences at the parliamentary level from 1992 on (as the CSCM proposal had gained support among parliamentarians). Similarly, the North Atlantic Assembly started a Mediterranean parliamentary forum in 1996. The Working Group on Arms Control and Regional Security (ACRS) of the multilateral track of the Madrid peace process established at the end of 1991, and the 1991 Egyptian proposal of establishing a Mediterranean Forum, which materialized in 1994, are additional initiatives covering all or parts of the Mediterranean (Selim 1997; Karsh and Seyigh 1994; Maoz 1997).

In the meantime, Europe's Mediterranean countries continued to lobby for giving greater importance to the southern Mediterranean— especially after the events around the Algerian elections of December 1991 and the subsequent outbreak of the civil war. Thus, Spain and France proposed the upgrading of cooperation with Maghreb countries, an idea that was formally endorsed at the June 1992 European Council in Lisbon, and later on extended to Mashreq countries as well (Commission 1992, 1993). In the following years, the Spanish and Italian governments sought to advance the Mediterranean on the agenda of the EU's Common Foreign and Security Policy (CFSP) as an area for joint action. At the same time, the EU Commission prepared its recommendations on establishing a Euro-Mediterranean Partnership (Commission 1994, 1995a), and started negotiating new bilateral trade agreements with Tunisia, Morocco, and Israel. The recommendations of the Commission were finalized in 1995 under the French EU presidency, and opened the way for the Barcelona Conference under the Spanish EU presidency at the end of the same year. In fact, the subsequent EU presidency of three "Mediterranean EU members," that is, France, Spain, and Italy in 1994/1995, notably favored the materialization of the Barcelona Process, since it permitted a pooling of agenda-setting efforts among Europe's Mediterranean countries.

Summary: The "Mediterranean Experience"

The EU's launching of the EMP in November 1995 was clearly an attempt to learn from previous mistakes of its Mediterranean policy.

These were identified as inconsistency, a lack of priority, and a lack of a regional perspective. At the same time, the EU's efforts to address the Mediterranean through a regional approach reflected the overall preoccupation of international players with Mediterranean security after the end of the cold war. Interestingly, however, the idea of a Mediterranean group of states in international relations has quite a long history. Its composition may have witnessed some change over time, and its designation was coined by international actors in relation to specific interests and international constellations, such as the cold war. However, major Mediterranean states gained some experience over the years in acting as "Mediterranean states" in different international institutions and fora. Thus, the beginning of the Barcelona Process was by no means the first experience of southern Mediterranean countries with regional and multilateral initiatives aimed at solving common problems and addressing common interests.

Euro-Mediterranean Relations since the 1990s

From 1995 on, the Euro-Mediterranean Partnership became the main framework of the EU's relations with its southern periphery—at least until the launching of the EU's Neighbourhood Policy in 2003–2004. As noted previously, several issues were linked up to the Barcelona Process, and the EU continuously sought to promote the regional component of the latter, along with a specific set of values (Patten 1999a, 2000, 2002; Commission 2000a). But how did the EMP partner states respond to these efforts? Which patterns characterize relations amongst southern Mediterranean states since the mid-1990s as well as their relations to the EU, the main promoter of the EMP?

Relations among Southern Mediterranean States

Relations outside the EMP Framework

While the Madrid peace process had entered a stalemate by the end of 1993, the Oslo process resulted in September 1993 in the mutual recognition between Israel and the PLO, and in May 1994 to the transfer of Gaza and Jericho to Palestinian civilian rule under the Oslo I agreement. The Oslo II accord of September 1995 stipulated the conditions and a time table for a further Israeli withdrawal from Palestinian territories, and the transfer of designated areas to the newly established Palestinian Authority (PA). With the start of the Oslo peace process, the wider Arab–Israeli conflict seemed on the verge of being solved. Jordan signed a "nonbelligerency accord" with Israel in July 1994, followed in October by a full-fledged peace treaty. Morocco established diplomatic contacts with Israel in September 1994, followed by Tunisia one month later. The trend toward peace in the region also included traditionally revisionist Arab states. Damascus had signalized its interest in a dialogue with Israel since mid-1992, and negotiations began shortly afterwards (Shlaim 2000: 508). The Syrian–Israeli track of the Madrid peace process, however, moved quite slowly, mainly because both sides insisted on rather incompatible preconditions for engaging in negotiations.[4] But the fact that Syria and Israel were negotiating on a "land-for-peace" basis was undoubtedly a novelty. Indeed, the argument of the late Syrian president Hafez al-Assad that peace with Israel was a "strategic option"—first announced in January 1994—was a significant departure from Syria's traditional stance (Al-Moualem 1997). Even Libya showed some reconciling signs. Although Muammar Qadaffi officially condemned Oslo and accused the late Yassir Arafat of treason, in 1993 he sent 200 Libyans pilgrims to Jerusalem, and invited Libyan Jews who lived abroad to visit Libya (Deeb 1995: 365).

Egypt reacted to the Oslo peace process in a less reconciling way, although it seemed to legitimize its 1979 peace agreement with Israel in retrospect. In 1995, Egyptian president Hosni Mubarak waged a rather unsuccessful campaign against Israeli nuclear weapons in view of the envisaged extension of the Non-Proliferation Treaty (NPT) (Landau 2003). Moreover, Mubarak ridiculed the late King Hussein for his promise to engage in a "warm peace" with Israel. Egypt's attitude has been linked to the domestic struggle against radical Islamist forces, to whose insurgence the state responded quite mercilessly (Ajami 1999: 202–207, 253–312). Certainly, the peace negotiations brought a number of regional rivalries and incompatible positions to the fore (Peters 1996), and there were also some less promising signs, such as developments in Algeria. All in all, however, by mid-1995, the Middle East seemed to have entered a new era, characterized by a convergence of interests and considerably improved regional relations.

Following the assassination of Israeli prime minister Itzhak Rabin in November 1995, the wave of Palestinian terrorist attacks within Israel in early 1996, and the election of an Israeli Center–Right government under Binyamin Netanyahu in May 1996, the Middle East peace process started to derail. However, already at the beginning of 1996, Israel concluded a strategic cooperation agreement with Turkey, which has been termed "one of the most important political developments in the region since the 1991 Gulf War" (Gresh 1998: 203). Reviving old fears of an anti-Arab alliance, Arab leaders immediately called upon Turkey to reconsider the agreement. In particular, the accord raised suspicion in Damascus, and if "there had been any prospects of Syria's coming to terms with Israel, the Turkish agreement ended it" (Shlaim 2000: 559). The new Israeli government under Netanyahu did not show much commitment to the peace process with the Palestinians, which entered a stalemate of over 19 months. In this period, Jordan and Egypt criticized Israeli policy in harsh tones, while Tunisia and Morocco temporarily withdraw their representatives from Israel. Within a few years, relations between Israel and Arab states had fallen to a low point.

The Netanyahu government lost its parliamentary majority in December 1998, and the succeeding government under Ehud Barak sought to put the peace process back on track. Since the negotiations with Syria did not move substantially forwards, Israel decided to unilaterally withdraw from southern Lebanon in June 2000. At the same time, the negotiations with the PA started to touch thorny issues such as the right of return of Palestinian refugees, Jerusalem, Jewish settlements, and the final status of the Palestinian entity. In September 2000, the second Palestinian uprising (the so-called *Al-Aqsa Intifada*) broke out. Tensions among Israel and its Arab neighbors rose to an unprecedented level since the beginning of Oslo. Morocco and Tunisia closed their representative offices in Tel Aviv in December 2000, and Cairo called back its ambassador. While the peace negotiations broke down shortly afterwards, the *Intifada* entailed a large number of suicide attacks within Israel. In March 2001, after the Barak government lost its parliamentary majority, Ariel Sharon was elected Israeli prime minister. While Sharon refused to negotiate "under fire," the violence continued, and various international efforts to broker a cease-fire failed. Israel's policy to retaliate against Palestinian terror attacks and prevent them witnessed numerous military raids and the reoccupation of the West Bank from 2002 on. While both Israel's policy in the territories and Palestinian suicide bombings led to the killing of many innocent civilians, the resulting spiral of violence lasted until after the election of Mahmoud Abbas (Abu Mazen) as the new PLO chairman in January 2005, following the death of Arafat. Israel's policy in the territories repeatedly caused large anti-Israeli demonstrations in the neighboring Arab states as well as harsh criticism by Arab leaders. Thus, if the early 1990s had raised the prospects of solving the

Arab–Israeli conflict, the Middle East seemed a hopeless case a decade later. In the summer of 2005, there were some positive signs at the horizon, including Abu Mazen's announcement that the Palestinian *Intifada* was over, and Israel's withdrawal from the Gaza Strip. However, although it is too early for predictions, the victory of *Hamas* in the Palestinian legislative elections of January 2006 do not bode well for Israeli-Palestinian peace-making.

However, in the late 1990s, the derailing Middle East peace process was not the only source of tension around the Mediterranean. Turkey had started to adopt a much more assertive foreign policy since the end of the cold war (Dagi 1993), leading to repeated confrontations with, and open threats toward, Syria over the Kurdish issue. Turkey was particularly disturbed by Syria's support of the separatist Kurdistan Workers Party, PKK, considered a terrorist group in Ankara, and Damascus's hosting of PKK leader Abdallah Öcalan (Sayari 2000). After the turn of the century, however, Turkish–Syrian relations notably improved, leading to the signing of two military cooperation agreements in June 2002. At the end of the 1990s, Turkey also threatened the Greek Cypriot government because of its intention to deploy Russian S-300 anti-aircraft missiles on Cyprus, thus causing serious tensions between Turkey and EU member Greece. However, relations between Ankara and Athens notably improved shortly afterwards— paradoxically prompted by two devastating earthquakes that struck Turkey and Greece in 1999 (Kasaba and Bozdoğan 2000).[5]

The western Mediterranean, which has a long history of rivalry, mutual suspicion, border disputes, and shifting alliances, similarly witnessed changing patterns of relations. At the beginning of the 1990s, there was a trend toward reduced tensions. This détente followed the acceptance of a UN initiative aimed at resolving the Western Sahara conflict, which traditionally pitted Morocco on one side, and Algeria, and Libya on the other (Zoubir 1999b). Similarly, the UMA initiative, involving Mauritania, Morocco, Tunisia, Algeria, and Libya, had been launched in 1989. But by the mid-1990s, this rapprochement showed the first signs of reversibility. The regional integration effort of the UMA had entered a stalemate, and so did the diplomatic efforts to resolve the Western Sahara conflict. As a consequence, relations between Morocco and Algeria once again deteriorated. They were additionally affected by the domestic violence in Algeria from the end of 1991 on. A hotel shooting in Marrakech in 1994, which was allegedly committed by Algerian fundamentalists, exacerbated the tensions, which led both governments to impose visa restrictions for nationals of the respective other state (Mortimer 1999). The UMA is still stalled, and in spite of UN pressure, the conflict over the Western Sahara remains unsettled. At the same time, the renewed tensions between Algeria and Morocco went hand in hand with a rapprochement between Tunisia and Libya from 1996 on (Zoubir 1999b). Thus, the old patterns of polarization in the Maghreb were reestablished.

Thus, the political situation in the Mediterranean and Middle East of the early 1990s notably differs from that at the end of the same decade and at the beginning of the twenty-first century. Relations among southern Mediterranean states before and since the beginning of the Barcelona Process have proven to be quite unstable indeed.

Relations within the EMP

In spite of the establishment of various Euro-Mediterranean networks, regional relations within the EMP framework have remained difficult. Certainly, the EU repeatedly stressed that the EMP was the only diplomatic forum in which Syrian, Lebanese, and Israeli officials would meet (Commission 2000a). But Syria and Lebanon boycotted some of the EMP meetings of foreign ministers after the eruption of the second *Intifada*, and regional EMP projects have generally not been able to bring Syrian, Lebanese, and Israeli participants together. For instance, although Syria and Lebanon are members of EuroMeSCo, they do not participate in practice. There are no youth programs in which the three countries participate together. Similarly, among the large number of projects for the preservation of cultural heritage, Syria and Lebanon participated in only one short-term project in which Israel took part. Israel, which was interested in breaking out of its regional isolation, recurrently complained that the EMP was held hostage to the Middle East peace process. Yet the position of Syria and Lebanon on regional cooperation and confidence-building measures is clear: perceived as steps toward the normalization of relations with Israel, in their view these measures should follow, and not precede, a fair and comprehensive Middle East peace agreement.

Similarly, Egypt voiced opposition to the normalization of relations with Israel whenever there were problems with the peace process, thus affecting the regional dimension of the EMP. Egypt also showed a far greater interest in economic cooperation with other Arab EMP partners. In this context, with the so-called Agadir Declaration of May 2001, Egypt, Morocco, Tunisia, and Jordan agreed on establishing a free-trade area among them within the EMP framework. Yet this development did not quite please Algeria, which, according to EU officials, temporarily aimed at becoming the *porte-parole* of Arab Mediterranean states vis-à-vis the EU.[6]

Altogether, Morocco and Tunisia were the most active participants in the EMP's regional track, while the other southern participants recurrently squabbled with each other over different issues. Turkey, on the other hand, participated in the EMP with a rather indifferent attitude, as it tended to view the EMP as a temporary phenomenon, EU membership being the real goal. The next section assesses relations between the EMP partners and the EU since the start of the Barcelona Process.

The EMP Partners and the EU

Traditionally, the EC/EU had been an important economic player in the Mediterranean and Middle East, yet with a limited political leverage. In the aftermath of the cold war, several Arab states were interested in improving their relations with Europe. This particularly applies to Maghreb states, which had maintained close political and economic relations to their former colonial powers. But also Egypt started to pursue a new foreign-policy strategy vis-à-vis the EC/EU. This became most visible with the Egyptian 1991 proposal to establish a Mediterranean forum, which preceded the launching of the EMP (Selim 1997).

Once the Barcelona Process started, it became increasingly difficult for most southern EMP partners to separate their bilateral relations to the EU from the EMP framework. This particularly regards those states the relationship with the EU of which was upgraded through the EMP. Officially, southern Mediterranean states have repeatedly reiterated their commitment to the EU and the EMP. This does not necessarily mean, however, that these states developed a regional approach while dealing with the EU. As discussed in the following sections, EU–Mediterranean relations were characterized by many disagreements and disputes.

Points of Criticism and Disagreement

The EU's policy toward the Middle East peace process was repeatedly criticized in harsh tones—by all the parties involved. Thus, over the years Syria and Lebanon regularly called for a stronger political involvement of the EU in the peace process. Similarly, Cairo repeatedly expressed its disappointment with the EU's political achievements in the Middle East (*Al-Ahram Weekly* February 22, 2001). Even Jordan, which generally refrains from voicing criticism, expressed its dissatisfaction with "Europe's long absence from taking part in the peace talks between the Palestinians and Israel and its neutral position in the Palestinian Intifada" (*The Star* November 29, 2000: 1).

On the other hand, in the context of the stalled peace process from 1996 on, Israel repeatedly accused the EU of an anti-Israel bias. Thus, the EU's Luxembourg Declaration of December 1998 calling for Israeli concessions in order to revive the peace process, along with the EU's 1999 statement on Jerusalem as *corpus separatum* (that is, a separated entity in terms of sovereignty), triggered a storm of protests from the Israeli side (Foreign Ministry of Israel 1997; Netanyahu and Sharon 1999). At other times, particularly Israeli Labor governments adopted a more accommodating and even friendly attitude toward the EU (Del Sarto and Tovias 2001). It is true that all Israeli governments were in favor of the EU's economic involvement in the peace process, along with the EU's massive financial assistance to the PA. A quite different matter, however, was the EU's political ambitions. Israel somewhat tolerated the latter as long as the peace process was moving ahead. However, after the eruption of the second *Intifada*, and in view of the EU's critical stance toward Israeli practices in the occupied territories, the EU's political ambitions were not particularly welcome in Israel.

However, the EU's involvement or noninvolvement in the Middle East peace process—depending on who is asked—was not the only source of friction in EU–Mediterranean relations. For example, Morocco had been fighting with the EU over fisheries and tomatoes. In this context, Moroccan officials recurrently complained of a lack of "real partnership" (*Le Matin* February 2, 2000). Similarly, Egypt and the EU disagreed on cotton exports and potatoes, prompting former Egyptian foreign minister Amr Moussa to quite sharply accuse the EU Commission of a "practice of double standards" (Moussa 1998). Israel, on the other hand, had a dispute with the EU over orange juice in 1997, which caused some diplomatic row. In general, southern EMP partners have been accusing the EU of a protectionist agricultural policy that does not compare to the efforts of opening their markets to EU competition in industrial products, as prescribed by the Euro-Mediterranean Association Agreements.

Human-rights issues have been the subject of additional Euro-Mediterranean disagreement, prompting complaints of some EMP partners about the EU's allegedly patronizing attitude (Aliboni and Said Aly 2000: 213). Algeria, the political reforms of which were being funded through the EMP budget, certainly adopted the most extreme stance. For instance, a 1996 resolution of the European Parliament calling for the introduction of democratic pluralism was denounced by Algerian government officials as a "flagrant, totally inadmissible and an unacceptable interference" in its internal affairs (*Agence France Presse* December 14, 1996). EU fact-finding missions to Algeria during a wave of killings between 1997 and 1998 met a similar official reaction. And a 2001 European Parliament resolution calling on the Algerian authorities to end the violence in the Kabylie region prompted Algerian representatives to declare a "total rejection of all forms of foreign interference in Algeria's internal affairs" (*Agence France Presse* May 19, 2001). At the same time, however, officials of the EU delegation in Algiers noted that Algeria supported the strengthening of the third basket, which, inter alia, envisages democratization programs.[7] Tunisia, as other southern participants, has also been critical of the EU's funding of nongovernmental organizations (NGOs) under MEDA Democracy without the government's explicit blessing (Desrues 1999: 108–110). Egypt may have been less critical in the verbal realm, but certainly not less opposed to foreign support for democratization. Thus, while passing restrictive NGO laws, the state has repeatedly harassed pro-democracy activists, as will be discussed further in the chapter on Egypt. Morocco has also voiced some criticism of the EU's human-rights policy. In this vein, Rabat reminded the EU that if human rights were so important to the EU, it better take care of the situation in the Palestinian territories (Benaïssa 2000).

Of all the EMP partners, Syria has maintained the most reluctant attitude toward the Barcelona Process. While insisting on the intrinsic link between Middle East peace-making and the EMP, Damascus remained suspicious toward economic liberalization (Abdel Nour 2001). At the beginning of 2001, negotiations on the bilateral free-trade agreement were broken off, since, much to the surprise of EU officials, Syria suspected the EU of wanting to "dictate" reforms.[8] Syria was the last country to sign a Euro-Mediterranean Association Agreement, which, as of early 2006, has not entered into force yet. But neither was Egypt particularly enthusiastic about economic liberalization, and negotiations on the bilateral free-trade agreement proceeded at a very slow pace. According to EU officials, this was due to Egypt's difficulties in "digesting" the idea of tremendous reforms, along with internal opposition.[9] This is somewhat surprising since Egypt initially counted as one of the most fervent supporters of the EMP.

Turkey's relations to the EU are dominated by Ankara's ambition of becoming an EU member, and the EU's feet-dragging on this issue repeatedly caused tensions between both sides. EU–Turkish relations reached an all-time low after the 1997 EU Luxembourg summit in which Turkey was excluded from the list of accession countries (*Turkish Daily News* April 30, 1998). The EU's decision to accept Cyprus as future member additionally infuriated Ankara. Following the rapprochement between Turkey and Greece in the aftermath of the 1999 earthquakes, Greece gave up its traditional opposition to Turkey's EU accession. However, the EU's insistence on far-reaching human-rights reforms as preconditions for EU membership prompted an ambivalent Turkish reaction. While some public figures expressed their support for both such reforms and EU membership, others criticized the EU for their patronizing attitude, thus questioning Turkey's EU membership altogether. Following the Nice European Council summit in December 2000, Turkish officials were extremely disappointed that Turkey, once more, was not listed as EU candidate country. Only at the end of 2004 did Brussels decide to start membership negotiations with Turkey, which officially began in October 2005. Yet the EU remains hesitant on whether Turkey's EU membership could be an asset (Del Sarto 2004). And while Turkey has met most of the EU's criteria, including far-reaching political reforms and the support of a compromise on Cyprus in early 2004, Ankara can hardly perceive the EU as having acted according to the spirit of "partnership."

The Euro-Mediterranean Motif and the Logic of the EMP
In spite of the initial enthusiasm accompanying the launching of the Barcelona Process, major EMP partners were rather critical of the EU toward the end of the 1990s. While the EU conveyed its bilateral relations with the "south" through a Euro-Mediterranean "lens," the EMP partners seemed far less convinced of the Euro-Mediterranean logic. Indeed, relations among southern Mediterranean states, as well as relations between the latter and the EU, indicate that the EMP partners did not develop any regional outlook.

This is also reflected in the official discourse. Indeed, the "Euro-Mediterranean" or "Mediterranean" themes were practically nonexistent in the foreign-policy discourse of most EMP partners—even while addressing the EU. In the foreign-policy discourse of Turkey, for instance, there are many references to Turkey's European vocation. And although Turkish newspaper articles and official statements quite frequently refer to Turkey's place in the "eastern Mediterranean," the Euro-Mediterranean theme is notably absent. According to Tayfur (2002), the Mediterranean was never conceptualized in Turkish foreign policy, and regional cooperation on a Euro-Mediterranean basis is quite irrelevant for Ankara. Seeking references to the Mediterranean theme in the official discourses of Egypt and Israel is a similarly futile exercise. Indeed, only an insignificant number of documents and declarations posted at the official websites of the foreign ministry of Egypt and Israel mentioned the EMP or the Euro-Mediterranean theme. In the case of Egypt, documents on the Euro-Mediterranean Association Agreement referred to it as a "Euro-Egyptian agreement," thus omitting the Mediterranean theme altogether.

A notable exception is Morocco. King Mohammed VI, who counts as a fervent supporter of Euro–Mediterranean relations, quite frequently refers to the Mediterranean and the EMP. Whether he addresses the Spanish king, Italian or French presidents, or his own diplomatic corps, Mohammed VI (2000a, 2000b, 2000c, 2000d) emphasizes Morocco's place within the Mediterranean. As discussed in the chapter on Morocco, speeches of senior Moroccan officials are similarly characterized by a Euro-Mediterranean narrative (Benaïssa 2000, 2001a). In a similar vein, French-language Moroccan newspapers, such as *Le Matin* or *TelQuel*, broadly cover the EU and the EMP, and mention Mediterranean values and identity themes.

Major EMP partners have also sought to reinterpret the logic of the EMP according to their own specific interests. In Jordan, for instance, parts of the political elite perceived enhanced Euro-Mediterranean cooperation as contradicting the concept of the "Arab world" (Joffé 2001). In view of the fate of the peace process, former Egyptian foreign minister Amr Moussa stated that closer *Arab–European* cooperation should be the goal of the EMP (Ezzat 1998), and Moroccan foreign minister Benaïssa (2001a) made a similar declaration in 2001. In this context, the above-mentioned Agadir process may well reconcile the Euro-Mediterranean idea with that of the "Arab world." Indeed, the Agadir Declaration states that the envisaged free-trade area is open to *other Arab states as well*. The necessary pragmatism notwithstanding, these positions do not really correspond to the original EMP logic.

Israel, on the other hand, repeatedly underlined its advanced economic relations with the EU. Therefore, it did not perceive itself as belonging to the group of southern Mediterranean states. In this vein, the Israeli Ministry of Finance repeatedly stressed that its bilateral economic relations with the EU are far more important than the Barcelona Process. From a political perspective, the fostering of economic development and democratization throughout the neighborhood in the framework of the EMP corresponded to Israel's own interest, along with confidence-building measures.[10] However, as discussed in the next chapter, Israel's commitment to the logic of the EMP was limited from the outset.

Thus, it is certainly no coincidence that at the beginning of 2001, Euro-Mediterranean parliamentarians jointly recognized that the EMP partners lacked a regional perspective, let alone an external policy for the region (Euro-Mediterranean Parliamentary Forum 2001). Governments and elites of most EMP partners maintained rather mixed attitudes towards the logic and benefits of the Barcelona Process, which remained irrelevant in public opinion (Joffé 2001). According to Aliboni and Said Aly (2000: 218):

> There is no parallel in the Middle East to the founding fathers of the European Community. Even when Shimon Peres, the former prime minister of Israel, called for a New Middle East, his ideas were mocked both in Arab countries and in Israel. . . . The end result has been a lack of strategic understanding among regional leaderships about the regional future; and the absence of active support for a Mediterranean Partnership or for a Middle Eastern community.

Euro-Mediterranean Relations and the EMP since 9/11

If the collapse of the Middle East peace process led to the reemergence of the traditional fault-lines, the events of September 11, 2001 and their aftermath negatively affected Euro-Mediterranean relations even further. On the one hand, 9/11, as well as the terrorist attack in Madrid on March 11, 2004 and in London in July 2005, demonstrated most dramatically that the dangerous phenomenon of Islamist terrorism builds on deep resentments against the "West" in many Arab and Muslim states (Eickelman 2002). Combined with the tendency in "the West" of equaling Islamist terrorism with Islam, along with raising anti-Muslim sentiments in many EU member states, the EMP participants have sought to counteract the emerging rift between "Europe" and "Islam" by establishing an intercultural dialogue and strengthening the EMP's third basket. In this vein, the EU Commission hosted a Conference on Inter-Cultural Dialogue in March 2002, and the EMP participants decided at the 2002 Valencia meeting to establish a Euro-Mediterranean Foundation for the promotion of dialogue between cultures. The so-called Anna Lindh Foundation with headquarters in Alexandria, Egypt, started its activities in early 2005. Yet, while the willingness to address prejudices across the Mediterranean is certainly a positive development, the intercultural dialogue phenomenon unfortunately risks reproducing the "clash of civilizations" logic that it aims at counteracting (Del Sarto 2005).

Moreover, 9/11 and the subsequent terrorist bombings in Djerba (April 2002), Bali (October 2002), Casablanca and Riyadh (May 2003), Istanbul (November 2003), Sinai (October 2004 and July 2005), Cairo (April 2005), and Amman (November 2005) demonstrated that Islamist terrorism not only threatens "the West," but also the governments of Arab/Muslim states. Not surprisingly, Euro-Mediterranean cooperation to combat terrorism has become a key issue of the EMP since 9/11. Corresponding to a general trend in many "Western" countries of curtailing democratic freedoms in the name of "security," the priority of fighting terrorism went partly at the expense of the EU's democracy promotion in Arab Mediterranean states (Gillespie 2006; Haddadi 2006). This attitude is very short-sighted, particularly since the persistent lack of democracy in most states of the Middle East is at least co-responsible for the rise of religious extremism to begin with.

Israel, on the other hand, came to see its policy toward the Palestinian *Intifada* as the legitimate right to defend itself in the global "war on terrorism" after 9/11. While the U.S. administration acquiescently supported Israel's policy—which included the liquidation of suspected terrorists, the reoccupation of Palestinian territories, curfews and military encirclement of Palestinian cities and villages—the Bush administration also largely ignored the Israeli–Palestinian conflict during much of its first term. The EU, however, has been far more critical toward Israel. Thus, it repeatedly called for an Israeli withdrawal from the territories, full access of humanitarian aid to the Palestinian territories, and the rehabilitation of the structures of the PA (Patten 2002). The EU has also been providing massive humanitarian assistance to the Palestinians. Israel, however, rejects the criticism of the EU, as well as that of Arab states, by pointing to the seriousness of Palestinian terrorist attacks. With it, 9/11 and its aftermath reinforced the patterns of Euro-Mediterranean disagreements that already emerged after the collapse of the peace process.

Finally, the U.S.-led invasion of Iraq in the spring of 2003 not only provoked a rift in transatlantic relations, but also within the EU itself. As Britain, (initially) Spain, Italy, and most new EU member states of eastern Europe entered the U.S.-led coalition in staunch opposition to France and Germany, the EU's policy towards the Mediterranean and Middle East seemed seriously compromised. But it was particularly the imminent EU enlargement of 2004 that prompted a reformulation of the EU's Mediterranean policy in 2003–2004. While embedding the southern Mediterranean in a broader policy framework that also addresses the EU's new neighbors in the east, the European Neighborhood Policy (ENP) abandons the EMP's regional logic and proposes a differentiated benchmarking approach instead (Commission 2003, 2004). Although the ENP partly overwrites the EMP (Del Sarto and Schumacher 2005), the Commission has been presenting both policies as compatible. While it is not clear whether and how the contradictions between the EMP and the ENP will be resolved, the future of the EU's Mediterranean policy will obviously also depend on developments in the region, particularly on the Israeli-Palestinian track. Yet the development of EU–Mediterranean relations will also depend on U.S. policy in the region as well as on the future of transatlantic relations.

Domestic Politics in the Southern Mediterranean

Adopting a broad regional perspective, the following sections discuss major domestic developments in the southern Mediterranean over the last decade. This exploration will keep in mind possible implications of domestic conflicts over state identity for the ability of states to engage in Euro-Mediterranean regional security.

Arab Mediterranean States

Political Liberalization Efforts

Against the backdrop of worsening living conditions, high unemployment, and rising poverty, most Arab Mediterranean states have been witnessing waves of public demonstrations and riots since the 1980s (Ibrahim 1993; Zoubir 1999c; Chartouny-Dubarry 2000).[11] While the economic decline starting in the 1980s resulted from falling oil prices, a dramatically growing debt burden, high military expenditures, economic mismanagement, corruption, and a rapid population growth (Sela 1998: 218), the economic discontent also gave rise to a growing dissatisfaction with the restricted space to voice opposition.[12] Larbi Sadiki (2000) suggests that the "bread riots," which were often sparked by the implementation of International Monetary Fund (IMF) structural adjustment programs, evidence the collapse of the socioeconomic basis of Arab rulers, which consisted in the provision of subsidized goods, such as basic food products, education, and health care. In return, the ruling classes demanded deference and political nonparticipation.

However, curtailing the providential platform eroded the domestic legitimacy of the "bread democracy" (*dimukratiyyat al-khubz*), thus prompting increasing public demands for political participation. Thus, half-hearted economic liberalization efforts in many Arab states had a negative social and political impact in the short run (Dawisha 1988a; Ibrahim 1998). Indeed, leaving the economic situation of the elites widely unaffected, the *infitah*, that is, the "opening" of the economy, often increased societal fragmentation, exacerbated the legitimacy crisis of the state, and alienated the weaker segments of society (Gerges 2000; Zoubir 1999c; Pioppi 2004).

With the notable exception of Syria and Libya, most Arab regimes reacted to the public discontent by introducing measures of political liberalization, albeit with a varying degree of determination (Salamé 1994b). Rather wide-ranging political liberalization efforts, at least initially, characterized Egypt, Jordan, and Algeria. Egypt embarked on a democratization process in the early 1980s, which however has not been maintained over the years (Kienle 1998b, 2001). In Jordan, the 1989 parliamentary elections were "among the most open in the Arab world at that time" (Chartouny-Dubarry 2000: 62), and the multi-party-system was reestablished after more than three decades of suspension. With these measures, the Jordanian monarchy also reacted to the eruption of the first Palestinian *Intifada* in 1987, Jordan's renouncing to territorial claims in the West Bank, and Israel's then preferred option of creating a Palestinian state in Jordan. Algeria under Boumedienne embarked on an extensive political liberalization process following the 1988 riots, introducing freedom of expression and association, and paving the way for the creation of a multiparty system. The subsequent developments, however, went in the opposite direction, as is well known.

Morocco's liberalization efforts since the early 1990s were more hesitant. The controversial 1993 parliamentary elections caused a deep political crisis, which prompted the monarchy to introduce additional electoral reforms prior to the 1997 elections. Although the former opposition leader Abderahman Youssoufi was appointed prime minister after the 1997 elections, Morocco's political reforms have been termed a "cosmetic response to domestic and international pressure" (Layachi 1999: 57). However, the reforms opened the way for political change, which continued under Mohammed VI, who ascended the throne in July 1999. Similarly, in Tunisia, the aftermath of the "bread riots" throughout the 1980s witnessed internal power struggles, the removal of President Bourguiba from office, and hesitant constitutional reforms.

Lebanon and the Palestinian territories are particular cases, since both are marked by the long experience with foreign domination, along with particular internal and external conditions. In spite of Syrian control on Lebanese politics after the end of the civil war, Lebanon resumed its model of a relatively liberal consociational democracy. The latter was born out of the need to soothe the communal-religious fragmentation of Lebanese society, although it had not prevented civil wars in the past. While Israel's occupation of southern Lebanon ended in 2000, and Syria withdraw its troops in April 2005, Lebanon still has to come to terms with the armed *Hizballah* militias in southern Lebanon. The demonstrations against Syria (and counter-demonstrations) after the assassination of former Lebanese president Rafik Hariri in early 2005 demonstrated that Lebanese civil society is vibrant, yet still fragmented along communal lines. In the Palestinian territories, democratic structures seemed most adequate for anchoring the political authority of the PLO leadership returning from the Tunisian exile, particularly in view of a traditionally vivid Palestinian civil society. Yet, Palestinian politics were challenged by the simultaneous task of state-building and nation-building, along with the oscillating prospects of peace with Israel (Khalidi 1996; Kamrava 1999). In spite of rather democratic elections in 1996, the regime of the late Yasser Arafat was characterized by autocratic lapses, corruption, the general absence of the rule of law, and serious human-rights violations, including the torture of prisoners, death sentences without court proceedings, and the imprisonment of critics of the PA.

Domestic Opposition: Islamism and Secular Forces
Much attention has been devoted to the rise of Islamism, which is "fully acknowledged as the main political and ideological force in the Arab world today" (Chartouny-Dubarry 2000: 64). It has been claimed that this development evidences the ideological bankruptcy of socialist ideologies and pan-Arab nationalism (Ajami 1992, 1999). Moreover, Edward Said (1995: 333) stressed that what appears as a resurgence of Islam "is in fact a struggle in Islamic societies over the definition of Islam." In this vein, moderate Islamist opposition movements must clearly be distinguished from radical Islamist groups, which do not refrain from the use of violence. Yet the general focus on Islamism tends to overshadow the presence of secular opposition movements, whose demands for political participation grew stronger over the last decades (Zoubir 1999c; Martín-Muñoz 2000). Arab

regimes have adopted quite different strategies in responding to the growing domestic opposition, including the Islamist challenge.

In the most prominent case of Algeria, the rulers had launched an electoral process the verdict of which—the victory of the Islamist FIS (Front Islamique du Salut)—they refused to honor. The annulment of the second round of elections, and the subsequent military coup in January 1992 led the country into a civil war.[13] However, an important segment of Algerian civil society supported the abortion of the second round of elections "because of the fears the radical Islamists provoked among many Algerians" (Zoubir 1999a: 32). The recurrent efforts to establish a political dialogue among the main political forces since 1995, along with the 1997 parliamentary and 1999 presidential elections, have evidenced the presence of additional important opposition forces. These include leftist and socialist parties, Berbers claiming cultural autonomy, and moderate Islamists (Martín-Muñoz 2000). Although political violence has declined in recent years, repressive measures towards all domestic opposition forces have been maintained.

Egypt, Syria, and Libya have also used repressive strategies toward Islamist forces and secular opposition. Syria widely succeeded in literally eradicating the Islamist movement. In Egypt, the initial "divide-and-weaken" strategy was replaced by plain repression of all Islamist forces after a wave of terrorist attacks between 1992 and 1994 and the Algerian crisis. By the end of the decade, the government widely succeeded in crushing the military capability of the radical Islamists. However, moderate Islamist movements have considerably expanded their societal standing, yet they are still excluded from politics. Secular opposition is similarly repressed in Egypt (Gerges 2000; Kienle 1998b, 2001). In 2003, however, the demands for political change grew louder, and the regime started with some very hesitant concessions. Libya, which witnessed various attempts to overthrow the regime in the last two decades, also reacted with plain repression of its increasing internal opposition, secular and religious alike (Deeb 1999).

Morocco and Tunisia responded quite differently to the growing domestic opposition. Whereas Morocco adopted a divide-and-rule strategy, the Tunisian regime chose a "divide-and-eliminate strategy" (King 1999: 70). The crisis in neighboring Algeria served as a justification for the repression of the Islamists, which was widely accepted by the public. Rather positive economic results in the late 1990s and the high popularity of President Ben Ali's social policy (thus reasserting the "bread-democracy model") accounted for the relative wide popular support of the Tunisian regime. In the case of Morocco, moderate opposition forces were co-opted into the system, while more radical opponents were repressed. The Casablanca bombings in May 2003 resulted in a quite merciless crackdown on suspected Islamist terrorists and their potential sympathizers, which, however, seemed to meet the approval of the wider public.

Co-option of Islamist forces also characterizes the experience of Jordan and Lebanon. In the case of Jordan, the Muslim Brotherhood has enjoyed a large "freedom of action in the spheres of culture, education, and public morality in exchange for the movement's loyalty to the monarchy" (Chartouni-Dubarry 2000: 66). However, Jordan's peace treaty with Israel put a strain on this arrangement. In the case of Lebanon, both moderate and radical Islamist forces, such as the political wing of *Hizballah*, are integrated into parliamentary politics, which may be explained by the communal structure of Lebanese politics. As far as the Palestinians are concerned, the situation was characterized by changing patterns of confrontation and cooperation between the PA and radical Islamist forces such as *Hamas* and Islamic Jihad, often correlating with progress or stalemate in the peace negotiations with Israel. Yet, toward domestic secular opposition, former chairman Arafat and his regime did not show much tolerance (Kamrava 1999).

Thus, our brief journey shows that most regimes have been struggling with both rising religious and secular opposition. The resulting political reforms, however, often led to a strengthening of the Islamists, which, along with the real or portrayed threat of Islamist fundamentalism, often served as a justification for repressing the opposition altogether. Although repressive policies prompted some temporary alliances between secularists and moderate Islamists, the religious–secular fault-line has deepened in many Arab states. Radical Islamists also recurrently targeted secular intellectuals, often in the physical sense of the word, while they did not refrain from attacking religious minorities, such as the Copts in Egypt (Hammond 2000). In addition, a growing presence of religion can be observed all over the Arab Mediterranean—and beyond. Although this phenomenon must clearly be differentiated from the rise of Islamist fundamentalism, it often entails a growing rift between the traditionally Western-educated, secular elites and the wider population. Against this background, many Arab regimes started to "frame political appeals in Islamic terms, since Islam is a means of legitimizing rule" (Roberson 1998b: 121). Thus, *traditionally secular* Arab leaders such as Egypt's Mubarak and Libya's Qadaffi increasingly portray themselves as defenders of Islam (Gerges 2000: 603; Deeb 1999). But these concessions—even if limited to the rhetoric realm—may actually back-fire and affect domestic politics, while curtailing a government's foreign-policy options. As Fouad Ajami (1992: 199) sharply formulated: "We are free to choose the symbols we wish to fight others with, but the symbols we use make their own demands."

Turkey and Israel: The Shattered Consensus

Turkey and Israel count as rare examples of Middle Eastern democracies with multiparty parliamentary elections. Turkey follows its democratic constitution "with legalistic precision" (Harris 1995: 19)—except when the whole system is overturned by the interventions of the military. Israel has an independent judiciary system and a free press, which is hindered only by censorship on military issues, and the opposition's criticism of government policies is usually quite vociferous. However, there are some difficulties in comparing Turkey and Israel to the model of a liberal democracy, even if we admit that there are no perfect examples of the latter in the real world. For instance, Amnesty International and Human Rights Watch repeatedly criticized Turkey for its human-rights record, particularly vis-à-vis its Kurdish minorities. Human-rights organizations also regularly denounce Israel's human-rights violations in the Palestinian territories under Israeli control. Moreover, the unclear separation between state and religion, along with discriminatory practices toward Israel's Arab minorities, casts a shadow on Israeli democracy (Smooha 1998; Sprinzak and Diamond 1993).

In recent decades, Israeli domestic politics has been characterized by an increasing polarization between supporters of territorial compromises in the search for peace, and advocates of peace without, or with limited, territorial concessions. The 1982 Lebanon war, the outbreak of the first *Intifada* in 1987, and the beginning of the Oslo process went hand in hand with the erosion of the national consensus on basic security issues (Weissbrod 1997). The assassination of Itzhak Rabin following the signing of the Oslo accords was probably the most serious evidence of this development. In addition, Israel has witnessed an increasing divide between religious and secular forces, a dormant, but still relevant, fault-line between Jews of European origin and Oriental Jews, and an increasing societal fragmentation after the Jewish mass immigration from the former Soviet Union (Evron 1995; Kimmerling 1998). Moreover, there is an important divide between Israel's Jewish majority and the widely ignored Arab minority, which however accounts for almost 20 percent of Israeli citizens. As discussed more in detail in the next chapter, the societal fragmentation and the challenges of the peace process have put a strain on Israel's governability, and early elections have become the rule. Government coalitions consist of different parties with partly incompatible platforms, and since they tend to enjoy a rather small majority, small parties are often the "king-makers" of Israeli politics. The fragmentation of Israeli society is also reflected in the large number of political parties that are voted into parliament, accounting for 13 in the 2003 elections. Moreover, the frequent alternation of Israeli governments, which run on diametrically opposed platforms, is striking. And while Sharon was the only incumbent prime minister to win a reelection since the 1980s, predictability has certainly not characterized Israel domestic politics over the last decades.

Volatility has also been characterizing Turkish politics. The gradual restoration of parliamentary procedures after the 1980 military coup went hand in hand with economic liberalization efforts under former prime minister Turgut Özal. The 1980s and early 1990s saw the emergence of new political parties, along with rising Kurdish violence in the southeast of Turkey, renewed Islamist agitation, and economic hardship resulting from increasing inflation. From the mid-1990s on, Turkey's secular establishment was confronted with the increasing political power of the Islamist Welfare Party, which emerged as the largest political force in the elections in March 1995. Two secular Center–Right parties, the True Path Party and the Motherland Party, formed a coalition in order to exclude the Welfare Party from political power, but it collapsed in June 1996. This opened the way for a coalition government between the True Path Party and the Islamist Welfare Party. In February 1997, however, the military stepped in through the National Security Council, outlawed Islamist parties, and forced the government to step down (Ergil 2000). The military establishment also imposed the closing of religious seminars, a halt of recruiting Islamists into government positions, and a careful scrutiny of the economic activities of Islamist groups (Yavuz 2000). However, in the parliamentary elections of November 2000, the Islamist-oriented AKP (Justice and Development Party) under Recep Tayyip Erdogan won a landslide victory. Turkey must also confront militant Islamists, who are held responsible for the murder of mostly Kurdish businessmen and moderate Islamist intellectuals in early 2002 (Kasaba and Bozdoğan 2000: 8), along with the bombings targeting Istanbul's Jewish community in November 2003. Yet the relation between state and religion is a complex matter, particularly since Sunni Islam has traditionally been part of Turkish national identity, albeit never explicitly. The role of the military in preserving Turkey's traditional secularism also raises some serious questions. And while the status of the Kurdish minority has not been sorted out yet, an important Shi'ite Alawi minority began protesting against its marginalization in the 1990s (Shankland 1999: 132). Although Turkey has implemented some serious democratic reforms in recent years, modern Turkey is increasingly internally divided, and it faces some difficult choices.

Domestic Fragmentation and National Politics

The domestic developments in the southern Mediterranean discussed so far build on preexisting patterns of fragmentation of Mediterranean societies, which challenge the state from within. One of the main features of Mediterranean societies is their pronounced ethnic and religious diversity. Indeed, there are more than 55 ethnic groups around the Mediterranean (Kliot 1989: 45). With its 18 religious communities or so, Lebanon certainly is an extreme example of religious diversity. Yet, maybe with the exception of Tunisia, the population of which is relatively homogeneous, important ethnic and/or religious minorities are present in all the states of the Mediterranean and Middle East. In some cases, ethnic minorities represent the ruling class, such as the Hashemites in Jordan or the Alawi in Syria. Moreover, through the ages, Mediterranean cultures have tended to be organized around ethnic, religious, and wider family structures, which remained largely unaffected by foreign domination. In this vein, Vatikiotis (1998: 24) still observes the imprint of "a tribal ethos on most Muslim Arab societies," while Israel's political cultural is characterized by a "tribal identity" (Ezrahi 1993: 259). Other scholars have identified a tendency of underlining differences as a basic pattern of Mediterranean societies (Isen 1998).

However, the political set-up generally does not reflect the pronounced diversity of Mediterranean societies. Indeed, Mediterranean and Middle Eastern states predominantly define themselves in ethnic-religious terms—much in contrast to, say, Western Europe. This implies that states necessarily give a preference to one ethnic and/or religious group over others. Thus, conceding equal standing to ethnic or religious minorities would entail a redefinition of a state's defining themes. Indeed, fully integrating the Kurds in Turkey, for instance, would necessitate a departure from Turkey's Kemalist self-definition, which is based on the dominance of ethnic Turks, and implicitly, Sunni

Islam. As for Israel, recognizing Israel's large non-Jewish minority as de facto equal citizens undermines the concept of the "Jewish state." Similarly, Berbers in the Maghreb and Copts in Egypt cannot stand on an equal footing as long as the respective states define themselves as predominantly Arab and Muslim.

But the demands for equality of ethnic groups that live across national borders—such as the Kurds, Berbers, Druze, Alawi, and Palestinians—also undermine the logic of the "nation-state" itself, since national distinctiveness laid the foundations of the modern "nation-state" in the Middle East and North Africa, as everywhere else. In a similar vein, the growing importance of religious ideology throughout the southern Mediterranean challenges the state from within. Indeed, religion—whether Islam, Judaism, or Christianity—does not recognize territorial boundaries (Halliday 2000: 26, 45–48). Certainly, most *moderate* Islamist movements are widely operating within the boundaries of the state (Sela 1998: 350), but the phenomenon of *Al-Qaeda* demonstrates that Islamist fundamentalism does not necessarily respect national borders. In Arab states, however, national identities already coexist uneasily with the broader discourse of (secular) pan-Arab nationalism since independence, often nurturing domestic conflicts and regional competition (Luciani and Salamé 1987). Certainly, the political fragmentation of the "Arab world" and its economic decline generated the crisis of pan-Arabism from the late 1970s on. Combined with the 1979 regime change in Iran, this paved the way for the rise of Islamism as political ideology (Heikal 1993). As a reaction, some Arab political leaders sought to construct *territorial* identities that were based on the pre-Islamic era. But in spite of the "triumph of the state" (Sela 1998: 350), the contradictions within different political identities and loyalties in Arab states still persist.

Turkey, on the other hand, has also repeatedly witnessed severe internal crises, such as the emergence of a revolutionary leftist movement in the 1960s, which prompted a military coup—one among several. As for Israel, contradicting religious and secular interpretations of Israel's political identity, along with the problems of defining the state and the nation, are as old as the state itself.

Thus, increasing economic and political discontent, the strengthening of both secular and Islamist opposition movements, Islamist fundamentalism and terrorism, globalization, and the advent of the peace process reinforce preexisting social and political tensions, or create new sources of friction. With it, there is a mounting pressure on the legitimacy of the state. Furthermore, the post–9/11 "war on terror," along with the "clash of civilizations" discourse, is prompting a redrawing of identities in the Mediterranean and Middle East, and beyond. In view of these challenges, the political survival of governments may well depend on the modification of the political discourse, for instance by absorbing religious themes, or by promoting an "authentic" political identity as a basis for state authority. Underlining *uniqueness and difference* thus becomes the name of the game. Yet, while restricting the space of maneuver of foreign policy, these attempts are hardly compatible with the promotion of values that a state allegedly shares with present enemies, former adversaries, or former colonial rulers. Against this background, then, fostering identity themes on a Euro-Mediterranean basis and developing a strategic outlook for the Euro-Mediterranean security region may be simply impossible.

Preliminary Findings

The EMP, which builds on a long history of Euro–Mediterranean relations, initially met on a positive response of most southern partners. This went hand in hand with dramatically improved relations among southern Mediterranean states, which were also interested in upgrading their relations with the EU. However, over the years, the EMP partners repeatedly questioned some of the underlying principles of the Barcelona Process, as well as the EU's role in, and commitment to, the region. At the same time, the apparent convergence of security interests around the Mediterranean of the early 1990s did not persist for long. A decade later, the traditional fault-lines across the Euro-Mediterranean had reemerged, reinforced by the collapse of the peace process and the events of 9/11. Whereas the EU nevertheless sought to uphold its vision for the Mediterranean, most EMP partners did not develop a consistent Euro-Mediterranean strategy in the time span under discussion.

Our discussion showed that most states in the southern Mediterranean are deeply divided over religion, culture, ethnicity, and the desirable way of life. Most states have been witnessing a deepening fault-line between more conservative, or even reactionary, domestic forces, and supporters of a more liberal and Western-oriented make-up of the state. In the Arab Mediterranean, a number of developments have exacerbated the domestic divisions, such as altered socioeconomic patterns, growing space to voice demands for political reforms, and rising religious ideology. At the international level, the beginning of the Arab-Israeli peace process partly eroded the thus far prevailing themes of state identity, thus challenging state authority from within.

More important, however, is that different domestic preferences potentially imply different types of Euro–Mediterranean relations, along with different concepts of regional order. Thus, Islamist forces may object enhanced relations with Europe and the "West," and are likely to be skeptical of the recipes for modernization prescribed by the latter. Moreover, the idea of a Euro-Mediterranean region, which includes Israel and originally Turkey, is likely to encounter important domestic opposition, particularly in light of deteriorating relations between Israel and the Palestinians.

In the case of Turkey and Israel, the question of regional order may also touch upon a number of domestic divides. As for Israel, we alluded to the significant domestic opposition to Shimon Peres's vision of the "New Middle East," even in the "good times" of the peace process. As for Turkey, the concept of a Euro-Mediterranean region may meet the suspicion of those who support Turkey's EU membership—and, at least theoretically, also of Islamist-oriented domestic forces. In the parliamentary political systems of Turkey and Israel, domestic politics have in fact evidenced a strong societal fragmentation and increasing polarization.

In the authoritarian systems of Arab Mediterranean states, the link between domestic fragmentation and altering patterns of Euro-Mediterranean relations is more difficult to trace. However, since the observed domestic fragmentation poses a threat to political authority, political leaders may be forced to promote identity themes based on cultural *distinctiveness* and *authenticity*. Similarly, in view of the challenges, most Arab governments will prefer not to affront the domestic opposition to the normalization of relations with Israel. In this context, the concessions that many Arab rulers have made to growing Islamist pressures are relevant. Indeed, Arab regimes cannot adopt religious motives in their discourses and simultaneously be indifferent toward the future of Jerusalem's *Al-Aqsa* mosque, Islam's third-holiest place. Similarly, it is difficult to stress the authenticity of Arab and/or Islamic culture, despise the "West," and concurrently embrace the United States or Europe without hesitation. Thus, internal fragmentation seems to exclude the search for common ground with Euro-Mediterranean neighbors, particularly in view of the historically conflictual relations between "the Arab world," Israel, Turkey, and Europe. In view of these constraints, Arab governments may find it extremely difficult to internalize the logic of the Barcelona Process, or develop a Euro-Mediterranean strategy of their own.

While the collapse of the peace process and the events of 9/11 may have prompted a closing of some domestic divides and reinforced Euro-Mediterranean divisions along the traditional fault-lines, the link between contested state identities and regional security on a Euro-Mediterranean basis in the time span before these events is intelligible. In the next three chapters, a close look at three different cases, namely Israel, Egypt, and Morocco, is offered, thus seeking to deepen and validate our preliminary findings.

Part II

Case Studies

4

Israel

This chapter explores the link between the setbacks of Euro-Mediterranean regional security and domestic identity conflicts in Israel.[1] We start by focusing on Israel's domestic scene. What are the country's main defining themes? Are there domestic divisions on these themes? The second and the third part of the chapter are dedicated to the impact of domestic identity divisions on Israel's ability to engage in Euro-Mediterranean region-building. Thus, we assess the development of EU–Israeli relations since the launching of the EMP as well as Israel's participation in the latter. Shifting to an identity-based analysis, the third part of this chapter discusses the implications of the EMP for Israel's state identity. How did Israel respond to the region-building logic? And how can it be linked to Israel's contested state identity?

Israel's Contested State Identity

Debates on the question of what Israel as a state and a society is—and is supposed to be—are as old as the state itself. Thus, since the founding of the state in May 1948, Israel's defining identity themes have been challenged, and different interpretations have emerged over time. This section starts by discussing the emergence and strengthening of Israel's core identity themes, which include Zionism, the Holocaust, a "Jewish state," self-reliance, and the identification with the United States.

The Defining Themes

The State of Israel was founded under quite particular conditions, which entailed the simultaneous tasks of nation-building and state-building, along with the defence against external enemies. Political

Zionism was certainly the main intellectual driving force. Taking shape in Eastern Europe from the second half of the nineteenth century on, Zionism was a reaction to persisting anti-Semitism, while it represented the Jewish form of nationalism, entailing the strive for independence and self-determination. Labour Zionism, which combined Zionism with socialist ideas, became the dominant branch of the movement toward the end of that century. Influenced by both German Romanticism and the East European type of nationalism based on ethnic groups (Shapiro 1993), Zionism incorporated the idea of "national uniqueness." In view of the exclusion of Jews in Europe, Zion—the biblical Land of Israel—became the place where the ideal "Jewish nation" was to be built.[2] Thus, from the early twentieth century on, encouraging emigration to Palestine became one of Zionism's most important aims.

In Israel's formative years, the Zionist narrative relied on selected periods of Jewish history. Mainly revolving around Jewish armed resistance against foreign oppression, specific historical events from Antiquity were presented as heroic past (Zerubavel 1995), and juxtaposed to those of the pre-state area, such as the battle of Tel Hai.[3] The Zionist narrative thus emphasized the principle of actively influencing fate, while dismissing the religious interpretation of events. But it also glorified the "readiness to sacrifice one's life for the nation" (Zerubavel 1995: 221). The biblical past was thus linked to the new "national revival" through the theme of "the few" defending themselves successfully against "the many," whereby the theme of "David versus Goliath" acted as underlying structure of meaning (Gertz 1984).

As probably most historical narratives, those promoted within Jewish collective memory—and commemorated until the present—do not always reflect the true course of events.[4] Yet the biblical past also served the aim of legitimizing Jewish statehood in what was to become Mandatory Palestine. Lilli Weissbrod (1997: 48) has remarked that "[i]n addition to differentiating themselves from other nation-states, the Israeli definition of who they are must also contain an assertion of their moral right to be where they are." Thus, a continuity between the biblical past and the present was established and transformed into a "taken-for-granted reality" (Aronoff 1993: 48). It became a central theme of the emerging identity of Israel.

The long history of discrimination and persecution that culminated in the Holocaust is an additional core theme of Israel's identity. The Holocaust provided the most dramatic evidence that assimilation and even conversion were no guarantee for avoiding the persecution and death of Europe's Jewish minorities. It thus justified Zionism's main tasks, namely to create a "safe haven" for the Jewish people, to establish collective and individual Jewish freedom, and to revive a rich Jewish history and tradition. In this vein, Israel's first prime minister David Ben-Gurion emphasized that the "State of Israel has a unique mission . . . in contemporary history, a mission which gives it its *raison d'être*" (Ben-Gurion 1976: 154, original italics).

Thus, Israel was founded as *the state of the Jews*. Encouraging Jewish immigration (*aliyah*, literally "ascension") from all over the world to Israel, irrespective of any socioeconomic considerations, attained an enormous ideological importance.[5] With it, Israel was conceived as a country of immigrants. Yet since the Jewish diaspora was extremely heterogeneous in cultural terms, the nation-building process had to rely on rather vague cultural themes. Combined with Israel's specific raison d'état, *Jewishness* thus became a core theme of Israel's identity. Additional themes of Israel's identity came to comprise the reactivated and modernized Hebrew language, the idea of statehood, the image of going "back to the roots," and the establishment of collectivist settlements (*kibbutzim* and *moshavim*) according to Labour Zionism's socialist and partly Marxist orientation. Moreover, given the trauma of the Holocaust, along with an increasingly hostile environment, a great importance was attached to national security, along with military virtues. In this context, Ezrahi (1993: 261) noted that Israel never witnessed the confrontation between people and state authority, which may explain why the development of a *civic* political culture has remained rather weak. At the same time, a basic *"conflict formula"* (Zerubvavel 1995: 218, original italics) based on the theme of "the few against the many" has been dominating the Jewish-Israeli collective experience.[6]

Labour Zionism clearly envisaged the creation of a secular and democratic state. But in accordance with Israel's particular raison d'état, a *state of the Jews*—which would be the correct translation of the title of Theodor Herzl's book *Der Judenstaat*—became synonymous to a Jewish state, although both things are not necessarily the same.[7] Consequently, the "*identity of the state* was constructed as 'Jewish' by means of various symbols and codes, such as a flag, the national anthem, its history, as well as the official days of celebration and memorial" (Kimmerling 1993: 411, original italics). In the international arena, Israel's political leaders portrayed themselves as "the representative of the Jewish people" (Rabin 1995a), and the references to Jewish religion and history underlined Israel's political legitimacy. As former foreign minister Abba Eban (1976a: 790) remarked before the UN Security Council: "It would seem to me that after 3,000 years the time has arrived to accept Israel's nationhood as a fact."

The long history of persecution and the Holocaust had nurtured among Israel's political leaders a considerable amount of suspicion toward the "Gentiles." The threats to its survival that Israel faced since its founding reinforced the sense of insecurity. Combined with the international criticism of Israel's policy, a clear definition of "the other" emerged—"Gentiles" in general, and "the Arabs" in particular. These factors delineated the cognitive boundaries between the State of Israel and the rest of the world, while strengthening the emphasis on the Jewish identity of the state.[8] But the history-rooted perception of "trust no one" and the will to survive also forged the emergence of the principle of self-reliance, implying the freedom to respond unilaterally to security threats, and the military ability to do so (Inbar 1996). In this vein, Ben-Gurion (1984) stated that "[w]e must not forget that our security depends on our own might," and in 2001, Ariel Sharon (2001: 12) similarly declared that "we must all know that we can never place our fate in the hands of anyone else, not even in the hands of those who are our best friends." Self-reliance also stands behind the investment in a strong and technologically advanced army, compulsory conscription, and a large reserve force, thus coining the concept of Israel as "a nation in arms" (Horowitz 1993: 15). Similarly, an emphasis was put on deterrence and a mixture of preventive, preemptive, and retaliatory military actions. Security considerations were—and have remained—Israel's main concern. Amos Perlmutter (1990: 120) remarked that "[t]he Israelis' search for security is an obsession, a quest for an almost metaphysical security."

After the 1967 war, Israel's self-definition witnessed an important shift, as the concept of *Eretz Israel*—the "Land of Israel"—gained currency, as discussed further below. Implying a stronger religious and/or nationalistic orientation, this perception became even more pronounced after the 1977 elections that ended the rule of the Labour party. In his speeches, former prime minister Menachem Begin hardly referred to the State of Israel, using the term *Eretz Israel* instead, while he even termed the Palestinians "Arabs of Eretz Israel" (Begin 1981b: 57). Initially, the victory and the conquest of territory seemed to confirm Israel's aspirations. Yet the threats pronounced by Arab leaders to "drive the Jews into the sea," along with the inactivity of the international community prior to the 1967 War, reinforced Israel's distrust of other states, and prompted fears of a possible repetition of the Holocaust. In his speech before the UN General Assembly, Eban (1976a) compared the aggression by Egypt, Syria, and Jordan to the Nazi's "final solution." Not surprisingly, Israel's leaders considered the accusation of being the aggressor, voiced by some states with regard to the 1956 Sinai campaign and the 1967 Six Day War, as outrageous (Eban 1976b: 812).

The almost-defeat in the 1973 Yom Kippur War, combined with the increasing diplomatic success of the PLO, nurtured more than ever the sense of isolation. Along with an anti-Zionist international mood—in 1975 the UN General Assembly had adopted Resolution 3397, which branded Zionism as racism—the criticism was perceived in Israel as anti-Semitism. While the early Zionist discourse had envisaged that Israel shall be "a light unto the nations," two very different perceptions emerged in the first decades of statehood. On the one hand, Israel repeatedly attempted to be "a nation like all nations," but on the other, the perception of "a nation that shall dwell alone" grew stronger. International criticism of Israel's invasion of Lebanon in 1982 as well as of its policy toward the first *Intifada* starting in 1987, nurtured the perception in Israel that "the whole world is against us." Former Prime Minister Itzhak Shamir (1989) probably best expressed Israel's distrust of the international community by stating: "I will never trust any decisions made by the UN or by any UN institution, because we know in advance that any UN body, no matter what its composition, will be against us."

Yet at the same time, Israel's strategic relations with the United States had deepened from the 1970s on. They were perceived as being based on similar values, namely "the American ideal of justice and the ideals of peace and democracy," as Itzhak Rabin (1976: 1142) declared. Israeli leaders also underlined Israel's Western orientation by pointing to its democratic system and the prevalence of "Western" values. While seeing itself as "a non-Arab island in an Arab Middle East" (Alpher 1995: 130), Israel's "Western" orientation also drew a cognitive border to "the Arab world" and accentuated Israel's *difference* to its Middle Eastern environment.

The beginning of the peace process in the early 1990s started to change the perception of being internationally isolated and misunderstood. In this vein, former president Ezer Weizman (1998: 10) called Israel's sense of isolation a "ghetto mentality" that was an obstacle to the peace process. In his opinion, Israel was never as secure as it was in the 1990s. Yet with the start of the second *Intifada* in September 2000, the themes of the "struggle for survival" and the general sense of isolation once more took hold of the Israeli polity.

Thus, in view of the threats of Arab leaders to destroy Israel over the decades, Israel perceived its righteousness as unquestionable, convinced that it had always acted out of legitimate self-defence. Only in recent years was this conviction challenged by Israel's so-called new historians (Morris 1999), as well as in the context of the post-Zionist debate (Elazar and Sandler 1997; Kelman 1998). Israel also traditionally stressed its unique security situation—a small state surrounded by enemies—which, however, some scholars define as a myth (Merom 1999). Based on the Jewish historical experience, the international criticism of Israel's policy reinforced the principle of self-reliance, while criticism is often viewed as hidden, or open, anti-Semitism.[9] Hence, since its establishment, Israel's cognitive boundaries between "us" and "them" were repeatedly reconfirmed, thus nurturing a defiant, and basically "realist," foreign policy (Arian 1995). Yet Israel's identity was born with a number of inherent contradictions. Some of them are linked to the historical constraints under which Israel was founded, while others reflect the divisions within the Zionist movement, as discussed in the next section.

The Divisions

The questions of what the State of Israel should be, whether it should be founded, and which territory it shall comprise prompted fervent discussions within and around the Zionist movement since the beginning. Indeed, Israel's acceptance of the 1947 UN partition plan and the 1948 Declaration of Independence was preceded by fervent internal disputes. Although both Labour Zionism and revisionist Zionism under the leadership of Zeev Jabotinsky were secular, they maintained different positions on whether there had to be a maximal congruity between the State of Israel and the biblical Land of Israel (Avineri 1981) the latter comprising Jerusalem, the West Bank, and the Gaza Strip. Revisionist Zionism supported a maximal congruity, and thus shared a basic belief with *religious Zionism*. The latter viewed the creation of the state as the beginning of the divine redemption process, which however had to be influenced "actively." This justified the cooperation with the secular Zionists. Conversely, orthodox and ultra-orthodox Jews traditionally opposed Zionism, as they considered the establishment of Israel through human action as a blasphemy. Yet their opposition to the Zionist project somewhat diminished after the Holocaust in Europe.

Given the state-building and nation-building efforts, it was actually quite functional to leave the core elements of Israel's identity ambiguous, such as the concepts of Zionism, "Jewishness," and "the Jewish State." Indeed, the first ambiguity concerns the relation between Jewish religion and the predominantly *secular* nature of Zionism. Since Israel did not emerge on a preexisting territory or on the basis of historical continuity,[10] secular Zionism paradoxically justified its territorial claims by relying on the Old Testament. The 1947 UN partition plan partly resolved this dilemma, since it provided a secular and legalistic basis for the territorial claims (Weissbrod 1997: 48). However, although the Zionist narrative promoted a nationalization of Jewish religion and tradition, it left its relationship to religion undefined. In the first decades of statehood, and despite some disputes on legislative issues, secular and religious interpretations of Israel's identity could coexist. Second, the *national* and *territorial* boundaries are not congruous in the case of Israel. Indeed, "the right to belong to the Israeli state was extended to Jews all over the world, who are by definition included in the Israeli collectivity" (Kimmerling 1993: 412). Third, the core element of Jewishness inherently links nationality to religion. Thus, until recently, Israeli identity cards had to contain the information on whether the holder is Jewish or not, paradoxically listed under the category of "nationality." Israel thus differs from the West European experience, in which national identities emerged as a substitute of religion (Del Sarto 1999). In fact, Israel's state-building endeavors sought to transform a religious community into a "nation-state," which, however, de facto also included non-Jews (Shapiro 1993: 66). Moreover, tying the "nation" to religion implies that the definition of who belongs to the "nation" must be decided in religious terms (Evron 1995: 188–202). This explains the importance of the fervently debated question of "who is a Jew" ever since the founding of the state.

Due to these ambiguities, the identity of Israel repeatedly witnessed the emergence of alternative interpretations, often triggered by questions of war and peace. The Jewish mass immigration from mainly Arab countries in the 1950s and 1960s prompted the emergence of an additional fault-line. While Jews of European origin (*Ashkenazim*) constituted Israel's ruling class and had hitherto dominated Israeli culture, this immigration wave challenged the idea that Israel is a European-type country, situated in the Middle East by coincidence only. The increasing protest of Jewish immigrants of oriental origin (termed *Mizrahim* or *Sephardim*) against *Ashkenazi* domination counts as a crucial factor for the change of government in 1977, which ended the rule of the Labour Party (Sprinzak and Diamond 1993).

The 1967 war certainly constituted a turning point in Israel's self-definition and foreign relations. The conquest of land that was part of "biblical Israel" affected the vast majority of Jewish Israelis, and "aroused religious and mystical sentiments even among circles that until then had considered themselves as secular" (Evron 1995: 228). This particularly concerns the conquest of the Temple Mount and the Western Wall in Jerusalem's Old City, which most Jewish Israelis consider as the "heart" of religious and Zionist aspirations. Unlike other occupied territories, East Jerusalem was immediately annexed to the state. Altogether, the conquest of "biblical land" provided a concrete material basis for the rise of the concept of *Eretz Israel*, maintained both by religious and revisionist Zionists. The "shock" of the 1973 Yom Kippur War additionally contributed to the strengthening of the *Eretz Israel* idea, since the war induced a "turning toward traditional Jewish values" (Sandler 1993: 146).

After the 1977 elections, Begin's government considerably intensified the construction of Jewish settlements in the conquered territories. While previous Labour governments had established "strategic" settlements by avoiding densely populated areas, *Likud* governments viewed the massive expansion of Jewish settlements all over the territories as the expression of rightful Jewish claims on biblical land (Sandler 1993; Avineri 1986). Similarly, religious Zionists interpreted Israel's control over "Judea, Samaria, and Gaza" as a messianic return to the Promised Land. But the conquest of "biblical" territory also affected the traditionally anti-Zionist ultra-orthodox sectors, as "[s]ome began to wonder if God had not blessed the Zionists after all" (Kimmerling 1998: 57). From the late 1960s on, ultra-orthodox Jews increased their participation in domestic politics, mainly through the veteran political party *Agudat Israel*.

However, the holding of conquered territory and the rule over the Palestinian population challenged Israel's identity from an additional corner. Israel's Declaration of Independence defined Israel as a *Jewish* and a *democratic* state. The possibility that these two principles may clash was not seriously considered from the outset, not even after the 1967 war, as long as the Palestinians in the territories remained silent. This changed with the eruption of the first *Intifada*. While persuading Israeli public opinion that the situation in the territories was not viable, the *Intifada* also prompted domestic disputes over the question of what kind of state Israel was supposed to be. Indeed, the *Intifada* made most disturbingly visible that the ongoing occupation of the territories compromises democratic principles. But enforcing democracy in the territories, and thus granting citizenship to the Palestinians, is incompatible with the aim of maintaining a Jewish majority in the long run, particularly in view of the higher birth rate of the Palestinians. This is certainly one of the reasons why the West Bank and Gaza have never been annexed to the state, but kept as a sort of settler-colony.

But already the 1982 Lebanon War had fueled fervent domestic discussions about Israel's moral standards. While introducing the dichotomy of "wars of no choice" versus "wars of choice," Begin considered the Lebanon War as a "war of choice," which, however, he considered as justified (Sandler 1993: 218). The justification of starting of a war not for preemption and prevention, but in order to achieve political aims, was certainly an attempt to manipulate a core element of Israel's identity, namely the theme of being repeatedly *forced* into wars in the struggle for survival. Begin's attempted manipulation of Israel's identity caused deep internal scissions. Indeed, the Lebanon War prompted the largest demonstrations against the government that Israel had witnessed until then.

In addition, the gap between religious and secular interpretations of Israel's identity widened further with the Jewish mass immigration from the former Soviet Union after the fall of the Berlin Wall. The "Russian" immigration, as it is commonly called, strengthened the secular segments of Israeli society, as the majority of "Russian" immigrants are secular. But it also fueled the domestic discussion over "who is Jew," since around 30–40 percent of the new immigrants are not Jewish according to religious law (Shepherd 1994; Central Bureau of Statistics 2004). However, under Israel's *secular* immigration law, they are entitled to receive Israeli citizenship. With it, the "Russian immigration" once more evidenced the incoherence between religious and "national" definitions of Jewishness.

Finally, Israel's domestic divisions considerably intensified with the beginning of the Oslo peace process. Since the conflict with Arab states and the Palestinians had accompanied the state ever since its establishment, the prospects of peace brought about a strong sense of uncertainty. As discussed below, in view of the option of territorial compromise in exchange for peace, the divide between nationalist and liberal interpretations of Israel's identity widened considerably. The assassination of former prime minister Itzhak Rabin in November 1995 was probably the most traumatic evidence of this scission.

With the outbreak of the second *Intifada*, debates on Israel's identity considerably receded, as the numerous terrorist attacks strengthened the "we-feeling" within Israeli-Jewish society. But this development also accentuated the *religious* and *ethnic* interpretations of Israel's identity, in which "Israeli" and "Jewish" are synonyms. With it, Israel's Arab minority—roughly one fifth of Israeli citizens—was increasingly identified as a security risk.[11] The demonstrations of Arab Israelis against the government's policy in the territories in October 2000, in which 12 Arab Israelis were shot dead by the police, were the most tragic case in point. Mainstream Israeli public opinion, including the usually rather liberal *Ha'aretz* newspaper, initially viewed the police's use of life ammunition and snipers against *Israeli citizens* as legitimate (*Ha'aretz* October 2–5, 2000).[12] Certainly, Israel's Arab minorities were never fully integrated into the Israeli collective. As Smooha (1993: 329) notes: "Most Jews even fail to perceive . . . differential practices as discrimination against Arabs. Instead they consider them as preferences rightfully accorded to themselves as Jews in a Jewish state."[13]

Competing Concepts of Israel's State Identity

Based on the discussion so far, we may distinguish between four main identity concepts prevailing in present-day Israel. These are termed here: *Eretz Israel* (the Land of Israel), a religious state, *Medinat Israel* (i.e., a Jewish and democratic state), and a state of all its citizens. While the boundaries between these categories are not clear-cut, some segments of Israeli society do not support any of these concepts, such as the Jewish ultra-orthodox (and anti-Zionist) *Neturei Kharta*, or the Islamic movement in Israel. While identifying the core values and supporters of the main identity concepts, the last part of this section will focus on an additional identity fault-line in Israeli society, termed here the "Middle East" versus the "West."

Eretz Israel

The concept of "the Land of Israel" (*Eretz Israel*) is basically a nationalist concept, which, by definition, promotes particularistic values. Its supporters favor a state that is supremely, or exclusively, committed to the interests of Israel's Jewish majority (Peleg 1997). It has been stressed that the narrative of *Eretz Israel* is comparatively gloomy, since it presupposes the endless persecution of Jews and the continuation of the Arab–Israeli conflict (Arian 1995: 230). These assumptions explain the perceived supremacy of "security" over other values. However, there is a secular and a religious version of *Eretz Israel*.

In its secular version, the concept is traditionally associated with the *Likud* party, and, in a more extreme version, by a number of smaller ultra-nationalist parties. This concept has an important territorial dimension. Indeed, it is rooted in revisionist Zionism, stating that the higher the territorial congruency between the "biblical Israel" and the State of Israel, the more the state is Jewish—in a national sense (Avineri 1986: 5). According to this concept, the Jewish people and the biblical territory are linked through an almost metaphysical bond. In this vein, Begin (1981a: 13) stressed that "the Land of Israel and the People of Israel are one." Similarly, Ariel Sharon declared on the possibility of evacuating Jewish settlements in Hebron: "No people has a monument like the Tomb of the Patriarchs, where the patriarchs and matriarchs of the nation are buried" (Sharon 2001: 15). However, for pragmatic reasons, single *Likud* leaders departed from the principle of never relinquishing parts of "biblical land." Thus, the Netanyahu government signed the Hebron redeployment agreement under U.S. pressure. In 2002, Sharon for the first time declared his support for an independent Palestinian state in (parts of) the West Bank, which however prompted a revolt of the *Likud* Central Committee (*Ha'aretz* May 14, 2002).[14]

In its *national-religious* version, the concept of *Eretz Israel* relies on the vision of messianic redemption, as noted above. In Israeli politics, the National-Religious Party (NRP or *Mafdal*) promotes this interpretation most notably. While stressing its loyalty "to the People of Israel, the Torah of Israel, and the Land of Israel" Jewish sovereignty over the territories is viewed as a fundamental right. Consequently, the expansion of Jewish settlements in the territories is an imperative, and the establishment of a Palestinian state between the Jordan River and the Mediterranean is rejected (Mafdal 2005). Extremist factions of the settler movement are not only more messianic in their interpretation of *Eretz Israel*, but also more prone to use violence to defend it—even against the state. According to this credo, the "uniqueness" of the Jewish people entails the *need* to isolate it from other peoples—which are viewed as eminently hostile (Rubinstein 1980: 120).

A Jewish Religious State

Israel's religious Jewish population can be subdivided into three main groups: ultra-orthodox, national-religious, and conservative. The latter comprises approximately half of Israel's Jewish citizens (mainly made up of Oriental Jews), who maintain a rather flexible way of religious observance (Elazar and Sandler 1997). The heterogeneity of the Jewish religious population also entails different positions on Zionism and the state. However, many Jewish Israelis sympathize with the idea that Jewish religion shall be a central feature of the state.

The idea of a theocracy comes close to the preference of Israel's ultra-orthodox Jews (*haredim*). Yet it is not defended openly, since the ultra-orthodox belief stipulates that only God can establish a theocratic Israel after the coming of the Messiah. For this reason, in theory the *haredim* reject the state and its institutions, although in practice, they participate in Israeli politics. Nevertheless, the ultra-orthodox sector defends the supremacy of religious law over any kind of state law, including the ruling of Israel's Supreme Court. In this vein, the ultra-orthodox party list United Torah Judaism (UJT) stated in its 1999 manifesto that it would fight any attempts to weaken the powers of religious courts, which ruled, for instance, against the drafting of ultra-orthodox *yeshiva* students to the Israeli army and against the recognition of Judaism's Reform and Conservative movements (Harris 1999).

Representing a *Sephardi* version of Jewish orthodoxy, *Shas*—the third-largest parliamentary faction from May 1999 until January 2003—also supports an observant state. Although many *Shas* voters are not necessarily orthodox religious, the more conservative *Shas* leadership maintains that Jewish religious law is superior to state law (Don-Yehia 1997; Peretz and Doron 2000). Finally, religious Zionists are committed to the Jewish character of the state, but they recognize the institutions of the state and the competence of secular courts in civilian matters. However, supreme authority is conceded to the Rabbinate (Mafdal 2005).

The different preferences regarding the religious character of Israel entail different positions on Israel's foreign relations, particularly regarding the question of territorial compromise. Thus, while religious Zionists generally oppose the relinquishing of territory, as noted above, the ultra-orthodox leadership elusively declared that "[a]ll decisions will be based on rulings of rabbis, taking into consideration the principle of the Land of Israel and the prevention of the loss of life" (Harris 1999: 4). Similarly, *Shas*'s spiritual leader Ovadia Yosef ruled that it is permitted to relinquish territory if it prevented the loss of life. The majority of *Shas* voters, however, are believed to oppose territorial compromise (Ilan 2000).

It is worth stressing that, in concrete situations, different interpretations of Jewish religious law (*halacha*) are possible. Thus, the murderer of Itzhak Rabin justified his deed by an interpretation of the *halacha*, according to which it is permitted to kill whoever endangers Jewish life and betrays the Jewish community. Although there was no official rabbinical ruling against the late Rabin, these issues were apparently discussed in extremist national-religious circles. Similarly, in July 1995 several rabbis affiliated with the settler movement issued a religious ruling that called upon resisting, even through the use of force, a possible evacuation of Jewish settlements by the Israeli Army. In the context of Israel's withdrawal from the Gaza Strip in August 2005, these events repeated themselves.

Medinat Israel

Corresponding to the vision of early Labour Zionism, the idea of a Jewish state in the form of a secular democracy has been the hegemonic cultural paradigm in Israel until the present (Aronoff 1993: 49). While putting the state and its institutions at the center, the concept of *Medinat Israel* however embodies frictions, which mainly revolve around the relationship of a "Jewish state" to democracy and secularism, as noted above. Thus, the concept permits for various interpretations.

Classical Labour Zionism, which stressed the importance of collective and particularistic values, is positioned on one end of the spectrum. Besides the Labour party and a number of smaller secular parties, the orthodox-religious *Meimad* party supports this concept of state identity in Israeli politics. This version of *Medinat Israel* more or less implicitly assumes that the state first serves the interests of the Jewish collective, which may be treated preferentially to non-Jewish citizens. The granting of formal citizens' rights to the latter is viewed as sufficient condition for defining Israel as a democracy. At the same time, the "Jewish character of the state" is ensured by official Jewish holidays, the state's political symbols, the principle of Jewish immigration and the secular-Zionist narrative. Within this concept, it is possible to grant supremacy to religious laws in specific realms (e.g., the personal status law), and to seek compromises whenever state law is not compatible with the *halacha*. Regarding the conflict with the Palestinians, this concept is compatible with territorial compromise, mainly because maintaining a Jewish majority is preferable to infringing on Israel's democratic character. In this vein, former prime minister Ehud Barak (1996) stated that "any type of full control by Israel over the whole area from the Mediterranean to the Jordan . . . means inevitably either a binational state, if it is democratic and so non-Jewish; or an apartheid state, which is non-democratic."

On the other end of the spectrum, a different interpretation of *Medinat Israel* gives priority to universal values and individualism.

While anchoring the "Jewish character of the state" in humanistic Jewish values, this interpretation still favors maintaining a Jewish majority within the state, but only in respect of democracy and equality. Thus, while supporting cultural and religious heterogeneity, there is a clear demand to separate state and religion. This position is anchored in Israel's civil-rights movement, and the *Meretz* Party (and since 2003 its successor *Yachad*) promote this identity concept in Israeli politics. Within this orientation, there is no contradiction between a state of the Jewish people and a state of all its citizens, Jewish and Arab alike (Meretz 2001; Yachad 2005). Moreover, it supports territorial compromise and an independent Palestinian state, whereby the justification ranges between pragmatism and the condemnation of Israel's occupation of the territories on *moral* grounds.

In-between the two edges, the party *Shinui* may be positioned. Although *Shinui* considered itself as a liberal party, its main characteristic was to be anti-religious, while it still promoted a collectivist concept of state identity. According to its party platform, "Shinui upholds the basic values of Israel as a Zionist and Jewish state, open to every Jew." Regarding the status of the non-Jewish minorities, the platform shortly stated that Israel is "a state ruled by law in which the minorities have equal rights, in the spirit of the Declaration of Independence" (Shinui 2005).

A State of All Its Citizens

The vast majority of Israel's political parties (and of Jewish Israelis in general) support one or another of the three concepts discussed thus far. Thus, the secular camp is divided over *Eretz Israel* versus *Medinat Israel*, the latter in the sense of a "Jewish democracy." On the other hand, except for *Meimad* supporters, the religious segments of Israeli society favor one of the variants of "a religious state," while religious Zionists support *Eretz Israel* in its religious version.

Defying Israel's dominant cultural paradigm, only a minority defends the concept of "a state of all its citizens" (*medinat kol ezraheiha*). Israel's president Moshe Katsav, for instance, refuted the option of an Arab Israeli becoming the president of Israel with the following words: "This is a Jewish state and there is no reason to conceal the fact. We have to be wary of the demand to turn Israel into a state of all its citizens . . ." (Katzav 2001: 14). Yet advocates of a "state of all its citizens" demand full equality of all Israeli citizens, irrespective of religion or ethnicity, along with equal access to financial and political resources. According to this concept, there would be no preferential treatment of any group, while the individual citizen would stand at the centre. Hence, this concept supports the abolishment of the state's Jewish political symbols, including the flag, the anthem, and the Jewish holiday cycle, and their replacement with symbols with which Jewish and non-Jewish Israelis alike may identify. Supporters of this concept are also in favor of abolishing the principle of Jewish immigration altogether.

"A state of all its citizens," which favors individualist and universal values over collectivism, attracts Jewish-Israeli intellectuals of what is commonly termed the "extreme Left." It is also supported by many Arab Israeli citizens (Ghanem 1997).[15] In Israeli party politics, a number of Arab parties promote this state identity concept—although in some cases, it is combined with some sort of Arab nationalism, or an Islamist orientation (as in the case of Israel's Islamic Movement). Most notably, the Arab-Jewish party *Hadash*—the successor of Israel's Communist Party—promotes this rather liberal concept of state identity (Hadash 2002), along with factions of *Meretz/Yachad*.

Cultural Patterns and Cognitive Regions

An additional division within Israeli society revolves around the preferred "cognitive region" (Adler 1997a) and cultural patterns. Geographically, Israel is undoubtedly part of the Middle East. But in terms of cultural orientation, not everyone agrees that Israel is a typical Middle Eastern country (if such a thing exists at all).

The different orientations can be linked to the inter-Jewish divide between *Ashkenazim* and *Mizrahim* (or *Sephardim*). The divisions and unequal distribution of resources and political power between the two groups may well have diminished over time, but the difference in cultural pattern is still relevant today (Smooha 1998; Kimmerling 1998). Israel may well be "a combination of Cracow and Casablanca" (Avineri and Weidenfeld 1999a: 5), but this combination is not always an easy one. With the "Russian" immigration of the 1990s, the balance once more shifted toward European cultural patterns. But it also woke up the temporarily dormant inter-Jewish fault-line between *Ashkenazim* and *Mizrahim*, particularly in the context of persistent socioeconomic inequalities, the economic success of the Russian immigrants, as well as the trend among the latter to voice their cultural difference (Smooha 1998). Moreover, in contrast to Israel's founding generation, who immigrated from a large number of different countries, the Israel-born population grew steadily over the years and represents now around 60 percent of Jewish Israelis (Central Bureau of Statistics 2004). This led to a strengthening of "Israeli" cultural patterns, which, however, are still far from being defined.

As argued elsewhere (Del Sarto and Tovias 2001), a large segment of Israeli society has difficulties in conceiving Israel as being part of the Middle East. For many Jewish Israelis, this option seems to contradict secular Zionism as well as Israel's political, economic, and cultural features. They perceive Israel as belonging to the democratic "West." For others, however, European cultural patterns appear alien to Israel's sociocultural features and geographic location. In their view, Israeli society has a high affinity for the Middle Eastern way of life, and Israel belongs to its geographical region, in spite of the conflict with the neighbors. Many *Mizrahi* Jewish and Arab Israelis tend to maintain this perception. Still others maintain that Israel is neither a Middle Eastern nor a Western country, but a country *sui generis*.

The support for "Middle Eastern" versus "Western" culture cuts through different segments of society and political affiliations. There are no large movements that explicitly propagate the different orientations, although *Shas*, for instance, promotes *Mizrahi* ethnicity, mainly out of protest against the still-dominant *Ashkenazi* elites. Altogether, the different identity concepts and domestic fault-lines discussed thus far impact on Israeli parliamentary politics, as the next paragraphs briefly assess.

Political Implications

Israeli society is highly polarized on questions related to Israel's state identity, and numerically almost equal groups maintain in fact incompatible preferences. Although voters may support a specific party for different reasons, Israel's democratic procedures permit to treat the composition of the Knesset, Israel's parliament, as mirroring more or less the domestic preferences. As the discussion thus far has shown, Israel's domestic identity polarization assumes different dimensions, which cut across each other.

To begin with, there is a deepening religious–secular divide. In the time-span under consideration, the increasing strength of the religious parties and the continuous decline of the two major secular parties *Likud* and Labour are a case in point (Peretz and Doron 2000; Hazan and Rahat 2000). The rise of the fervently antireligious *Shinui* party in the 2003 elections, which became the third-largest faction instead of the declining *Shas*, also points to an increasing polarization of Israeli society along religious–secular lines.

The second fault-line revolves around territorial–political questions. The *secular* supporters of *Eretz Israel* held roughly one fourth of seats in the fifteenth Knesset (May 1999–January 2003), while supporters of *Medinat Israel* were represented with 48 out of 120 mandates.[16] In relative terms, this is a majority, but not enough to govern. Facing the option of territorial compromise in the context of the peace process, secular defenders of *Eretz Israel* could ally with the national-religious NRP and the ultra-orthodox party list (with five seats each). Conversely, supporters of *Medinat Israel* were backed by the 10 seats of the Arab parties, which are however not considered as legitimate enough to actually enter a government coalition. The remaining two major parties (*Shas* with 17 mandates, and the 6 seats of the former Russian immigrant party *Israel B'Aliyah*[17]), ran on a restricted sectarian platform. This also applies to the ultra-orthodox UJT. Indeed, these three parties were primarily preoccupied with ensuring government funds for their specific constituencies, that is, the religious sectors and the "Russian" immigrants (Peretz and Doron 2000: 266). Capable of entering a coalition with either Labour or *Likud*, the sectarian parties finally decided on who governs the country, thus determining its foreign-policy course. Moreover, the territorial–political axis divides between inclusive and particularistic interpretations of state identity. Thus, it positions the different versions of *Eretz Israel* and the religious parties on one side of the divide, and *Meretz/Yachad*, most Labour representatives, and most Arab parties on the other, while leaving a grey field in the middle.

The third fault-line revolves around ethnicity and cultural patterns, which assumes several dimensions. Over the last decades, the divide between the Arab minority and the Jewish majority has grown deeper. Both the diminishing support of Arab Israeli voters for Zionist parties at the polls (Peretz and Doron 2000), and the October 2000 events and their aftermath clearly support this observation. Yet this fault-line also cuts through the Jewish majority. With the rise of *Shas* between the mid-1980s and the late 1990s, inter-Jewish ethnicity once more became a political issue (Sandler 1993: 161). Similarly, the electoral strength of the "Russian" immigrant parties since the 1990s underscores the importance of ethnic sectarianism.

A fourth fault-line divides Zionists from non-Zionists (or even anti-Zionists). Although the voting pattern of Arab Israelis remains highly fragmented, there is a growing opposition to the Zionist rationale, if it implies the preferential treatment of one group over another. However, while there are very different interpretations of Zionism, as we have seen, the non-Zionist camp is similarly heterogeneous, comprising most Arab parties, the Jewish-Israeli extreme Left, along with segments of the Jewish ultra-orthodox community.

The polarization of Israeli society along different fault-lines has produced fragile parliamentary majorities. While governments are often forced to accommodate the requests of small coalition partners, the parties making up a government tend to maintain partly incompatible identity concepts and foreign-policy preferences. With it, governments may be quite incapable of simultaneously pursuing internal reforms and take important foreign-policy decisions. Barak, for instance, was unable to simultaneously advance the Oslo process—for which he needed *Shas*—and implement the promised "civil revolution." Since the latter also entailed the containment of religious power, Barak could certainly not count on the blessing of *Shas*, or of any other religious party. Conversely, the *Likud* and the ultra-nationalist secular parties may have supported the domestic reforms, but they opposed Barak's foreign-policy course.

Hence, Israeli governments may fall over minor domestic disputes, not to mention crucial foreign-policy issues. Considering the importance of floating votes, internal or external events may easily tip the balance. This explains why Israel has been witnessing frequent changes of governments, along with a high incidence of early elections. Indeed, in the 1990s, Israel went from the hitherto most "nationalist" government in its history under Shamir to an extremely "dovish" one under Rabin after the 1992 elections. Following Rabin's assassination in 1995 and the interim government under Peres, the 1996 elections saw the victory of Binyamin Netanyahu, who ran on an *Eretz Israel* platform (although he honored the Oslo accords). After the anticipated elections in May 1999, a Labour-dominated coalition under Ehud Barak sought to revive the moribund peace process. And when Barak lost the parliamentary majority after the outbreak of the second *Intifada*, the new *Likud* chairman Sharon took over, forming a grand coalition with Labour. The collapse of the latter led to the early elections of January 2003, after which Sharon's *Likud* party initially formed a coalition with the religious and ultra-nationalist parties which was later on reshuffled in view of the planned withdrawal from the Gaza Strip.

Finally, it is relevant that the domestic fault-lines cut across party lines. Recent events show that this also applies to the territorial–political axis. Thus, most *Likud* members oppose Sharon's support for an independent Palestinian state. His withdrawal from the Gaza Strip divided his cabinet, provoking a fracture within both the *Likud* and the national-religious NRP (which faced the choice between loyalty to the state and commitment to *Eretz Israel*), and Sharon's subsequent founding of the "centrist" *Kadima* party. Entailing the reassessment of the original *Eretz Israel* concept, the Gaza withdrawal in August 2005 in fact resulted in a redrawing of Israel's political landscape. Thus, Israel is not only difficult to govern, but it also faces serious obstacles in pursuing a coherent foreign-policy course on issues that touch the nerve of the domestic dispute over state identity. This particularly concerns territorial questions, relations to Israel's traditional "enemies," and the favored regional order.

Israel, the EU, and the EMP

Leaving Israel's domestic scene aside for now, this section focuses on Israel's participation in the Euro-Mediterranean Partnership since 1995. The following questions will be addressed: First, how did Israel react to the launching of the Barcelona Process and its underlying principles? Second, how did the EMP affect EU–Israeli relations? Third, what characterizes Israel's participation in the EMP? The development of EU–Israeli relations before and after the beginning of the peace process in the early 1990 provides the starting point of our investigation.

Bilateral Rapprochement after Oslo

Due to the burden of history, Israel's relationship to Europe has never been an easy matter. Although economic relations between the EC/EU and Israel had developed positively over the decades, Israeli political leaders had generally remained quite skeptical toward the countries of Europe, the EC/EU, and their political aspirations.

In the aftermath of the 1967 war, and, even more so, the Yom Kippur War, Israel's political leaders perceived that the EC did not—or did not want to—understand Israel's situation. However, in 1975 the EC and Israel concluded the first bilateral free-trade agreement, in spite of OPEC's threats to use the "oil weapon" against Europe. Yet at the beginning of the 1980s, relations between Israel and the EC witnessed a low point. Israel reacted with outrage to the 1980 Venice Declaration, which called for recognizing the Palestinian right to self-determination and the involvement of the PLO in future peace negotiations (European Council 1980). In retrospect, the EC was well ahead of its time. But since the PLO at that time still openly called for Israel's destruction, Israel rejected the Venice Declaration. The subsequent Israeli invasion of Lebanon in 1982, along with Israeli policy toward the first Palestinian *Intifada*, additionally troubled EC-Israeli relations. In light of the heavy criticism expressed by EC member states, former prime minister Shamir (1989) remarked on the Europeans: "They don't exactly understand us or our motives." Consequently, Israeli governments by default opposed any attempts of the EC to play a greater political role in Middle Eastern affairs.

The signing of the Oslo Agreements induced a rapprochement between Israel and the EU. Departing from the traditional Israeli reluctance, Rabin and his foreign minister Peres urged the EU to support Israel in its quest for peace. This "structural reevaluation" (Sachar 1999: 342) also comprised the quest for the EU's participation in the multilateral structures of the Madrid peace process, along with European financial assistance to the Palestinians. The EU followed suit. Moreover, EU–Israeli negotiations on a new trade agreement started shortly after the beginning of Oslo. In the previous decade, the EC/EU had disregarded Israel's request for updating the 1975 free-trade agreement, mainly out of political opposition to Israel's settlement policy in the occupied territories. After the beginning of Oslo, the EU publicly acknowledged Israel's advanced economic status, much to Israel's satisfaction. Thus, in the 1994 Essen Declaration, the EU explicitly stated that "Israel, on account of its high level of economic development, should enjoy a *special status* in its relations with the European Union" (European Council 1994, italics added). In return, the EU's political ambitions in Middle Eastern politics started to gradually face less resistance in Israel. As one Israeli Foreign Ministry official put it, Israel became used to see former EU special envoy to the Middle East, Miguel Ángel Moratinos, on almost every picture taken in the framework of Middle Eastern political events. In this context, EU Commission officials also pointed to the EU's increasing acknowledgement of its own political limitations. According to this argument, Israel reacted positively to the EU's realization that it can play only a complementary role to the U.S. in the region.[18]

Thus, before Oslo, there was a gap between the EC/EU's advanced economic ties with Israel and rather oscillating political relations, mainly due to disagreements over Israel's policy toward the Palestinians. For the EU, the prospects of peace in the Middle East offered the possibility of resolving these tensions, while reconciling its economic interests vis-à-vis both Israel and Arab states. At the same time, Middle East peace-making permitted the EU to effectively address its "security interests," while increasing European political and economic influence in its southern periphery through a regional approach. Israel's reaction to the launching of the EMP is the subject of the next section.

The Launching of the EMP

Although the EU's launching of the EMP was certainly not an exercise in altruism, the initiative was nevertheless meant to support political change in the Middle East after the beginning of the Oslo process. The Barcelona Process offered a legitimate "alternative to America's four-decade role as guardian of Western interests in the Middle East" (Sachar 1999: 354), which had not proven to be that successful either. However, some Israeli observers were skeptical of the "real aims" of the EMP. Regretting that the United States would not participate in the Barcelona Conference, Israeli critics maintained that the only purpose of the EMP was to increase European influence in the region (*Jerusalem Post* October 13, 1995). Others viewed the EMP as a smokescreen for the EU's key concern of wanting to reduce illegal immigration from the Maghreb.

Yet for the incumbent Israeli government, the EU's vision for the Mediterranean was compatible with its efforts to build a "new Middle East" (Peres 1993). In this vein, Shimon Peres declared: "We hope Europe will play a genuine role in this historic attempt to construct a new Middle East. This would be consistent with its destiny; it would be an outgrowth of its historical commitments" (Peres 1995: 168). According to this perspective, economic development and democratization throughout the region was in Israel's own interest. Thus, the EU and the Israeli government under Rabin had similar interests, a fact that positively influenced EU–Israeli relations. In addition, the EMP was certainly a diplomatic success for Israel. Indeed, Syria and Lebanon, which had refused to take part in the multilateral structures of the Madrid peace process, participated with Israel in the EMP from the outset.

Both for Israel and the EU, the launching of the Barcelona Process implied a somewhat increased role for the EU in the region. However, both sides disagreed over the degree of this involvement. For the EU, the multilateral and regional character of the EMP seemed to entail a greater European role in peace-making. But this position met on Israel's resistance. Certainly, Israel perceived the EMP as a means to support the peace process, both financially and through regional confidence-building measures. Yet, Israel insisted on wanting to separate the EMP from the Middle East peace process, in spite of the efforts of other participants to link one to the other. According to the Israeli position, the peace process was subject of another forum and mediated by a different player, namely the United States (*Jerusalem Post* November 27, 1995). The EU eventually gave in to Israel's demands, and the Barcelona Declaration (1995) explicitly stated that both processes are separated.

From the EU's perspective, the regional and multilateral character of the EMP entailed that bilateral relations with southern Mediterranean countries were embedded into the Euro-Mediterranean logic as soon as the partnership started. Consequently, new trade agreements with the southern parties were termed "Euro-Mediterranean agreement," even if the respective negotiations had started long before the launching of the EMP, as in the case of Israel. Indeed, the Commission's suggestion to call the 1995 bilateral agreement at a very late stage of the negotiations "Euro-Mediterranean Association Agreement" caught Israeli Finance Ministry officials by surprise. While arguing that the EU itself recognizes that Israel notably differs from other southern Mediterranean countries, as the Essen Declaration attests, the Israeli Finance Ministry disapproved of Israel being classified as a *southern Mediterranean country* in economic terms.[19] The fact that Israel's 1975 free-trade agreement in industrial goods with the Europeans was fully implemented in 1989, whereas the EMP envisages the same trade regime with other EMP participants by the year 2010, supported this argumentation. Yet EU officials stressed the importance of the new EU–Israeli trade agreement for stabilizing the southern Mediterranean (*Associated Press* November 20, 1995), although this claim is obviously doubtful.

Thus, from the outset, Israel maintained a quite different interpretation of the EMP logic. In fact, Israel consented to a greater EU role in the region as long as it remained confined to the financial dimension, along with the facilitating of cooperation and confidence-building measures. In exchange, Israel was willing to involve the Europeans through consultations, and to accept their presence on pictures of Middle Eastern events, so to speak. Yet due to Israel's perception of being in a particular security situation, along with its traditional (and history-based) suspicions of the EU's neutrality in the Arab–Israeli conflict, the only mediator in the peace process was to remain the United States. At the same time, Israel viewed its "special" bilateral relations to the EU as independent of the Barcelona Process.

EU–Israeli Relations and the EMP

Since the beginning of the EMP, Israel has been participating in an impressive number of projects within the three baskets. The Barcelona

Process succeeded in facilitating Euro-Mediterranean cooperation in various domains indeed, such as on the highly sensitive issue of water, while involving government representatives, academics, businesspeople, and various segments of civil society.

However, Israel repeatedly regretted that the separation between the peace process and the EMP was more difficult to maintain than it had hoped. Syria and Lebanon, for instance, refused to participate in most regional EMP projects in which Israel took part. Against the backdrop of the recurrently derailing peace process over the years, other Arab partners also repeatedly boycotted EMP events because of Israel's participation. Similarly, confidence-building measures remained difficult, since many Arab states simply rejected any development that resembled the "normalization" of relations with Israel in the absence of a resolution of the conflict. In fact, the expression "confidence-building measures" had to be dropped altogether from EMP documents and replaced with the more neutral word "measures." However, Israeli Foreign Ministry officials point to a few successful confidence-building projects, most notably EuroMeSCo activities, along with a project on the prevention and management of natural and man-made disasters, in which all the EMP signatories participated. Interestingly, even after the collapse of the peace process, EMP activities involving Israeli and Palestinian and/or other Arab participants continued, albeit on a reduced scale. Thus, all EMP participants took part in the 2001 Euro-Mediterranean meeting of Foreign Ministers in Brussels as well as the EMP meeting of Trade Ministers in May 2001. Similarly, at the NGO level, various projects involving Israeli and Palestinian youth continued.

Yet, the different interpretations of the EMP maintained by Israel and the EU repeatedly caused irritation and disputes between the two sides. The most contested issue remained the EU's political involvement in Middle East peace-making, which for the EU, was an almost natural consequence of its increased financial commitment in the framework of the EMP and beyond. In this vein, the EU de facto started to define the Middle East peace process as an area of its Mediterranean policy, as various EU documents clearly show. But particularly with the recurrent stalemates of the peace process from 1996 on, the EU's ambitions deeply annoyed Israel. Thus, Israeli governments remained disturbed by repeated visits of EU representatives to Palestinian officials in the former "Orient House" in East Jerusalem, since this seemed to imply the EU's recognition of Palestinian sovereignty over the eastern part of the city. The EU also sought to exert pressure on Israeli governments regarding its policy in the occupied territories. Thus, in 1998, the EU started to produce a twice-a-year Human Rights Watch Report that chronicled the treatment of Palestinian prisoners, border closures, demolition of Palestinian homes, and various human-rights violations. In the same year, the EU also protested against Israel's construction of the *Har Homa* Jewish settlement near Jerusalem by officially visiting the site over Israeli objections. This step angered Israel profoundly. Similarly, the EU's 1997 Luxembourg Declaration that called on Israel to show more flexibility in order to reinvigorate the derailing peace process was decisively rejected by the Israeli government (Foreign Ministry of Israel 1997). In January 1999, the EU issued a similar statement that held Israel responsible for the delay in the implementation of the Wye River Memorandum, which stipulated a further Israeli withdrawal from occupied territories. This statement also met with a harsh Israeli response. And the EU's 1999 statement defining Jerusalem as *corpus separatum* in accordance with the 1947 UN partition plan—thus denying Israel's legitimate sovereignty over any part of Jerusalem—infuriated the Israeli government (Netanyahu and Sharon 1999), and prompted an official complaint before the summoned European ambassadors to Israel.

Israel also repeatedly moaned the EU's attempts to use economic tools for exerting political pressure. While there is nothing specifically European about such a policy, it is certainly the other side of EU economic power that, conversely, also offers economic benefits as incentives or reward. In this vein, several EU members delayed the ratification of the EU–Israel agreement in response to the serious clashes between Israel and the Palestinians in 1996, provoked by the opening of an antique tunnel in Jerusalem's Old City. Israel reacted sharply to what it perceived a threatening tone from the European side. The issue of the Israeli "origin" of products manufactured in Jewish settlements in the occupied territories was an additional point of controversy. For decades, Israel benefited from the duty-free export to the EU of these products. Much in contrast to the EU's political stance of considering the occupied territories as not a part of Israel and Jewish settlements as not compliant with international law, the EU maintained a laissez-faire attitude toward this practice for years. Yet after the first serious derailments of Middle East peace-making during the Netanyahu government, the EU started to publicly voice doubts on the "Israeli origin" of these products. The EU's firm position on this issue over the years eventually compelled Israel to give in. Thus, Israel no longer marks the products that are produced in the settlements as having originated in Israel, with the effect that they are excluded from duty-free access to the EU.

Moreover, Israel repeatedly criticized the EU for its multilateral logic in economic terms, as noted above. In contrast to the EU's narrative, Israel tended to distinguish between the 1995 bilateral trade agreement, seen as the main pillar of EU–Israeli relations, and the economic benefits of the Barcelona Process, which are indeed limited for Israel. As high-tech is far more important than, say, the export of oranges for Israel's economy today, Israel's Finance Ministry disagreed with the EU's practice of officially considering Israel as a southern Mediterranean country. Similarly, Israeli Finance Ministry officials disliked the EMP's underlying north–south approach, which is most visible in the allocation of development aid to most EMP partners—Israel excluded. Thus, Israeli officials preferred to divide the EMP participants into "16 and 11," instead of "15" (the then–EU member countries) and "12" (the then-EMP partners). Alternatively, they stressed that Israel is a *particular* case, as neither a receiving nor a donor country.[20] Yet EU officials did not see any contradiction in maintaining a coherent approach toward its southern periphery and individual economic arrangements with the different partners.

Another long-standing argument between the two sides revolved around the rules applying to the so-called origin of products according to the bilateral free-trade agreement. Originally, the EMP offered the prospect of diagonally cumulating origin rules among EMP participants.[21] Besides economic considerations, Israeli scholars first proposed the cumulation of origin rules as a means to consolidate peace among former adversaries over 20 years ago (Arad et al. 1983). While Israel was interested in cumulating origin rules with Jordan (and with Turkey), the EU Commission maintained that the respective parties first had to conclude free trade agreements among them. On the Israeli side, the EU's wait-and-see attitude on this issue raised doubts on the seriousness of the EU's Mediterranean policy. In this vein, Zohar Peri of the Israeli Trade Ministry declared that the "Europeans are strong when it comes to politics and declarations, however, when there is a concrete opportunity to do something and help along, they shy away" (*Jerusalem Post* August 3, 1995).

Altogether, the EMP certainly affected EU–Israeli bilateral relations. Thus, Israeli officials repeatedly mentioned that the EU's *multilateral* Mediterranean policy positively affected bilateral relations as long as the peace process was proceeding, and negatively as soon as the latter started to derail.[22] Generally, Israeli officials stressed that Israel felt quite uncomfortable with the EU's regional and multilateral logic. From an Israeli perspective, promoting democratization and economic reform in its Arab neighborhood is independent of the peace process, and being put into the category of "Mediterranean countries"—particularly in economic terms—disregards Israel's "European-type" political and economic features. Hence, Israel did not develop a strategy or policy of its own toward Euro-Mediterranean regional security, as argued in the next section.

A Lack of Strategy

Although Israel occasionally stressed the potential benefits of the EMP in the future, it did not identify with the principles of the EMP over the years. As one EU official remarked at a conference in Tel Aviv in 2001, there was a lack of a "national strategy" from the Israeli side (Di Cara 2001). Indeed, the EMP did not figure in Israel's foreign-policy preoccupations and discourse, and it was not the subject of any broad public debate.

For Israel, there were different explanations of why the EMP lagged behind its expectations, and of why Israel did not develop a Euro-Mediterranean perspective. Some Israeli officials stressed that due to its conflict-laden history, Israel has not much experience with multilateral ventures, which may explain why it is such a bad regional player. Thus, Israel's political situation distorted priorities and impeded the development of any regional outlook. Another frequent explanation pointed to the fate of the peace process, along with the tendency of Arab Mediterranean participants to link the latter to the EMP. Others blamed the Palestinians for the fate of both the EMP and Oslo. Still other officials mainly held the EU responsible for the discrepancy between theory and practice of the Barcelona process.[23]

In fact, complaints about the EU's patronizing, insensitive, and incoherent attitude toward southern Mediterranean states, including Israel, were a recurrent theme among Israeli officials—mostly off-the-record. Examples include the EU's practice of employing exclusively European experts in EMP projects, as if there were no experts in the EMP partner states, or the EU's repeated statements describing the southern Mediterranean—and North Africa in particular—as a "security problem." According to this argument, the Europeans do not comprehend that such statements would raise suspicion among the EMP partners, especially in the context of the EU's attempts to develop the common European Security and Defence Policy (ESDP). Moreover, these practices were perceived as contradicting the EU's recurrent emphasis on the principle of "partnership." However, the EU was also criticized for not promoting more aggressively democratization and the respect for human rights in neighboring states, or for not exerting more pressure on former PLO leader Arafat in order to stop terror.

A quite common argument remained that reducing unwanted immigration from its southern periphery was the EU's key concern, or at least among its most important interests. Alternatively, one foreign ministry official argued that the Barcelona Process was initially meant as an economic enterprise, which only later (and somewhat accidentally) developed into a political project. Finance ministry officials, on the other hand, stressed the economic irrelevance of the Barcelona Process for Israel, and insisted that Israel decided to "play the game" out of courtesy.[24] Similarly, in an internal paper, Israel's Delegation to the EU recommended the use of the EMP framework for promoting Israel's *particular economic interests* vis-à-vis the EU. Officially, however, the foreign ministry stressed the EMP's potential political benefits and insisted that Israel must participate at the EMP as a *southern Mediterranean country*. Thus, the former director-general of the Israeli Ministry of Foreign Affairs publicly stressed the "great importance" of the EMP and praised it as a "great opportunity" (Liel 2001). Yet it is remarkable that, while acknowledging that the Barcelona Process facilitated confidence-building measures, Israeli Foreign Ministry officials in charge of regional security claimed that the EMP had nothing to do with security, not even in the long term.

Some of these arguments may be founded, but the assessment of their validity is not our objective here. The interesting point is that these arguments evidence that Israeli policy-makers who were actively involved in the EMP, along with close observers, did not internalize the principles of the EMP. While the EMP was largely irrelevant for Israel, there was no strategy toward Euro-Mediterranean region-building. This is particularly striking if we consider that Israel was actively involved in the Barcelona Process for many years.

Israel's Contested State Identity and the EMP

Israel and the EU indeed maintained different opinions on the question of what the EMP was finally about. The Israeli position is best characterized by the assessment that Israel was not satisfied with the EMP but was interested in its continuation, as the EMP coordinator at the Israeli Foreign Ministry once put it.

After the collapsed peace process, the Euro-Mediterranean vision seemed particularly abstract and unrealistic. Not surprisingly, Israel reacted positively to the EU's 2003–2004 European Neighbourhood initiative, which disconnects bilateral relations to the regional perspective (Del Sarto and Schumacher 2004). However, an identity-based perspective permits for an alternative explanation of the difficulties of the EMP, which is also significant for the time span before the outbreak of the *Intifada*. As the next section argues, the EMP implied an attempt to alter Israel's identity, thus touching upon a number of domestic identity divides.

The EMP's Implicit "Identity Manipulations"...

The underlying logic of the EMP had a number of implications for Israel's self-perception, three of which deserve a special attention here. First, the EU's Euro-Mediterranean vision envisaged dramatically altered relations between Israel and its neighbors, which include Israel's most important enemies—its "significant other." Indeed, the EMP logic presupposed some sort of ongoing peace negotiations, along with the commitment of the conflict parties to achieve peace in spite of the difficulties. In the long run, the EU's Euro-Mediterranean logic—whether explicitly or not—envisaged the establishment of an independent and viable Palestinian state. In addition, the idea of achieving peace, prosperity, stability, and regional integration necessitates constructive relations and the building of confidence among southern EMP partners.

Second, the EMP sought to redefine "Israel's place in the region," while forging a link between Israel's self-perception and its geographic surroundings. This aspect directly touches upon the type of favored relations to Israel's "other"—which are its geographic neighbors. While increasingly referring to Israel as a southern Mediterranean country in the time span under consideration, the EU's discourse also implied a disregard for Israel's "special" economic and political features. Similarly, the regional and multilateral logic of the EMP envisaged the promotion of a Euro-Mediterranean regional order.

Third, the EMP implicitly sought to redefine Israel's relations to the EU, as the Euro-Mediterranean logic implied an increasingly political EU role in the region. At the same time, the EU's downplaying of Israel's "special" status in its Euro-Mediterranean narrative entailed a "normalization" of EU–Israeli relations themselves, since bilateral relations were no longer considered as "special," but "different" at best. Thus, in view of these three aspects, the EMP has far-reaching implications for Israel's state identity. These implications exceed by far the aim of promoting an overarching Mediterranean identity, which is relevant per se and is discussed separately below. But how did Israel respond to the EU's attempted "identity manipulations"?

... and Israel's Response

Israel and its "Significant Other"

Relations to the Palestinians and the so-called Arab world certainly touch the nerve of Israel's internal identity divides. Irrespective of subsequent events, the beginning of the peace process marked a turning point, as the Middle East conflict had been a constant feature of Israel's collective experience. Interestingly, with the beginning of the peace process, Israel's political leaders sought to redefine the identity of the state. In this vein, the late Rabin (1995b: 298–299, italics added) stated:

> One might say that Arab hostility and political isolation hurt us—we lost our trust in others. We suspected everyone and developed a siege mentality in a sort of political, economic and mental ghetto. . . . In face of the new reality in a changing world, we must design a new dimension for the Israeli image. . . . This is new reality, we must be part of it and it obliges us to *revolutionize our thought and behavior patterns* in the coming years.

Rabin thus implicitly made the point that identity themes are not only dependent on external situations, but also influence a state's perception of the outside-world, and thus its international behavior. Yet Rabin's proposed "revolution" encountered pronounced resistance from large segments of Israeli society, and, along with the prospects of territorial compromise, fueled fervent discussions on Israel's identity. Certainly, this development may be explained in terms of declining external threat perceptions that had thus far provided the "glue" for a deeply divided society. But the fervent debates in Israeli society on the desirability of an Israeli withdrawal from the territories brought most visibly the incompatibility of different interpretations of Zionism and a "Jewish state" to the fore, since it implied *a need to choose*. In essence, the rift between nationalist and/or religious interpretations of Israel's identity on the one hand, and secular-liberal interpretations on the other hand widened most notably (Barnett 1999; Hermann and Yuchtmann-Yaar 1997; Alpher 1995; Dowty et al. 1997; Newman 1997).

In view of the fragile parliamentary balance, and the usually very heterogeneous government coalitions, embarking on the redefinition of Israel's relations to its "significant other"—and therefore of Israel's "self"—was bound to face enormous difficulties even if the peace process had proceeded smoothly. Yet, taken the unclear prospects of the latter, coupled with repeated terror attacks that were perceived as assaults on Israel's security, fragile majorities were easy to reverse. Although Israel's domestic debates receded after the collapse of the peace process, Israel's crucial identity conflicts are only postponed, and are far from being solved. Since the EMP sought to reshape Israel's relations with its adversaries, it is easy to see how Israel's contested identity impeded the development of a consistent Euro-Mediterranean strategy from this perspective. Although Israel refuted any link of the EMP with the peace process, the former is inherently based on the latter. Israel's contested identity—with all its political implications—makes it almost impossible for Israel to consistently embark on the reshaping of relations with its "significant other" in the first place.

Israel's "Place in the Region"

In general terms, the beginning of the peace process gave rise to an alternative perception of Israel's "place in the world." While Shimon Peres propagated the idea of an Israel that is firmly anchored in a "New Middle East" (Peres 1993, 1995), Itzhak Rabin (1995c: 2) stressed:

> No longer are we necessarily "a people that dwells alone," and no longer is it true that "the whole world is against us." We must overcome the sense of isolation that has held us in its thrall for almost half a century.

Yet various identity concepts prevailing at the domestic level resist any attempts to redefine Israel's "place in the world" and to become "a nation like other nations," albeit to a different extent. These potentially include religious interpretations of state identity, as all religions emphasize "uniqueness" and thus stress particularistic values. More specifically, this concerns the value system of the Jewish ultra-orthodox sector that obliges it "to close in on itself and to differentiate itself from the world around it" (Friedman 2001). Similarly, the extremist version of the nationalist-religious credo entails the desire for the international isolation of the state (Rubinstein 1980: 120). As for the secular concept of *Eretz Israel*, it is linked to the idea that Israel shall "live by the sword." This does not mean that the concept is isolationist in general terms. In fact, many defenders of this concept are favorable to an "Americanization" of Israeli society and politics, support economic globalization, and—as the *Likud* platform does—stress Israel's high cultural affinity with the United States (Likud 1999). But this orientation nevertheless puts an emphasis on Israel's difference with regard to its *regional* environment, and stresses Israel's detachment from its geographic surroundings.

Due to the frequent alteration of Israeli governments over the last decades, Israel has been defined in several ways in its foreign-policy discourse. The same applies to its "place in the region" and "place in the world." Israel's political leaders have recurrently used the ambiguous term of the "Jewish state," along with *Eretz Israel*, and *Medinat Israel*. They have emphasized Israel's high affinity with "the West," while stressing that Israel must "dwell alone"—at least in the region. Alternatively, the idea of a "normal," secular, and democratic state that is firmly anchored in a (new) Middle East has been promoted (Medzini 1976–1995). Yet given the need to choose, there is not much room for compromise, as the idea of being part of a region and the idea of not being part of it are quite incompatible. In terms of cognitive regions and cultural boundaries, the EMP's vision for the Mediterranean is similar to Peres's vision of a "New Middle East." The latter, however, did not find much support within his own Labour party, mainly because it was perceived as being too exotic (Weissbrod 1997). Had it become a topic of public debate, the Euro-Mediterranean idea would have faced comparable difficulties. Needless to say, the already meager domestic support for a New Middle East, and by extension, of a Euro-Mediterranean regional order, further diminishes in situations of renewed conflict with Israel's regional neighbors.

The different opinions on the logic of the Barcelona Process maintained by Israeli officials in charge of EU–Israeli relations in general, and the EMP in particular, clearly reflected Israel's undefined "place in the region." Thus, as noted above, Israel's finance ministry stressed the country's European-type socioeconomic features, while voicing the conviction that Israel's economic place *is in Europe*, and not in the Mediterranean.[25] An emphasis on Israel's difference to the region also characterized the position of Israel's diplomatic representatives to the EU, who identified the development of the states of the Middle East (Israel excluded) as main objectives of the Barcelona Process. The recommended strategy, thus, was to stress more assertively Israel's "special" standing in the region vis-à-vis the EU, while advancing sub-regional cooperation with similar countries, namely Turkey, Malta and Cyprus.

And indeed, Israel's relations with Turkey developed positively in the time span under consideration (Del Sarto 2004), described as a "honeymoon" by one Israeli official.

In general, however, Israel was eager to point out the difficulties in fitting into many regional EMP projects because of its distinct political and socioeconomic features. A case in point was Israel's participation in Euro-Mediterranean democratization projects, since many projects are not applicable to Israel, and most Arab countries rejected having Israel as a "teacher" of democracy, given Israel's human-rights violations in the occupied territories. Conversely, Israel's foreign ministry stressed that Israel was always interested in participating in the EMP as a *southern Mediterranean country*. Yet while disagreeing with the finance ministry's assertion that Israel's place is *in Europe*, foreign ministry officials were neither convinced that Israel firmly belongs to the Middle East, or the Mediterranean for that matter.

In fact, in conferences on EU–Israeli or EU–Mediterranean relations, and in the presence of EU officials, Israeli officials often simultaneously voiced different assessments of whether Israel participated at the EMP as a European-type state, a Mediterranean country, or a "special" case. One may argue that that there is no contradiction in being a European-type economy and Western-style democracy that is located in the southern Mediterranean/Middle East. However, in view of the EMP's aim of creating a Euro-Mediterranean region, which, by definition, must be based on common themes, it is relevant whether the participants emphasized common features or, alternatively, difference. Yet, although the tendency toward the latter was more pronounced, Israel gave very different signals, somewhat in "yes-but-no" manner.

In one way or another, most Israeli officials involved in, and observers of, the EMP maintained that Israel was somewhat caught between Europe and the Middle East (Del Sarto and Tovias 2001). Thus, while generally acknowledging that Israel has some Mediterranean cultural features in the realms of food, music, and mentality, most interview partners expressed the opinion that Israel is actually a "mixture" that does not really belong to any region. The argument of Avineri and Weidenfeld (1999a: 5) that Israel is a mixture between "Cracow and Casablanca" resonates here. With it, Israel's dissonant identity discourse can be linked to the domestic divide in terms of cultural patterns, which, at least implicitly, also entails different preferences of regional order.

Altogether, Israel's dissenting identity discourse evidenced its difficulties in deciding on whether it belongs to a "Western" or "Middle Eastern" cognitive region, whether it is part of the Mediterranean or different and detached from it. Although the EMP narrative actually aimed at reconciling "East" and "West," it emphasized Israel's Mediterranean character and anchorage in the region. Yet the question of whether Israel's geographic location is relevant for its self-definition cannot be separated from the question of what kind of state Israel wants to be. These questions touch upon different dimensions of Israel's contested state identity, and have not been sorted out in the first place.

Relations to the EU

There is a broad consensus in Israel on the type of favored relations to the EU, which clearly affected the interpretation of the EMP logic. As long as the peace process was proceeding, Israel wanted the EU to financially back Oslo, stay out of politics, and further develop bilateral relations. This consensus rests on the Jewish historical experience with "the Europeans," which was additionally nurtured by the EC/EU's positions on the Arab–Israeli conflict in the past. In view of Israel's key preoccupation with security, many Jewish Israelis believe that Europe is biased and opportunistic, and can therefore not be trusted when it comes to matters of war and peace (Alpher 1998). Israel's two major parties *Likud* and Labour, which have traditionally dominated Israel's foreign-policy making,[26] implicitly or explicitly share this assessment. The religious parties were never directly involved in foreign-policy making, but particularly the ultra-orthodox parties would most probably reject closer relations to the EU, as the motive of persecution plays a central role in their value system.

Yet in spite of the general consensus, there are differences regarding the favored type of EU–Israeli relations among Israel's political elites. In fact, EU–Israeli relations fluctuated in correlation with Israel's alternation of governments. Thus, Labour-led governments in general had a rather positive attitude toward the EU. In particular, the former Barak government maintained a somewhat "Europeanist" foreign policy. In this vein, Barak and his ministers Shlomo Ben-Ami and Shimon Peres frequently consulted European leaders on issues related to the peace process, and their discourse toward the EU was quite amicable and value-oriented. Thus, upon the entering into force of the 1995 EU–Israel agreement in June 2000, Barak's first foreign minister David Levy (2000) described EU–Israeli relations as constituting "an extensive framework of long-standing democratic principles, membership in the free world, economic gains and shared cultural values." And while Levy stressed the "important role" that the EU played in the Middle East peace process, his successor Ben-Ami declared that the EU foreign-affairs representative Javier Solana "has an important role to play in this part of the world as key member of the European Union leadership." In the same declaration, Ben-Ami also addressed the former EU special envoy to the Middle East Moratinos, as "our friend" (Ben-Ami and Solana 2001).

Under the Netanyahu government, however, the same "friend" Moratinos was repeatedly confronted with accusations that the EU is profoundly biased against Israel, and that its positions are an undesirable interference. The Netanyahu government even called the EU's criticism of Israel's insufficient commitment to the peace process a "distortion of justice" (Sharon and Moratinos 1999). At the same time, the EU's decision to approve Israel's participation in its so-called Framework Program for Research and Development as equal partner met a comparatively tepid official Israeli reaction. Although Israel became the first non-EU member to fully participate at EU research activities and funds, the then–foreign minister Sharon declared that Israel is "satisfied," referred briefly to EU–Israeli common interests, but said nothing beyond this (Sharon 1999). This attitude seems to correspond to the position of the *Likud* in general, the platform of which refers to the EU only in terms of common *economic* interests (Likud 1999).

Conversely, during the grand coalition under Prime Minister Ariel Sharon starting in early 2001, the then–foreign minister Peres expressed "gratitude and appreciation" for the visit of an EU delegation to Israel in March 2001 (Peres et al. 2001). The visit occurred in the context of the efforts of the U.S.-led Mitchell Commission to revive the peace process. Yet while Peres considered the visit "another important page in the book of European-Mediterranean relations" (Peres et al. 2001), Sharon was far less enthusiastic about the EU's backstage-role within the Mitchell Commission, according to the Israeli media.

In the first place, thus, the quality of EU–Israeli political relations and the degree of cordiality between the two sides depended on Israel's relations with the Palestinians and the status of the peace process. Labour-led governments and the EU usually pursued similar interests in the Middle East, which may explain their affinity. Moreover, the variation in EU–Israeli relations has to do with different positions toward multilateralism maintained by different Israeli governments. While the EU is undoubtedly an advocate of multilateralism in international politics (Kagan 2003), Israel's foreign relations were traditionally bilateral. But while pursuing the aim of building a New Middle East, to use the words of Peres, or to open up to the world, to paraphrase Rabin, Labour governments were somewhat more open to experience with multilateralism than their *Likud* counterparts. Personal and political affinities may have been an additional factor. Indeed, Barak and his European colleagues of the so-called New Left, namely Britain's Tony Blair and Germany's Gerhard Schröder, shared a similar ideological platform. Similarly, one Israeli official stressed that Ben-Ami and Peres—the latter being described as "European in his blood"—knew how to play the European game, and thus succeeded in gaining access to the close elitist club of EU decision-makers.

More important, however, is that the EMP aimed at reshaping EU–Israeli relations. Indeed, presupposing an increased political leverage of the EU in the region implies that Israel will accept the EU's support and advice as much as its criticism. In addition, as discussed above, the EU's Euro-Mediterranean narrative abandons the "Essen logic," as Israeli officials and academics repeatedly regretted. To be clear, the argument here is not about trade relations alone. In fact, EU–Israeli economic relations continued to be much more advanced than those between the EU and most other southern EMP participants. The problematic aspect of EU–Israeli relations clearly concerns politics and perceptions (Dachs and Peters 2004). The EU's Euro-Mediterranean narrative, in which Israel is no longer a "special" case, clearly implied a step toward the "normalization" of EU–Israeli relations. This, however, touches upon the most sensitive themes of Israel's self-definition, namely recent history and the Holocaust (Zerubavel 1995). Indeed, references to this dark historical chapter are frequent in Israel's public discourse toward EU officials and European politicians, independent of party affiliations. Similarly, the prevailing perception in Israel is that the EU has a historic responsibility toward Israel (Medzini 1976–1995; Sachar 1999). Yet references to recent history may turn into harsh accusations in the context of political disagreements. An illustrating example is the reaction of former prime minister Netanyahu and his then–foreign minister Ariel Sharon to the EU's 1999 statement on Jerusalem as *corpus separatum* (Netanyahu and Sharon 1999):

> It is particularly regrettable that Europe, where one third of the Jewish people perished, has seen fit to try and impose a solution which endangers the state of Israel and runs counter to its interests.

Only a minority of Israel's political elites of the Center-Left—such as Peres, Ben-Ami, and Yossi Beilin—seemed willing to get acquainted with the idea of "normalizing" EU–Israeli relations. These "Europeanists" are certainly committed to the central role of recent history for Jewish collective memory, but apparently draw slightly different conclusions on how this is to affect present and future EU–Israeli relations. Yet due to the centrality of this issue for Israeli identity, along with its sensitivity, even a gradual reinterpretation of this theme is significant.

After the beginning of the EMP, Israel's altering government coalitions indeed gave different signals regarding the EU's role in the region. Thus, the EU was invited to play a (slightly) greater political role, increase its financial assistance to the peace process, but it was also repeatedly harshly rebuffed for its political opinions. However, in the long run, engaging in the EMP entailed a need to choose between competing concepts of state identity, as the "normalization" of EU–Israeli relations presupposes that Israel will become a "normal" country. This idea already faces important domestic opposition, as discussed above. Yet by touching upon a central and sensitive theme of Israel's self-definition, the EMP's attempts to "normalize" EU–Israeli relations, and thus, Israel's "self," were bound to face an even larger domestic opposition.

Israel, the EU, and the Compatibility of Values and Identities
A further dimension of EU–Israeli relations concerns the values that the EU sought to promote in the EMP framework and their compatibility with different identity concepts maintained within Israeli society. With regard to the higher affinity of Labour politicians with both the EU and the principles of the EMP mentioned above, one foreign ministry official mentioned that, particularly in the first years of his premiership, Ariel Sharon was like a "red flag" in Europe, no matter what he did or said. But, by using the same figure of speaking, European governments also perceived Itzhak Shamir and Binyamin Netanyahu as "red flags." Is it then really a matter of personalities, or is it rather a question of the set of values these politicians represent? In fact, most Israeli officials have referred in one context or another to the compatibility of values between Labour governments and the EU, in spite of Israel's traditional reservations toward the EU.

Notwithstanding the contradiction between the EMP's theory and practice, the EMP is based on a set of liberal values, which, as discussed above, are at the center of both the EU's self-definition and normative power. Thus, the aims of the EMP are compatible with liberal and adaptive interpretations of Israel's state identity, such as *Medinat Israel* or "a state of all its citizens." In addition, by favoring democracy and territorial compromise, both identity concepts permit for a regional order that complies with the EU's Euro-Mediterranean project. On the other hand, the EU's vision of the Mediterranean is rather incompatible with nationalistic or religiously oriented state identity concepts, and their regional policy-orientation. It is illuminating in this context that fervent supporters of the *Eretz Israel* concept repeatedly criticized the EU's practice of funding Israeli NGOs that promote peace, territorial compromise, and human rights. Thus, according to the *Jerusalem Post* (June 27, 2001: 3), Michael Kleiner of the ultra-nationalist *Herut* Party called this practice "disgusting," while former NRP chairman Shaul Yahalom commented on this issue: "The biased intervention of foreign nations in the democratic processes in Israel is unprecedented and shameful."

Hence, the EU and *Likud*-led Israeli governments may clash over the future of the occupied territories and Jewish settlements, but there is an underlying lack of mutual understanding, which is based on incompatible sets of values defended by both sides. The EU, which has written "post-national liberalism" and regional integration on its flag, does not share the underlying assumptions of the concept of *Eretz Israel*, nor its regional policy-implications, such as "living by the sword." In return, the value system embedded in the concept of *Eretz Israel* does not lend itself to comprehend the EU's self-image, and consequently, the type of its favored international and regional relations. In practical terms, the frequent alternation of Israeli government coalitions did not impede Israel's participation in the EMP with more or less enthusiasm. But given the different values and identities maintained by subsequent Israeli governments, the frequent change of governments did put a strain on the development of EU–Israeli relations according to the EMP's prescriptions as well as on Israel's development of a strategy toward Euro-Mediterranean regional security.

Israel's Quest for Unity and the Mediterranean Theme

In view of Israel's contested state identity and its significant political impact, could the Mediterranean theme be helpful in soothing Israel's internal divisions? In the time span under consideration, the Euro-Mediterranean theme did generally not feature within Israel's foreign-policy discourse. The few exceptions to this rule mainly occurred in the context of official EMP events, and they were mainly pronounced by Shimon Peres.

Before the start of the EMP, Israel did not seriously consider the option of being part of the Mediterranean. And even after the beginning of the Barcelona Process, discussions on the "Mediterranean option" remained confined to a relatively small group of Israeli academics and policy-makers. Yet since identities are multiple, an overarching Mediterranean identity is an interesting option for Israel, since it could serve as "a common cultural platform for the discussion of tensions on separate identities" (Ohana 1999: 86). Theoretically, the inclusive nature of a Mediterranean regional identity may soothe the friction between different interpretations of Israeli identity indeed, while reconciling Israel with its neighbors and geographic location. In the case of present-day Europe, Brigid Laffan (1996) has pointed out that there is no longer a contradiction in being, for instance, simultaneously German, Bavarian, *and* European, or alternatively Italian, Tuscan, *and* European. In analogy, and as pointed out elsewhere (Del Sarto 1999), in the case of Israel, an overarching Mediterranean identity could comprise Jewish, *Ashkenazi* (or oriental), and Israeli sub-identities, or a Muslim (or Christian), Arab, and Israeli identity. Similarly, a Mediterranean identity is compatible with both a religious and a secular-ethnic interpretation of Jewishness, while it does not contradict Islam, Christianity, or Arab culture.

In this vein, some Israeli scholars highlighted the importance of the Mediterranean in the Jewish past, stressing that even the early Zionists, who came from the Mediterranean Sea, primarily settled on the coast. David Ohana (1999) also argued that Israel's integration into the Middle East is not a viable option at present, since such a perspective raises suspicions both among Arab countries and Israel. These are linked to fears of economic domination on the one side, and fears of cultural assimilation into Arab culture on the other side. Nevertheless, the Mediterranean model would certainly entail a departure from the dream of Israel's founding generation, the "socialist world reformers, the fathers of the kibbutz," as the Israeli writer Amos Oz (1998) pointed out. For a large majority, however, the Mediterranean theme remained pure romanticism, a nice idea that lacks any concrete political implications (Shavit 1988; Benvenisti 1996). Some viewed the Mediterranean idea as a euphemistic version of "Middle Easternism"—which they refute. Others suggested that the Mediterranean idea was relevant in the past, when the Mediterranean Sea was central to trade routes, but it is no longer today, in the era of the Internet and e-commerce. Similarly, some insisted that the Mediterranean image of the lemon tree no longer applies to Israel, where high-tech development has become much more important than lemons. Hence, according to this view, the Mediterranean idea will hardly succeed in serving as integrating theme for Israel, let alone for the region. Thus, Israel's incapacity of developing a strategy vis-à-vis the Euro-Mediterranean was well reflected in the skepticism toward a Mediterranean identity among the majority of Israel's political and academic elites. Certainly, given Israel's identity conflicts, the Mediterranean theme could develop into an integrative force. But as long as Israel's political elites do not promote it, its relevance is limited indeed.

However, Israel's political establishment sought to address the problem of increasing internal divisions in mainly two ways. First, it decided to reform the electoral law in order to reduce the fragmentation of the Knesset and to reduce the excessive power of the smaller parties. But the electoral reform—first applied in the 1996 election and abolished prior to the January 2003 elections—achieved the opposite result. The introduction of the direct election of the prime minister, along with the proportional vote for a political party, permitted the splitting of the vote, and thus further encouraged the emergence of one-issue parties. One result was that the number of political parties that entered parliament augmented (Reuven and Hazan 2000). With it, the fragmentation of Israeli politics actually increased.

Second, particularly since the assassination of Itzhak Rabin, political leaders have advocated internal "unity" in order to heal the wounds. But the real dilemma is that there are no unifying identity themes that appeal to all the citizens of Israel. The lowest common denominator is certainly the theme of "Jewishness." But while harboring pronounced contradictions, as discussed above, it also leaves *by definition* Israel's Arab citizens out. In this context, Kimmerling (1993: 415) remarked that all of Israel's official holidays and memorial days refer to Jewish religion and history, while the only Israeli civic day of festivity—namely Independence Day—"is a bitter reminder of Palestinian Arabs of their political and social devastation." Similarly, former prime minister Netanyahu's calls for unity invoked the "Jewish heritage, which is the basis of our unity *as a people*, and from which we draw the principles of justice and equality for all of Israel's citizens, Jewish and non-Jewish alike" (Netanyahu 1996, italics added). In spite of the nice wording, the subtext clearly refers to the unity of the *Jewish people*. Netanyahu's statement thus rather resembles an attempt to square the circle. Hence, Israel's quest for unity potentially entails an emphasis on the particularistic and communal element of Israel's identity, and thus in principle contradicts an inclusive and liberal conception of the state. With it, there is not much room for the promotion of regional themes of any type.

Finally, since competing identity concepts call for different foreign-policy behavior, postponing any crucial decision may temporarily soothe the domestic divisions. It has also been argued that the closing of societal schisms generally occurs only amidst situations of external threat (Newman 1997). Thus, with the outbreak of the second *Intifada* and the collapse of the peace process, the sense of unity among Israel's Jewish population has certainly increased. But this went hand in hand with a growing sense of insecurity, international isolation, and an emphasis on *difference* with regard to other peoples and "nations." In this situation, there was definitely no room for developing any regional outlook. It seems, thus, that Israel is confronted with a serious dilemma. Postponing foreign-policy decisions that concern the region increases societal cohesion (at least among the Jewish majority). Conversely, moving toward a different regional order in fact exacerbates internal divisions. Yet, due to the relations of forces in the Knesset and the multidimensional nature of Israel's domestic identity conflicts, the domestic divisions also impede the consistent evolution toward any alternative regional policy.

While reinforcing Israel's traditional identity themes and accentuating the resulting boundaries between "us" and "them," the terror attacks of 9/11 and their aftermath pushed the Euro-Mediterranean option further away, as the next section briefly discusses.

9/11, Israel, and the Mediterranean

Long before 9/11, Israel was directly affected by terrorist attacks. Indeed, Palestinian suicide bombings against Israeli civilians not only accompanied the second *Intifada*, but actually the whole period of the peace process. As much as the wave of terror attacks prior to the 1996 elections has been held responsible for the victory of Netanyahu over Peres (Sprinzak 1997), the unprecedented rise in the number of suicide bombings inside the Green Line after the start of the second *Intifada* may well explain the election of Ariel Sharon in 2001. For most Israelis, suicide bombers killed the peace process in the final analysis. Considering Israel's defining themes, it is not surprising that Israel tended to perceive the suicide bombings as existential threats, notwithstanding its military superiority. Israel's core identity themes and the "realist" foreign policy they nurtured also explain why Israel viewed its repressive policy against the Palestinians as legitimate self-defence against the terror of the *Intifada*, irrespective of what the international community may think.

For Israel, the events of 9/11 confirmed this assessment. Accordingly, the "war against terrorism" started to dominate Israel's official discourse, while the conflict with the Palestinians was exclusively interpreted in these terms. In this vein, one Israeli journalist (Rosenblum 2002: 5)ironically noted that since 9/11

> every form of combat and military operation has been upgraded to a "war against terrorism". . . . It is not surprising that the chief of staff and his cabinet ministers make sure to stick the word "terrorism" into every sentence three times . . . which just goes to show that when everything is terrorism, anything goes.

Certainly, this interpretation of events propagated by the Israeli government also followed political and strategic reasons. However, in 2001–2002, Ariel Sharon led a grand coalition the tough policy of which toward the Palestinians enjoyed a large public support, as different polls demonstrated (*Ha'aretz* July 7, 2002; Barzilai and Barzilai 2002). This shows that for a majority of Israelis, these identity-based perceptions of reality were "real." Thus, while 9/11 prompted Israel's unconditional positioning on the side of the "free world" versus "terrorism," it undoubtedly strengthened Israel's identification with the United States.

Yet this development also reinforced Israel's *difference* to its Euro-Mediterranean neighbors. For many Palestinians, the *Intifada* was a legitimate means to fight Israeli occupation and to struggle for national liberation, while a suicide bomber is termed *shahid*—a martyr for the cause. Similarly, other Arab neighbors did not follow Israel's interpretation of reality, and neither did the EU as "civilian power." Thus, considering the EU–Israeli identity dissonance, the EU's criticism of Israel's policy against the Palestinians was as self-evident as Israel's prevailing perception that, in times of terror, the EU's emphasis on human rights and international law is out of touch with reality. The EU's anger at Israel's military incursions into Palestinian territory, which also partly destroyed EU-financed infrastructure (such as the Gaza airport), did not change Israel's prevailing perception of the EU. At the same time, Israel's dismissal of European criticism as anti-Israeli or anti-Semitic positions reflected, and reinforced, Israel's history-rooted perceptions of "us" and "them." While EU–Israeli relations reached an all-time low, Euro-Mediterranean region-building seemed more unattainable than ever.

Conclusions

Between 1995 and 2002, the Euro-Mediterranean Partnership was not the focus of Israel's foreign-policy discourse and actions. The collapse of the peace process and the increased Euro-Mediterranean dissonance after September 11, 2001 overshadow any alternative explanation of the difficulties of Euro-Mediterranean region-building. Yet an identity-based analysis permits to link Israel's lack of strategy toward Euro-Mediterranean regional security to questions of identity and domestic constraints. This explanation is also relevant for the time span before the outbreak of the second *Intifada* and the terrorist attacks of 9/11.

The defining themes of Israel's state identity entail a strong tendency to *underline difference* to begin with. The Zionist rationale of the "Jewish state," the Holocaust, the idea of "Jewishness," and the principle of self-reliance correspond to the underlying principles of Jewish religion that promotes the concept of the "chosen people" and does not proselytize.[27] At the same time, the sense of existential threat and international isolation are perceived as a continuation of the Jewish historical experience, which fuels Jewish-national sentiments further. Israel is still in a nationalist phase, in which "state" and "nation" are intrinsically linked, and the "nation" is defined through an ambiguous mixture of ethnicity and religion. Although all states and "nations" are characterized by an in-group/out-group bias, Israel's identity themes are a somewhat negative precondition for region-building ventures in general. Yet engaging in regional security on a Euro-Mediterranean basis had a number of crucial implications for Israel's identity. Indeed, it entailed a redefinition of Israel's "significant other," a reconsideration of its "place in the region," a different definition of the concept of security, along with the reshaping of its relations to the EU. This necessitated a departure from Israel's prevailing perception of having "no choice" in its regional relations, the principle of "trust no one," and the sense of regional and international isolation. Thus, for Israel, the EMP's prescriptions for Euro-Mediterranean regional security demanded a fundamental change of how it defines itself.

While Israel's state identity was born with inherent ambiguities and contradictions, a number of developments were responsible for the emergence of mutually exclusive identity concepts. Most notably, territorial questions in the context of peace-making triggered a competition among political actors to impose their vision of state identity. However, the different domestic preferences remain highly incompatible. As the beginning of the Oslo peace process clearly showed, moving toward a different (and peaceful) regional order implies a *need to choose* between competing and mutually exclusive concepts of Israel's state identity. Indeed, the beginning of the peace process went hand in hand with the attempt of the Rabin government to alter Israel's self-perception, and, thus, its behavior. Yet large domestic groups resist any attempts to change Israel's identity. In view of Israel's multi-dimensional identity polarization and fragile parliamentary balance, policy choices that involve one or several aspects of Israel's contested identity have produced policy oscillation or, alternatively, stalemate. With it, Israel's identity discourse remained contradictory and dissonant.

The option of a Euro-Mediterranean security region, however, went even further than Peres's vision of a New Middle East, as it also touched upon Israel's relations with the Europeans. At the same time, the Euro-Mediterranean option is based on a rather "exotic" geographic dimension, namely the Mediterranean. The different elements of the EMP's attempted identity manipulations—the implicit side effects of Euro-Mediterranean region-building—all touch upon Israel's central identity themes. Yet since the interpretation of these central themes is contested at the domestic level, they have remained unsettled in the first place.

Thus, in the case of Israel, several aspects of how its contested identity impedes the development of a consistent strategy toward Euro-Mediterranean regional security became visible. First, frequent changes of governments, which in themselves are an expression of Israel's domestic identity polarization, entailed discontinuity regarding the favored type of EU–Israeli relations, as well as regarding the question of how far the EMP shall go. Second, Israel's dissonant identity discourse showed that Israel had not sorted out the question of what and where it wants to be. In the framework of the EMP, the EU's attempts to decide these questions for Israel have failed, as Israel's dissonant and partly reluctant responses toward both the EMP and the EU have demonstrated. And finally, in view of the domestic identity-divisions, Israel's quest for unity promoted the strengthening of themes and values that basically contradict the emergence of regional identity themes on a Euro-Mediterranean basis.

Thus, the breakdown of the Middle East peace process certainly reduced the EMP's chances of success. And the events of 9/11 reinforced Israel's identity-based perception of difference with regard to most of its Euro-Mediterranean neighbors, Arab and European alike, while they generated a further drifting apart of identity-based perceptions of reality across the Euro-Mediterranean. However, independent of these developments, as long as the questions of what and where the state of Israel wants to be are not sorted out, Israel will be quite incapable of engaging consistently in the emergence of any alternative regional security order.

5

Egypt

In our investigation of whether contested state identities explain the lack of strategy toward Euro-Mediterranean region-building, this chapter analyzes the case of Egypt. Officially the Arab Republic of Egypt, *Al-Gumhuriyat Misr al-Arabiyya*,[1] Egypt is probably the best-researched Arab country in the literature. With around 70 million inhabitants (there are no precise figures), Egypt is also the most populous Arab country. For decades, Egypt stood at the center of Arab culture and politics, and it played a central role in the wider Arab–Israeli conflict, both in terms of war and peace. In view of these facts, along with the strengths of the Egyptian army, Egypt is a central player for any regional security scheme. Thus, the first part of this chapter concentrates on Egypt's state identity, its construction and reconstruction, along with the challengers. The main focus here is the time–span starting with the 1952 coup of the Free Officers and Nasser's rise to power in 1954. As Egypt was and is governed by an authoritarian regime, the institutional power to shape identity is discussed separately. The second part of the chapter shifts its attention to Egypt's participation in and strategy toward the EMP, along with the development of EU–Egyptian relations. In the last part we explore whether and how Egypt's state identity, along with the domestic fault-lines, can be linked to its policy toward Euro-Mediterranean regional security.

The Identity of Egypt

Since Egypt reached formal independence from British colonial rule in 1922, the definition of its identity has witnessed three major reassessments. The first rupture occurred with the 1952 coup d'état and the rise to power of Gamal 'Abd-el Nasser in 1954. Subsequent reassessments occurred with the change of leadership from Nasser to Anwar al-Sadat and from Sadat to Hosni Mubarak. The ability of Egypt's presidents to impose their vision of state identity is based on the president's extensive institutional powers, yet alternative domestic preferences have always existed and are relevant until the present, as the next sections argue.

Egypt's Defining Themes Between Revolution and Evolution

Ruptures: From Independence to Nasser and Sadat

Although Egypt always maintained a certain degree of political autonomy and the control over a well-defined territory, the country has a long history of colonial interference. It witnessed Ottoman rule from 1517 on, the invasion of Napoleon Bonaparte's army in 1798, British occupation from 1882 on, and the formal establishment of a British Protectorate at the beginning of World War I. Egypt's independence movement grew stronger during the war, and crystallized around the *Wafd* (the Delegation) under the leadership of Sa'ad Zaghlul.[2] When Britain recognized Egypt's independence in February 1922, it still retained control over the Suez Canal and Egypt's defense, while it continued to support an increasingly powerful Palace against the *Wafd*. Egypt's independence movement started to disintegrate along different ideological lines once independence was reached—Egypt not being unique in this respect. Due to dire economic conditions, political repression, fraudulent elections, and factionalism, the calls for ending parliamentarism and British interference grew stronger during the 1930s and 1940s (Vatikiotis 1978). The 1952 coup of the Free Officers was to satisfy these calls, as it indeed set an end to the monarchy while dissolving all political parties.

The period before the coup witnessed a struggle between very different patterns of defining Egypt's identity. The first concept was based on territoriality and revolved around the idea of "nation" (*watan*). Emphasizing the importance of the "Land of the Nile" for defining Egypt, it relied on pre-Islamic motives that traced Egypt's roots back to the times of the Pharaohs. Supported by liberal intellectuals, this concept also stressed Egypt's anchorage in the Mediterranean and its high affinity with the "West" (Hourani 1983; Gershoni 1977). The second interpretation focused on the importance of Arab ethnicity, culture, and language. Embedded in pan-Arabism, which had emerged in the Fertile Crescent toward the end of the nineteenth century, this concept propagated the idea of *qawm* (Arab nation). The third concept emphasized the belonging of the Egyptian people to the Islamic community of believers (*umma*). In contrast to the territorially defined concept of "nation," the concepts of *qawm* and *umma* in principle transcended territorial borders. Moreover, unlike the Western-inspired concept of "nation" that was anchored in modernity, the transnational preferences relied on traditional loyalties (Gershoni 1981: 29; Lewis 1998). From the 1930s on, against the backdrop of rising fascist ideologies and the persistence of British colonial allures, three development countered the attempts to construct a national-territorial identity: first, the resurgence of revivalist Islamic thought of *Salafi* inspiration,[3] second, the rise of pan-Arabism as political ideology, and third, the strengthening of anti-Western sentiments. Indeed, a number of political parties, along with the Palace, increasingly defended pan-Islamic and/or pan-Arab ideas.

The struggle over how to define Egypt's identity was to be decided after Nasser took power in 1954. Nasser succeeded in coining Egypt's identity according to the principles of Arab unity and solidarity, a socialist economic order based on agrarian reform and nationalization, anti-Imperialism, and anti-Zionism. Within Nasser's pan-Arabism, Islam served as a *cultural* reference point. With it, religion was nationalized, or "Arabized," to be more precise. While Egyptian history was reinterpreted within an Arab context, Egyptians started "regarding themselves as Arabs living in Egypt" (Dekmejian 1971: 51). But Nasser's pan-Arab ideology also served to legitimize Egypt's quest for regional hegemony within the Arab state system. This explains why Nasser's pan-Arabism stressed Egypt's distinctiveness as traditional center of Arab and Islamic culture, its unique *national* history, its geostrategic location and population size (Abd al-Nasser 1959: 75–66). Thus, pan-Arabism was combined with what has been termed Egyptocentrism (Dekmejian 1971: 80; Jankowski 1997).

Foreign policy became the main expression of Nasser's way of defining Egypt (Dawisha 1988b; Cooper 1982). In 1956, Nasser negotiated the gradual withdrawal of British forces from the Suez Canal Zone and thus asserted Egypt's independence. An increasing involvement in Arab, Islamic, and African affairs followed, which also included the interference in the domestic politics of other states. Against the background of decolonization, Nasser adopted a strong anti-imperialist stance against "the West," and he played a leading role in the nonaligned movement in the cold-war context. In 1956, Cairo turned to Czechoslovakia and, indirectly, the USSR for military supply after the Western powers had refused to grant support, and it campaigned most vociferously against the 1955 Baghdad Pact.[4] Continued low-scale military confrontations with Israel, and the nationalization of the Suez Canal in 1956—which prompted the war against Britain, France and Israel in the same year—additionally served to underline Egypt's anti-imperialist and anti-Zionist stance.[5]

Opposition against Israel and the identification with the Palestinian cause were crucial in the crystallization of Nasser's pan-Arab ideology. Nasser's continuous confrontation course toward Israel, the entering of defense alliances with a number of Arab states in the mid-1950s, along with the short experience of unification with Syria between 1958 and 1961 (under the name of "United Arab Republic of Egypt") cemented Nasser's pan-Arab ideology, which in the context of the fierce inter-Arab struggle of the 1950s and 1960s obviously also followed Egypt's quest for regional hegemony (Vatikiotis 1978: 229 ff.; Kerr 1971). Nasser's propagated antipathy toward the "West" went hand in hand with a rapprochement to the Soviet Union from the late 1950s on. His strong rhetoric appealing to Arab solidarity and pride made pan-Arabism a powerful ideology in the 1950s and 1960s. As Avraham Sela (1998: 19) notes, "[p]ersonifying Egypt's quest for regional hegemony, Nasir played the role of the rebuking prophet, a standard bearer whose choices and interpretations were beyond debate." With it, Nasser's Egypt became the ideological and political center of the "Arab world."

Nasser's leadership, along with his way of defining Egypt, enjoyed a broad domestic support. However, there was also opposition, mainly deriving from the Muslim Brotherhood (*Ikhwan al-Muslimun*) that had plotted against Nasser in the mid-1950s, and allegedly again in 1965 (Vatikiotis 1978: 182–185; Beattie 1994). Since the country was on the verge of economic bankruptcy in the mid-1960s, popular discontent grew. But it was the 1967 military defeat against Israel that shook Egypt to the roots as "the whole edifice of Nasserism came crashing down" (Ajami 1999: 234). In February 1968, demonstrations against the light court sentences passed against senior officers for their responsibility in the 1967 defeat turned extremely violent. Nasser's cautious turning toward the "West" for economic aid toward the end of his presidency may well have prompted a turn within his foreign-policy course, but this remains a speculation.

This course of action occurred under Anwar al-Sadat, who succeeded Nasser after his death in September 1970. By the end of Sadat's regime, most identity themes of Nasserist Egypt had been redefined. Symbolically, this was reflected in the change of Egypt's flag, the national anthem, and its official name—from "United Arab Republic of Egypt" to "Arab Republic of Egypt." In May 1971, Sadat propagated his "corrective revolution" (*thaurat at-tashih*), announced the sovereignty of the law (*siyadat al-qanun*), and promised political liberalization. With it, Sadat sought to anchor his regime, at least formally, in legal-constitutional provisions (Heikal 1983: 39–42; Cooper 1982). A major change was the reintroduction of the multiparty system, which led to the 1978 parliamentary elections. Yet Sadat defined the consensus, as the parties had to commit themselves to the principles of the 1952 and 1971 "revolutions," which included "national unity," and socialism. However, the adoption of the so-called *infitah* policy in the mid-1970s, entailing measures of economic liberalization and privatization, was a clear departure from Nasser's "Arab socialism" (Waterbury 1983). In addition, Sadat increasingly propagated the principle of "Egypt first" (*Misr al-awwal*) (Krämer 1986: 153–155). Thus, without renouncing his rhetoric commitment to pan-Arabism, Sadat somewhat recurred to the narrower definition of Egyptian patriotism that had characterized the era of liberal thought of the 1920s and 1930s. However, in contrast to the secular character of the liberal era, Sadat portrayed himself as "the Pious President," thus forging an increasingly religious interpretation of Egypt's identity (Kepel 1993: 247 ff.). The May 1981 constitutional amendment eventually declared the *shari'a* (Islamic law), which hitherto had been one of the principal sources of Egyptian law, as *the main source* of legislation. This development, however, eroded the principle of "national unity," which had been defined as the peaceful coexistence between Egypt's Muslim majority and the Coptic minority.[6] Indeed, increasing tensions between Copts and Muslims accompanied Sadat's regime and intensified toward the end of his tenure (Ansari 1984; Heikal 1983: 139–217).

Sadat's attempted manipulation of Egypt's identity was most visible in the foreign-policy realm. Despite displaying an initially anti-Western rhetoric, Sadat sought foreign aid from the conservative Gulf monarchies and the "West." At the same time, Egypt increasingly distanced itself from the Soviet Union, starting in 1972 with the dismissal of Soviet advisers and ending in 1976 with the annulment of the Friendship Treaty with Moscow (Dessouki 1991: 171–175). Yet particularly the principles of pan-Arabism and anti-Zionism witnessed a dramatic reassessment. Certainly, Sadat fought the 1973 October War under exactly these principles, and the myth of the 1973 Arab "victory" over Israel was portrayed as counter-balancing the 1967 defeat. Indeed, the success of the Egyptian army in "crossing the Canal" to the eastern bank, which corresponded to Cairo's strategic objective, considerably strengthened Sadat's domestic standing (Hudson 1977: 248 ff.; Sela 1998: 140–145).[7] The October War thus permitted an overlap of the national and pan-Arab dimensions of state identity. Sadat's rather surprising trip to Jerusalem in November 1977 was also justified in terms of Egyptian leadership of the "Arab world," this time in the realm of Middle East peace-making (Heikal 1983; Perthes 2002: 60–61). Sadat's new approach, however, gave priority to the recovering of lost *national* territory at the expense of the Palestinian cause. Thus, it broke away from Nasser's commitment to pan-Arab "unity of action."

As the strong domestic criticism of Egypt's separate peace agreement with Israel showed, Sadat's attempt to manipulate Egypt's identity was probably too abrupt. Egypt was increasingly isolated in the "Arab world," and its portrayed pan-Arab identity was left without a basis (Ajami 1999). At the same time, Sadat's attempts to reshape relations to Israel, the country's traditional "enemy," proved a complete failure. Particularly after Israel annexed East Jerusalem in 1980, the perception in Egypt grew stronger that Israel, on its part, did not intend to honor the provisions of the Camp David agreements relating to the Palestinians. Opponents of the peace treaty insisted that Israel had paid a minimal price for peace, while "Sadat made Egypt the center of nowhere" (Heikal 1983: 275). As in the short term, the expected economic benefits of peace did not materialize either, Sadat's regime started to lose legitimacy. The September 1981 mass arrests against critics of the Camp David accords—Islamists, Nasserists, and liberals alike—did certainly not increase Sadat's popularity (Heikal 1983: 227–241). Sadat's assassination in October 1981 by a religious fundamentalist "and the sheer nonchalance with which the ordinary Egyptian reacted to his death" (Dawisha 1988b: 269) most dramatically showed the unpopularity of Sadat's new foreign-policy course, along with his attempted redefinition of Egypt's identity.

Synthesis and Ambiguity: Egypt under Mubarak

Under Hosni Mubarak's regime, Egypt's identity once more witnessed a reassessment, which, however, has been gradual. This corresponds to Mubarak's political style. Mubarak certainly lacks the personal charisma of his predecessors, he is not an ideologist, and unlike Nasser and Sadat, he is not inclined toward dramatic foreign-policy actions. Instead, Mubarak has been characterized as a "balancer" (Springborn 1989: 19), displaying a style that is "nonsensationalist and non-confrontational" (Dessouki 1991: 157). Moreover, Egypt's difficult political legacy, namely its aspirations for *grandeur* and leadership and the disillusionments of reality, exerts pressures on the regime, since "[t]o rule Egypt is to rule against the background of these expectations and disappointments" (Ajami 1999: 234).

Rhetorically, Mubarak is committed to both the legacy of Nasser and Sadat—in spite of their incompatibility. In practice, the regime maintains an ambiguous course in between both orientations. After coming to power, Mubarak released political prisoners incarcerated under Sadat and co-opted both Nasserists and supporters of Sadat into important positions. He repressed radical Islamists without mercy during the 1990s, but also increasingly adopted an Islamic discourse. And, while promoting economic liberalization, the state maintained an extensive control over the economy. Thus, Mubarak's political choices are "pitting secularism against theocracy, authoritarian control against liberalization, and those who venerate the memories of Sadat, Nasser, Saad Zaghlul, and Hassan al-Banna against one another" (Springborn 1989: 19).

Mubarak's foreign policy is similarly ambiguous. Giving approximately U.S.-\$ 2.2 billion in military assistance and another U.S.-\$600 million in economic aid a year, the United States has remained Egypt's most important supplier. Yet the regime treats U.S.–Egyptian relations with discretion and consents to regular attacks on U.S. policy in the government-controlled press, such as *Al-Ahram*. At the same time, Egypt revived its role in the nonaligned movement and in African affairs (Dessouki 1991: 166–168). And while Cairo repeatedly confirmed its commitment to the peace treaty with Israel, it has not engaged in "normalizing" relations to Israel either. But even amidst domestic calls for canceling the Camp David agreements during the second *Intifada*, Mubarak has not refrained from meeting Israeli officials for discussions (*Ha'aretz* August 6, 2002). During the 1990s, Mubarak also succeeded in bringing Egypt back to the "Arab world" and to increasingly reaffirm Egypt's leadership ambitions. Indeed, the 1991 Gulf War and the beginning of the Middle East peace process provided the playing fields for Mubarak's new role as mediator and consultant to the different parties (Sela 1998: 324–334; Perthes 2002: 74–78).

However, in the absence of a resolution of the Palestine problem, opposition to Israel remains a central motive in Egypt's official discourse. In this vein, Cairo ridiculed the late King Hussein of Jordan for his commitment to "warm peace" with Israel, and vociferously campaigned against Israeli nuclear weapons in the context of the planned extension of the NPT in the early 1990s (Ajami 1999: 253–255). Similarly, in the multilateral ACRS talks of the Madrid peace process,

Egypt sought to set the "Arab agenda" by focusing on WMD, thus building on the opposition to Israel (Landau 2003). Mubarak also "allowed" his former foreign minister, Amr Moussa, to employ a rather strong anti-Israeli rhetoric, to the point that during the second *Intifada* a song with the title "I hate Israel, I love Amr Moussa" became a hit in Egypt. References to "the Arab position" and to "Arab solidarity" are frequent in Egypt's official discourse, along with the rhetorical commitment to the Palestinian cause.

Traditionally, the regime party NDP (National Democratic Party, *al-hizb al-watani al-dumuqrati*) best reflected the ambiguities of Mubarak's regime. The party, which had not altered its party platform in two decades, used to promote both the continuation of the *infitah* policy and a tight state control over the economy. The party stressed the importance of "national values," but also supported *shari'a* law from 1986 on. It advocated a nonaligned foreign policy, but also close relations to the United States. And while stressing Arab solidarity, the platform expressed support for Egypt's peace policy (Krämer 1986: 60–61; Gamblin 1997). Although the party presented itself as the true heir of Nasserism, it maintained a notably different interpretation of the latter from its inventor. Due to relatively scarce results in the 2000 elections, the party reformed its platform and adopted a modern-reformist outlook (while Mubarak's son Gamal became the party's policy secretary). The new platform stresses Egypt's *national* identity, but still affirms Egypt's affiliation with both the Islamic and Arab "nations" (NDP 2003). The role of pan-Arabism for Egypt's self-definition deserves a brief separate consideration, the subject of the next section.

Pan-Arabism, Egyptocentrism, and the Quest for
Regional Hegemony
Pan-Arab nationalism played an important role in the formation of Arab states, yet its relationship to the state remained ambiguous. In practice, Arab leaders used the commitment to Arab solidarity to strengthen both the state and their legitimacy as national and regional leaders. Yet on several occasions, the ideological commitment proved to be a burden imposing action against an otherwise nationally defined foreign-policy interest (Ajami 1992; Luciani 1990; Dawisha and Zartman 1988). Similarly, it is widely acknowledged that inter-Arab regional politics recurrently contradicted pan-Arab ideology (Kerr 1971; Luciani and Salamé 1987). Yet pan-Arab loyalties became central in the self-definition of Arab states. Given Nasser's crucial role in coining pan-Arabism, this is particularly relevant for Egypt,

which entered Arab regional politics relatively late (Gershoni 1981; Kienle 1995).

In fact, Egypt's leaders have repeatedly altered the interpretation of pan-Arabism. Under Nasser, it implied a compulsory "unity of purpose" and, later on, a "unity of action"—even at the expense of purely Egyptian concerns (Sela 1998: 57–59). Sadat, on the other hand, downgraded pan-Arabism as he gave priority to Egypt's state-based identity (and therefore *national* interests), at the expense of pan-Arab unity. And Mubarak somewhat combined the idea of pan-Arab solidarity and the rhetorical commitment to the Palestinian cause with the priority given to Egypt's nationally defined identity and interests. But in all cases, Egypt's perceived centrality as political and cultural leader of "the Arab world," which was linked to the country's distinctive *national* identity, serves as an identity frame. Non-Egyptian Arabs may well refer to Egypt as *um al-dunya* (mother of the world) with an ironical undertone, and Egypt's rivals in the quest for regional hegemony may reject Egypt's self-perception. However, many regional and global actors implicitly or explicitly recognize Egypt's centrality in Arab regional politics, and with it, the existence of an "Arab world" with Egypt as its center of gravity.

Institutional Factors and the Power to Shape Identity
In view of Egypt's experience with centralized power over various millennia, the regime could build on a "historical pattern of autocracy and bureaucratic control" (Hudson 1977: 243). Since the 1952 coup, the country is an authoritarian state; executive and legislative powers, along with the command over the army and multiple security services (*mukhabarat*), are concentrated in the hands of the president. In spite of various reforms and the different style of Egypt's presidents, the country continues to be an example of what the 2005 Arab Human Development Report has termed a "black hole" state, "which converts its surrounding social environment into a setting in which nothing moves and from which nothing escapes" (UNDP 2005: 15).

While Nasser possessed personal charisma and the ability of delivering stirring speeches, he also had the powers to suppress any alternative preference. Under Nasser, there was no political opposition whatsoever, and the regime's unitary political party Arab Socialist Union (ASU) was meant to prevent political pluralism (Waterbury 1983: 310–322). While relying on the army and the military-bureaucratic elites (Ayubi 1980a), Nasser co-opted potential political adversaries, who, however, were also "periodically fought by the coercion of a repressive security and intelligence service" (Vatikiotis 1978: 175). As Nasser had relied on adventurous foreign-policy actions to legitimize rule and deviate attention form internal problems, the degree of coercion considerably increased after the 1967 defeat.

Sadat initially sought to play opposition forces against each other. Thus, following the 1972 and 1973 student demonstrations led by Nasserists and Marxists, Sadat repressed the left-wing opposition while assenting to a growing role of the Muslim Brotherhood (Kepel 1993: 139–145). The transformation from one-party rule to a multiparty system after the 1973 war led to the emergence of organized opposition, yet Sadat retained far more powers than parliament. The president also relied on popular referenda with suspiciously high approval rates. In this vein, a referendum in April 1979 even approved Sadat's peace policy with 99.9 percent of the votes. In addition, Sadat sought to lend religious legitimacy to his rule, which was regularly attested by the government-appointed Sheikh of the *Al-Azhar* University. At the same time, the emerging *infitah* bourgeoisie became linked to the state through a complex patronage system (Heikal 1983: 183). Following the January 1977 "bread riots" that were sparked by IMF-prescribed reforms, and in view of the growing opposition to Sadat's peace initiative, the regime forced political parties to "voluntarily" suspend their activities. In October 1978, Sadat founded the regime party NDP, which has won parliamentary majorities ever since. After violent clashes between Muslims and Copts in June 1981, Sadat declared a state of emergency. Mass arrests of intellectuals and political activists followed (Krämer 1986; Heikal 1983: 227–241). With it, the experiment of political pluralism was terminated.

Mubarak's Egypt has been described as "controlled pluralism" (Zartman 1988: 73). Indeed, there are many opposition newspapers, but they are regularly harassed (Kienle 2001: 98–107). Egypt has around 16,000 registered NGOs, yet the 2002 law governing associations notably restricts their space of maneuver (UNDP 2003: 68–74). Similarly, more than 10 political parties have been licensed under Mubarak, yet most of them only after lengthy judiciary battles. The state-controlled committee that decides on the admission of political parties clearly prefers negative answers, indeed.[8] Moreover, 10 out of 18 licensed parties are currently frozen (UNDP 2005: 131). Egypt's electoral system has also witnessed fairer procedures, but this was mainly the result of Supreme Court rulings. Thus, prior to the elections in October–November 2000, the court ruled that judges should supervise the ballot stations. The court also ruled that the party lists had to be replaced with a two-round majority voting of individual candidates. This put an end to the provision that party lists that did not pass the 8-percent threshhold had to transfer their votes to the largest party, usually the NDP.

Parliamentary elections have continued to be manipulated. Relying on the emergency laws that are still in force, the regime can considerably restrict the activities of opposition parties, and the voters' registry is believed to be rigged (Kienle 2001: 27). Thus, although the 2000 elections were among the less fraudulent in decades, the NDP accounted for 87 percent of MPs, of which more than half ran as independent candidates that joined the NDP after the elections. And in the parliamentary elections of November–December 2005, the NDP once more became the largest faction, obtaining 311 out of 454 seats. Since parliament used to propose with a two-third-majority the presidential candidate(s)—voted through a popular referendum every six years—Mubarak was repeatedly the only candidate. Following a constitutional amendment in mid-2005, for the first time several candidates ran in the presidential elections of September 2005, which, however, Mubarak won with 88.6 percent of the votes. In addition, Mubarak ran still dissolve parliament and pass decrees without its approval. The president also appoints the government and its ministers, the NDP executive committees, high military and civilian officials, 10 members of parliament and one third of the indirectly elected second chamber. While strengthening the role of the military (Staloff 1988), Mubarak also established special (and military) courts with an extremely restricted possibility of appeal.

During the 1990s, Mubarak's regime has become even more repressive. While the regime regularly harasses opposition activists, members of the Muslim Brotherhood tend to be arrested prior to elections (Perthes 2002: 147; Kienle 2001: 137–139; *The Economist* December 8, 2005). One of the most prominent examples of Mubarak's dealing with unwanted criticism was probably the arrest of the known sociology professor Saad Eddin Ibrahim and his trial at a high security Court in 2000 (Weaver 2001).[9] The detention in 1998 of Hafez Abu Seda, the secretary-general of the Egyptian Organization for Human Rights, was another prominent case (Stacher 2001). The latest one was the temporary jailing of Ayman Nour, opposition leader and co-founder of the new *Al-Ghad* (Tomorrow) Party, in January 2005 and his subsequent conviction to five years in prison in December 2005—after he had "dared" to run as a presidential candidate in September.[10] These cases caused international uproar, but it is no secret that Mubarak's regime extensively relied on emergency measures in its campaign to crush militant Islamists in the 1990s. Arrests and detentions without charges or legal protection, torture, and death penalties, became the rule. It is estimated that between 15,000 and 16,000 Islamists—not all of them militant—are detained in Egyptian prisons, many of them without ever having been charged or tried (Gerges 2000; Singerman 2002). The crackdown on Islamists has obviously intensified ever since 9/11 and in particular after the various terrorist attacks in the Sinai Peninsula and in Cairo in 2004 and 2005. Mubarak's announcement of greater political liberties in early 2005, following the emergence of the popular protest movement *"Kifaya!"* (Enough!) that opposed a fifth term of Mubarak, has remained insignificant, as the results of the parliamentary and presidential elections, along with the imprisonment of Nour, clearly demonstrate.

Alternatives and Challengers

Robert Springborn (1989) has argued that Egypt's fragmented political order is a result of the regime's deliberate strategy of staying in power. But Egypt's opposition parties are also internally weak. There is a general lack of internal democracy, personal rivalries and infighting, and a greater focus on personalities than content (Stacher 2001). In addition, the traditionally geriatric leadership of Egypt's political parties reduces their appeal to the country's large young generations. Thus, most legal opposition parties have a restricted popular basis, maybe with the exception of the left-wing *Tagammu'*.[11] However, this party held meager 6 parliamentary seats, out of 454 after the 2000 elections, and gained only 2 seats in the 2005 elections. Conversely, the Muslim Brotherhood, which had 17 "independent" members in parliament between 2000 and 2005, and considerably increased its strength to 88 "independent" members of parliament after the 2005 elections, does not lack popular support, but is officially still illegal. Altogether, Egypt's broad population is rather politically apathetic, partly fearful, and distrusts politics. Polls indicate that between 65 and 70 percent of Egyptians do not care about politics (Fergany 1995; Stacher 2001). And while the identification with a political party is very low, many voters are not registered in the voters' registry and do not know how to register. Other organizations that could articulate political alternatives, such as the professional syndicates, face similar restrictions (Kienle 2001: 84–87). However, as in other Arab states, there are different domestic preferences regarding the political and societal set-up in Egypt (UNDP 2005), as the following sections highlight.

Background

Many of the domestic preferences in present-day Egypt have their roots in the prerevolution period, and after Sadat reintroduced the multiparty system, major political forces of the prerevolution era reemerged. Thus, the New *Wafd* sought to revive the *Wafd*'s liberal tradition, and the Socialist Labor Party (SLP) followed the nationalist ideology of the *Misr al-fattah*. The Muslim Brotherhood, founded in 1928 by Hassan Al-Banna', started to operate rather freely as social organization. The *Tagammu'*, which defended socialist and Marxist ideas, along with Nasser's pan-Arabism, also emerged in this period. In fact, Sadat's liberal experiment brought an impressive diversity to the fore, as more than 40 groups applied for recognition (Cooper 1982: 182–203). Yet most applications were denied, and even the newly recognized parties were soon to suspend their activities, as noted above. Conversely, the Muslim Brotherhood deepened its anchorage in society, and after it publicly renounced the use of violence, its members succeeded in entering parliament on the list of other parties. Departing from the original (Islamic-inspired) socialist orientation, and increasingly adopting an anti-Israel and anti-"Western" rhetoric, the Brotherhood became Egypt's most important opposition force.

On the other hand, militant Islamist groups, such as the *Gama'at Islamiyya* and the *Gihad*, among which was Sadat's murderer, were increasingly fighting the state from the late 1980s on. Denouncing the state as un-Islamic, these militants engaged in terror attacks against tourists, assassinations of politicians, police officers, and intellectuals. In this vein, Farrag Foda, a fervent supporter of the separation between state and religion, was assassinated in 1992 by Islamist fundamentalists, and an unsuccessful attack on the life of Nobel Prize winner Naguib Mahfuz followed in 1994. While facing the state's harsh response, the fundamentalists somewhat lost popular support after the 1997 terrorist attack in Luxor, in which 58 tourists were killed (Gerges 2000; Perthes 2002: 146). In 1999 and 2000, incarcerated leaders of Islamist terrorism declared an end to the armed struggle, and *Gihad* members sought to obtain recognition for their *Shari'a* party, which, not surprisingly, was refuted (Lübben and Fawzi 2000).

Liberal and secular intellectuals were caught in the battle between militant Islamists and a coercive regime. It is also illustrative that under Mubarak the *Tagammu'* has "been more harshly and consistently repressed than any other party" (Springborn 1989: 174). And while Egypt is witnessing a growing presence of Islam, liberal thought was constantly on the retreat (Ajami 1999)—at least until the founding of the liberal-oriented *Al-Ghad* party in November 2004. As for pan-Arab ideologies, it is true that they have been contradicted by political realities. But the support for an Arab common position is still very much alive in Egypt.

The Islamization of Society and Politics
As in other Arab and Muslim states, the most important domestic development in Egypt has been the rise of Islamist preferences since the mid-1970s (Krämer 1986; Ayubi 1980b). In this context, pan-Arabism's "nationalization of religion" explains the relative ease with which the dominant discourse could shift from nationalism to Islamism (Sela 1998: 32–33).

Today, Islamists dominate Egypt's student organizations, which were controlled by Nasserists during the 1960s and early 1970s. They have increased their influence in Egypt's professional associations, including the lawyers' syndicate, which used to be close to the *Wafd* (Fahmy 1998). Islamist sectors have also emerged within the *infitah* bourgeoisie, visible for instance in the increasing number of Islamic investment companies. In a similar vein, many formerly secularist intellectuals are by now propagating political Islam (Flores 1988: 28–30). And most legal political parties have adopted some of the Islamists' demands over the years. These include the originally secularist *Tagammu'*, which has been stressing Islam's compatibility with socialism since the mid-1980s (Ramsès 1997). The regime party, NDP, started to support the spreading of Islamic values after its 1986 congress (Springborn 1989: 159) and favors *shari'a* law until the present (NDP 2003). As for the *Wafd*, the party linked up with the Muslim Brotherhood prior to the 1984 elections. Although the alliance was dissolved in 1986, the *Wafd* has remained internally fragmented on the question of religion. At its place, the formerly secularist SLP, which changed its name to Labor Party, became the *Ikhwan*'s main electoralally (Makram-Ebeid 2001). And the Brotherhood's 88 "independent" candidates who were voted into parliament in the 2005 elections represent the largest parliamentary opposition block at the present.

The growing power of religion has undoubtedly been exerting pressures on the regime's space of maneuver. The 1994 conference of the UN Population and Development Fund, which took place in Cairo, was an interesting case in point. The provisions on women's rights on education, reproduction, and equality in the preliminary document of the conference caused fervent protests from religious conservatives, including the Mufti of Egypt, *Al-Azhar* scholars, and the *Ikhwan* (Daoued 1994).[12] Claiming that these "Western" provisions violated the principles of Islam, they protested against Egypt's participation at the conference altogether. Absurdly, the host of the conference Mubarak eventually maintained that the final conference document was not binding.

The courts have become the battlefield of the Islamists' struggle to impose their vision on state and society. Thus, in 1995, appeal courts confirmed the conviction of Nasr Hamid Abu Zayd of apostasy and declared him as divorced from his wife according to the principle of *hisba* (Sfeir 1998).[13] Abu Zayd, then a professor at Cairo University, had angered his opponents by calling upon his students to apply their own rational interpretation of the Qur'an without relying on the interpretation of the early Islamic scholars. The principle of *hisba* was also employed in the charges against the prominent Egyptian doctor and feminist Nawal Al-Sadawi in 2001. Accused of abandoning her faith in Islam, the court ruled that she would have to divorce her husband, to whom, at that point, she had been married for 37 years (Darwish 2001).

Seeking to fight the Islamists on their own terrain, Mubarak has increasingly presented himself as the "defender of Islam." With the backing of the state, the *Al-Azhar* University turned into a religious censorship authority (Zeghal 1996). Indeed, the number of banned publications grew steadily over the years, and includes the books of the assassinated Farrag Foda, *A Banquet for Seaweed* of the Syrian author Haidar Haidar, Khalil Gibran's *The Prophet*, and the classic *Thousand and One Nights*, to name a few. Similarly, the state tolerates the recurrent harassment of liberal intellectuals by the Islamists (Najjar 2001). The appeasing strategy of a once secular regime also included the 2001 arrest of 52 Egyptian homosexuals and their trial in a high security court on charges of "practicing sexual immorality." In general, the Islamization process entails a greater emphasis on morality, which is often expressed as contrasting the "West" and the perceived sexual permissibility and "decadence" of the latter (Ferrié 2000).

As in other authoritarian Arab states, political and economic factors are certainly co-responsible for the growing appeal of the Islamists as the only "real" and uncorrupted opposition. Yet in the case of Egypt, the glorification of tradition (Al-Jabri 1999a) is also a result of the ruptures in Egypt's recent history, along with the deep malaise it caused (Ajami 1999). The next sections elaborate on the domestic identity fault-lines in present-day Egypt.

The Identity Fault-Lines

The alternative preferences regarding Egypt's identity mainly revolve around three issues. The first dimension invokes the definition of Egypt's identity in national, pan-Arab, or pan-Islamic terms. The second fault-line concerns the preferred socioeconomic order, whereas the third concerns the question of state and religion. In the following typology, the positions of organized opposition groups serve as indicators, since, due to Egypt's authoritarian system, a precise assessment of the relevance of different preferences is hardly possible.

Umma, Qawm, and "Egypt First"

This dimension goes back to the prerevolutionary fault-line, which separated a nationally and territorially defined identity concept from transnational ones. The latter include the idea of appertaining to the pan-Arab *qawm* and the Islamic *umma*. However, distinctions became blurred under Nasser, as Egypt's *national distinctiveness* became firmly embedded in pan-Arabism, while it became common to use the term *umma* to designate the "greater Arab nation" (Lewis 1998: 82–83). This indicates that pan-Arab and pan-Islamic concepts of Egypt's identity may easily overlap. However, there are different priorities. Thus, the first reading prioritizes Egypt's anchorage in the Islamic *umma*, treats Islam as a religious reference point, and defines Egypt's identity as predominantly Islamic. The second version puts Egypt's anchorage in the Arab nation, *qawm*, at the centre, and treats Islam as a *cultural* reference point. A third interpretation affirms Egypt's Arab and Islamic identity, yet it puts a greater emphasis on Egypt's *national* distinctiveness. Within this "Egypt first" orientation, a territorially defined Egypt stands at the center, followed only in second place by pan-Arab and/or pan-Islamic loyalties. The distinct identity preferences have different implications for foreign policy.

Thus, the concept of *qawm*, which is most notably promoted by the *Tagammu'* and the Nasserist Party, entails a clear preference for nonalignment, anti-imperialism and anti-Zionism (Makram-Ebeid 2001; Moheiddin 1995; El-Said 2000). Particularly the Nasserist Party strongly supports Nasser's dream of "Arab unity." Thus, in its 2000 platform, the party promoted enhanced relations with Libya and the Sudan while asserting "Egypt's leading role in the Arab-African-Islamic sphere" (quoted in Al-Nahhas 2000). While opposing U.S. hegemony in the Middle East, this stream also tends to interpret the Arab-Israeli conflict as a "conflict of the Arab people on the one hand,

Zionism and American imperialism on the other hand" (*Al-Ahram Weekly* November 9, 1995).

Conversely, the priority given to Egypt's anchorage in the religious *umma*—which characterizes most Islamist groups and intellectuals—implies an Islamic orientation of Egypt's foreign relations. For Islamist militants, such as the *Gihad*, this may entail a divine command to fight unbelievers world-wide, which is most visible in their former engagement in fighting the Soviets in Afghanistan, and their connections to *Al-Qaeda*. For moderate Islamists, this concept may entail solidarity with the plight of Muslims in other countries, yet without recurring to armed resistance or terrorist activities. In this vein, the *Ikhwan* launched a campaign of solidarity with the Bosnian Muslims during the war in former Yugoslavia (El-Sayyid 1994). Yet there are also Islamist streams that explicitly recognize the Egyptian nation-state as a central reference point. Two (unrecognized) political parties that were founded in 2000, the *hizb al-wasat* (Center party) and the *hizb al-islah* (Reform party), serve as examples here (Lübben and Fawzi 2000).

Finally, the preference for "Egypt first" is somewhat more open toward Egypt's relations to the "West." Traditionally, the *Wafd* best represented this orientation. Thus, while promoting Egyptian nationalism and the idea of national unity, the *Wafd* usually refrained from adopting clear anti-U.S. or anti-Israel positions (Krämer 1986: 83–84; Hinnebusch 1984). Yet, as articulated in its 2000 platform (*Al-Ahram Weekly* September 28, 2000) the party has been adopting a stronger commitment to Arab unity over the last decade, and became more outspoken in its opposition to Israel. The newly established *Al-Ghad* party is another example of the "Egypt first" orientation, which is also reflected in a cautious call for "openness" toward the United States and the West (Roumani 2004). The (still suspended) Labor Party also tended to support the concept of "Egypt first," but it traditionally combined it with an Islamist vision (Krämer 1986: 68). This, however, did not impede the party from supporting nine Coptic candidates in the 2000 elections, as compared to the *Wafd*'s 12 Coptic nominees.

Socialism versus Economic Liberalism

The preferred economic order also forges a fault-line involving questions of Egypt's identity, particularly since in the Egyptian context, the classical Left–Right divide pits supporters of Nasserism against defenders of Sadat's *infitah* policy. Thus, both the *Wafd* and *Al-Ghad* support economic liberalism—yet supported by a social welfare system (Al-Nahhas 2004). Conversely, the *Tagammu'* and the

Nasserist Party, along with Marxist and other left-wing intellectuals, adhere to Socialism, central planning, and state intervention (Ramsès 1997). However, after the collapse of the Soviet Union, the *Tagammu'* started to support some measures of economic liberalism within its socialist orientation (Moheiddin 1995; El-Said 2000). This fault-line also runs through the Islamist stream. Indeed, by now many supporters of the Muslim Brotherhood are part of the *infitah* bourgeoisie. Thus, they prefer economic liberalism, provided that it respects social justice (Springborn 1989: 47–50). However, a number of Islamist intellectuals, such as the late 'Adel Hussain of the Labor Party and Khalil 'Abd-el Karim of the *Tagammu'*, advocate a socialist *and* Islamist set-up of the state, viewed as the only option for achieving social justice. Similarly, the Labor Party, which represents "an alliance between certain leftists and Islamists" (Kienle 2001: 30), supports an Islamic-inspired socialism.

In terms of foreign relations, the preference for economic liberalism and market economy generally tends to imply more openness toward "the West," the *Wafd* being the best example. Conversely, "leftist" economic preferences clearly give priority to Egypt's self-reliance and independence, while there is a higher sensitivity to perceived Western imperialism or neo-colonialism. The combination of these positions with Islamist preferences generally tends to strengthen anti-Western perceptions even further.

"An Islamic State," Its Interpretations, and Its Opponents
By now, the question of whether Islam is to play a role in Egyptian public life is far less contested than the questions of what Islam means, how much it is to influence politics, and who has the right to decide on these questions (Gresh and Ramadan 2002; Al-Ashmawy 1989). Indeed, there are very different interpretations of the *shari'a*, and with it, of the constitutional provision that defines it as Egypt's main source of legislation (Lombardi 1998). This relates to the questions of which school and parts of the Islamic jurisprudence are binding besides the Qur'anic scriptures and the Prophetic Sayings, and whether contemporary interpretations of the Qur'an are admissible. Moreover, there are quite different prescriptions of how to establish a state and society that respects "Islam."

Only a few intellectuals openly advocate the separation between state and religion. The attention drawn to the discrimination of Copts often accompanies the demand for confining religion to the private sphere. Similarly, many women organizations embed their struggle for gender equality in the same demand (Al-Ali 2000). This stream was recently boosted by the *Al-Ghad* party, which defends the separation of state and religion, along with the empowerment of women (Al-Nahhas 2004; Roumani 2004).[14] Yet this position, which stands on one side of the divide, is not to be confused with atheism. In fact, the argument that what the Prophet Mohammed did or said several centuries ago may be irrelevant for present-day society is unthinkable in Egypt, as in many other Arab and Muslim states.

The Islamists, on the other hand, are a very heterogeneous group. Radical Islamists want to revolutionize state and society by force, whereby the end justifies the means. Other radical groups changed strategy, and, as noted above, applied for recognition as political parties. They nevertheless retained a radical interpretation of the *shari'a*, along with a pronounced black-and-white thinking that distinguishes between good and evil, believers and unbelievers, Islam and "the West" (Lübben and Fawzi 2000: 240–247). Conversely, the Muslim Brotherhood's prescription for establishing an Islamic state focuses on the education of the *individual* (Sullivan and Abed-Kotob 1999). Yet, while rejecting the exegesis of the radical Islamists, the *Ikhwan* also opposes contemporary interpretations of Qur'anic scriptures, as do the even more conservative *Al-Azhar* scholars (Zeghal 1996). Interestingly, over the last decade the *Ikhwan* started to promote political reforms, along with women's rights according to Islam, democratic elections, and political pluralism (UNDP 2005: 6). Finally, some Islamists maintain a rather liberal interpretation of the religious texts, such as the Islamists of the *Tagammu'* and the so-called Sina group, along with the leaders of the not legalized *Wasat* party—who eventually founded a cultural organization. While being committed to religion, this position often supports full equality between Muslims and non-Muslims, as well as between men and women, a position that is also defended by Islamist feminists (Badran 2002).

Between the outspoken "secularists" and the various types of Islamists, there is a large middle field. Thus, many intellectuals condemn the Islamist discourse and the exploitation of religion for political aims, yet without being "secularists." In fact, their critique often takes Islam as reference point, which, considering the general mood, is in part also a necessity (Zakariya 1991: 20; Ghalioun, 2000). In this vein, the judge Mohammed Said Al-Ashmawy (1989) for instance deconstructs the Islamists' key concepts, such as the "Islamic government" or the concept of *jihad*, while arguing that the codification of Islamic law has always been man-made in a specific historical context. Thus, along with Abu Zayd and others, Al-Ashmawy supports contemporary interpretations of Islam, which he views as compatible with democracy. The middle field also includes the *Wafd*, which however opposed the right of women to divorce and supported the accusations of apostasy against Abu Zayd. This, however, does not impede the *Wafd* to condemn the radical Islamists and to define itself as a "liberal" party.

Political Implications

The discussion thus far has shown that there is a considerable degree of diversity regarding the preferred set of values that are to determine Egypt's state identity. But what are the political implications of this finding?

Certainly, the regime's power to manipulate Egypt's identity discourse and, above all, the rules of the political game limits the relevance of alternative domestic preferences. However, extensive powers do not guarantee the domestic acceptance of specific identity concept, Sadat's attempted identity manipulation being the best example. Indeed, this case supports the claim that any "successful" identity manipulation must be gradual (Norton 1988: 48)—whereas Sadat's peace policy shattered Egypt's identity as coined by Nasser. It is also relevant here that the domestic protest against the Camp David accords dramatically increased when it became clear that the "Arab world" did not follow Egypt's lead (Heikal 1983). Thus, if only material factors mattered, one could ask why most Egyptians rejected the peace agreements, given that Egypt recuperated Sinai and its oil fields, and was granted massive aid by the United States. Ali Hillal Dessouki (1991) has argued that economics determine Egypt's foreign policy, as the country has been dependent on foreign aid ever since independence.[15] This certainly explains why Egypt continues to rely on the United States and adheres to the peace agreement with Israel, in spite of unfavorable popular sentiments. Yet Mubarak's strategy of "muddling through" very different lines of domestic and foreign policy (Perthes 2002: 136) shows that the domestic identity fault-lines are relevant.

In fact, Mubarak's leadership ambition in Arab and Islamic affairs, which partly builds on confrontation toward Israel, and partly on the role of mediator in the Arab-Israeli conflict, bridges between the identity concepts of *qawm, umma*, and "Egypt first." Similarly, Cairo's increased role in the nonaligned movement and the general diversifi-cation of its foreign relations reconciles the concept of "Egypt first" with the preferences of Arab nationalists. And the mix between market economy and state intervention soothes the fault-line between supporters of the *infitah* policy of Sadat's legacy and the defenders of Nasser's

"Arab socialism." Moreover, this mix is also compatible with the Islamists' demand of "social justice," at least theoretically. Cairo's increasing involvement in Islamic affairs and the confrontation course vis-à-vis Israel are also in line with the Islamization of Egyptian politics and society, which restricts the regime's foreign-policy choices. In this vein, given Egypt's mass demonstrations against Israel after the outbreak of the second *Intifada*, Mubarak's regime did not cease to stress the solidarity with the Palestinians. Cairo withdrew its ambassador to Israel in 2001, but also increased its mediation efforts, for instance by hosting the Sharm Al-Sheikh conference in November 2000, which sought to reach an Israeli-Palestinian ceasefire.

It is significant that, in view of Palestinian suffering, anti-Israel positions unite all political and social groups in Egypt. Even Islamist and pan-Arabic preferences converge on the Palestine issue and the question of Jerusalem. Thus, in the large anti-Israel demonstration of September 2001, Islamists marched under the banner "Palestine is Islamic," and left-wing protesters with the slogan "Palestine is Arab," but they marched together. In the same demonstration, prominent Brotherhood members and the secretary-general of the *Tagammuʻ* Rifʻat Said—until then no friends of each other—hugged "to confirm unity among Egyptians when it comes to the Palestinian cause," as *Al-Ahram Weekly* (September 13, 2001) stressed.

Hence, although the regime has the power to engage in foreign-policy options that are unpopular, domestic developments and identity contestations exert pressures on the regime. Mubarak's ambiguous and partly contradictory foreign policy in fact succeeded in alleviating "the struggle for Egypt's soul" (Ajami 1979) by giving a new meaning to Egypt's Arab-Islamic identity and leadership role.

Egypt, the EU, and the EMP

In our investigation of whether Egypt's contested identity impacted on its engagement in the EMP, this section shifts from Egypt's domestic scene to the realm of foreign relations. It starts with a short historical background of European-Egyptian relations, followed by a discussion of the development of bilateral and regional relations after the launching of the EMP.

Background

The extent of Egypt's attachment to Europe greatly varied in the course of history. Before the Arab-Muslim conquest of Egypt in 614 C.E.,

Egypt's interaction with the European maritime powers was intense. It was to decline after the conquest, but reemerged with the French invasion in 1798 and the rise of Mohammed Ali's modern Egypt. Particularly his successor Khedive Ismael aimed at turning Egypt into "a part of Europe." With the expansion of British control over Egypt from 1882 on, the country became structurally dependent on Europe (Selim 1995). Yet at the beginning of the twentieth century, Egypt's European orientation became increasingly contested with the emergent nationalist movement, and under Nasser, Egypt's relations with Europe were confrontational at best. A gradual rapprochement between the two sides occurred under Sadat. His initial attempts to seek diversified sources of financial aid coincided with the first round of the Mediterranean policy of the then-EC. In 1972, the first EC–Egyptian trade agreement, providing for preferential trade concessions, was signed. With it, Egypt became one among the last countries in the southern Mediterranean to sign an agreement with the EC (Grilli 1993: 182–195).

After the 1973 war, the EC launched the Euro–Arab dialogue, and in the framework of the "Global Mediterranean Policy," it signed a new cooperation agreement with Egypt in 1977. In spite of the flaws of the GMP discussed above, the new bilateral agreement nevertheless respected some of its principles. Thus, besides granting far-ranging trade preferences to Egypt's industrial products and some concessions in agricultural exports, the agreement stipulated cooperation in social matters, and established bilateral institutions for consultation and dialogue. In addition, the new agreement provided for economic assistance under the EC's financial protocols. In fact, compared to other Maghreb and Mashreq countries, Egypt by far received the largest amount of EC aid and loans, particularly since the actual disbursement of committed funds was higher than in the case of other southern Mediterranean states (Grilli 1993: 196–197). Certainly, this observation becomes relative if we consider that Egypt was, and still is, the most populous country in the region. Moreover, it has been argued that the EC's "generosity" toward Egypt was meant to support Cairo's shift toward "the West" after Sadat's visit to Jerusalem (Parfitt 1997: 866). Yet Sadat's "Western" foreign-policy orientation remained almost exclusively focused on the United States (Dessouki 1991: 167). In view of Washington's extensive financial aid and its role in the Camp David process, Cairo did not consider the EC as a serious alternative (Selim 1995). In fact, in scholarly analyses of Egypt's foreign relations under Sadat, Europe is often not mentioned at all.

In the mid-1980s, Cairo started to reassess its relations to the European neighbors, and the idea of linking European, Mediterranean, and Middle Eastern security started to emerge. Egypt first raised the idea of establishing a Mediterranean Forum during the 1987 meeting of the nonaligned movement in former Yugoslavia, which, however, was not followed up any further. After the end of the cold war, Cairo reinvigorated this idea, which Mubarak formally presented in November 1991 to the European Parliament. The reasons for Egypt's Mediterranean proposal were fourfold: First, Egyptian policy makers feared that after the end of the cold war, Egypt's strategic importance to the United States would decline. Thus, Cairo's interest in Europe and the Mediterranean represented an attempt to diversify its external relations. Second, in view of Egypt's economic needs, Cairo looked to the North in order to secure export markets, supply of technology, and sources of financial aid.[16] Third, the Madrid peace process had just started, which seemed to legitimize Egypt's separate peace with Israel a posteriori. Thus, it was now possible for Egypt to promote the establishment of a forum in which Israel would participate without embarrassment, while boosting Egypt's position as mediator and speaker of "the Arab world." Finally, Egypt sought to counter the EC's Euro-Maghreb "5 + 5" proposal of 1991 from which it was excluded (Selim 1995: 16–17).

However, Cairo was interested in keeping the degree of institutionalization of the proposed Mediterranean Forum as low as possible, and rather envisaged a platform for an exchange of ideas (Al-Sharkawy 1997). At the same time, Egypt initially envisaged including only north and south Mediterranean countries, with the option of expanding cooperation to all of the EU in the future. Cairo also argued that beyond the Mediterranean, other Arab countries should be admitted to the Mediterranean Forum, otherwise it "would serve as a tool of division among Arabs" (Selim 1997: 74).

The Launching of the EMP

The Euro-Mediterranean Partnership went far beyond Egypt's ideas on Mediterranean cooperation. Indeed, Cairo's preliminary proposals had focused on economics, the transfer of technology, and social affairs, and far less on security or political cooperation. According to Cairo's reasoning, the latter should be envisaged only after a solution of the wider Arab–Israeli conflict was reached. In this context, Cairo reacted with reluctance to Shimon Peres's idea of a "New Middle East," which accompanied the beginning of the Oslo peace process. As most Arab states and Israel participated at the MENA (Middle East and North Africa) conferences in Casablanca and Amman in 1994 and 1995 respectively, this concept had indeed started to become relevant. Cairo's profound dislike of the "New Middle East" originated in the perception that increased Middle Eastern economic cooperation would justify Israel's growing political and economic involvement in the region. Particularly in view of Israel's advanced economic and technological status, this seemed to entail Israel's regional hegemony, thus undermining Egypt's self-perception of being the natural regional leader (Sela 1998: 71–75).

In view of the EU's preoccupation with "security," the Egyptian government put forward a number of ideas on Euro-Mediterranean cooperation on soft security issues, such as the implementation of a Mediterranean nuclear-free zone, the cleaning of landmines, the establishment of conflict prevention and resolution mechanisms, and measures to mitigate and manage ecological disasters (Foreign Ministry of Egypt 1994). Yet by 1994, the EU had taken the lead in Euro-Mediterranean cooperation, and while the EMP's principles clearly differed from what Egypt had in mind, Mubarak's regime decided to present the EMP as a further development of the Egyptian proposals. Thus, at the 1995 Barcelona Conference, former Egyptian foreign minister Amr Moussa (1995) stressed that the EMP was a "response" and a "positive reaction" to genuine Egyptian aspirations. However, the same speech is also illuminating regarding Egypt's position and expectations toward the powerful European neighbors, as Moussa declared:

> We are committed before our people to strive together for peace and security, to reject policies of hegemony, discrimination and superiority, to establish homogenous societies based on democracy, freedom, and respect of human rights, primary among which is the right to development, progress, and the right of peoples to self-determination.

Furthermore, Moussa declared that "[w]e Arabs have come to Barcelona from countries in the South and East to forge ties with Europe as new model for co-operation," while stressing "Egypt's position, history, and contribution to human civilization beginning with its unique pharaonic history, its dominant cultural role in its Arab and Islamic environment, its African and European dimensions" (Moussa 1995). Hence, the speech is also informative regarding Egypt's self-perception and prevailing concept of regional order. As for the envisaged type of regional relations, the Egyptian government had made it clear on several occasions that the Barcelona Process would not make any sense without progress in the Middle East peace process (Selim 1995). Initially, Cairo also supported the endorsement of the NPT in the Barcelona Declaration, a position which met the outright rejection of Israel, as noted above. Although Cairo signed the Barcelona Declaration without the provision, Egypt would reiterate the NPT issue in the following years, within the EMP framework and beyond it.

Euro–Egyptian Relations and the EMP

Mohammed El-Sayed Selim (1995, 1997) has argued that Egypt's new Mediterranean orientation of the early 1990s was the result of a long-term strategic policy choice. Yet Egypt's participation in the EMP has been ambiguous and contradictory.

The fate of the peace process was the most crucial factor influencing Egypt's stance toward the EMP. However, while opposing the normalization of relations to Israel in the absence of a comprehensive Middle East peace agreement, Cairo also sought to promote its own economic interests. Thus, Egyptian diplomats stressed that the country's economic interests should not be trapped into the Middle East peace process, from which the Barcelona Process was separated (quoted in Ezzat 2000). But on the other hand, Cairo constantly underlined the interlinkage of the two processes. Egypt also requested that the chapter on the political dialogue of the *bilateral* EU–Egyptian agreement should include provisions relating to the peace process (Selim 1997: 80). After the collapse of the peace process, former foreign minister Ahmed Maher (2001a) categorically ruled out any regional cooperation that included Israel.

Yet given the difficulties of the peace process, the EMP also served Egypt as a regional forum for defining the "Arab position" and ensuring EU support for the latter. In this vein, Moussa declared that "[s]ince Europeans have a position favorable to that of the Arabs in peace-making, closer Arab-European co-operation should be the target [of the EMP]" (quoted in Ezzat 2000). Similarly, President Mubarak expressed his hope "for a more active . . . European role to press upon Israel the necessity of respecting its commitments" (quoted in *Al-Ahram Weekly* May 21, 1998). Cairo also repeatedly criticized the EU for its allegedly pro-Israeli bias, and expressed disappointment with the EU's role in the region (*Al-Ahram Weekly* February 22, 2001).

In this vein, former foreign minister Maher (2001a) urged the EU to act "and not to rely only on statements and declarations."

Defying Israel within the EMP framework remained an important rule of the game. Hence, as long as the peace process was proceeding, Cairo insisted that Euro-Mediterranean cooperation on soft security issues had to tackle nonconventional, and in particular nuclear, weapons (El-Shazly 1996; Landau 2003). And after the derailments of the Oslo peace process, regional EMP meetings regularly witnessed Egypt's expression of solidarity with the Palestinians, the condemnation of Israel's policies, and the celebration of the "unified Arab stand" (Foreign Ministry of Egypt 2002a). For this policy, however, Egypt preferred the *complete* EMP arena. Thus, when Syria and Lebanon refused to participate at the 2000 EMP foreign ministers meeting in Marseille out of protest against Israel, Moussa stressed the importance of "Arab participation" in order to defend the Palestinians, counter Israel's arguments, and "clarify the real situation to the European side" (Moussa 2000). Officially, Egypt expressed understanding for the decision of Syria and Lebanon to boycott the Marseille meeting. Subsequently, Cairo also played the boycott card itself—namely by refusing to grant entry visas to Israeli participants at a planned 2001 EMP meeting of chambers of commerce in Cairo, which led the EU to cancel the event. But in the wake of the 2001 EMP meeting of foreign ministers in Brussels, Maher underlined the importance "of the full participation of all Arab members," while arguing that "[t]his is expected to provide an impetus to Euro-Mediterranean cooperation that *has been obstructed by the absence of members*" (Maher 2001b, italics added). At the same time, Egypt continued its role as a mediator within the EMP (and beyond). Thus, Moussa for instance met separately with his Israeli counterpart at the EMP meeting in Marseille.

From the outset, Egypt also gave a high priority to the EMP's contribution to *Arab-European* economic cooperation, sometimes defined as the real aim of the EMP. In this vein, at the 2002 Valencia meeting, Egypt stressed that the adoption of a strategy served the "reinforcement of Euro-Arab cooperation" (Foreign Ministry of Egypt 2002a). Reflecting the government's positions on this issue, *Al-Ahram* columnist Ibrahim Nafie (1999) stressed Egypt's economic interests in the EMP, arguing that it will help in strengthening "Arab unity, as closer ties with Europe mean better Arab integration."

Another constant feature of Egypt's participation in the EMP was the criticism of, and suspicion toward, the EU's commitment and real intentions, as voiced by other EMP partners as well. Thus, Egypt joined the chorus of criticism of the initial slow disbursement of MEDA funds and EU red tape (Ezzat 2000)—irrespective of the fact that Egyptian bureaucratic squabbles over how to handle the funds notably reduced Egypt's absorption capacity (Commission 2002a: 16). Off the record, Egyptian diplomats also repeatedly questioned the EU's commitment to the Mediterranean, given that for instance the Balkan wars and the issue of EU enlargement attracted much of the EU's attention.[17] And the EU's plans for developing an ESDP equally prompted suspicion in Egypt (*Al-Ahram Weekly* December 21, 2000). In this vein, Wafa'a Bassim, former deputy-assistant foreign minister for European affairs, stressed that the EU needed to be more transparent and sensitive vis-à-vis its EMP partners (*Al-Ahram Weekly* June 1, 2000). Interestingly, while Egyptian officials repeatedly praised the importance of EU–Egyptian relations, unofficially they also expressed their concern for Egypt's independence.[18] In this vein, chief political advisor Osama Al-Baz stated that "Egypt will not act hastily" in the realm of Euro-Mediterranean cooperation (quoted in *Al-Ahram Weekly* June 1, 2000).

The lengthy bilateral negotiations of the Euro-Mediterranean Association Agreement showed what this meant in practice. Indeed, they lasted between 1994 and June 1999, yet another 20 months passed before Egypt initialed the agreement in February 2001, and another 4 months went by before Cairo finally signed it. During the negotiations, disagreements revolved around standards, rules of origin, competition, the rights of Egyptian immigrants in the EU, along with the amount of financial aid. But from the outset, trade in agriculture was the most controversial issue (Selim 1997: 83–84; Parfitt 1997: 879). Egypt dismissed the EU's initial offers of slightly increasing Egyptian export quotas in agricultural products and demanded trade liberalization instead. As other EMP partners, Cairo complained about the EU's protectionist agricultural policy that did not match at all the task of liberalizing trade in industrial goods to be made by the EMP partners. In addition, Egyptian negotiators stressed that Egypt was a net importer of agricultural products from the EU and that among southern Mediterranean economies, Egypt was most dependent on agriculture.[19] According to Cairo, these facts requested a different European approach toward Egypt. As the EU insisted that the export quota demanded by Egypt partly exceeded Egyptian production, the negotiations entered an impasse in 1996 (Parfitt 1997: 880).

At the 1997 EMP foreign ministers meeting in Malta, Moussa (1997) openly declared that the negotiations "caused us grave frustration and stirred our suspicion of the existence of a genuine and equitable political will on the European side to conclude an agreement with Egypt which runs consonance with the true spirit of partnership." Moussa (1997) also expressed the suspicion that

> Barcelona is no more than a tactical move which does not ensure security or the objective of the establishment of the free-trade area referred to, unless the intention is to make the countries of the South pay the price of this development in the long term in return for the assistance it needs for the short term.

Although unrelated to the association agreement, the controversy over textiles that erupted between the two sides in 1998 did not improve bilateral relations either. Cairo reacted with outrage to the EU's dumping accusations regarding Egyptian cotton textile exports. While refusing to negotiate on possible penalties, former trade minister Ahmad Goweili (1998) stressed that Egypt was ready to defend its trade interests and reputation, and maintained that Egypt, as the most important country in the region, had the right to a different treatment. The year 1998 also witnessed a trade dispute over Egyptian potato exports to the EU, along with a similarly uncompromising Egyptian stance (*Al-Ahram Weekly*, August 13, 1998).

The EU eventually granted some concessions to Egyptian agricultural exports and increased its economic assistance.[20] Egyptian chief negotiator Gamal Bayoumi (1998) immediately interpreted these concessions as the EU's acknowledgement of Egypt's special role in the region. Yet, Egypt remained nervous about the stipulated trade liberalization and the gradual reduction of import duties on EU products, which were comparatively high. Considering the structure of Egypt's industry, which is largely controlled by a "notoriously inefficient and massively overstaffed" public sector (Parfitt 1997: 878), this is not surprising. Thus, the Egyptian government fears that competition with the EU might destroy some of Egypt's industries and lead to a further rise in unemployment, of which the Islamists would profit most (Selim 1997). Yet disagreements between different Egyptian ministries and internal bureaucratic squabbles delayed the signing of the bilateral agreement further. The minister of trade and the economy minister had approved the list of sensitive industries for which import duties would be reduced at a later stage, but they subsequently had second thoughts. Thus, after the end of the negotiations, the two ministries launched a media campaign against the agreement (*Al-Ahram Weekly*

May 25, 2000), and Mubarak himself intervened to end the quarrel. Cairo's subsequent request for "further clarifications" on specific issues, however, left the EU perplexed.[21] The 2001 cabinet reshuffle and the unfamiliarity of the new cabinet with the agreement caused additional delays, which seriously annoyed the EU. But even after its final signing, fervent discussions on the desirability of the agreement continued among Egypt's political elites (Essam El-Din 2002).

The EU Commission's previous experience with Egypt's economic reform programs had proven similarly problematic. Regarding a multidonor project that started in 1998, the Commission expressed "reservations in repeating the relatively open funding model," while stressing the need for "a clearer relationship with line social ministries, a revised mandate and a proper state funding base" (Commission 2002a: 17). A project on industrial modernization—with € 250 million, it was the largest external project funded by the EU—faced outright resistance from key ministries. This prompted the Commission to note that "the problems encountered in launching [the project] have significantly changed perceptions on the limits to achieve significant economic reform in the face of resistance from individual ministers, and the risks in Egypt associated with very high budget programmes" (Commission 2002a: 17–18).

After the events of 9/11, Egypt championed for strengthening the cultural dialogue, and, as other Arab states, reacted with dismay to the growing anti-Muslim sentiments in Europe. However, it is not without irony that back in 1996, Cairo proposed a convention among the EMP countries to combat terrorism, which was to include the "exchange of data of suspected persons and information on their whereabouts" (El-Shazly 1996). In view of the "European connection" of some of the 9/11 terrorists (such as the Hamburg cell), and the involvement of Egyptian nationals in *Al-Qaeda*, Egypt's repeated claims that it had warned of such dangers, but no one would listen, cannot be dismissed.[22]

Finally, the case of Saad Eddin Ibrahim clearly demonstrated Egypt's position toward democratization and EU involvement in this issue. It is indeed paradoxical that the accusation of illegal foreign funding and embezzlement of funds directed against Ibrahim revolved around an EU grant of € 145,000 within the EMP's MEDA Democracy program. The EU vehemently denied that Ibrahim had presented false financial documentation, as stated in the verdict. Certainly, the EU did not protest Egypt's grave violations of human rights as long as they were directed against the Islamists (Parfitt 1997: 875). Yet, while the

U.S. administration threatened to suspend additional foreign aid in protest against the prosecution of Ibrahim—who is both an Egyptian and a U.S. citizen—the EU did not engage in any similar action.

Summary: The EMP According to Egypt

To sum up, Egypt's attitude toward the EMP did not fully correspond to the image of an "active participant" as depicted by the EU Commission (2002: 2). Mainly dictated by Egypt's interest in development cooperation with the EU, Cairo initially accepted the EMP, but maintained a specific interpretation of its objectives and principles. While insisting from the outset on the EMP's interconnectedness with the peace process, Cairo hoped for a stronger European role in Middle Eastern politics, favorable to "the Arab side." Egypt's initial focus on the issue of nuclear weapons entailed a collision course toward Israel, which is widely believed to possess such weapons. After the derailments of the peace process, Egypt sought to become the *porte-parole* of the "Arab position," while strengthening its role of mediator among the conflicting parties. Accordingly, Egypt condemned other Arab states from boycotting high-level EMP meetings out of protest against Israel, as it undermined Egypt's all-Arab leadership ambitions.

The constant emphasis on Euro–Arab cooperation within the EMP also shows that Cairo perceived the region under construction as Euro-Arab at best. This position clearly preceded the EU's decision to accept Cyprus, Malta, and Turkey as EU members, which indeed changed the architecture of the EMP. Yet Egypt also remained suspicious of the EU. Thus, while Cairo agreed on EU-funded reform projects, its ministries sabotaged their implementation in practice. Similarly, the delay of two years between the end of the negotiations and the signing of the bilateral agreement points to a certain lack of enthusiasm on the Egyptian side, to say the least. As the EU Commission (2002: 7) noted, these delays "called into question the extent of Egypt's commitment to the Barcelona process." Moreover, the case of Saad Eddin Ibrahim most clearly illustrates Egypt's attitude toward political reforms: participating in a EU-sponsored democratization program and subsequently convicting the recipients of EU funds for, indeed, accepting foreign funding does not point to a high affinity with the EMP's principles. Thus, Egypt did not fully lack a strategy toward the EMP, but its policy remained contradictory, while it ran counter to the promotion of regional security on a Euro-Mediterranean basis.

Egypt's Identity and the EMP

The EMP's implicit identity manipulations discussed in the previous chapter are also relevant for Egypt. The most crucial aspect for Egypt is the realm of regional relations, and in particular the envisaged normalization of relations to Israel in the framework of regional co-operation. In spite of the formal peace agreement, Israel still counts as an adversary for Egypt, and, with it, as "significant other." Still in the realm of regional relations, the EMP also aimed at significantly upgrading EU–Egyptian relations. The EMP's second "identity manipulation" regards Egypt's stipulated anchorage in an axiomatic Mediterranean, or Euro-Mediterranean, region, thus seeking to redefine Egypt's "place in the region." The idea of a Euro-Mediterranean regional order also touches once more upon Egypt's relations to its regional neighbors, including Israel and the EU. Third, following the normative power rationale, the EMP sought to promote European-type "Western" values, including economic liberalism, democratization, and the respect for human rights. Thus, the EMP's attempted "identity manipulations" touched upon a number of key issues related to Egypt's difficult identity history and domestic divides, as argued in the following sections.

Regional Relations

Relations to Israel

Egypt's official position of ruling out "normal" relations to Israel as long as the Palestinians are deprived of their rights, along with the domestic unpopularity of the Camp David accords, is well known. However, although scantly covered in the Egyptian media, both sides maintain business relations, including Egyptian oil exports to Israel (*Middle East Times* March 31, 2001).[23] Before the outbreak of the second *Intifada*, Israel also provided the fourth-largest number of tourists, ahead of any Arab country; and during the Netanyahu government, Israeli exports to Egypt even increased (Sobelman 2000).

It is important that Egypt's opposition to Israel is articulated in terms of identity, entailing an emphasis on the country's Arab and/or Islamic features. Thus, reacting to Israel's raids on Gaza in July 2002, the Grand Imam of *Al-Azhar*, Sheikh Mohammed Sayed Tantawi, called on Muslims to "unite against Israeli arrogance or else they will be punished by God" and proclaimed that "Israel is the enemy of God" (*Agence France Presse* July 26, 2002). At the same time, with regard to the Palestine conflict, the references to Arab solidarity in Egypt's official discourse are too numerous to mention. As Gerges (2002) rightly observes, "problems of modernization, relations with the West, the appropriate role of religion, the balance between national and Arab identities are often defined in relation to Palestine and Israel."

Not surprisingly, the domestic opposition to the "normalization" of relations to Israel grew considerably after the collapse of the peace process. This also included those domestic groups that economically profited most from the "cold peace" with Israel. Thus, as Egyptian businessmen in the tourism sector in the Sinai Peninsula put it to the author in October 2000, their identification with the Palestinian cause actually contradicted their own economic interests, that is, their business with Israeli tourists. A similar shift also occurred among Egypt's moderate political elites.[24] In this vein, the journal of the *Wafd* party, which usually refrained from pronounced anti-Israeli positions, condemned Mubarak's 2002 meeting with former Israeli foreign minister Peres and categorically ruled out the prospects of normalizing ties with Israel (*Al-Wafd* August 6, 2002: 14). In this period, there were also repeated domestic calls for annulling Egypt's peace treaty with Israel, while some suggested that to defend the Palestinians, Egypt should go to war with Israel (*The Economist* June 4, 2002: 24). The domestic situation exerted a considerable amount of pressure on the Egyptian regime. However, the regime affirmed that war was not an option since "the Arabs want peace" (Mubarak 2002a).

However, the picture looked different at the beginning of the peace process. A survey of Egyptian public opinion conducted in 1994–1995, that is, in the rather optimistic times of Middle East peace-making, is illuminating here. True, a large majority of the 1500 Egyptian respondents opposed normalizing relations with Israel, as both the survey (Fergany 1995) and the publication of the preliminary findings in *Al-Ahram Weekly* (December 29, 1995) stressed. In this vein, 75 percent of respondents were against the establishment of Israeli factories in Egypt, 53 percent disproved of Israelis visiting Egypt, 71 percent opposed buying Israeli products, and 62 percent were against visiting Israel (Fergany 1995: 12–13). What the survey did not stress, however, was the percentage of *positive replies*, which varied between 20 and 42 percent. Thus, although only 20 percent approved of Israel establishing factories in Egypt, 36 percent of the respondents answered that they would like to visit Israel, 27 percent said that they did not oppose buying Israeli goods, and 42 percent approved of Israelis visiting Egypt. If we add the 2–4 percent of "no opinion" on each question, Egypt's alleged domestic consensus vis-à-vis Israel becomes very relative.

A similar observation applies to Egypt's elites, who allegedly tend to oppose closer relations with Israel (*Al-Ahram Weekly* July 2, 1998). However, the preferred type of relations to Israel repeatedly caused internal disputes, thus showing that different opinions on this issue indeed existed. Thus, as Egyptian officials and businesspeople admitted off the record, some groups are in favor of improving relations to Israel, but they cannot maintain this position openly due to social pressure. However, with the beginning of the peace process, Peres's vision of a New Middle East caused several public debates among Egyptian (and other Arab) intellectuals. Supporters of the revival of an Arab regional system most fervently opposed the concept of "Middle Easternism," or *sharqawsatiyya*, arguing that it endangered Egypt's Arab and/or Islamic identity (Sela 1998: 339–340). But the "crack in the intellectual consensus" (Ajami 1999: 308) occurred with the 1997 Copenhagen meeting of Arab and Israeli intellectuals, which stirred fervent debates in Egypt. It is revealing that a Marxist and former opponent of Sadat's peace policy, the late Lutfi Al-Khuli, led the Egyptian delegation. Moreover, even during the difficult period of peace-making in early 1999, a parliamentary bill that proposed the annulment of the Camp David accords—supported by the Nasserist Party, the Islamist-oriented Labor party, and the *Tagammu'*—caused considerable polemics. Due to the opposition of the NDP and the hesitant position of the *Wafd* (which proposed amendments to the bill), the draft legislation did not pass. With the new prospects of peace-making in mid-1999, the scissions among Egyptian intellectuals became even more visible. In July 1999, the "Cairo Peace Society," an organization promoting peace with Israel, which was founded two years earlier, held its first open conference in a Cairo hotel along the Nile, chaired by the NDP deputy secretary. In reaction to this event, the "Organization to Combat Zionism and Normalization" held a meeting on the other side of the Nile on exactly the same days. Fervent debates and mutual accusations between supporters and opponents of "normalization" followed in the media, including in the government-affiliated *Al-Ahram* (Howeidy 1999; Ezzat 1999; Sid-Ahmed 1999).

Support or opposition to the peace treaty with Israel and "normalization" of relations with the latter broadly corresponded to the domestic identity divide positioning pan-Arab and pan-Islamic identity concepts on one side, and the idea of "Egypt first" on the other. In this vein, supporters of normalization, such as Amin Al-Mohdi, explicitly criticized "the official and ruling Arab thought" (quoted in Sobelman 2000), and others openly praised Sadat's peace policy for having served *Egypt's interests*, such as enabling the *infitah* policy and the reestablishment of a multiparty system (Said 1999). Similarly, the late veteran diplomat and writer Tahsin Bashir stressed that the Camp David accords led to the recuperation of "Egyptian land" (quoted in Sami 2001). And the newspaper of the *Wafd* Party rejected the option of going to war with Israel since it would be disastrous for the Egyptian economy (*Al-Wafd* April 3, 2002: 14). Thus, this stream pragmatically argues from an Egyptian view and defends purely Egyptian interests (Khalil 1998). While it generally comprises personalities that are (or were) close to the regime, this position was also defended by some members of the political opposition and independent intellectuals, such as Naguib Mahfuz.

Conversely, the pan-Arab *Tagammu'* and the Nasserists continue to be among the most outspoken opponents of enhanced Egyptian–Israeli relations, as the proposed annulment of the Camp David accords demonstrates. However, in the period of Middle East peace-making, the *Tagammu'* witnessed an internal scission on the normalization issue, as some of its members started to question the traditional party line (*Al-Ahram Weekly* January 6, 2000). As for the Islamist streams represented by the Labor party, the Muslim Brotherhood and the *Al-Azhar* establishment, the outspoken opposition to normalizing relations to Israel remained constant (Zeghal 1996; Lübben and Fawzi 2000). In this vein, even during the "good times" of Oslo, the Grand Imam of *Al-Azhar* refused to meet former Israeli president Weizman during his state visit to Cairo on the grounds that Israel still occupies Jerusalem (Gerges 1995). And in 1999, the journal of the Labor Party accused former agriculture minister Yusuf Wali of "high treason" for having allegedly worked toward normalizing relations with Israel (Essam El-Din 1999). This caused both a libel suit by Wali and the regime's banning of the journal.

To sum up, the EMP's implicit objective of altering Cairo's relations with Israel touches upon a highly emotional identity divide within Egypt. This gap, however, is dependent on Middle East peace-making. Indeed, Israel's repressive policy toward the Palestinians during the second *Intifada* united the population in anti-Israeli sentiments and pro-Palestinian feelings of solidarity. In this situation, the regime's efforts of both mediating between the conflicting parties and defining the "Arab position" also contributed to the reconciliation between very different domestic preferences. Conversely, the prospects of resolving the Middle East conflict brought the incompatibility of different identity concepts to the fore, and, in the long run, demand a choice between them. Touching upon relations to a "significant" other, the resolution of the conflict would also require a redefinition of Egypt's state identity, of which some elements came to be defined in relation to Israel.

Relations to the EU

Compared to the question of how to deal with Israel, relations to the EU were far less an issue of public debate—or interest—in Egypt. True, there is a certain admiration for the European integration process, which is contrasted to the meager achievements of economic integration among Arab states (*Al-Ahram Weekly* January 7, 1999). But these voices were rather rare.

In general, due to the experience with European colonialism, Egyptian elites display a distrust of the EU and its regional ambitions (Said Aly 1996: 24–16; Guazzone 1996; Perthes 1996). Indeed, criticism of the EU is often embedded in the history-rooted perception that "the West" does not live up to its commitments vis-à-vis the Arab people.[25] In this vein, in view of Egypt's growing disillusionment with the EU's role in peace-making, *Al-Ahram Weekly* (February 15, 1999) quite bluntly stated that "Europe, which played such as crucial role in creating the conflict that continues to tear the region apart, is only willing to contribute cash to the peace efforts." On another occasion, *Al-Ahram Weekly* (May 25, 2000) criticized the EU for treating Israel as "special case," while contending that Egypt and the EU need to build trust, which, following this reasoning, is apparently nonexistent. After the collapse of the peace process, this type of criticism grew stronger (Ezzat 2000), and Mubarak (2002b) even pointed out (albeit wrongly) that the "EU is the biggest financer of Israel."

Similarly, fears of European political and economic domination persisted. In this vein, Mubarak's chief political advisor Al-Baz claimed that closer EU–Egyptian relations may narrow down Egypt's independence (*Al-Ahram Weekly* June 1, 2000), and leading Egyptian academics warned against relations "of total dependence" (quoted in *Al-Ahram Weekly* November 19, 1998). This went hand in hand with the emphasis on Egypt's right to a different treatment (Goweili 1998). It goes without saying that the gap between the EU's rhetoric of "partnership" and its far less collegial (agricultural) policy only strengthened these perceptions.

However, distrust of the EU tended to be more pronounced among supporters of the concepts of *qawm* and *umma*. In this vein, a former leading thinker of Egypt's communist movement, Mohamed Sid-Ahmed, quite bluntly considered the EU's interests in its southern periphery as an "updated version of the imperialist project" (Sid-Ahmed 2000). In the past, Sid-Ahmed was in favor of developing closer relations to Europe, but mainly because he reckoned that Egypt would benefit from an emerging rivalry between the EU and the United States in the Middle East (Selim 1997: 85). Similarly, a survey of attitudes toward the EMP among Egyptian elites found that liberals tended to welcome the EMP initiative, while socialists, Arab nationalists, and Islamists tended to opposed it. Regarding the Islamists, the study stressed that Israel's participation in the EMP was the main reasons for their opposition, along with a traditional cultural animosity toward Europe and "the West"(Joffé 2001).

This cultural animosity, however, also affected Egyptian "liberals" after 9/11. Thus, the chief editor of *Al-Wafd* denounced the growing hostility against Arabs and Muslims in "the West," and called for a common strategy of Arab and Muslim states (*Al-Wafd* September 16, 2001). And the comments of Italian premier Berlusconi on the alleged superiority of the West over the Islamic civilization (*Corriere della Sera* September 27, 2001) prompted a furious reaction. Thus, while sharply criticizing that Berlusconi, "who thought of himself as mafia leader," did not even apologize for his inappropriate statements, *Al-Wafd*'s commentator called for cutting all ties to Italy. At the same time, *Al-Wafd* termed the attitude of "the West" toward Arabs and Muslims as "US-European terrorism" (quoted after *BBC Monitoring Middle East* October 7, 2001). Thus, it may be argued that the post–9/11 "civilizations narrative" induced a greater affinity with pan-Arab or pan-Islamic loyalties among the traditional supporters of the "Egypt first" concept.

With regard to the economic dimension of EU–Egyptian relations, another domestic fault-line proved to be relevant. Indeed, the issue of economic liberalization according to the EMP's prescriptions pitted Nasserists and socialists against the defenders of Sadat's legacy of economic liberalism. In this vein, the *Wafd*, which represents large parts of Egypt's business elites, openly endorsed the new association agreement (*Al-Wafd* June 25, 2001), while the Nasserist Party, the *Tagammu'*, and the *Ikhwan* opposed it.[26] In this context, it is interesting that Mohammed Al-Azaburi of the Brotherhood argued that instead of opening Egyptian markets to European competition, the increased willingness of Egyptians to boycott American and Israeli products during the *Intifada* should be used to strengthen Egypt's economy (Essam El-Din 2002). Besides revolving around the preferred sociopolitical order and questions of political legacy, positions on the agreement may obviously also be linked to the different economic interests. However, this reasoning is not clear-cut, since, for instance, in early 2001 the Federation of Egyptian Industry supported the agreement, but not the ministry of trade and industry (*Al-Ahram Weekly* May 10, 2001).

To sum up, although it is not an issue of top priority, Egypt's preferred relations to the EU are subject to some domestic debates. While suspicion toward the EU is common, the question of EU–Egyptian relations touches upon the question of Egypt's national, religious, and regional identity, along with the question of the preferred socioeconomic order. Indeed, opposition to the EU is most pronounced among supporters of Egypt's pan-Arab and socialist orientation "à la Nasser," as well as among Islamists. On the other hand, supporters of "Egypt first," which broadly correspond to the defenders of economic liberalism according to Sadat's *infitah*, tended to support closer economic relations with the EU, along with the economic reforms it prescribes. At the same time, this support also remained anchored within the "Egypt-first" concept, since it is expected that the EU acknowledges Egypt's *special* political role in the Arab state system and its *particular* socioeconomic needs.

The EMP and Egypt's "Place in the Region"

Taha Husayn, the famous Egyptian writer, professor, and minister for education in the prerevolutionary *Wafdist* government, believed in Egypt's anchorage in the Mediterranean and was favorable to enhanced relations with Europe (Husayn 1954). His position was typical of the prerevolutionary liberal thought that defined Egypt's identity in national-territorial terms. However, in present-day Egypt, these ideas do not find many supporters. Said Aly (1996: 26) stressed that "regional security in the Southern Mediterranean area has been defined traditionally by Arab writers and academicians only from a pan-Arab posture." Indeed, dominant perceptions of regional order take the Arab, and possibly Islamic, identity dimension as a key reference point. Since leadership in the "Arab world" is a constitutive element of Egypt's identity, the country's dominant perception depicts an Arab cognitive region with Egypt at its center.

As we have seen, this perception impacted on Egypt's attitude toward the EMP, and the EU in general, which, interestingly enough, the EU came to recognize. Thus, the EU Commission (2003, 9) explicitly stated that

> Egypt, as an Arab country, has had to rebuild its position as the natural leader and spokesman of the Arab world that it totally lost immediately after Camp David and Egypt's peace treaty with Israel. President Mubarak's achievement in successfully restoring Egypt's leadership is a remarkable one, all the more so since the Arab World [*sic*] no longer needs a 'spokesman' in the way it did in the immediate post-war era.

Indeed, it remains questionable whether the heterogeneous "Arab world" presently needs a leader, but it is also worth noting that there is nothing natural about Egypt's leadership role. The country certainly has the largest army and population among Arab states, along with a truly impressive cultural heritage and an important movie industry. However, its economic strength, innovation capacity, and cultural power are limited (UNDP 2003). According to Ajami (1999: 221), in the 1990s the country produced merely 375 books a year.

However, the conceptualization of an Arab regional order may have different meanings. In this vein, Milad Hanna (1994) argued for instance that Egypt is characterized by four layers of civilization—Pharaonic, Graeco-Roman, Coptic, and Islamic. They describe three different geographical spaces, namely the link to Europe through the Mediterranean, the Arab world, and Africa. For most Islamists, Egypt is obviously part of a much broader "Islamic world"—which may be combined with pan-Arab loyalties. In this vein, Ibrahim Shoukri, the former leader of the (still frozen) Islamist Labor Party, declared in the party journal *Al-Sha'b* that "Arab and Islamic unity" should be "the basis of a strategy that proposes to turn the Arab-Islamic nation from a nation merely protecting itself and its interests into an active one influencing the course of events." In the same article, Shoukri also called for an Arab and Islamic summit to "counter hostile schemes seeking to undermine our interests and our unity" (quoted after *Africa News Service Egypt* June 16, 1999). This position expresses a clear resistance to any attempt of redefining Egypt's "place in the region."

The idea of a Mediterranean region potentially raises similar suspicions as Middle-Easternism, new or old.[27] Thus, with reference to the ideas of Taha Husayn, Egyptian academics argued that Egypt's Mediterranean link is "dangerous, since it paved the way, and still does, for a Middle-Eastern vision" (quoted in Khallaf 1998). Others dismissed Egypt's Mediterranean identity by arguing that Husayn underestimated Egypt's Arab culture. Reflecting a wide-spread perception among Egyptian politicians and intellectuals, the idea of the Mediterranean is thus viewed as an attempt to redraw the regional map, put Israel at the center, and thus erode Egypt's Arab and Islamic identity (Khallaf 1998). Other scholars, however, suggested that the Mediterranean idea is not unacceptable in Arab states, since the southern Mediterranean is, at any rate, predominantly Arab and Islamic (Kodmani-Darwish 1998: 45). In a similar vein, Sid-Ahmed (2000) stressed that the broader concept of the Mediterranean entails constructive relations with the EU, while the idea of the Middle East places the Arab–Israeli conflict at the center. Most interview partners agreed, however, that a Mediterranean regional order could only emerge if it does not challenge Egypt's Arab and/or Islamic identity.[28] Amr Moussa's assertion, mentioned above, that closer Arab–European cooperation should be the target of the EMP can clearly be put into this context, along with the remarks in the government-affiliated press on the EMP's attempts to build a "Euro-Arab partnership . . . across the Mediterranean" (Sid-Ahmed 2000). Hence, the inter-Arab Agadir initiative in the framework of the EMP is highly compatible with this conceptualization of the preferred regional order.

To sum up, Egypt's predominant idea of its "place in the region" is defined by pan-Arab, and to a lesser extent, pan-Islamic loyalties. In general, regional security on a Euro-Mediterranean basis potentially deprives Egypt of its predominant identity frame, particularly if it implicitly builds on the scenario of a New Middle East. This explains the absence of the Mediterranean theme in Egypt's official discourse. Yet the question of regional order is also intrinsically linked to Egypt's type of regional relations, most notably to Israel and the EU. Arab nationalists and Islamists can hardly accept the idea of a Euro-Mediterranean regional order if, besides including Israel and Europe, it potentially divides Arab states and Muslims into "Mediterraneans" and "non-Mediterraneans" (Selim 1997: 85). However, in the absence of a settlement of the Middle East conflict, the reformulation of Egypt's concept of regional order, which the EMP demanded in the long run, could be postponed. Conversely, Egypt could use the EMP to *reaffirm* its identity through its reasserted leadership role and focus on Euro–Arab cooperation.

The EMP, Domestic Reforms, and Liberal Values

Since Egypt's Euro-Mediterranean association agreement only entered into force in June 2004, it is too early to assess its impact on the

Egyptian economy. Yet in the long run, implementing the treaty may entail processes of socioeconomic restructuring, such as a greater transparency and accountability of the state bureaucracy, the implementation of the rule of law, along with reforms of Egypt's patronage system. Certainly, as noted above, the EU has not been consistent in promoting democracy in the southern Mediterranean (Bicchi 2004). And it also remains highly questionable whether economic liberalization triggers political reforms (Solingen 2003)—particularly since Egypt's *infitah* policy did not have these effects (Pioppi 2004). However, the EMP's aim of promoting reforms in the southern Mediterranean raises the question of whether its values and principles are compatible with Egypt's political culture and domestic preferences.

Certainly, Egypt's political opposition has constantly called for reforms, including a fairer electoral process and the repeal of the emergency legislation. However, political reforms may have quite different meanings to the various groups. Thus, while some opposition parties called for a greater freedom of expression, other forces may have a different agenda. Parliament member Mohammed Mursi of the *Ikhwan*, for instance, identified "strengthening the role of *Al-Azhar* in promoting and disseminating religious values" as the most important aim of political reforms (quoted in *Al-Ahram Weekly* March 15, 2001). *Al-Azhar*'s censoring activity and the support it received from conservative Islamists also shows that freedom of expression is not the priority of these domestic groups—unless it concerns their own right of free speech, of course. But it is also important to note that parts of Egypt's elites silently approved of the regime's repressive strategies, particularly after the 1991 Algerian elections, and in the aftermath of 9/11 (Stacher 2001; Singerman 2002: 34). On the other hand of the spectrum, liberal forces, such as represented by the new *Al-Ghad* party, not only demand the replacement of the presidential system with a parliamentary one, but also the full participation of all political forces in Egyptian politics, including the (conservative and moderate) Islamists (Roumani 2004).

The question of political reforms often raises debates revolving around questions of tradition versus modernity. The issue of gender equality remains one of the main battlefields in this context (Al-Ali 2000). An illustrative example was certainly the 2000 reform of Egypt's personal status law, which made it easier for women to obtain a divorce—provided that they renounce all financial rights. Yet while the Grand Imam of *Al-Azhar* approved the reform, other conservative Islamists fervently opposed it on religious grounds. As one Islamist parliamentarian put it, "[g]iving women the right to divorce is an explosive bomb in Egyptian society" (quoted in *Al-Ahram Weekly* February 3, 2000). Even representatives of the *Wafd* rejected the reform—interestingly enough by arguing that it contradicted the *shari'a*. Given the wide-spread popular resistance against the bill, some of the original provisions—such as permitting a woman to travel abroad without her husband's explicit consent—were dropped altogether. Another prominent example is the above-mentioned trial of 52 homosexuals in September 2001, which was justified by prevailing religious and cultural norms. As Mohammed El-Sayed Said (2001) denounced, "flagrant violations [of human rights] are made in the name of our cultural specificity."

It is important that this "cultural specificity" tends to be contrasted to the values of the "West" (Ferrié 2000; Dupret 2000). In discussions with the author on these issues, Egyptians—male, female, intellectuals and nonintellectuals alike—often mention the allegedly low moral standards of most "Westerners," visible for instance in the comparatively low importance given to marriage, high divorce rates, single parenthood, and the tolerance of homosexuality. Egyptian men tended to add to this list the greater sexual liberties and alleged immodesty of "Western" women, and generally, their status in society. In fact, the critics may highly appreciate German cars, Finnish portable phones, American satellite dishes, Italian fashion, and British Pop music. But when it comes to the imperatives of "morality" and Islam, the admiration of "Western" inventions has its limits. As an Egyptian businessman once put it bluntly to the author, "if democracy means that everybody can do what he wants and that women can walk half-naked on the streets, we don't want democracy!"

Thus, the domestic support for "Western-type" political liberalism remains limited in Egypt. While this partly corresponds to the Arab intellectual tradition of seeking a genuine path toward modernization, without blindly imitating "the West" (Hanafi 1990; Arkoun 1994; Al-Jabri 1999a), the persistence of patriarchal and authoritarian patterns puts a strain on the promotion of individualism (Sharabi 1988; UNDP 2005: 17–18). Moreover, as Milad Hanna (1998) noted, "tolerance and acceptance of the other are in the retreat, because liberal or left-wing ideas no longer prevail." Indeed, until the emergence of *Al-Ghad*, there were no political parties in Egypt that defended truly liberal values, such as the respect for the individual, gender equality, let alone the separation between state and religion. Even the *Wafd*'s traditional support for political reform had its limit in the realm of women's rights. At the same time, individuals who openly defended a liberal agenda, such as Abu Seda, Ibrahim, and recently Ayman Nour, not only risk state repression, but also face the accusations of intellectuals and the press of being agents of the "West" (Ibrahim 1998; Stacher 2001; *Le Monde* April 27, 2005). The legislative elections of 2005 may be a further indication of the persisting decline of political liberalism in Egypt, given that around 15 legal parties representing the nonreligious opposition failed to gain a dozen seats together. It goes without saying that the regime's affinity for liberal values provides an even bleaker picture.

It has often been claimed that the Islamists would probably most benefit from the democratization process in Arab/Muslim states. In the case of Egypt, this may be true, although this is obviously not a reason for rejecting political reforms altogether. Moreover, in the time-span under discussion, political reforms may have strengthened those political forces that were most hostile to a Euro-Mediterranean regional order, such as the various conservative forces and the left-wing opposition. In general, however, serious political reforms would certainly accentuate the existing domestic fault-lines while adding new ones. With it, questions of authenticity and modernity, cultural specificity, and difference to the "West," would most likely become an even greater issue of domestic debates.

Conclusions

Although Egypt was initially interested in Euro-Mediterranean co-operation, its participation in the EMP between 1995 and 2002 was much more ambiguous. Cairo has been reluctant vis-à-vis the economic dimension of the EMP, and its interpretations of the EMP rationale, along with its commitment to the latter, remained very contradictory.

Egypt has undoubtedly a difficult legacy in terms of identity, which has witnessed several ruptures. Mubarak sought to bridge these ruptures by merging the identity concepts of his two predecessors and the respective foreign policy courses related to it. As a result, Egypt under Mubarak is defined by its Arab and Islamic identity, along with its role as "natural" regional leader, which is ambiguously justified by its *national distinctiveness*. Therefore, combined with Egypt's profound suspicion of Europe in view of the colonial experience, the core themes of Egypt's self-definition are not conducive to regional security on a Euro-Mediterranean basis in the first place. Egypt's identity as coined by Mubarak influenced Egypt's attitude toward the Barcelona Process from the start. Thus, Cairo sought to employ the regional dimension of the EMP for strengthening its leadership role among Arab states. Thus, while insisting on the link between the EMP and the peace process, Cairo sought to win European support for what it defined as the "Arab position," while it also stepped up its role as mediator in Middle Eastern affairs. Moreover, Cairo depicted the EMP as contributing to enhanced Euro–Arab relations and economic cooperation among *Arab* states.

The question of whether Egypt's lack of commitment toward Euro-Mediterranean regional security can be linked to the country's internal identity problems faces a number of methodological problems. Most notably, they concern the regime's extensive powers in determining Egypt's identity discourse, its foreign policy, and the rules of the political game. However, as the case of Sadat has shown, the domestic acceptance of the policies of an authoritarian regime has its limits. Hence, the regime of Mubarak has been sensitive to frame policies in terms of identity, while downplaying policies that may contradict important domestic preferences—such as Egypt's relations to the United States and the peace agreements with Israel. Moreover, as the regime's increasing adoption of a religious discourse demonstrates, domestic sentiments and developments—such as the strengthening of religion and their political exponents—do exert pressures on authoritarian regimes. They may restrict a regime's space of maneuver in foreign policy, and sometimes demand cautious balancing acts. This became particularly visible after the outbreak of the second Palestinian *Intifada*, which caused widespread anti-Israeli—and anti-U.S.—sentiments among Egyptians.

Yet a closer investigation into domestic politics and developments shows that Egypt's state identity is domestically more disputed than it may seem from an external, state-centered perspective. In spite of a large domestic consensus around Egypt's Arab and Islamic identity, there are very different positions on what this means in detail, and whether Arab, Islamic, or purely Egyptian interests and loyalties are to determine Egypt's foreign relations. Moreover, in the Egyptian context, the rather classical fault-line that separates supporters of a socialist economic order from defenders of economic liberalism reflects the divide between the adherents of Nasser's and Sadat's legacy, respectively. Finally, against the backdrop of the strengthening of religion in Egyptian society, the preferred role of Islam in Egyptian politics, along with its meaning and interpretation, is fervently disputed. These fault-lines are multiple and intercrossing, while they partly also cut across the organized political opposition.

The EMP, according to the EU's interpretation, touched upon several of the domestic identity divides. Thus, its implicit redefinition of Egypt's relations to Israel remained a highly emotional and history-laden issue. As long as the Middle East conflict is not solved, a majority of Egyptians may well oppose "normal" relations with Israel. Yet as the beginning of the Oslo peace process showed, this issue caused several internal clashes and debates, broadly pitting supporters of "Egypt first" against the defenders of Egypt's pan-Arab and/or pan-Islamic loyalties. Second, in spite of a general suspicion toward Europe, the domestic preferences on EU–Egyptian relations followed similar patterns. This was even more pronounced as far as the economic dimension of the bilateral relations is concerned, which directly touches upon the divide between the defenders of Nasserism and supporters of Sadat's *infitah* policy. Third, the EMP's implicit manipulation of the preferred concept of regional order is domestically contested. The predominant perception revolves around the image of the "Arab world"—and Egypt at its center, but Islamist preferences may conceive of the region as including a broader "Islamic world." Finally, the EMP's prescriptions for reforms followed the "Western" model of economic liberalization and democratization. Yet the support for liberal values was relatively limited at the domestic level, which may well be a result of Egypt's political experience with authoritarianism. At the same time, the question of political reforms is interlinked with the already thorny debates on modernity versus tradition, specificity versus liberalism, and, once more, role and meaning of Islam. Positions in these debates clearly cut across the commonly assumed divide between Islamists and non-Islamists.

Thus, while involving questions that are contested in the first place, the EMP in fact demanded a profound *change* of how Egypt defines itself. Indeed, it required a departure from the Egyptian state that defines itself in primarily pan-Arabic and Islamic terms, maintains a mixed socialist and liberal economic order, views the Europeans with suspicion but remains an important interlocutor of the "West," and perceives itself at standing at the center of a predominantly "Arab world." In view of the existence of quite different, and potentially mutually exclusive, identity preferences at the domestic level, the regime is well advised to avoid policies that entail the choice of one identity concept over another. Engaging consistently in the EMP would have been such a policy. Paradoxically, the nonresolution of the wider Arab–Israeli conflict permitted Cairo to maintain its course without notable domestic resistance or pressures, as opposition to

Israel's policy toward the Palestinians and its continuing control over the Islamic sites in East Jerusalem indeed unite inherently incompatible domestic preferences. Moreover, the collapse of Middle East peacemaking permitted the reinforcement of Egypt's unifying identity themes within the EMP, and seemed to justify the regime's hesitant position toward Euro-Mediterranean regional security. Thus, the fate of the peace process was not the reason for Egypt's reluctance toward Euro-Mediterranean region-building. Rather, this reluctance is a result of Egypt's self-definition, along with the imperatives imposed by Egypt's domestic identity divisions.

6

Morocco

In our investigation of the link between contested state identities and Euro-Mediterranean regional security, Morocco is the last of our case studies. According to the preliminary findings, Morocco is less plagued by domestic identity conflicts, while it was also actively participating in the Euro-Mediterranean Partnership in the time span under consideration (November 1995 until the end of 2002). Thus, Morocco seems to provide an "inverse" example of our argument. While seeking to test and explain the preliminary findings, this chapter starts with a discussion of Morocco's state identity, its main themes and challengers. In this context, it is necessary to explore the monarchy's institutional powers over domestic and identity politics. Subsequently, alternative concepts of Morocco's state identity are assessed. When and why did alternative interpretations emerge, what characterizes competing concepts, and how significant are they in present-day Morocco? Shifting the attention to the state level, the second part of this chapter concentrates on Morocco's participation in and strategy toward the EMP. The last part of this chapter seeks to link Morocco's identity features to its policy toward Euro-Mediterranean regional security.

Morocco's State Identity

According to John Entelis (1989: 25) "Moroccan society is diverse but not divided." While elaborating on this observation, what are both the cognitive and the institutional dimensions of Morocco's state identity? Of what does the portrayed consensus exist, what are the inherent ambiguities, and which concepts challenge, or outright defy, the prevalent interpretation of Morocco's identity?

The Monarchy and Islam

Historical Background

Although Morocco—officially *al-Mamlaka al-Maghrebiyya* (the Western Kingdom)—reached political independence from European colonial rule in 1956, the country "was not a creation of colonial map-making" (Pennell 2000: 297). Since the founding of the first Muslim kingdom in the eights century, a sultan-king had more or less continually ruled the space that was formerly known as *al-Maghreb al-Aqsa* (the farthest West), and the 'Alawi dynasty has been governing the country in a constant chain of rule since the seventeenth century. Morocco was never part of the Ottoman Empire, and compared to other Maghreb states, the period of European colonial rule, namely 44 years, was relatively short.[1] Thus, while the sociocultural impact of colonialism remained limited, modern Morocco relies on a long political tradition that has seen the centralization of powers around the 'Alawi monarchy (Laroui 1977).

The role of the monarchy and its portrayed anchorage in religious tradition are crucial for understanding Moroccan politics (Kably 1999). Through inheritance, the king is believed to possess *baraka*, that is, divine blessing, which must be validated through successful action (Bourqia 1999; Munson 1993).[2] The king's investiture is legitimized through the oath of allegiance (*ba'ya*) by religious scholars (the *'ulama*), thus drawing a parallel to the allegiance granted to the Prophet Mohammed by his early followers. Above all, this practice has a symbolic importance, since religious scholars have seldom objected to a future sultan or king (Tozy 1999: 103 ff.; Hassan II 1993: 93). Moreover, *baraka* and the oath of allegiance are combined with the concept of *sharifian* rule, that is, descent from the Prophet Mohammed through his daughter Fatima and his son-in-law Ali. According to the dominant historical narrative, *sharifian* rulers repeatedly saved the country from foreign invaders, and succeeded in preserving internal unity through their divine standing (Hammoudi 1997: 14–17).

Paradoxically, French and Spanish colonial rule reinforced the legitimacy of the *sharifian* monarchy, which had witnessed a period of relative decline between the end of the nineteenth and the early twentieth century. Indeed, after the death of Sultan Moulay Hassan in 1894, the monarchy was challenged by tribal chiefs allied to religious leaders, wars between tribes, and a growing independence movement that initially aimed at establishing a republic (Laroui 1977; Julien 1978). After the establishment of the French Protectorate in 1912, the colonial powers sought to forge political alliances with rural notables, who were part of the sultanate's traditional power base. The colonialists also adopted a decree that would have divided the country between Arabs and Berbers. The sultan's refusal to sign the decree turned him into a central figure of the growing popular resistance against colonial rule. As Entelis (1989: 17) remarks, "French colonial insensitivity and/or stupidity, in the manner in which it treated the sultan personally (he was imprisoned) and the sultanate institutionally (it was expressly bypassed), almost guaranteed that nationalist sentiments would crystallize around man and throne."

Indeed, after the sultan returned from exile in 1955 and became king in 1956, Mohammed V was a national hero for his leading role in the struggle for independence.[3] In popular perception, his ability to liberate the country was a proof of his *baraka*. Thus, Morocco's independence fused with the institution of the monarchy and its religious foundations. Clifford Geertz (1968: 81) remarks in this context that there are probably few other cases "in which the hero-leader of the revolution and independence was engulfed in religious authority, over and above the political, as Muhammed V was in Morocco in 1956." At the same time, the monarchy inherited from the colonial powers a centralized bureaucracy, a modern army, and control over areas that had previously resisted to the sultanate's rule (Julien 1978).

Symbolic Politics, Coercion, and Reforms

We may agree with the contention that "the celebrated link between the King and his subjects is in fact a recent slogan which has been transformed into an explanatory construct" (Hammoudi 1997: 16). However, the monarchy has remained the leitmotif of Morocco's identity and political life. This is partly due to the monarchy's extensive institutional powers, its control over religious narratives, along with a mixed strategy of coercion and accommodation toward the opposition.

Institutionally, Morocco is an absolute hereditary monarchy. Although the 1962 constitution established a multiparty system and confirmed the separation of powers, it also stipulates that the king is the sovereign and the supreme representative of the nation, and the guardian of Islam and of the constitution itself (Tozy 1999: 92). *Qua* constitution, the king enjoys judicial immunity, and the law forbids to criticize the monarch, or to depict him in a humorous way (Maghraoui 2001). The king is also the supreme religious authority in Morocco, and his title of "Commander of the Faithful" (*amir al-mu'minin*) is justified through his *sharifian* lineage. Hence, the monarch could occupy the center of the religious discourse, which arguably narrows down the playing field of *religiously framed* political opposition (Waterbury 1970; Tozy 1999: 75–82). Over the decades, a number of constitutional amendments have strengthened the role of parliament.[4] But the Palace still appoints and may dismiss the prime minister, dissolve parliament, pass royal decrees, and revise the constitution by national referendum. In addition, the king appoints judges and magistrates, all governors, prefects, and directors of public agencies, along with four key ministers—interior, foreign affairs, defence, and religious affairs. The interior ministry has traditionally been extremely powerful, as it supervises the police and various security services, approves the allocation of regional budgets, and grants the necessary license to associations and political parties. More than that, it is in charge of organizing and supervising all elections. Indirectly, this provides the king with the exclusive control over the electoral process, which has repeatedly been accused of fraud.

In terms of symbolic politics, the Palace has embedded its powers into Islam and traditional cultural themes. This is certainly facilitated by the fact that religion has traditionally been an integral part of Moroccan culture and school education. Thus, the monarchy as a monolithic concept of power is presented as corresponding to Islam's principle of monotheism. Similarly, Islam has served to justify the need for obedience to the ruler by pointing to the threat of anarchy (*fitna*), which the Qur'an considers as a calamity. In fact, after the harsh suppression of the 1965 uprisings, King Hassan II maintained that the prevention of *fitna* would justify the sacrifice of two thirds of the community of believers (Tozy 1999: 32). Hence, the constitution defines obedience as a civil duty, the *shari'a* makes of it a religious obligation, while *sharifism* transforms it into a source of blessing (Tozy 1999: 82).

Different religious narratives and ceremonies construct and reproduce the bond between the monarchy and Islam, between the king and his people, and between past and present. In fact, the monarchy's staging of cultural-religious performances has been described as a real innovation in post-independence Morocco (Combs-Schilling 1999). In this vein, the monarchy celebrates the allegiance (*ba'ya*) of the people—represented by religious scholars, merchants, and aristocratic families—during the annual Feast of the Throne ever since Rabat annexed large parts of the disputed Western Sahara in 1979. This followed the 1975 "Green March," a royally orchestrated popular march in which 350,000 Moroccans participated. The Palace thus linked its religious authority to Morocco's "territorial integrity," thus reinvigorating the former (Mednicoff 1998). The monarchy also depicted Morocco's claims on the Western Sahara as a struggle against *secular* Algeria, which, as ally of the Polisario Front, traditionally supported the territory's independence (Leveau 1984: 22). In addition, the king plays a symbolic role in the Feast of the Prophet's birthday by presenting himself as "the first under equals." Certainly, in contrast to the king's religious importance as portrayed in the state-controlled media, Henry Munson (1993: 115–118) noted that the monarchy is irrelevant in Muslim rituals and prayers. Nevertheless, the monarchy's religious legitimacy is widely accepted.

Besides symbolic politics, Morocco's kings employed means of plain coercion in order to forge consensus around the Palace and the state bureaucracy—termed *makhzan*.[5] In fact, Mohammed V and, after his death in 1961, Hassan II, waged a permanent power struggle with opposition forces, which reached a peak with the 1971 and 1972 attempted military coups and the unsuccessful Marxist insurrection in 1973. In this struggle, the monarchy relied on the suppression of demonstrations, incarcerations, torture, exiling, and the assassination of political rivals. While Mohammed V was partly venerated because of his personal charisma and moderation, Hassan II relied on a system of repression and fear. The degree of coercion slightly decreased after 1975, as the Western Sahara issue created a new pillar of national consensus. This strategy of coercion, along with the co-option of other political forces, builds on a powerful "master-and-disciple" schema, which exploits persisting patriarchic and authoritarian patterns in many Arab societies (Ben Haddou 1997; Sharabi 1988; UNDP 2005: 17–18). Thus, Morocco's king became the central figure in a complex patronage system, which attaches groups and individuals to the Palace through the granting of favors, prestige, and power. Within this system, the king also cultivates the role of an arbiter who stands above private interests. Of course, this is more of a fairy tale, but as Abdallah Hammoudi (1997: 23) argues: "So we are dealing with a fiction—but a fiction which is accepted by the political actors for a variety of reasons."

Since the early 1990s, the monarchy has been engaged in a gradual political reform process, while the treatment of political opponents notably improved. Thus, as a reaction to growing international criticism, Hassan II established a human-rights ministry in 1993 and reformed the procedures for administrative detention. A comprehensive amnesty for political prisoners followed in July 1994. Similarly, the king supervised the drafting of the 1992 constitution, which stipulated that the prime minister, instead of the king, appoints the cabinet ministers. After the 1997 elections, the king appointed the leader of the former opposition as prime minister, termed *alternance* (Layachi 1999: 43–60; Martín-Muñoz 2000). And reacting to the demands of women's associations, Hassan II set up a royal committee to study a reform of the personal status law in 1992. King Mohammed VI, who ascended the throne in July 1999, has been continuing the path of incrementally administered and royally orchestrated change initiated by his father. Thus, he dismissed the powerful and long-term minister of interior Driss Basri, who had become the symbol of the *makhzan*'s suppression. Furthermore, Mohammed VI granted an encompassing amnesty to political prisoners, and allowed exiled political adversaries to return to Morocco, such as Abraham Serfaty and the family of the assassinated Mehdi Ben Barka. Similarly, Mohammed VI started to promote women's rights and eventually reformed the family code in 2003. In view of the Berbers' increasing demand for autonomy in neighboring Algeria, the king also founded a royal institute for Berber—or, better, *Amazigh*—culture. Still under the sign of reform, dossiers about "disappeared" persons were made public, and the state started to pay compensation to the victim's families. Mohammed VI also set up a reconciliation commission to cope with the iron rule of his father (*Le Monde* April 13, 2005). And the fight against corruption—until recently no common word in Morocco—became a public issue (Denoeux 2000). Finally, the parliamentary elections of September 2002 were comparatively fair.

Morocco's Royally Manipulated Identity Discourse
Relying on its extensive institutional powers, the Palace has traditionally defined Morocco's identity by emphasizing Morocco's cultural inclusiveness, juxtaposing "tradition" and "modernity," and promoting a tolerant version of Islam.

Rahma Bourqia (1999: 253) asserts that while Islam is the core element of Morocco's identity, "Moroccans find themselves within concentric circles of identities (Moroccan, Arab, Berber, African, North African, Muslim)." Indeed, the monarchy has a long tradition of depicting Morocco as a link between different worlds (Zartman 1983: 105), which is regularly presented as an asset. In this vein, King Mohammed VI (2001b) referred to the different origins of Moroccans—Berber, Arab, African, Andalusian—as expressions of the "Moroccan spirit" (*"le génie marocain"*).[6] Similarly, the late King Hassan II declared that Morocco's history "rests on multiple foundations, which are solid and healthy, on foundations that are rich through their diversity, spirit, and authenticity" (quoted in Mohammed VI 2001a). Addressing the Moroccan people in the 2001 Feast of the Throne, Mohammed VI maintained that Morocco is as much "characterized by its diversity and its pluralistic character, as it distinguishes itself through its homogeneity, its unity and its originality throughout history" (Mohammed VI 2001a). On another occasion, the monarch stressed that Morocco is a "real melting-pot. It is the country of North Africa that is most diverse. One can find here Andalusian, African, Jewish, and Arab culture" (Mohammed VI 2001c). Similarly, he emphasized that Morocco is committed to the "values and objectives of unity, solidarity, cooperation, and good neighborhood with its brothers and friends of the Arab Maghreb, Africa, and the Arab and Islamic world," while he designated Morocco as a "factor of stability and peace in its Maghreb, Arab, Islamic, Euro-Mediterranean, African and American [*sic*] environment" (Mohammed VI 2001d).

Regarding the depicted harmony between tradition and modernity in Morocco's official discourse, Hassan II (1998) for instance asserted the aim of building "a nation that is proud on its authenticity and endowed with a value system, which is open towards other experiences and permeable to external contributions." Similarly, the former king emphasized that Morocco "remains true to its tradition of being the land of encounter, of brewing of cultures and civilizations, always open towards its immediate, regional, and international environment" (Hassan II 1997a). On another occasion, Hassan II (1999) stated that Morocco is a country "of faith, tolerance, openness, justice and solidarity." His successor, Mohammed VI, has been reiterating that Morocco's tolerant version of Islam always coexisted with modernity. Thus, he depicted the outstanding feature of Moroccans to be "at the same time Muslims, wholehearted and faithful to all principles, proud of their spirituality and their convictions, and nevertheless fully inscribed in the universal values of humanism and modernity that are most widely shared in the world" (Mohammed VI 2001c).

Consensus, Diversity, and Divisions

According to Entelis (1989: 25), "male-female, urban-rural, sedentary-nomadic, secular-religious, scripturalist-saintly, and Arab-Berber differences remain as socioanthropological categories relevant" in Morocco. Yet in his opinion, "these axes are at best understood as complementary parts of a single cultural tradition." Entelis's assessment may underestimate the monarchy's coercive role in forging consensus, since different domestic preferences regarding Morocco's political set-up have always existed. The complex relationship between diversity, consensus, and challengers is explored in the following sections.

Background

From the outset, Morocco's independence movement, which emerged in the 1930s, comprised very different ideas on the future political set-up of the country. It included religious scholars of the *Salafi* movement, who opposed divine kingship on religious grounds and advocated a return to "true" Islam (Munson 1993; Al-Fassi 1954). But it also comprised Morocco's bourgeoisie, along with secularist intellectuals who promoted Marxist-Leninist ideas. For strategic reasons, the movement and its leading political party *Istiqlal* (Independence) rallied around King Mohammed V in their fight against European colonial rule.

However, there was a broad popular support for limiting the king's powers once independence was reached (Leveau 1997: 105). While the monarchy refused to do so, the ideological differences within the *Istiqlal* prompted the breakaway of the socialist-oriented *Union Nationale des Forces Populaires* (UNFP) under Mehdi Ben Barka in 1959. John Waterbury (1970) observed a difference between devout *Salafi* scholars and secular, French-educated intellectuals among Morocco's elites. In practice, however, this distinction was blurred, as many UNFP supporters were religious, such as the *Salafi* reformist and former minister of the crown Mohammed bin al-'Arbi al-'Alawi (Munson 1993: 109). While the *Istiqlal* decided to participate in the government in the early 1960s, the UNFP returned to the opposition after a short government intermezzo in 1959–1960, and denounced the Moroccan monarchy for its archaic nature (Munson 1993: 132). Since socialist and Marxist ideas enjoyed a growing popular support, the monarchy harshly repressed the opposition organized around the UNFP and the trade unions during much of the 1960s and 1970s. The repressive measures included for instance the 1963 trial of prominent Marxist leaders on charges of having plotted to kill the king, the 1965 kidnapping and assassination of Mehdi Ben-Barka in France, the temporary banning of the UNFP in 1973, and the outlawing of the Marxist-oriented student organizations between 1973 and 1979 (Zartman 1988; Waterbury 1970; Munson 1993). On the other hand, the failed military coups of 1971 and 1972 also brought the existence of a "militarist culture" (Entelis 1998: 9) to the fore. While the plotting officers were imprisoned or liquidated, the attempted coups prompted Hassan II to increase the royal oversight over the army.

Islamist preferences became salient from the late 1970s on, particularly following the "Islamic revolution" in Iran in 1978–1979 that prompted widespread enthusiasm among Moroccans. The monarchy also reacted with repression toward the Islamist challenge, particularly since the mentor of Morocco's largest Islamist movement, Abdessalam Yassine, had openly criticized the monarchy's allegedly heretic rule. While the Islamist movement remained illegal, Yassine was alternatively jailed, hospitalized in a psychiatric clinic, or put under house arrest. Yet the large demonstrations during the 1991 Gulf War evidenced the "enormous capacity of the Islamists to rally support" (Desrues and Moyano 2001: 38), and prompted Hassan II to ensure that the Moroccan troops dispatched to Kuwait under the U.S.-led alliance would not engage in the fighting. The 1991 Gulf War also animated some of Morocco's rather lethargic political parties, along with labor federations and civil society organizations, giving them the opportunity to mobilize opposition to the monarchy (Hegasy 1997: 82; Ibrahim 1993).

Facing economic difficulties and an astronomic external debt in the early 1980s, Morocco started an economic reform process following the prescriptions of the IMF and the World Bank. Entailing the erosion of the providential (and legitimizing) basis of the *makhzan*, the resulting elimination of food subsidies sparked popular protests. Yet the "bread riots" of 1981, 1984, and 1990 also prompted demands for *political* reforms (Layachi 1999; Sadiki 2000). At the same time, high unemployment, poverty, a flawed education system, and high illiteracy rates—particularly among rural women—continued to exert pressures on the regime (World Bank 1996). Hence, the monarchy started a cautious political reform process, which also aimed at preparing the country for the royal succession in view of Hassan's ailing health. Indeed, according to Gema Martín-Muñoz (2000: 98), these challenges "led the Moroccan élite to the conclusion that, given the profound changes affecting the country, it would have to redefine itself through institutional reform." But with the growing space for voicing opposition conceded by the monarchy, the politicization of Morocco's civil society grew, and the calls for democratic reforms have increased ever since (Hegasy 1997; Denoeux 2000; Roque 2004). With it, different domestic preferences became more visible than before.

The "Consensus"

Pluralism characterizes Moroccan politics and society. In the previous legislature, the parliament comprised fifteen political parties of which nine formed the government. Twenty-three parties entered parliament after the 2002 elections, and the current government comprises six political parties. Compared to other Arab states, Morocco has a relatively free and diverse press, although it is recurrently subject to state intervention. Moreover, an impressively large number of NGOs are operating in Morocco (Hegasy 1997; Roque 2004). However, in Morocco's "manipulated pluralism" (Zartman 1988: 64), the monarchy determines the predominant cultural paradigm, along with the rules and playing field of politics. Although some scholars claim that the royally determined "frame" is accepted by both the elites and the broad population (Tozy 1999: 131; Suleiman 1985), the Palace's control over the *culturally possible* and *politically admissible* poses a methodological problem, as in the case of Egypt. Indeed, most Moroccan government officials usually refrain from expressing positions that deviate from the "official line," which casts a doubt on whether the portrayed consensus fully corresponds to reality.

However, three factors are significant here: First, the concept of "tradition" is widely accepted. In this vein, the prominent Moroccan philosopher Mohammed 'Abed Al-Jabri (1999a) maintains that tradition (*turath*) is a pivotal reference point of both Arab-Islamic philosophy and current Arab-Islamic political thought. Second, there is a certain consensus around the idea that Islam shall play a role in Moroccan public life. Indeed, there are no major political forces in Morocco that promote a clear-cut separation between state and religion (Hegasy 1997; Al-Jabri 1999a, 1999b).[7] This, in turn, implies a critical position toward, or an outright rejection of, the "Western" concept of a secular democracy. Finally, the stipulated consensus around monarchy, Islam, and Moroccan culture is quite inclusive, as it allows for a combination of *Salafi* scripturalism, *Sufi* mysticism, orthodox elements, and popular beliefs (Tozy 1999). Similarly, Morocco's identity allows for a "cultural synthesis" (Entelis 1998: 6), combining European (and particularly French) cultural pattern with Islam, Arabic, and *Amazigh* culture, along with a variety of local sub-identities.

Diversity within the Consensus

Often led by high-ranking officials or individuals who are close to the Palace, several political parties defend the status quo in Moroccan politics. The explicitly pro-royal *Wifaq* (Entente) comprises a party that represents the Berber movement, the *Mouvement Populaire* (MP), along with the *Union Constitutionnelle* (UC), and the *Parti National Démocratique* (PND). Moreover, the allegedly independent *Rassemblement National des Indépendants* (RNI) supports the monarchy. In the 1997 parliamentary elections, the *Wifaq* and other pro-royal parties gained more than half of the total 325 parliamentary seats (Layachi 1999; Desrues and Moyano 2001; Martín-Muñoz 2000).[8]

A slightly different interpretation within the consensus corresponds to the *Salafi* tradition of aiming to limit the monarchy's absolute power. Embedded in conservative values, this concept asserts Islam's dominant role in Moroccan politics and society. At least implicitly, the *Salafi* preference aims at resuscitating a glorious past as a means to reaffirm Morocco's identity (Al-Jabri 1999a). In parliamentary politics, the *Istiqlal*—the second-largest party in the current legislature—promotes this concept most notably.[9] Although the party belongs to the "democratic bloc" (*al-Koutla*) and is part of the government coalition since 1997, its rhetoric has been characterized as nationalist-religious of *Salafi* inspiration (Martín-Muñoz 2000: 126).

Another preference within the consensus combines the support for a constitutional democracy with socialist or social-democratic ideas, while the relation between Islam and politics is left obscure. In Moroccan politics, the *Union Socialiste des Forces Populaires* (USFP), which split from the UNFP in the late 1970s, promotes this concept most notably. It became the largest party of the *Koutla* after the 1997 elections, and its former leader, Abderrahman Youssoufi, served as prime minister in the *alternance* government between 1998 and 2002.[10] Yet while supporting a social market economy and a pro-Western foreign-policy orientation, the party's most outspoken ideologue Al-Jabri (1999a) warns of blindly adopting "Western" concepts without relying on the rationalist and liberal achievements of Arab-Islamic philosophy. In general, this concept finds a large support among Moroccan intellectuals and Morocco's independent NGOs.[11] But while obviously refraining from calling for the abolition of the monarchy, Islam often remains a reference point in one way or another. Thus, it is illustrating that Fatima Mernissi, Morocco's most prominent women's rights activist, anchors the demands for gender equality in the Qur'an and the Prophetic Sayings, showing that Islam permits for such an interpretation (Mernissi 1994).

Still within what is commonly termed the Moroccan Left, some promote Marxist ideas and may question the role of religion. But even this orientation implicitly treats Arab-Islamic tradition as a reference point (Al-Jabri 1999a). This orientation is represented by the formerly communist *Parti du Progrès Socialiste* (PPS), which currently holds 11 parliamentary seats, and the new *Front des Forces Démocratiques* (FFD), holding 12 seats, along with other splinter parties. The Marxist-oriented parties that traditionally accepted the legitimacy of the monarchy have been termed "the Leftists of Her Majesty" (*Jeune Afrique* 1306, January 15, 1986).

Finally, in the last decade, a moderate Islamist preference was admitted into the royally manipulated "consensus." Following the integration of an Islamist group into the pro-royalist party of Abdelkarim Khatib, a former minister, the *Parti de la Justice et du Développement* (PJD) represents a pro-royal Islamist preference. While obtaining only nine seats in the 1997 elections—probably due to electoral fraud (Leveau 1998)—the PJD gained 42 seats in the 2002 elections, thus becoming the third-largest party. This preference envisages the implementation of *shari'a* law, while the "return to pure Islam" is portrayed as the solution to various problems. Yet in contrast to the strategy of radical Islamists, the PJD aims at imposing its vision with the support of society. In addition, the PJD thus far refrained from opposing the monarchy *on religious grounds* (Tozy 2000b; Willis 2000). Certainly, the PJD's moderation is also dictated by the limits of Moroccan politics, particularly considering the events of the 1990s in neighboring Algeria, along with the post–9/11 climate. However, the domestic support for this orientation is probably stronger than the electoral strength of the PJD. Indeed, worried to perform too well and thus prompting the regime's repression, the PJD had deliberately limited its electoral campaign and number of candidates in the 2002 elections (Willis 2004).

The Challengers
Three main concepts challenge the consensus as defined by the monarchy. The first one espouses the separation between state and religion and characterizes what is usually termed the "radical Left." Although distinctions are sometimes blurred, there are two main versions of this orientation. One favors a liberal, "Western"-style democracy, whereas the other is embedded in the pan-Arab tradition of the 1950s and 1960s and envisages the establishment of a socialist republic. As a result of the monarchy's repression, the radical Left, which in the past had openly called for an overthrow of the monarchy and questioned the legitimacy of Morocco's occupation of the Western Sahara, went

underground or into exile—in the event that its leaders were not jailed or liquidated. With the return of many former opposition leaders from exile or their release from prison in the 1990s, there has been a certain revival of socialist-inspired secular ideas. Thus, the fusion between Morocco's "mainstream Left" and royal power increasingly became the subject of open criticism—not always without consequences. Indeed, following a number of critical articles on these and similar issues, the weekly newspapers *Le Journal / As-Sahifa* and *Demain* were closed in December 2000, along with the paper of the USFP's youth organization *Shabiba Ittihadia* (Jamaï 2001).[12] In addition, many human-rights and women's associations advocate a liberal and secular set-up of the state (Hegasy 1997). While the radical Left was absent from Moroccan politics until 2002, the *Parti de la Gauche Socialiste Unifiée* (GSU) obtained three seats in the 2002 legislative elections.

Second, the failed military coups of 1971, 1972, and 1983 showed that specific segments of Moroccan society, notably among the officers of the armed forces, support the establishment of a military regime. Embedded in paternalistic and authoritarian values, this preference favors "discipline, honesty, and sacrifice at the expense of democracy, liberty, and justice" (Entelis 1989: 89). Although many of Morocco's army officers are Berbers, the prevalence of this preference seems to be linked to their rural and bourgeois background rather than to ethnicity (Leveau 1997: 106). At the present, the military appears loyal to the throne, but the significance of this domestic preference remains uncertain.

Finally, the most important challenger to Morocco's royally orchestrated consensus remains the (illegal) Islamist movement that is mainly organized around Abdessalam Yassine's *al-'Adl wa-al-Ihsan* (Justice and Charity). Partly combined with *Sufi* mysticism, this orientation promotes the message that Islam is the "salvation," and openly criticizes the existing political order for its corruption, incompetence, and submission to "Western" influence. Similarly, the fusion of Islam and the monarchy, the king's religious authority, the idea of *baraka*, and the concept of hereditary power are rejected on *religious* grounds (Tozy 1999: 258–267). Certainly, different religious traditions, such as the *Salafi* movement, have made similar claims beforehand, yet Yassine's criticism is comparatively harsh and polemic. This became visible in Yassine's memorandum of February 2000, which attacked both the present king and the late Hassan II for their moral and material corruption, and proposed to use the monarchy's personal fortune in order to pay off Morocco's foreign debts.[13]

Altogether, the growing domestic support for Islamist preferences has mainly three reasons: First, as in other Arab states, the Islamists are not associated with the corrupt political system and thus represent the "real" opposition. Second, the Islamists succeeded in establishing an extensive social network for the poor and deprived, thus increasing their legitimacy. Third, with diminishing state repression, the Islamists' space of maneuver has grown. As in other Arab states, Morocco's Islamists particularly appeal to the young generation—university students and uneducated youth alike (Tozy 1999: 129–131). Yet there are different assessments of how strong and "dangerous" Morocco's Islamists are. Not surprisingly, the king usually dismisses the "Islamist threat" (Mohammed VI 2001b, 2001c). Mohamed Tozy (2000b) estimates that around 25–30 percent of the population supports either moderate or radical Islamist preferences. It has also been claimed that the potential for Islamist-inspired violence is limited in Morocco, as the monarchy traditionally occupied the religious discourse (Tozy 1999; Desrues and Moyano 2001: 26). However, the Islamist terror attacks in Casablanca in 2003 cast a doubt on this assessment. Moreover, the electoral success of the PJD in the 2002 elections undermines the argument that the king's status as "Commander of the Faithful" would prevent the Islamization of Moroccan politics, as Michael Willis (2004: 5) rightly pointed out.

Political Implications

Our discussion has shown that there are quite different domestic preferences regarding the set of values that are to define Moroccan politics and society. But what are the potential political implications of this finding?

There is no doubt that the monarchy's absolute powers restrict the relevance of alternative domestic preferences. As most political parties are not a full-fledged opposition, but rather part of the system, they support the status quo in the final analysis. Indeed, comparable to the case of Egypt, most legal Moroccan parties have a rather limited popular basis—maybe with the exception of the *Istiqlal*, the USFP, and the Islamists, the radical stream of which, however, remains illegal. Moreover, most parties lack of internal democratic structures, and rather rally around personalities than programs. Morocco's "atomized political system" (Desrues and Moyano 2001: 29) is accompanied by persisting fears over the *makhzan*'s arbitrary use of power, and a general popular distrust in the state and its institutions

(Leveau 1997: 111; Entelis 1998: 51; Mednicoff 1998). Thus, as in the case of Egypt, the experience with authoritarianism has left its traces on Morocco's political culture. Moreover, as the monarchy is highly skilled in what could be termed identity politics, it managed to "integrate the nationalistic and religious discourses, reflecting the importance of both in the process of formation of individual and collective identities in Moroccan society" (Desrues and Moyano 2001: 26). As the Palace traditionally defined Morocco's identity in a quite inclusive way, the potential for domestic fragmentation was reduced, while different policies were potentially legitimate and intelligible.

Nonetheless, the monarchy cannot ignore domestic preferences and developments. By integrating the most important legal opposition force into the *alternance* government after the 1997 elections, the regime reacted to the growing calls for political liberalization, along with the rising strength of the Islamists. Thus, the *Istiqlal* has been "used to confront doctrinal Islamism, and the USFP, together with the trade-union movement linked to it, for mobilising the disadvantaged population which would obviously resonate to [the Islamists'] propaganda" (Leveau 1997: 107). Moreover, in view of the Islamists' appeal to the poor and deprived, Mohammed VI started to publicly address the issue of poverty and illiteracy. Choosing to face the Islamists on their own terrain, the king launched a pilot literacy course for 10,000 men and women that took place in mosques throughout the country (Howe 2001).[14] Similarly, Mohammed VI visited the rural provinces in southern and central Morocco, which had not seen any royal visit in 30 years. Finally, although the admission of the PJD into parliamentary politics followed the old principle of *divide et impere*—both vis-à-vis the illegal Islamist movement and the *Istiqlal*—this example shows that domestic pressures forced the monarchy to alter the boundaries of the politically admissible. The September 2002 elections are a further evidence of this course of action. The decline of most pro-royal parties and the strengthening of both the *Istiqlal* and the PJD indicate that the electoral process has become fairer indeed. Yet the king still maintained his extensive political prerogatives, and the appointment of Driss Jettou as prime minister, a party-less technocrat, after the 2002 elections clearly underscores this fact.

In the realm of foreign policy, Pennell (2000: 391) asserts that the "monarchy's great flexibility, the ability to mobilize and manipulate different lines of authority, patronage and power, helped it to adapt itself to external pressures brought to bear by forces that were stronger than itself." Indeed, during the cold war, Morocco cultivated strong economic and military ties with the "West," in particular France and the United States, while it also succeeded in maintaining informal contacts with the former Soviet Union (Pennell 2000: 259–345).[15] Similarly, Morocco upheld a strong identification with the aspirations for Arab unity, along with the opposition to Zionism. Due to his status as *amir al mu'minin*, the Moroccan king presides the Al–Quds Committee of the Islamic Conference, which was created for protecting Islam's holy places in East Jerusalem. At the same time, however, Morocco used to defend quite independent positions vis-à-vis the Arab–Israeli conflict—for instance by meeting Shimon Peres in 1986 in Ifrane to discuss the Palestinian question, in spite of the protest of other Arab states. In the 1980s, Zartman (1983) sought to explain the "nearly inexplicable" absence of Islam in Moroccan foreign policy by pointing to the monarchy's exclusive powers to define foreign policy, along with the royally manipulated identity discourse that legitimized different lines of action. Thus, the Moroccan king "used the monarchy as a way of bridging the segments of Moroccan society, turning that diversity into a strength of his regime, and allowing him to face down the challenges from the victims of the modern economy inside Morocco, and his Arab rivals internationally" (Pennell 2000: 391). Yet the strengthening of Islamism in Morocco also affected the parameters of Moroccan foreign policy. Thus, the monarchy was repeatedly forced to reassess specific foreign policy decisions, such as during the 1991 Gulf War, as noted above. The monarchy had also to react to Israel's policy vis-à-vis the Palestinians after the collapse of the peace process, given the Islamists' ability to mobilize Morocco's population, as discussed below. Thus, against the backdrop of Morocco's political liberalization, and given the persistence of internal and external pressures, it remains to be seen whether the Moroccan monarchy will continue to be able to master the political identity game—the rules of which seem to be changing.

Morocco, the EU, and the EMP

While leaving Morocco's domestic scene aside for now, the following sections discuss the development of EU–Moroccan relations before and after the launching of the EMP. Subsequently, we assess Morocco's attitude and strategy toward the EMP.

Background

Since independence, Morocco had maintained intensive ties to Europe, particularly to the former colonial power France, and, to a lesser extent,

Spain. In cultural terms, Moroccan elites have been reluctant to abandon French language and culture, in spite of various, and partly successful, "Arabization" initiatives over the decades. In economic terms, France has remained Morocco's most important trading partner and investor, and it supplies the kingdom with bilateral aid and weapons up to the present.

From the outset of Euro-Moroccan relations, Brussels has been treating Morocco preferentially, but it also repeatedly declined to fully respond to Morocco's aspirations. Thus, the 1957 Treaty of Rome, which founded the EC, explicitly invited Morocco (and Tunisia) to negotiate association agreements, as noted above (Grilli 1993: 183–184). Yet during much of the 1960s, Morocco refrained from doing so since it would have entailed more disadvantages than benefits. Indeed, at that time, most Moroccan products—including agricultural products—enjoyed duty free entry to France. Rabat's aspirations of extending this practice to all the six EC founding members faced the resistance of first Italy, and then of the EC Commission, which, at that time sought to implement the Common Agricultural Policy (CAP). Initially, Brussels also rejected Morocco's wish of obtaining technical and financial assistance.

The first association agreement between the EC and Morocco, signed in March 1969, granted duty free access to Morocco's industrial products, which, however, had a marginal relevance for the Moroccan economy. The agreement fell short of Morocco's expectations, as it granted neither economic assistance nor far-reaching trade concessions in agriculture (representing 50 percent of Moroccan exports at that time). The 1976 bilateral trade agreement introduced economic assistance in form of financial protocols, but again, it did not grant access to Moroccan agricultural exports.[16] Similarly, immigration remained a contentious issue between the two sides, as EC member states had started to adopt an increasingly restrictive immigration policy from the 1970s on. Following the EC's southern enlargement in the 1980s, which led to a further discrimination against Moroccan products and nationals (Tovias 1996; White 2001), Rabat applied for full EC membership in 1984 and in 1987. The Moroccan minister in charge of the first membership application, Azeddine Ghessous, asked how it could be that "Europe [shall] not include Morocco" since "Spain is only fourteen kilometers away" (quoted in Lister 1997: 90). But Brussels rejected the applications on the ground that Morocco was not part of Europe.[17] In the 1980s, Morocco "voluntarily" accepted quotas on certain commodities, yet the EC repeatedly suspended free trade provisions regarding Moroccan textile products, and the EC's increasingly protectionist CAP further restrained the access of Morocco's agricultural products to EC markets (White 2001: 76 ff.; Grilli 1993: 191–195). Although, in turn, the EC's bilateral aid to Morocco had constantly grown over the decades, the total amount was still "modest in relation to Morocco's developments needs" (Damis 1998: 96).[18] At the beginning of the 1990s, Morocco continued to be economically dependent on its European neighbors, as 64 percent of its total exports went to the EC (IMF 1992). Europe was also the main origin of tourists visiting Morocco (Pennell 2000: 358).

With the European efforts to develop an encompassing Mediterranean policy from the early 1990s on, Morocco witnessed several political gestures. Thus, Brussels started a new dialogue on Euro–Maghreb relations in February 1992, France announced a new partnership with Morocco in November 1992, and the former EU Commission president visited the kingdom after Morocco's 1993 parliamentary elections. The events in Algeria in the early 1990s clearly provided the background to the pampering attitude of Brussels vis-à-vis Morocco. Indeed, "Morocco had the advantage of not being Algeria" (*The Economist* January 9, 1993: 38). In addition, Europe's energy interests were crucial, as the natural gas pipeline linking Algerian gas fields to Spain and Portugal through Morocco and the Strait of Gibraltar, which became operational in 1996, was under construction at that time (Khene 1997). The kingdom was also the first country that Brussels invited to renew its trade agreements while the EMP started to take shape, and preliminary discussions started in May 1992. But the usual pattern of European–Moroccan trade relations repeated itself. Indeed, in the exploratory talks Rabat maintained that the European proposals "fell short of Europe's desire to turn the agreement with Morocco into a model for a new generation of agreements" (quoted in Damis 1998: 99). Specifically, Rabat criticized the lack of concessions regarding trade in agriculture, the limited amount of financial aid, and the EU's unwillingness to address non-tariff barriers to trade. Thus, not seeing any substantial gains in a new accord, Morocco initially preferred to keep its 1976 agreement.

But at the beginning of 1994, Morocco reviewed its position. The bilateral negotiations on a new trade agreement, however, proved to be long and difficult. Indeed, although technically separated, the negotiations soon became intertwined with the mid-term review of the four-year bilateral agreement on fisheries of 1992, which granted Spanish and Portuguese fishing fleets access to Moroccan territorial waters. Rabat insisted that Europe had to reduce its fishing capacity, and since both sides could not agree, the accord lapsed in April 1995, prompting Morocco to ban European fishing fleets from its waters.[19] Due to the EU's interests in negotiating fisheries and Morocco's insistence to first address the issue of agriculture within the new trade agreement, the negotiations temporarily broke down at the beginning of 1995. This period was accompanied by serious tensions between Morocco and the EU, and particularly Spain, which is most concerned by the issue of fisheries.

The Launching of the EMP

When the EU launched the EMP in November 1995, a new Euro-Mediterranean Association Agreement with Morocco had just been initialed. After Israel and Tunisia, Morocco was the third country to eventually sign a Euro-Mediterranean agreement in 1996. As for most southern EMP partners, the prospect of upgrading bilateral trade relations with the EU was Morocco's key interest in the Euro-Mediterranean project.

The EU Commission, on its part, was interested in concluding the negotiations with Morocco and resolving the thorny issue of fisheries before the Barcelona Conference of November 1995 would take place. Given the asymmetry of the respective bargaining power, Morocco's ability to play its trump card in the negotiations, namely fisheries, was limited. Thus, Morocco eventually attenuated its original demands regarding European fishing rights, and it also accepted the terms of the new association agreement (Commission 1995b). With the aim of establishing a free-trade area in industrial goods until 2010, the agreement applies different time-tables for the gradual reduction of customs duties on EU imports.[20] The agreement also stipulates a slight overall reduction (and in few cases the elimination) of EU import duties on Moroccan agricultural exports. Yet quotas and seasonal restrictions on products that are competitive to the EU's products persist, which comprise some of Morocco's most important agricultural products, such as tomatoes and citrus fruits (Commission 1995b). Since most Moroccan *industrial* products already enjoyed duty-free access to European markets under the previous agreement, the real challenge for Morocco is to open up its markets to EU competition. For Morocco, this challenge entails far-reaching economic, social, and financial reforms.[21] The funds allocated to Morocco under the MEDA I program (1996–1999) accounted for € 630 million, of which € 265 million were earmarked for economic restructuring (*Middle*

East Economic Digest February 11, 2000: 18). Yet only the costs of dismantling tariffs on EU imports were estimated at € 130–140 million a year (Commission 2001). In spite of the EU's meager financial support, for Rabat the EMP nevertheless represented an opportunity to receive assistance for a course of action in which it had started to engage *before* the EMP was launched.

In addition, the EMP provided an institutionalized framework for political consultations, while it also permitted to address the issue of immigration. However, both sides maintained notably differed perspectives on this issue. In fact, during the bilateral negotiations, Morocco also sought to use immigration as a bargaining card. "Give us a deal," Morocco threatened, "or we will give you our people," as *The Economist* (September 9, 1995: 47–48) put it. The 1996 agreement explicitly states the aim of improving the conditions of Moroccan migrant workers in Europe. Yet the rules for "regulating" Moroccan immigration to Europe, along with the question of who is in charge and under which conditions, caused several disputes between the two sides.

Hence, although the EMP fell short of Morocco's aspirations, it was compatible with Rabat's overall objectives in view of its course of cautious economic and political reforms that had started in the early 1990s. It is important to stress that Morocco has traditionally considered its relations to Europe as its most vital foreign-policy interest, as the Moroccan regime and the media have not ceased to stress (Benaïssa 2002; Mohammed VI 2000a).

Morocco, the EMP, and EU–Moroccan Relations

EU officials constantly stressed the importance of Morocco ever since the EMP was launched (Patten 1999a). In this vein, Pascal Lamy, former EU trade commissioner, described Morocco as a "privileged partner" (quoted in Mansour 2001: 5) and Javier Solana termed it a "major Mediterranean interlocutor" (quoted in *European Report* July 11, 2001: 528). As a Moroccan official has put it to the author, the kingdom was a very dynamic and constructive partner in the EMP in the time-span under consideration.[22] Rabat also repeatedly called for reinvigorating the Barcelona Process whenever it was stalled, for instance due to the events in the Middle East (Mohammed VI 2000b, 2000c). And the EMP Action Plan adopted at the 2002 Euro-Mediterranean foreign minister meeting in Valencia (Commission 2002b) incorporated many of Morocco's official propositions, such as strengthening sub-regional cooperation and establishing a cross-cultural dialogue in the post-9/11 era (Fassi Fihri 2002). In general, Morocco was engaged in a reform process according to the "spirit" of Barcelona, and it has been participating in a large number of EMP projects over the years. Much to the EU's satisfaction, Morocco also improved its human-rights records over the last decade, which, compared to most other EMP partners, is quite advanced. Rabat was also active in fostering sub-regional cooperation in the framework of the Agadir process, a development the EU strongly favored (Commission 2001: 3).[23] In the same spirit, Morocco concluded a free-trade agreement with Tunisia in March 1999.

Until 2001, almost half of the € 630 million under MEDA I were utilized for structural adjustment programs and the improvement of Morocco's socioeconomic balance. Thus, EMP projects covered privatization, standardization and quality management, vocational training, and enterprise competitiveness. Others programs aimed at the improvement of the standard of living in Morocco's urban and poor rural areas, thus addressing water supply and sanitation, infrastructure, land irrigation, health care, education, housing, and job creation. The EU also financed the institutional development of Morocco's public administration as well as of NGOs. Similarly, the € 500 million of EIB loans between 1996 and 2001 targeted the improvement of infrastructure, the environment and the business sector (Commission 2001). Altogether, the EU was satisfied with the implementation of the bilateral association agreement, which officially entered into force in March 2000—although some EU officials occasionally criticized Morocco's slow pace of reforms (Mansour 2001).

In spite of the efforts, however, Morocco's socioeconomic indicators did not improve considerably in the time-span under review. Economic growth was slow and unstable, mainly due to Morocco's heavy dependency on agriculture and repeated periods of drought. Coupled with an annual increase of the labor force by 2.6 percent, unemployment and poverty actually increased (Commission 2001). Morocco's fiscal policy recurrently caused "preoccupations," as the EU stated. Yet in spite of the 2001 devaluation of the dirham by 5 percent, Morocco's macro-economic stability was maintained. Rabat has engaged in far-reaching privatization schemes, and its external debt decreased over the last decade, mainly due to the debts rescheduling and conversion by the EU and single EU member states (Commission 2001: 12–13). However, raising unemployment, reduced state revenues, and growing trade dependency on the EU characterize Morocco's economic development until the present.

In spite of an overall positive picture of Morocco's EMP participation, there were some contested issues. To begin with, as other EMP partners, Morocco criticized the initial slow disbursement of MEDA funds, which according to Moroccan officials had only reached 14 percent of the commitment at the end of 1999 (*Africa News Service* January 1, 2000). In this context, Rabat was also unsatisfied with the EU's red tape and centralized decision-making procedure on MEDA-funded projects. Similarly, Moroccan officials (along with their colleagues of other EMP partners) lamented the unequal distribution of EU aid to the southern Mediterranean as compared to Eastern and Central Europe (*Maghreb Arab Press* November 6, 2000). Rabat also voiced its incertitude regarding the impact of the EU's eastern enlargement on EU–Mediterranean relations (Benaïssa 2002).

Yet immigration remained one of the most controversial issues between the two sides. Much in accordance with the EU's rhetoric, Rabat repeatedly stressed that the stability of the Mediterranean region substantially depended on the reduction of developmental gaps between the two shores. Thus, in view of the approximately 2 million Moroccans living in the EU, Rabat repeatedly argued that the living conditions of legal Moroccan workers residing in the EU had to be improved. On one occasion, Foreign Minister Benaïssa (2002) even declared that this was the most important concern of Moroccan foreign policy. At the same time, Morocco was (and is) interested in increasing the number of legal Moroccan workers in the EU, thus reducing domestic unemployment and boosting the remittances of foreign workers, which is one of the largest sources of foreign currency (after the revenues from the sale of phosphates and tourism).[24] Thus, during a visit to the European Parliament in October 2001, Moroccan parliamentarians maintained that the "improvement of the circulation of people" was a key element for the "Euro-Mediterranean construction" (quoted in *Le Matin* October 5, 2001).

For the EU, however, improving the circulation of people was certainly not the objective of the EMP, but rather to reduce migration, particularly the illegal one—which is often associated with "security threats." In response, Foreign Minister Benaïssa called upon the EU to go beyond this *"vision sécuritaire"* and to adopt a global and humanistic approach to immigration (quoted in Mansour 2001: 4). Similarly, Morocco's former ambassador to the EU, Aïcha Belarbi, criticized the concept of "fortress Europe" (*Maghreb Arab Press* November 6, 2000). And at the 2002 Euro-Mediterranean meeting in Valencia, the Moroccan representative stressed that immigration must clearly be separated from the issues of organized crime and terrorism (Fassi Fihri 2002). Yet illegal immigration continuous to touch a sensitive nerve in EU–Moroccan relations, and as Spain is the main entry point of Moroccan illegal immigrants, this issue particularly concerns Spanish–Moroccan relations. Following European complaints that Morocco was not doing enough to prevent illegal immigration to the EU, King Mohammed VI argued that European (and particularly Spanish) traffickers, who are wealthier and better equipped than their Moroccan counterparts, were also involved in the lucrative business. Moreover, he stressed that the EU had more financial means and a better technical equipment to fight illegal migration than Morocco (Mohammed VI 2001b).

Besides migration, agricultural exports and the EU–Moroccan "fish war" (*The Economist* September 9, 1995: 47) negatively impacted on EU–Moroccan relations. In 1999, when the bilateral fisheries agreement of 1995 expired, the old game repeated itself. Morocco refused to renew it automatically, and the EU rejected Rabat's proposition of reducing the access of European vessels to Moroccan territorial waters. Spain, which was most concerned by the lapse of the agreement, accused Morocco of exceeding the quotas of tomatoes stipulated in the trade agreement, and prompted the EU to impose additional quota certificates on Moroccan tomatoes. Much to Spain's displeasure, the Commission subsequently lifted the restrictions (*The Financial Times* February 4, 2000). Yet the continuing dispute over fisheries between Rabat and Madrid led to the recalling of the Moroccan ambassador to Spain in 2001. In July 2002, tensions between Spain and Morocco raised to an unprecedented level, prompted by the dispute over the uninhabited, Spanish-controlled Parsley islet, as noted previously. Morocco's claims on Ceuta and Melilla, which are still under Spanish control, partly provided the background to this dispute, particularly since Spain and Britain started discussing the possible transfer of sovereignty over Gibraltar to Spain.

Critical undertones emanating from Morocco also concerned the EU's human-rights policy, although Rabat's criticism was more restrained than that of Algeria, for instance. While Rabat benefited from € 2.47 million under MEDA Democracy (Commission 2001: 18), it remained disturbed by what it perceived as EU double standard vis-à-vis the Israeli-Palestinian conflict. Thus, in January 2001 Foreign Minister Benaïssa (2000) remarked that if human-rights were so important to the EU, it should be more sensitive to Israel's human rights violations in the Palestinian territories.

Finally, cannabis production in Morocco's Rif region and its export to Europe was a point of controversy. In 2002, Morocco's export of cannabis and hashish was estimated at 2,000 to 2,500 tons a year, believed to cover 70 percent of consumption in the EU (*Libération* March 12, 2002: 25). According to a study of UNODC and the Kingdom of Morocco, cannabis cultivation employs around 800,000 Moroccans (UNODC 2003: 5), thus providing an income for one of the country's poorest rural regions. While the EU had financed measures to develop alternative crops with € 1.18 million between 1996 and 2001 (Commission 2001: 18), Moroccan officials argued that European demand, not Moroccan supply, was the problem. Pointing to the decriminalization policy regarding the drug in many EU member states, Rabat maintained that it was not logic that a poor country such as Morocco shall bear the responsibility for hashish consumption in Europe (*The Economist* August 10, 2000: 40). Needless to say that the EU was not very content with this situation, particularly since Morocco's cannabis production actually increased over the last years. The EU was also disturbed by the fact that Moroccan farmers partly cultivated cannabis within EU-sponsored alternative crops programs, which enjoy a comparatively good irrigation.[25]

The various contentious issues between the two sides repeatedly prompted Rabat to question the EU's commitment to, and sense of, "partnership." In this vein, King Mohammed VI maintained that the EU should refrain from political correctness, and instead develop a partnership that reflects "the geography and the daily realities of the economic, social and cultural life of our countries" (quoted in *Agence France Presse* March 21, 2000). Similarly, Moroccan officials repeatedly called for an honest dialogue on common interests, while stressing the need for solidarity and a "real" partnership across the Mediterranean (Fassi Fihri 2002).

Morocco's Strategy

In the time-span under consideration, Rabat constantly stressed the importance of the EMP and its relations to Europe. Morocco's foreign ministry published a large number of documents on EU-Moroccan and Euro-Mediterranean affairs, and the Barcelona Process was also extensively covered in Morocco's media. Certainly, Rabat may not have fully been satisfied with the EU's conduct of the EMP. Thus, off-the-record, Moroccan officials criticized the EMP for being over-ambitious, and regretted its de facto interlinkage with peace and war in far-away Palestine. One official also remarked that the main flaw of the EMP consisted in its grouping together of states among which relations are tense. And while the EU aspired to resolve all the political problems in its periphery, it did not have the adequate means to do so.[26]

De facto, Morocco was arguing with the EU over fish, tomatoes, cannabis, and immigration, and it demanded more aid and trade concessions than the EU was willing to offer. Interestingly, Moroccan officials were well aware of all these difficulties from the outset (Académie du Royaume du Maroc 1996). However, given that Morocco has traditionally been seeking closer ties to Europe, it welcomed the EMP as a potential tool to achieve its objectives. Mohammed VI may be more realistic than Hassan II, who had applied twice for EC membership, but he is certainly no less "Europeanist" than his father. Indeed, before becoming king, Mohammed completed a law doctorate on EU–Maghreb relations, published under the name of Mohamed Ben El Hassan Alaoui (Alaoui 1994), and he worked in the office of former EC/EU Commission president Jacques Delors for his doctoral research. This "specialization was a clear sign of the path that he expected Morocco to follow in the twenty-first century," as Pennell (2000: 372) noted. Hence, Rabat repeatedly conveyed the message to Brussels that the EMP was but one step on the path towards closer EU–Moroccan relations (Youssoufi 1999, 2001) In this vein, during the first and second meeting of the bilateral Association Council in October 2000 and October 2001 respectively, Morocco expressed its wish of obtaining a status between accession and association ("*entre adhésion et association*") (quoted in Mansour 2001: 4). Subsequently, Rabat proposed a customs union between the EU and Morocco (Commission 2001). According to the former Moroccan ambassador to the EU Belarbi, the opening of negotiations on agricultural trade in January 2002, along with the establishment of a working group on migration and social affairs, pointed to the increasing institutionalization of EU–Moroccan relations, which Rabat warmly welcomed (*Le Matin* January 16, 2002).

Similarly, Rabat regularly embedded bilateral relations to single EU member states into the wider European or Euro-Mediterranean context (Mohammed VI 2000b, 2000c). Conversely, it sought to separate its quite strained relations to Spain from the Euro-Mediterranean context. Within the EMP, Morocco obviously emphasized those issues with which it was most concerned. For instance, given Rabat's traditional cooperation with France and the United States in "hard security" matters, Morocco strongly favored the establishment of a Stability

Pact in the Mediterranean. In light of growing xenophobia in EU countries and Rabat's concern for its nationals living in Europe, Morocco stressed the importance of enhanced cooperation in social and cultural matters. In this vein, former prime minister Youssoufi viewed the third EMP basket as potentially contributing to the improvement of the "living and working conditions of our respective resident communities" and to the promotion of "tolerance and a better knowledge of the respective cultures and civilizations" (Youssoufi 1999). Following the events of 9/11, the king proposed at the November 2001 Euro-Mediterranean meeting in Brussels to organize a conference on intercultural and interreligious dialogue in Morocco. And while stressing that Islam must be separated from terrorism, Morocco reiterated its interest in strengthening the intercultural dialogue at the EMP meeting in Valencia (Fassi Fihri 2002).

Obviously, the fact that the EMP's objectives largely corresponded to Morocco's development strategy explains the country's positive attitude toward the EMP. Mohammed VI stressed that there was no alternative to economic modernization and Morocco's integration into the global economy in order to break the cycle of unemployment and poverty (Mohammed VI 2000a). In order to achieve this aim, he reckoned, better relations to the EU, along with increased financial assistance, were crucial. Similarly, for Youssoufi the future of EU–Mediterranean relations largely depended on the political and economic reforms that the EMP partners would implement (Youssoufi 1998). In this context, the compatibility between Morocco's development plan for the period 2000–2004 and EMP documents was so striking that one could suspect EU officials of having drafted the development plan (Ministry of Economic Prevision and Planning 2000).[27] At any rate, Rabat was pleased that the EMP's 2002–2006 "National Indicative Program" for Morocco (Commission 2001), which lined out the priorities of EU funding under MEDA, fully respected Morocco's development strategy (Youssoufi 2000).

Moreover, the monarchy understood well before the start of the EMP that some sort of political reforms were necessary, not only for relieving internal pressures, but also for attracting aid, trade, and investments. In this vein, Mohammed VI praised Morocco's "new image that was accredited among the international public opinion, the image of a democratic and modernist Morocco, mobilized around its sovereign, an example of moderation and tolerance." Similarly, the king explicitly called upon his diplomats to further promote "Morocco's image as a fortress where the banner of democracy, of modernization, of human dignity, of moderation and of Islamic tolerance is waving" (Mohammed VI 2000a).

Finally, although the UMA initiative is stalled until the present, Morocco's strategy within the EMP also included the aim of fostering sub-regional cooperation, as the Agadir initiative shows. In this vein, Morocco emphasized on several occasions the importance of the EMP's multilateral track, which, however, shall be strengthened at a "differentiated rhythm" (Fassi Fihri 2002). As one foreign-ministry official put it to the author, differentiation would avoid the need to find a common position on every single issue in the heterogeneous southern Mediterranean area.[28] Moreover, for Rabat, enhanced sub-regional cooperation was important for the development of "the south," the main reason being that an economically integrated region is more attractive for foreign investments (Youssoufi, quoted in *Le Matin* October 6, 2001). In view of our discussion thus far, how can Morocco's "Mediterranean" policy be linked to its diverse, and partly contested, state identity?

Morocco's Identity and the EMP

Altogether, Morocco was playing the "Euro-Mediterranean game" quite well in the time-span under consideration, and it "used" the EMP to support its developmental strategy and to foster a stronger attachment to the EU. However, and as discussed in the previous chapters, the EU's original vision for the Euro-Mediterranean has several implications for the southern participants in terms of regional relations, regional order, and identity. Indeed, vis-à-vis all the EMP partners, the EU stipulated their anchorage in an axiomatic Mediterranean region and sought to promote a Mediterranean regional identity, however it may be defined.

Thus, the EMP's regional design touched upon Morocco's difficult relations with Algeria, which are intrinsically linked to the Western Sahara issue. As for the type of EU–Moroccan relations envisaged by the EMP, our discussion has shown that Morocco's objectives exceeded the Euro-Mediterranean logic as Rabat wanted far more than the EU was (and still is) willing to concede. In addition, the EMP touched upon the issue of modernization and reform, given that Morocco, as compared to most other EMP partners, is comparatively "advanced" in its reform process. Against this background, the efforts of the EU to promote and export its values of "Western" political and economic liberalism must be taken into account. Thus, the following sections assess Morocco's official response and identity discourse, along with the question of whether the EMP's attempted identity manipulations triggered domestic divisions.

Morocco and Its Euro-Mediterranean Environment

Morocco's "Place in the Region"

Morocco's official discourse traditionally stresses the country's multiple identity dimensions and the closeness to Europe. A good example is the king's statement that "Morocco is the country of Africa that is closest to Europe, the Arab country that is closest to Europe and the country of the Maghreb that is closest to Europe" (Mohammed VI 2001b). Within a multiple identity discourse, a Mediterranean identity dimension is quite easy to accommodate. Indeed, the Mediterranean and the Euro-Mediterranean themes were frequently mentioned in Morocco's official discourse, within the framework of Euro–Mediterranean relations and beyond. The late King Hassan II (1997a) stressed for instance that "geography has put my country at the crossroads of two seas and two continents, where the Mediterranean communicates with the Atlantic Ocean and where Europe is closest to Africa." In a similar vein, Rabat has repeatedly called for the establishment of "*un nouvel espace méditerranéen,*" or a new Mediterranean space (Benaïssa 2001b). References to a common history, to the cultural affluence of the Mediterranean ("*richesse culturelle et civilisationnelle de la Méditerranée*"), and to a Mediterranean identity are frequent (Benaïssa 2001b). Similarly, former prime minister Youssoufi (1998) repeatedly called for the "construction of a Euro-Mediterranean area of peace, stability and shared prosperity" ("*construction d'un espace euro-méditerranéen de paix, de stabilité et de co-prospérité*").[29]

Moreover, Morocco's official discourse generally affirms the existence of a Mediterranean or Euro-Mediterranean area. In this vein, during the 1998 Speech of the Throne, the late Hassan II (1998) underlined the objective of "enhancing cooperation between the nations of the eastern and southern Mediterranean region." Similarly, while addressing his diplomats, Mohammed VI (2000a) stressed that Moroccan diplomacy aims at going "beyond the Euro-Mediterranean space" ("*au-delà de l'espace Euro-Méditerranéen*"). Addressing the Moroccan people, the monarch also called attention to Morocco's constructive role in the "Mediterranean region" and declared that Moroccan diplomacy is committed to work toward the "development of the Mediterranean region" (Mohammed VI 2001a). Addressing the

Italian president, Mohammed VI also stressed the "common belonging to the Mediterranean region, the cradle of civilizations" (Mohammed VI 2000b). Morocco's ministers and government officials adopted the same narrative. Thus, Youssoufi referred to "the Euro-Mediterranean economic space of which we are an integral part" (quoted in *Le Matin* October 6, 2001). And the former minister in charge of the condition of women and the protection of the family, Nouzha Chekrouni, stressed that Morocco is continuously working for "a global, solid, and efficient partnership with the Euro-Mediterranean area" (quoted in *Le Matin* September 15, 2001).

The official discourse also regularly describes Morocco as a "country of the southern Mediterranean" (Mohammed VI 2000c; Hassan II 1997b). Similarly, while addressing the representatives of neighboring states, Youssoufi (1998) stressed that "we, the countries of the southern and eastern Mediterranean and of the Maghreb in particular must seek to gain the best advantages of the Barcelona Process." But at the same time, and vis-à-vis Europe, Morocco repeatedly stressed that it is "closer" to Europe than, and different from, the other southern neighbors. Thus, as a response to France's "security reflex," King Mohammed VI stressed that it is a mistake to put Morocco into the same category as "other southern Mediterranean countries." According to the king, Morocco "has a different identity" due to the proximity to Europe, both in geographical and cultural terms (Mohammed VI 2001b). And in the aftermath of 9/11, the monarch dismissed the possibility of a "clash of civilizations" by pointing to Morocco's particular features. "For the West," he stated, "Morocco is the Orient, while for the Orient, Morocco is the West. We are the buffer zone, the lock chamber. We are a real blotting pad" (Mohammed VI 2001c).[30]

Thus, the Mediterranean theme is one among several identity dimensions within Morocco's official discourse. It characterizes both the Palace and the government, which also included the former political opposition. We may assume that Morocco's French-educated elites generally consent to this assessment, as most discussion partners have claimed.[31] The fact that Morocco's prestigious Al-Akhawayn University in Ifrane offers a Masters course in "Mediterranean and North African Studies" may further support this argument. Yet Moroccan government officials are well aware that the EMP's Mediterranean vision is the EU's brain-child. Thus, off-the-record one official stressed that "this Mediterranean, as stipulated by the EU in Barcelona, will only be realized by and for Europe."[32] Moreover, the extent to which Morocco's portrayed Mediterranean self-image is accepted among the broad population remains questionable. But it is also true that the Palace's long tradition of presenting Morocco's "place in the region" as multidimensional narrows down the space for domestic contestation. As the Mediterranean area is depicted as bridging "East" and "West," "North" and "South," different interpretations of Morocco's regional identity may coexist, since, to put it bluntly, "anything goes." Similarly, in view of Morocco's inclusive identity discourse, the country may well perceive itself as being part of the Mediterranean region while stressing its closeness to Europe. Thus, the EMP's attempts to promote a Mediterranean regional identity for the EMP partners did not seem to pose a major problem for Morocco.

Regional Relations in the Southern Mediterranean
In theory, Morocco's multiple identity discourse permits the strengthening of regional relations under a shared Mediterranean identity. In practice, however, this is overshadowed by the Western Sahara dispute and, more recently, the fate of Israeli-Palestinian peace-making.

Certainly, the importance of inter-Maghreb and inter-Arab co-operation is a constant theme in Morocco's official discourse. In this vein, Hassan II (1999) stressed the "community of destiny that links our country to our Arab brothers," along with the "attachment to the Maghrebi ideal." The initial efforts of Mohammed VI to reinvigorate the UMA initiative and insert it into the EMP framework were accompanied by statements that "the Arab Maghreb Union is where the Arab, Islamic, African and Mediterranean circles of our foreign policy converge" (Mohammed VI 2001a). However, the sub-regional Agadir process that was initiated by Rabat excludes Algeria. Although Mohammed VI described his personal relations with the Algerian president Bouteflika as "excellent" (2001b), Algeria's traditional support for the independence of the Western Sahara collides with Rabat's firm position of claiming sovereignty over its "southern provinces."[33] Hence, Morocco's official discourse constantly refers to the country's "territorial integrity," which is depicted as a key element of Morocco's identity (Hassan II 1997, 1998; Mohammed VI 2002, 2003a). De facto Moroccan control over the Western Sahara became an element of national consensus—out of conviction or necessity. Indeed, there are no major political parties or organizations that dare to question "*la Maroccanité de notre Sahara*" (Mohammed VI 2001a). Those who did so in past and present suffered the *makhzan*'s repression, such as the radical Left in the 1970s, and more recently a number of journalists, as noted above.

Yet the Western Sahara issue is still unsettled. Although the UN-brokered cease-fire between Morocco and the Algerian-backed Polisario Front of the early 1990s still holds, the proposed UN referendum on the future of the territory has not materialized, mainly due to severe differences over the question of who is entitled to vote. While the International Court of Justice had ruled in the 1970s that Morocco's occupation of the Western Sahara is illegal (Hassan II nevertheless insisted that the court had ruled in Morocco's favor), the UN proposed in 2001 that the disputed territory should remain under Morocco's rule as largely autonomous province. The new proposal of the UN has been linked to pressures of the United States and France, given that American and French oil companies signed deals with Morocco to search for oil in Western Saharan waters (*The Economist* December 8, 2001: 44–45). Yet the UN Security Council rejected the proposal in May 2002, and in June 2004 the UN special envoy to the Western Sahara, James Baker, stepped down after his unsuccessful attempts over seven years to broker a political settlement. Yet a solution involving Rabat's withdrawal from the territory would certainly demand a profound reshaping of one of Morocco's central identity themes. This, in turn, harbors the risk of eroding the legitimacy of the monarchy. Not surprisingly, the Palace has thus far not shown any signs of reconsidering Morocco's "territorial integrity."

Regarding the Arab-Israeli fault-line, Rabat had traditionally identified with the Palestinian cause, voiced a special concern for Jerusalem, and simultaneously maintained a moderate stance toward Israel, as noted above. While regularly referring to the tolerance of Islam, the Palace also explicitly asserted that "Moroccan Jews belong to the national patrimony" (Mohammed VI 2001b).[34] The Palace's balancing act was possible as long as it firmly controlled Moroccan politics. But it became much more difficult during the second *Intifada*, particularly in view of the opposition's increased space of maneuver. Indeed, Israel's repressive policy toward the Palestinians prompted several large demonstrations, mainly organized by Abdessalam Yassine's Islamists. Given the large mobilizing effect of the Palestinian issue, planned demonstrations received the regime's permission a posteriori. Thus, in autumn 2001, former prime minister Youssoufi and his long-time companion Abraham Serfaty led a march of solidarity with the Palestinians through the streets of the capital (Howe 2001). King Mohammed VI also sharply criticized the Israeli government for its "bad inspiration of wanting to profit from the current situation [after September 11, 2001] in order to radicalize and accentuate its repression . . . against the Palestinian people" (Mohammed VI 2001c). In April 2002, following Israel's military incursion into formerly Palestinian-controlled areas, around 2 million people demonstrated in Rabat against Israeli policy. Once more adopting the strategy of "riding the tiger," the Palace permitted the demonstration, which was preceded by spontaneous protests of Morocco's Islamists, along with their efforts to enlist Moroccans for the "*jihad* in Palestine." In March 2002, both moderate and radical Islamists protested the planned visit of Israeli parliamentarians to a meeting of the Interparliamentary Union, scheduled in Marrakech for that month (*Agence France Presse* March 11, 2002). And considering the popular feelings, Mohammed VI postponed the royal marriage festivities that were planned for the second week of April 2002 (they were held in June 2002).

Although the king depicted the solidarity with the Palestinians as his personal conviction, the Palestine conflict potentially puts Morocco's monarchy and internal balance at risk. Certainly, most political parties in Morocco identify with the Palestinians, as the various party-affiliated newspapers attested.[35] Yet particularly the Islamists, Morocco's most important opposition force, draw political advantages from the mobilizing power of the "Palestinian cause." Thus, the Palace was no longer able to simultaneously maintain a "neutral" position and portray Morocco's identity as Islamic and Arab. Similarly, due to altered parameters of domestic politics, the monarchy by default had to identify with the Palestinians' *Al-Aqsa Intifada* unless it wanted to undermine its religiously constructed authority. Thus, in view of Palestinian suffering, the king was forced to choose among different layers of Morocco's state identity, and to act according to the country's portrayed Arab-Islamic identity. Hence, in the past Morocco's identity discourse may have been able to accommodate the EMP's model for a Mediterranean region that comprises Israel, in spite of the unsettled Palestine conflict. Yet due to Morocco's domestic developments, this option has become dependent on Israeli-Palestinian peace-making.

Relations to the EU and "the West"
Rabat traditionally identifies Moroccan-European relations as an "interdependence of destiny" (Mohammed VI 2000c). According to Youssoufi (1999), the Euro-Moroccan "community of destiny," which is "as much evident as natural," is based on "the geographic proximity,

the cultural affinity, a long common history, and the strong overlapping of our interests." Both sides also share the "respect of liberties, democratic principles and universal values of human rights" (Youssoufi 1999). Within this generally pro-European attitude, France is treated with particular cordiality—and not only while addressing a French audience (Mohammed VI 2000c). Thus, Hassan II (1996) considered French president Jacques Chirac as "our great friend," and his son underscored Morocco's friendship with the French Republic ("*République Française amie*") by terming bilateral relations as "family relations" (Mohammed VI 2001b). Yet as we have seen, Rabat's traditional allusions to its proximity to Europe went hand in hand with its demands for a greater European commitment, so as to provide "a strategic, political, and economic content to the de facto interdependence between Morocco and Europe" (Mohammed VI 2000c).

On the domestic political scene, there are no outspoken challengers to Morocco's pro-European and pro-Western orientation. This was particularly visible in the electoral year of 1997, in which all political parties declared their aim to further promote Morocco's relations to "the West." This domestic "consensus by default" also included the Islamist PJD, whose member Abdelillah Benikrane affirmed that "we are conscious of our capacity, the reality of our country, its interests and its international environment" (quoted in *Agence France Presse* January 15, 2002). There may be several reasons for this consensus, the first being that the country's political elites—including the king himself—have generally remained attached to the French language and "Western" culture (Pennell 2000: 382). Second, most politicians may pragmatically consider good relations to the "West" as inevitable for the country's developmental needs.[36] Third, the domestic unanimity could be the result of the *makhzan*'s coercion. Finally, the monarchy's identity discourse may have succeeded in persuading Moroccans that the country's pro-European and pro-Western orientation "does not infringe on Morocco's sociocultural identity and its personality," as an editorial in *Maroc Hebdo International* (March 25, 1998) stressed. Once more, this would point to the political advantages of multiple and inclusive identity politics.

Thus, as long as the king retains his powers, and as long as the elites remain Francophile, it is unlikely that EU–Moroccan relations will face major domestic opposition. However, the Islamists may challenge this orientation. Indeed, while Benikrane of the PJD denounced Morocco's "powerful secular and francophone elites" (quoted in *Agence France Presse* January 15, 2002), the more radical Yassine never concealed his contempt for the monarchy's Western influence. His daughter Nadia, often acting as the speaker of the movement, maintained a similar position. "We are not the West," she repeated in fluent French during a demonstration against the allegedly decaying morality on Morocco's beaches (*BBC World* 2002).

Moreover, the monarchy's relations with the United States came increasingly under assault. Following the monarchy's harsh condemnation of the 9/11 terrorist attacks, Mohammed VI organized a memorial ceremony for the terror victims in Marrakech's St. Peter's Cathedral on 16 September, in which Muslim, Christian, and Jewish representatives participated. However, 16 *'ulama* issued a *fatwa* (religious ruling) that denounced the ceremony as a "great sin", and 200 intellectuals, including PJD parliamentarians, supported the *fatwa* (*El País* November 2, 2001: 11). The monarchy also prevented a number of demonstrations against the prolonged U.S. strikes on Afghanistan in 2001. Particularly the Middle East policy of the first Bush administration prompted widespread domestic criticism. Most Moroccan party-affiliated newspapers, along with the largely independent press, criticized the U.S. administration for its support of Israel during the *Intifada*, not to mention its invasion of Iraq. The mass demonstration on April 7, 2002, which took place during the state visit of former U.S. Secretary of State Colin Powell, also showed the growing salience of anti-American popular sentiments in Morocco. Not surprisingly, the more radical Islamists marched with the most extreme anti-American slogans (*Le Figaro* April 8, 2002). Thus, with a high degree of violence on the Israeli–Palestinian track, and given the Middle East policy of the Bush administration, Morocco's "Western" orientation and identity layer became increasingly contested. Yet this development noticeably limited the foreign-policy options of the monarchy, while further strengthening the Islamist opposition. In the long term, rising anti-Western sentiments may also affect Morocco's attachment to Europe.

The Internal Dimension

For Morocco, the major challenges of the EMP were related to the realm of domestic politics. Occasionally, Morocco's newspapers criticized the tough time schedule for implementing the Euro-Mediterranean free trade agreement, which Youssoufi termed *"lourd d'implications"*—with "heavy" implications (Youssoufi 1998). Indeed, implementing the agreement is more than a technical matter. Increasing the international competitiveness of Morocco's economy, along with its attractiveness for foreign investments, necessitates transparency and accountability, including the establishment of the rule of law. This entails, however, reforms of the state bureaucracy and the judicial system, and the dismantling of the patronage system—which, less diplomatically, may also be called corruption. Given that Morocco already engaged in a political reform process, further socioeconomic restructuring touches upon at least three thorny issues, namely the relation between political power and opposition, the interpretation of Islam and its role in public life, and, herewith related, the issue of modernity and tradition.

Corresponding to the monarchy's practice of legitimizing the challenges of modernity through tradition and religion, the king declared to his people that the monarchy "counts on the will of total mobilization and efficient adhesion to the nearly-sacred struggle that we are leading in the economic and social realm" (Mohammed VI 2001a). He continued by stressing that in "this type of jihad [*sic*] your best weapon will be your faith in the values laid down by your religion and dictated by your patriotism." Certainly, in view of the far-reaching socioeconomic implications of the reform processes, it may be questioned whether faith alone will suffice to face the challenges, as the following sections discuss.

Political Power and Opposition

Although the "Western" model of a liberal democracy may not be the only option for Morocco, further political reforms nevertheless entail the limitation of the monarchy's absolute powers. Ideally, the reforms would also comprise the internal democratization of the political parties, an increased freedom of expression, the strengthening of civil society, and the political participation of the broad population—and not only of small elites.

After a quite promising start, the king's democratization efforts receded in the time-span under consideration (Tozy 2000a; Deneoux 2000; Howe 2001). This went hand in hand with a drop of his popularity among Moroccans, who had affectionately nicknamed the young king "M6." Given the king's interests in winter ski and expensive cars, the popular humorist Bziz (who is banned from state-controlled television) coined the phrase "Sa Majeski," thus contradicting the monarch's portrayed self-image as "the king of the poor." Within the process of decentralization that started in July 2001, the king also appointed regional prefects with quite extensive powers in February 2002, without consulting the government or parliament (*Le Monde* February 14, 2002). In addition, there was a growing influence of the king's personal advisors, such as the long-time financial advisor André Azoulay, who did not refrain from publicly blaming the inclusion of Youssoufi and his party into the government for the persistence of Morocco's economic malaise (*Le Monde* January 25, 2002).

While the government complained about the king's authoritarian steps, the slow pace of reforms also damaged the credibility of the Youssoufi government. The opposition frequently criticized the government for its indecisiveness, but it came also under the attack of *Istiqlal* leader Abbas Al-Fassi (*Maroc Hebdo International* May 5, 2000, January 11, 2002). Apparently, Al-Fassi forgot that he himself was the minister of social affairs and that the *Istiqlal* participated in the *alternance* government. Altogether, Youssoufi's government and the nine parties composing it showed a certain unwillingness to further promote democratization. Indeed, the government and the parliament generally abided to the royally orchestrated political game, shed away from thorny issues, and repeatedly adopted the *makhzan*'s authoritarian style. In this vein, USFP and *Istiqlal* sponsored a bill that would have granted the president of a parliamentary commission the authority to imprison citizens up to five years for refusing "to cooperate." Similarly, in December 2000 the USFP favored the shutting down of the newspapers *Le Journal* and *Demain* because they had questioned the role of generals and politicians (including Premier Youssoufi) in the failed coup against Hassan II in the 1970s (Howe 2001). Morocco's elites, which are the basis of the patronage system, for obvious reasons also rejected altered relations between power and opposition that would damage their standing (Maghraoui 2001). One Moroccan author claimed that the predominant political culture of "paternalism, authoritarianism, exploitation, and repression" (Ben Haddou 1997: 215) paralyzed any democratization effort. This argument may be correct, but it once more raises the question of the hen and the egg, as a predominant political culture is, at least partially, the result of a society's political experience.

The more interesting question is why the monarchy and the elites consented to democratic reforms in the first place, since they potentially undermine their power, status, and personal interests. Certainly, some have argued that Morocco's cautious reform process was only a means to de-politicize and tame the opposition, whereby the Palace framed democratization in terms of "morality" (Ferrié 2000). Yet, to paraphrase Ajami (1992: 199), the themes we use make their own demands. Indeed, stipulated themes may function as a "trap" in specific cases, develop their own dynamics, and require that actors adhere to them, even against their utilitarian interests (Schimmelfennig 2001). This may explain the monarchy's apparent illogical behavior of engaging in political reforms to begin with.[37] At the same time, it explains the regime's wavering between reforms and reactionary measures in terms of the frictions between identity constraints and personal interests. However, in the final analysis the regime's inconsistency undermined the credibility of the monarchy and the political institutions, while it further nurtured the alienation of large segments of society, particularly urban youth (Maghraoui 2001). Again, the Islamist movements, whose commitment to democratic principles is even more questionable than that of the so-called democratic parties, most benefited from this development.

Morocco's cautious reform process undoubtedly raised the question of what kind of democracy the country envisages. Yet democratic procedures would most likely demand the departure from the cultural "master-and-disciple" pattern (Hammoudi 1997), while it would jeopardize Morocco's corrupt, but effective, balancing system between rural and urban sectors, different tribes and families. With it, Morocco's societal cohesion may diminish, at least in the long run. Increasing democratization would also erode the monarchy's unifying frame, for better or for worse. Thus, the "democratization paradox" also applies to the Moroccan case: if implemented too fast or too slow, democratic reforms endanger the country's stability and societal cohesion. Thus, the EMP envisaged a transition process that is basically risky, and which potentially strengthens those forces that reject the idea of a democratic and inclusive Euro-Mediterranean region in the first place.

Tradition and Modernity

As repeatedly illustrated so far, the juxtaposition of tradition and modernity was (and still is) a constant feature of Morocco's official narrative. Yet since the traditional elements of Morocco's political life revolve around the monarchy and Islam, democratic reforms touch upon the royally defined balance between tradition and modernity, while limiting the monarchy's power to impose its interpretation of these concepts. This issue is particularly sensitive since Morocco is characterized by a cultural duality, comprising the culture of modernity of a small and wealthy elite, and the culture of tradition of a vast, and often impoverished, population (Al-Jabri 1999b).

Yet even Morocco's elites maintain profoundly different interpretations of what tradition and modernity actually mean. One reading of tradition, termed "fundamentalist" by Al-Jabri (1999a: 9), focuses on how to revive tradition in order to regain the greatness of the past. A glorious past that is firmly anchored in an alleged "pure" Islam, is projected in the future and serves as a means to reaffirm identity. "Western" values are rejected theoretically, although this discourse in fact integrates "Western" concepts and developments (Tozy 1999). In this vein, Sheikh Abdessalam Yassine for instance has his own Internet website. This interpretation of tradition characterizes moderate and radical Islamists, but also the *Salafi* school of thought that is defended by the *Istiqlal*. A quite different reading defines tradition through a "Western" frame of reference, and views the "Western" path towards modernity as the only option. Potentially espousing an orientalist discourse (Said 1995), this orientation tends to deny the distinctiveness of Arab-Islamic history and its relevance for a "modern" future. Finally, the Marxist reading of tradition embeds the idea of a (Marxist) revolution into tradition (Al-Jabri 1999a: 11). In present-day Morocco, this interpretation is far less relevant than the other two.

In spite of the analytical difference between these readings of tradition, different combinations are possible. Indeed, opponents of an orientalist discourse are not necessarily fundamentalists, against modernization, or against "the West" (Al-Jabri himself being the best example). And not every sympathizer with "Western" concepts believes that Arab-Islamic history is only a footnote of a Western-dominated history. Implicitly or explicitly, the interpretation of tradition influences the answer to the questions of what modernization entails for Morocco and whether the "Western" model of a liberal democracy is desirable. This debate is certainly not new, but it came to the fore ever since Morocco implemented its first political reforms. Thus, PJD member Benikrane for instance called upon the government to conduct a reform program that is consistent with the *shari'a* (*Africa News Service* August 14, 2000). Others, such as Al-Jabri (1999a, 1999b), advocate an epistemological self-critique in order to define Morocco's genuine path between tradition and modernity. This line of thought entails the demand that Morocco must eliminate "moribund" elements of its sociocultural heritage, develop its positive elements, and reassert Morocco's identity without falling into the trap of classical or contemporary orientalism.

The issue of women's rights clearly illustrated Morocco's problem of redefining the balance between tradition and modernity. Although democratic reforms do not necessarily improve the status of women (Brand 1998), democratization nevertheless requires the abolition of any *legal* discrimination against women, often upheld in the name of tradition.

From the outset, Mohammed VI stressed that he would promote gender equality, and, unlike his father, he regularly referred to women in royal speeches. Yet any effort to implement concrete steps, such as reforming the family code (*mudawwana*) according to the demand of women organizations, brought deep divisions within Moroccan society to the fore, which cut across Morocco's political elites and society.[38] Thus, while the government's reform proposal of the family code of March 2002 triggered a march of support of 100,000 participants in Rabat, a far larger protest demonstration took place in Marrakech. Organized by the Islamist movements, many (veiled) women participated in the latter. Yet many parliamentarians, including USFP and *Istiqlal* representatives, opposed the bill as well (*Maroc Hebdo International* May 5, 2000). Positioning supporters of patriarchal, non-egalitarian cultural pattern against advocates of liberal and egalitarian values, gender equality inevitably demands a departure from Morocco's patriarchal culture. Certainly, the divisions on the issue of gender occasionally took curious forms. For instance, Nadia Yassine, who became the speaker of the radical Islamist movement during her father's imprisonment, is certainly Morocco's most famous woman politician. And in May 2002, a parliamentary majority approved the adoption of a women quota of 30 out of 325 seats (corresponding to 9.2 percent). Interestingly, *Istiqlal* leader Al-Fassi, whose party had opposed the reform of the *mudawwana* on religious grounds, wanted to increase the women quota to 20 percent (*El País* May 8, 2002: 11).

Somewhat exploiting the popular indignation with radical Islamism after the Casablanca terrorist attacks of March 2003—and assumedly the increased fears of attracting the regime's anger—Mohammed VI pushed through a far-reaching reform of the *mudawwana* in October 2003. Not surprisingly, the king justified the reform by pointing to the tolerance and egalitarian nature of Morocco's Islam (Mohammed VI 2003b). With it, Morocco achieved the most liberal family code of all Arab Mediterranean states (Alami M'Chichi et al. 2004). Although the debate over the family code is over for now (implementing the reform is certainly another matter), this example shows that questions of modernity and tradition pit defenders of very different sets of values against each other, transgressing party lines, gender, and socioeconomic categories.

Islam, Its Interpretation, and Its Role
Questions of tradition and modernity are intrinsically linked to the "valid" interpretation of Islam and the role it is to play in Morocco's

politics and society. We may agree with Al-Jabri's contention that, at least in the near future, the separation between state and religion is an unlikely scenario for Morocco (Al-Jabri 1999a). As discussed in the case of Egypt, such an option seems to contradict Arab-Islamic tradition, political thought, and reality (Zakariya 1991; Halliday 2000; Ghalioun 2000). Nevertheless, as we have seen before, there are very different answers to the questions of what Islam means and which public role it is to play. Thus far, the king insisted on his exclusive powers to define the "valid" interpretation of Islam. And unlike Egypt, Morocco's struggle over the definition of religion does not take place in the courts. Yet Morocco's political reforms gave more room to alternative preferences, triggered the attempts of different forces to impose their vision, and, with it, their interpretation of Morocco's political identity.

Promoting a messianic vision of Islam for political ends obviously characterizes Islamist movements in general. Not surprisingly, Morocco's Islamist forces repeatedly called for respecting the *shari'a*, whether this concerns the status of women, or other political and social reforms. While the monarchy traditionally allowed the coexistence of different elements and interpretations of Islam, most Islamist forces are clearly not in favor of inclusiveness. Thus, *moderate* Islamists attacked the allegedly heretic elements of popular Islam, such as the *Sufi* tradition and its mysticism (Willis 2004). Similarly, the opposition to the Palace's interpretation of Islam grew, as the above-mentioned *fatwa* against the memorial ceremony for the victims of 9/11 clearly illustrates. Stressing his status as superior religious authority, Mohammed VI dismissed these critics with the argument that they lacked the authority to issue the ruling (Mohammed VI 2001c). Yet this example shows that segments of Morocco's elites, including legal political players such as the PJD, started to enter in a public competition with the monarchy over imposing the valid interpretation of Islam. Other political forces may be less clear on the preferred type and role of Islam, such as the "political center" around the USFP. Yet considering the *Salafi* tradition of the *Istiqlal* and the preferences of the radical Left, it is evident that there are partly incompatible domestic preferences on these questions. They compete with the vision of both the Islamists, which are a quite heterogeneous group, and the monarchy.

The EMP, the EU, and Morocco: Compatibility of Values

How compatible is Morocco's political culture and identity with the EU's "normative power exercise," that is, the attempts to export key values such as human rights, democracy, the rule of law, and liberalism to Morocco in the framework of the EMP?

Certainly, there are Moroccan political forces and individuals that support the European-inspired vision of the country's future set-up. Yet in view of the discussion so far, the EMP's set of values still differs from the predominant cultural and political features of Moroccan society, including the elites. Critics of a "Western" prescription for Morocco's future clearly exceed the Islamist forces, since many non-Islamist Moroccan intellectuals voiced concern for the EU's allegedly orientalist perception of, and attitude toward, its southern periphery. However, the reform process also triggered debates around the desirable political system, values, and identity, whereby the "Western" model was but one of several options. Thus far, Morocco is in a phase of transition, in which old and new coexists. The combination of power and symbolic politics, along with the sociocultural features of Morocco's elites, permitted the acceptance of the EMP's Mediterranean construct in broad terms. But the breaking down of the EMP's narrative into concrete elements showed that there was no consensus on the concrete meaning, implications, and desirability of the EMP's "Western" prescriptions for Morocco. Quite to the contrary, these issues just started to become the subject of domestic debates. In discussions with the author, Moroccan government officials contended that Morocco undoubtedly necessitated the EU's commitment for the success of its transition process, whose end, however, is open. Whether the EU's projection of its self-definition on the southern Mediterranean was helpful, in this respect, remains questionable.

Abandoning the support for human rights in favor of security in the post–9/11 era is even more problematic in this context. According to the *Frankfurter Allgemeine Zeitung* (December 4, 2001: 4), France's president Chirac conveyed exactly this message to Morocco, and at least unofficially, the EU has been following this trend in recent years (Gillespie 2006; Haddadi 2006). Yet without entering the debate on whether such a stance may be justifiable or not, there is no doubt that this development entails the erosion of the values that the EU seeks to promote in the international arena. For Moroccan NGO activists, who tend to demand a greater assertiveness from the EU when it comes to supporting human rights, this is certainly bad news.[39] And if a more or less *coherent* projection of the EU's self-definition on the southern Mediterranean already prompted the sense that the EU is not committed to its principles, an incoherent one will certainly not improve Euro-Mediterranean relations in the future.

Conclusions

Given that Morocco traditionally sought closer political and economic ties with the EU, it used the Euro-Mediterranean Partnership for promoting its particular interests. Indeed, both the economic and the regional logic of the EMP largely corresponded to Morocco's development strategy, which was formulated well before the EMP was launched. Thus, in the time-span of our investigation, Morocco was an active partner in the EMP. It favored reinvigorating the EMP whenever it was stalled, and it repeatedly launched new initiatives. However, the aspirations of the monarchy vis-à-vis Europe traditionally exceeded what the EU was willing to concede. Thus, Rabat desired a stronger European commitment, improved trade conditions, more aid, and institutionalized political relations.

In the time-span under consideration, Morocco's official discourse frequently referred to the Mediterranean theme. Since the royally defined narratives traditionally present Morocco's identity as inclusive and multiple, the Mediterranean theme was easy to accommodate. Rabat's promotion of the Mediterranean theme may partly have been instrumental, but it also reflects the concept of Morocco's "place in the region" as maintained by Morocco's elites. Thus, Morocco's regional identity is not unsettled and disputed, but rather appears stable by force of its inclusiveness.

While the EMP was not the subject of major domestic dissent, the type of regional relations envisaged by the EMP nevertheless faced some difficulties. Most notably, they concern Rabat's relations to Algeria that are interlinked with the Western Sahara dispute. Since Morocco's "territorial integrity" became attached to both Morocco's state identity and the legitimacy of the monarchy, any territorial compromise would necessitate a departure from prevalent narratives, while it potentially undermines the powers of the Palace. This partly explains the monarchy's intransigent position on this issue so far. Moreover, with the collapse of the Israeli–Palestinian peace process in September 2000, Morocco witnessed a broad popular mobilization against Israel's policy. Thus, in contrast to the monarchy's rather moderate positions on the Arab-Israeli conflict in the past, the support for a Mediterranean region that includes Israel became difficult to maintain. Morocco sought to circumvent this problematic dimension of regional relations by supporting the idea of sub-regional cooperation and the development of Euro-Mediterranean relations at a variable pace. In this context, it is not surprising that Rabat welcomed the explicitly differentiated approach of the EU's European Neighbourhood Policy, launched in 2003–2004.

However, Morocco's support for the EMP must be linked to the king's traditional control over all aspects of the country's political life. Thus, the monarchy has the powers to impose its vision of Morocco's state identity and to legitimize Morocco's "European" foreign policy orientation through a multiple identity discourse, in which "East" and "West," "North" and "South," "tradition" and "modernity" coexist. Through a mixture of co-option, coercion, and symbolic politics, the monarchy constituted Morocco's unifying frame in spite of the existing social and political diversity. The cautious political liberalization process that has been characterizing Morocco since the 1990s was prompted by various internal and external pressures, lags behind expectations, and witnessed recurrent authoritarian backlashes. In a way, the Palace and the political class are caught between the will to live up to the portrayed "modern" identity of Morocco and the self-interested reluctance to relinquish powers. But while gradually undermining the monarchy's exclusive control over the definition of Morocco's politics and identity, the reform process also made visible that quite different domestic preferences regarding Morocco's political set-up exist. With it, the country started to face a number of complex questions, which revolve around the relation between power and opposition, tradition versus modernity, and the role and interpretation of Islam. Facing the need to choose between different options, Morocco's domestic scene, along with the political parties themselves, is quite divided. At the same time, Morocco's "Westernized" elites differ from the large and often uneducated population, which tends to be entrenched in traditional values.

Thus, for Morocco, the real challenge of the EMP is related to the reform process it prescribed and supported. It confronts the country with the need to choose between conflicting values and different identity preferences, which the powers of the regime had kept together hitherto. In spite of the *mahzan*'s strategy of dividing the opposition and co-opting the moderate factions, the Islamist forces thus far benefited most from Morocco's reform process for a combination of reasons. Hence, the king was forced to make concessions to the Islamist opposition, particularly in the realm of foreign policy. The Islamists are certainly the strongest opposition in Morocco—and those most closely observed in the European media. But while Morocco's more radical (and illegal) Islamists are explicit in opposing the EU's values and prescriptions, the position of the moderate Islamist party on these issues remains partly unclear. However, the opposition to "Western" ideas of modernity and democracy is not confined to the Islamists, and large parts resist the Western reading of "development" for a variety of reasons. In general, there may be a large domestic consensus on supporting political (and economic) liberalization. But the moment it calls for concrete decisions and requires a departure from predominant cultural patterns, the consensus noticeably weakens. Overall, there are quite different, and partly incompatible, domestic preferences regarding the aim of Morocco's reform process. Provided that Morocco's political reform process continues, the incompatibility of different domestic identity preferences is most likely to increase in the future.

Conclusion

Explanations of the difficulties of the Euro-Mediterranean Partnership have generally focused on the fate of Middle East peace-making, the inherent inconsistencies of the EMP, or the institutional flaws of EU foreign-policy making. Moreover, in the aftermath of the terrorist attacks of September 11, 2001, the "clash of civilizations" thesis also affected Euro–Mediterranean relations. The explanation that EMP partners states may have been reluctant, or perhaps unable, to positively respond to the EU's region-building initiative *for mainly domestic reasons* has rarely been considered. This book took up precisely this line of thought.

More specifically, it has argued that internal divisions on the favored political set-up of the state in some of the EMP partners have put a strain on their ability, or willingness, to engage with the EMP, which was the main policy framework of Euro–Mediterranean relations over the last decade. Although the European Neighbourhood Policy, launched in 2003–2004, started to partly overwrite the original rationale of the EMP, the latter must be understood as an alternative type of security project, aiming at constructing a security region across the Euro-Mediterranean area that is based on common interests and the sense of belonging to the same political region. However, while supporting economic and political reforms in the southern Mediterranean, this region-building initiative also sought to change the way the EMP partner states define themselves and their regional surrounding. Hence, this book assessed the possibility of altering the definition of "self," "other," and regional order toward the emergence of a Euro-Mediterranean region in three different EMP partner states, namely Israel, Egypt, and Morocco. While concentrating on the first seven years of the EMP's existence, we analyzed the prevailing concepts of state identity and "cognitive regions" in these three cases, along with the political significance of alternative, and outright defying, concepts.

In a nutshell, the study permits to draw five general conclusions: First, the self-definition of states determines their foreign-policy behavior, including their policy toward Euro-Mediterranean regional security. The empirical evidence fully supports the argument that the way a state defines its main features is intrinsically linked to the definition of its foreign-policy interests. Second, states the identity of which is domestically disputed had difficulties in engaging in Euro-Mediterranean region-building. There is a correlation between the degree of domestic conflict over state identity, its impact on foreign-policy making in general, and the lack of a strategy toward the Barcelona Process in particular. Third, the degree of domestic polarization on questions of state identity and the type of state–society relations are the most important variables that determine whether contested state identities are significant for foreign-policy making in situations of choice. Fourth, a liberal constructivist framework is useful for studying the questions addressed in this research, while the research findings, in turn, corroborate the theoretical premises of this approach. Finally, while other explanations may be partly useful, contested state identities offer a significant and independent explanation for the EMP's difficulties and repeated backlashes.

Social identities are difficult to study, since they are "real" but abstract, multiple, and context-dependent. Identities are not direct *causes* of behavior, but they legitimate and justify certain actions. Since identities are deep-rooted and intrinsic, they tend to remain under the surface when influencing the perceptions of actors and their behavior. In the realm of international relations, state identities are a plainly *political* phenomenon. They justify the existence of states, along with state authority and policies, but they also influence the perception of social reality. While this research faced the analytical difficulties resulting from the hybrid nature of identities, our three case studies also represent three worlds apart. Indeed, Israel, Egypt, and Morocco notably differ from each other in their self-definition, political system, socioeconomic features, foreign policy, culture, and history. Moreover, assessing domestic preferences in Egypt and Morocco faced methodological difficulties related to their authoritarian political system.

To elaborate on the first conclusion on the correlation between state identity and foreign relations, the prevailing self-definitions of both Israel and Egypt are a rather negative precondition for Euro-Mediterranean region-building to begin with. Israel's dominant identity themes, such as the Zionist rationale of the "Jewish State," the Holocaust, the concept of "Jewishness" that combines religion with ethnicity and nationality, and the principle of self-reliance, entail the tendency to *underline difference*. This tendency, which also results from the long history of regional conflict, somewhat contradicts the EMP's first "rule of the game," namely to promote common themes. And Egypt's self-perception as the center of the "Arab world," which underlines its particular history and legitimizes its quest for regional hegemony, is not compatible with the concept of a Euro-Mediterranean region either. While the Mediterranean theme was notably absent in the official discourse of both states, they both lacked of a strategy toward the Barcelona Process, disliked some of its key features, or sought to interpret the initiative to their liking. Conversely, Morocco's multiple and inclusive identity discourse, which also comprises a European "layer," permitted to accommodate the Mediterranean narrative. Of our three case studies Morocco was also most actively engaged in the EMP.

There is no doubt that the construction of state identity in Israel, Egypt, and Morocco follows different patterns than in (Western) Europe. Religion remains a key element in the self-definition of these states, thus prompting specific delineations regarding the question of who belongs to the collective and who does not. Moreover, defining state identity in religious terms somewhat contradicts the concept of a liberal democracy that the EMP implicitly sought to promote. In the case of Egypt and Morocco, and assumedly in the case of most Arab Mediterranean states, the importance of religion also entails a specific concept of regional order, such as "the Muslim world." While transnational identity concepts based on religion and ethnicity already coexist with national ones in the southern Mediterranean and Middle East, the emergence of a Euro-Mediterranean security region would have demanded a departure from prevailing concepts of regional order. Particularly in Egypt, the self-definition of which depends on the existence of an Arab and Muslim "world," this option faced important domestic opposition.

The second conclusion regards the impact of domestic factors on foreign-policy making in general, and Euro–Mediterranean relations in particular, which is the most important finding of this book. In the sample of case studies, there is a clear correlation between the extent to which a state's identity is domestically contested and the degree of engagement in the creation of a Euro-Mediterranean security region. Thus, Israel's strongly contested state identity affects its foreign relations, including its attitude toward the EMP, which remained contradictious and ill-defined. Egypt's state identity may seem less unsettled than

Israel's, and domestic divergences over state identity may not *directly* affect foreign-policy making as in the case of Israel. However, Egypt's latent domestic divisions have produced a definition of "self," "other," and regional order that corresponds to the country's *unifying* quest for regional hegemony. Egypt's inclination to preserve this self-definition for mainly domestic reasons explains its reluctance toward the EMP. Conversely, Morocco, which is far less plagued by domestic identity conflicts for a variety of reasons, maintained a clear strategy toward the EMP. Considering the three cases jointly, the correlation between contested state identities and policy toward the EMP is significant in absolute terms. However, a number of variables intervene, thus determining why, when, and how unsettled state identities impede the formulation of national policies toward regional security on a Euro-Mediterranean basis. For each case, a specific constellation of factors was relevant.

Israeli society is deeply divided regarding the question of what Israel is and wants to be, and some domestic preferences are mutually exclusive. The domestic conflicts revolve around a number of cross-cutting fault-lines, entailing different territorial preferences, different ideas on the role of religion within the state, and different regional and cultural orientations. Since Israel's type of political representation is, broadly speaking, democratic, the domestic divisions translate into the realm of foreign policy. Facing significant political decisions, such as territorial compromise in the context of peace-making or the relationship between religion and politics, Israel's domestic identity polarization and fragile parliamentary balance have produced oscillating policies, or alternatively, stalemate. Frequent changes of government are a direct result of Israel's contested identity. As a consequence, Israel's identity discourse has remained ambiguous and contradictory. However, the EMP directly touched upon a number of domestically contested issues, such as the country's relations to its traditional "enemies" and the definition of its "place in the region." The EMP's implicit attempts to reshape Israel's relations to the EU have also remained problematic in view of history. In addition, the EMP demanded a departure from Israel's prevailing perception of having "no choice," the principle of "trust no one," and the sense of regional detachment and international isolation. With it, the Barcelona Process implicitly called upon Israel to choose one identity concept over others. The inability to decide on these issues in the first place explains Israel's lack of strategy, and partly its reluctance, toward the EMP. While Israel's identity discourse remained dissonant, the political implications of

Israel's unsettled identity were also reflected in a changing degree of cordiality toward the Europeans, along with rather oscillating regional relations, even during the peace process.

Indeed, Israel's contested identity affected its engagement in the EMP long before the outbreak of the second *Intifada* and the collapse of the peace process. More than that, Israel's domestic identity conflicts were particularly significant during the years of the peace process, since the country faced crucial choices that also demanded a change of identity. In this vein, it is not surprising that the Gaza withdrawal, which similarly demanded a choice between competing identity concepts, provoked deep internal scissions. Conversely, situations of threat and conflict, in which the traditional "enemy" reemerges, have a unifying effect. In fact, Israel is facing a serious dilemma: The option of moving toward a peaceful regional order aggravates Israel's domestic identity conflicts. The threat of serious domestic unrest, however, makes it extremely difficult for any government to adopt a policy that abandons some of Israel's founding myths. Conversely, postponing crucial policy-decisions, combined with the sense of threat, increases social cohesion, at least among Israel's Jewish majority, yet without solving Israel's crucial identity questions. In fact, it inevitably reinforces Israel's *particularistic* self-definition and accentuates Israel's cognitive boundaries between "the Jewish State" and "the other"—whereby the latter also includes its non-Jewish citizens.

Egypt has witnessed several ruptures and manipulations of its state identity since independence. However, competing, and mutually exclusive, domestic preferences of the political set-up, the concept of regional order, and the type of foreign relations persist. The main domestic fault-line revolves around the support for the legacy of Nasser and Sadat respectively, which has important implications for the preferred socioeconomic order. This fault-line partly overlaps with different preferences regarding the question of whether Egypt is predominantly defined in a national-territorial way, or whether pan-Arabic and/or pan-Islamic elements are prevailing. In addition, while the role of religion has notably increased over the last decades, the question of what Islam is and what role it is to play in public life are fervently disputed. But since Egypt is an authoritarian state, it remained difficult to assess the significance of competing identity preferences. Moreover, as a result of Egypt's unrepresentative and repressive political system, domestic identity conflicts do not *directly* affect foreign-policy making.

However, the concept of state identity as maintained by Mubarak's regime amalgamates different, and in fact incompatible, domestic preferences. Thus, while assenting to an increasing Islamization of domestic politics, the regime of Mubarak reassessed Egypt's pan-Arab identity and promoted the country's self-definition as the center of the "Arab world" *qua* its particular *national* history. This concept goes hand in hand with Egypt's role as mediator in the Arab–Israeli conflict and the attempts to set the agenda among Arab states, particularly in relation to Israel. For Cairo, engaging in the EMP implied a departure from the prevailing concept of state identity, as the herewith related type of regional order and Egypt's role within it are not compatible with regional security on a Euro-Mediterranean basis. Moreover, in view of Egypt's difficult "identity history," the state's self-definition as coined by the current regime resembles a balancing act between very different preferences, which also aims at keeping the internal frictions under control. But as in the case of Israel, the EMP implicitly demanded from Egypt a choice of one identity concept over others, which, however, faces domestic opposition and increases internal tensions. Furthermore, the Egyptian regime has a conspicuously low affinity with the liberal principles of the EMP as well as with any type of democratic reform. Taken together, these factors well explain Egypt's reluctance to engage in Euro-Mediterranean region-building. In fact, Egypt maintained an interpretation of the EMP that fully corresponded to its prevailing perceptions of "self," "other," and regional order from the outset. Thus, it used the EMP as another forum to underline its all-Arab leadership ambitions and set the regional agenda. In accordance with Egypt's prevailing concept of regional order and, herewith related, its state identity, Cairo also maintained that the aim of the EMP was the emergence of a *Euro-Arab* region.

Morocco has served as inverse example for our argument. Although different domestic preferences exist, the domestic fault-lines are far less pronounced than in both Israel and Egypt. Morocco has a unifying frame in form of a religiously legitimized monarchy, which, in spite of interruptions, has been in power for several centuries. Unlike Egypt, Morocco's identity history has not witnessed major ruptures. However, although Morocco is far less autocratic than Egypt, institutional factors are also relevant here. Indeed, the Palace thus far defined not only the rules of the political game, but also Morocco's identity discourse, which has traditionally been inclusive and multidimensional. While the key element of *diversity* within Morocco's state identity potentially legitimizes different lines of foreign policy, the monarchy has also been able to integrate the Mediterranean and Euro-Mediterranean themes into the identity discourse. Reflecting the perception of cultural closeness to Europe, as maintained by large parts of Morocco's political elites, the Mediterranean theme does not contradict the Maghreb, Arab, Islamic, and African layers of Morocco's self-definition. In the realm of regional relations, there are problems with Morocco's neighbors, most notably Algeria in the context of the Western Sahara dispute. However, considering the different identity layers, Morocco's regional identity is not fervently contested or unstable. At the same time, Rabat maintained a clear strategy toward Euro-Mediterranean regional security, also because closer ties to Europe and improved regional cooperation were identified as corresponding to the country's development needs.

In fact, Morocco was already engaged in hesitant economic and political reforms before the launching of the Barcelona Process. As the reform process was consistent with the EMP's prescriptions for development, Rabat benefited from European support. However, the reform process has been moving some difficult questions to the top of the political agenda. These revolve around relations between power and opposition, questions of tradition versus modernity, and the desired role of Islam in Moroccan public life. With a growing degree of political freedom in general terms, quite different domestic preferences have become visible, while the clout of Morocco's moderate (and less moderate) Islamists has been growing. Certainly, Morocco's reform process has repeatedly witnessed autocratic backlashes, and it has been criticized as a purely cosmetic instrument within the monarchy's strategy of self-preservation. However, some important changes have been taking place in Morocco, the ground-breaking reform of the family code being but one example. Yet the case of Morocco also suggests that a cautious reform process is perhaps the best way of avoiding internal ruptures, along with the unintentional strengthening of potentially undemocratic domestic forces. At the same time, the Moroccan case also confirms that the key objectives of the EU's Mediterranean policy, namely democratization, economic reform, and stability, are potentially contradictory, and at best difficult to obtain simultaneously.

A comparison of the three case studies permits our third conclusion on the variables that make domestic identity conflicts salient in the first place, and relevant for foreign-policy making in the second. First, the cases of both Israel and Egypt showed that processes of transition from war to peace, or the prospects of such a development, may "trigger" domestic conflicts. Since an external enemy is a powerful unifying factor, the prospects of its disappearance may erode the sense of internal unity. Moreover, the transition from war to peace, or its prospects, implies that the previous concepts of "self" and "other" are no longer compatible with the new reality. Second, domestic conflicts over state identity unquestionably increase in situations of *choice*. Third, the cases of both Egypt and Israel confirm that altered patterns of amity and enmity at the international level necessitate conscious and cautious *identity politics*. Sudden attempts to manipulate identity that considerably exceed the boundaries set by the previous definition of identity may have fatal results—literally. Indeed, both Egypt and Israel have witnessed the assassination of a peacemaker, who had lost political legitimacy in the eyes of some domestic groups. Conversely, we may identify four factors that alleviate domestic fragmentation. First, a leader who provides a unifying frame certainly counts as such a variable, as the case of Morocco has shown. However, the monarchy's unifying power also partly results from coercion, mixed with skilful symbolic politics, and more recently from a number of intelligent political moves of Mohammed VI. Second, the Moroccan case indicates the usefulness of multiple and inclusive ways of defining state identity, since it potentially legitimizes different lines of foreign policy. Third, the existence of a powerful adversary is certainly a factor that appeases domestic identity conflicts; both Israel and Egypt serve as examples here. Finally, postponing foreign-policy decisions that imply a choice between competing identity preferences temporarily soothes the domestic fragmentation. However, this option only delays the problem without solving it.

As for the variables that transform domestically contested state identities into a foreign-policy constraint, the type of political representation and state–society relations are the most significant variables. Indeed, domestic identity conflicts will only directly affect foreign-policy making in states with a fairly democratic representation, Israel serving as example here. Conversely, the cases of both Egypt and Morocco indicate that authoritarian states may control the political effects of domestic fragmentation. Yet, domestic fragmentation nevertheless exerts pressures on foreign-policy making, even if these effects may be less direct, and therefore, less traceable. As the case of Egypt shows, the regime has been promoting a concept of state identity that reconciles very different domestic identity preferences. Similarly, the once secular regime of Mubarak has largely given in to the strengthening of Islamist preferences by adopting religious laws and discourses, somewhat in exchange for the ongoing exclusion of all Islamist forces from politics. But these developments have undoubtedly reduced the regime's space of maneuver in the realm of foreign policy. In Morocco, the growing restriction of the monarchy's foreign-policy options partly results from the regime's co-option of the moderate Islamists, but it is in particular related to the generally increased space to voice opposition.

The fourth set of conclusions concerns IR theory. Studying the political implications of state identities, analyzing their emergence, contestation, and possible transformation, and linking the findings to questions of regional security undoubtedly benefited from a constructivist framework. These questions cannot be compared to the study of material factors and resources, for which other theoretical approaches may be useful. For our study, a constructivist framework had three main advantages: First, because of its different ontological and epistemological premises, constructivism considers international politics as part of the social world. It is a world in which human beings give things names, attach meanings to objects, classify items, delineate groups and boundaries, and agree on these meanings and categories through intersubjective processes. For this reason, constructivism permits to consider identities of groups and states as a result of specific delineation processes that *can be changed*. With it, the region-building logic of the EMP as alternative security project becomes intelligible—independent of self-interested motivations. Second, constructivism permits to treat interest and identities as mutually dependent variables, and link change in the former to change in the latter. This was the starting point for the question of whether *unsettled* state identities may impact on foreign policy in general, and on Euro-Mediterranean regional security in particular. Finally, as constructivism explicitly relies on the foundations of social theory, it has been unproblematic to integrate the insights on identities of other social sciences and apply them to states and international relations. However, since this study considered both domestic factors and foreign policy, it integrated a premise of liberal theory, namely the consideration of domestic preferences, into a broader constructivist framework. This permitted the switching between the domestic and the state level of analysis and the integration of the findings obtained at both levels. In fact, although the level-of-analysis problem has produced lengthy debates in IR theory, the problem is less significant in empirical terms once the analytical premises are defined.

In turn, the study confirmed the central role of identities in foreign-policy making, along with the interdependence of interests and identities, which are basically constructivist claims. Similarly, the finding that the way a state defines "self," "other," and regional order are central for the prospects of forging peaceful change corroborates a number of assumptions that are constructivist in nature. However, this research also suggested that domestic factors must be studied more consistently within the constructivist research agenda, and a liberal-constructivist approach, as adopted here, may be useful in other cases as well. A final point concerns the allegedly idealistic orientation of constructivist approaches. This book has evidenced the negative impact of domestic identity conflicts on region-building, and the rather bleak prospects of surmounting them. This finding obviously refutes the accusation that constructivism is intrinsically romantic, as critics have occasionally claimed. Certainly, constructivist thinking does challenge the deterministic premise that states and their interests, and consequently relations among states, follow materially defined and therefore unchangeable patterns. Instead, it asserts the possibility of peaceful change while postulating that in international relations, as elsewhere in the social world, people and states *do have choices*.

These observations lead us to the type of explanation that this book offers, which is our last conclusion. Although domestic constraints to Euro-Mediterranean regional security are significant, there were certainly different factors that impeded the emergence of a Euro-Mediterranean security region in the time-span under consideration. For example, the EU's tendency of giving a far greater importance to its own economic and security interests than to the liberal principles of the EMP inevitably nurtured the suspicion of neo-colonialism in many EMP partners, most of whom experienced European colonialism in the past. Moreover, the EU's role as security actor may be questioned, particularly since "hard" security issues are relevant in the Mediterranean and Middle East. Yet, the development of EU military capabilities is still in an embryonic state. Similarly, there is no doubt that persisting conflicts in the region—most notably the Israeli–Palestinian conflict—are a serious obstacle to Mediterranean security. But on this point our study made an interesting observation. The discussion of the cases of Israel and Egypt showed that domestic identity constraints to Euro-Mediterranean regional security clearly *preceded* the collapse of the peace process. Moreover, in both cases the breakdown of the Middle East peace process actually *soothed* the domestic divisions that otherwise constituted an impediment to the EMP. This finding points to a paradox. It implies that Middle East peace-making negatively influences the emergence of regional security-schemes, whether peace-making proceeds or collapses. While the explanation is almost self-evident in the second case, the negative impact of peace-making on the emergence of regional security can only be detected through an identity-based analysis. Thus, Israel's deep domestic divisions put a strain on moving toward a different regional order that demands territorial compromise, and thus, a reshaping of its identity. Egypt, which is mistakenly considered as a "moderate" state, in a way profits from the unresolved Palestine problem and its "cold peace" with Israel, as it permits the regime to increase its prestige through its mediating role, to unify a potentially divided population in anti-Israel feelings, and to simultaneously shy away from democratic reforms. In a similar vein, it can be predicted that the Palestinians will face a number of fervent internal conflicts over questions of political identity and core values once peace-making is again at the horizon. It can be argued that the threat of internal conflict, which undermines political authority, is one of the reasons of why the late Yasser Arafat was reluctant to prepare his people to abandon some key elements of Palestinian political identity that peace-making inevitably demands. With regard to Israel, Itzhak Rabin at least tried this course of action. Thus, while rejecting mono-causal explanations of complex phenomena in international relations, our findings permit the conclusion that domestic identity conflicts in the states of the southern Mediterranean are a significant factor impeding the construction of a Euro-Mediterranean security region. With it, the explanation for the setbacks of Euro-Mediterranean region-building that this book offers is independent of other factors and explanations.

Finally, a number of lessons may be drawn for the future of Euro–Mediterranean relations as well as for future IR research. First, processes of delineating boundaries between "us" and "them" deserve a special attention in the study of world politics, particularly in the post–9/11 era. Indeed, facing the threats of international terrorism, foreign-policy interests seem to be objectively given, yet often without defining what terrorism is and who qualifies as a terrorist. And as in the cold-war era, whole states, and potentially "civilizations," are defined as "evil." But definitions of "us" and "them" are not self-evident at all. Thus, given that Islamist terrorists also attack targets *within* Arab and Muslim countries, the latter obviously share the same concerns as the "West" on this point. Similarly, the existence of an "Arab world," or of an "Islamic world," is more of a fiction, particularly when it comes to politics, as argued elsewhere (Del Sarto 2005). Indeed, state–society relations and domestic policies in, say, Morocco, Egypt, Iran, Turkey, and Indonesia are very different from each other, and serious rivalries within the alleged Arab or Islamic world are not a new phenomenon either. More important, Arab and Muslim states themselves are not internally homogenous, as our discussion has abundantly shown. Thus, an Imam may have more in common with a Christian cleric, or a Rabbi for that matter, than with, say, a women's rights activist of his own country. While the struggle over the role of religion in the Middle East—and beyond—is often a conflict between patriarchic-authoritarian structures and individualistic-egalitarian values, the configuration of diversity and affinity in international relations may thus be depicted in very different ways. Yet, in world politics, there are serious consequences of how these categories are defined, the risk of a self-fulfilling prophecy related to the "clash of civilizations" thesis being but one case in point. In fact, the mechanisms that theoretically enable the creation of security regions are the same mechanisms that can make "civilizations" clash. For this reason, a far greater awareness of how boundaries are delineated is imperative for the study of world politics.

Second, in the post–9/11 era, the importance of the Mediterranean and Middle East in world politics is most likely to increase. While the EMP did not even come close to the objectives it set out in 1995, region-building remains a legitimate alternative approach to security, particularly in view of the other available options, Iraq being a case in point. In addition, most informed observers would agree that democratic reforms in the southern Mediterranean and Middle East have become crucial, not only for regional, but also for international, security. But peaceful reforms and security in the Mediterranean and Middle East also depend on incentives. Theoretically, the EU's recently launched Neighbourhood Policy responds to these requirements. Indeed, it introduces the principles of "positive conditionality" and differentiation, thus offering enhanced trade and aid in exchange for reforms. In practice, however, the EU's financial and economic incentives behind this policy remain limited, thus raising a serious question mark on its effectiveness. And EU membership, the most important incentive for inducing reforms and expanding regional security, has been ruled out for the remaining EMP partners. Thus, the negative reaction of reform-reluctant Egypt to the EU's Neighbourhood Policy is understandable given that the EU's "incentives" are pale compared to the economic assistance Egypt receives from the United States—to which no specific "conditions" are attached. Similarly, Israel has a clear alternative to Europe, an obvious interest in relying on the United States as the main broker of Middle East peace-making, and so far only few incentives to end the occupation of the territories. But as much as reforms in the region will not work without massive financial assistance and the fight against poverty, there is also an urgent need to acknowledge the potential friction between wanting to achieve stability, security, democracy, and economic reforms at the same time. Thus, it is crucial to set the priorities straight, develop adequate policies, and avoid contradictions. Indeed, preaching human rights in the Middle East while the practice of torture of suspected terrorists is tolerated in the name of security is plainly counterproductive, to say the least. And neither will it increase the credibility of "normative power Europe," or of the United States for that matter.

Third, domestic factors deserve a special attention in the study of world politics, as they influence national foreign-policy making. With regard to the southern Mediterranean, domestic factors may not only dictate the pace of future region-building attempts, but also determine the chances of whether specific regional identity themes may work or not. Similarly, domestic factors often impact on whether the incentives, policies, and values promoted by the "West" are acceptable. In other words, domestic factors related to political identity may be decisive for the success of the EU's normative power in world politics. At the same time, a cautious pace of reforms in the southern Mediterranean and Middle East is not necessarily negative, as it permits governments to balance economic and political reforms and soothe potential risks. Similarly, the emergence of regional security, along with any reform process, necessitates conscious and cautious *identity politics* within the respective state. This, however, requires the commitment of key domestic actors. It is certainly not sufficient if an external actor, such as the EU in the case of the EMP, is the main promoter of an alternative regional narrative. At the same time, identity manipulations must be cautious and require some time. Political leaders cannot simply change the definition of "self," "other," and regional order overnight without running the risk of losing their legitimacy and provoking domestic upheaval.

Finally, the actors involved in Euro–Mediterranean relations must take into account that identities influence the perception of reality, and that, therefore, different interpretations of reality are possible. If a peaceful order in the Mediterranean and Middle East is to emerge, a better understanding of the self-definition of the respective "other," along with its consequences for the perception of reality, is absolutely imperative.

Notes

1   Region-Building and Contested State Identities

1. The EMP originally included the EU and Morocco, Algeria, Tunisia, Egypt, Israel, Jordan, Lebanon, Syria, Turkey, Malta, Cyprus, and the Palestinian Authority. Malta and Cyprus entered the EU in May 2004, and Turkey officially became an EU candidate country in December 2004. Moreover, after the lifting of international sanctions, Libya was granted observer status to the EMP and may become a full member in the future.
2. In the present study, the terms "Islamism" and "Islamist" will be used to refer to political Islam and its proponents.
3. Although Islamist terrorism is real and serious, the portrayed threat of "Islam" does generally not imply any deeper understanding of the religion *per se*, let alone a differentiation between religion and the politically motivated, fundamentalist versions. These undifferentiated perceptions obviously grew stronger after 9/11.
4. The attempts to deal with military security resulted in two distinct proposals on a "Stability Pact" in the Mediterranean (Tanner 1994, 2000), which, however, did not materialize thus far.
5. If the perception of sharing common values grows stronger, a security region may well develop into a security community in the long term. On the other hand, a "security complex," referring to the "interdependence of rivalry and shared interests" (Buzan 1991: 190) among a group of states, is a purely instrumental concept that does not permit consideration of perceptions, values, and identity themes.
6. For this reason, it seems unlikely that the EU's current attempts to develop a common ESDP will considerably change the EU's distinctive foreign policy identity, precisely because the EC/EU has been defining itself through the particular traits of a civilian power over the last decades.
7. The EU publications *Euromed, Euromed Special Feature* and *Euromed Synopsis* are available at <http://europa.eu.int/comm/external_relations/med_mideast/euro_med_partnership/euromed_info.htm>, last accessed throughout February 2005.
8. MEDA differs from previous bilateral financial protocols in not having fixed country allocations. The priority of specific areas of cooperation is agreed between the EU and each Mediterranean partner for a period of three years,

and may be reviewed on a yearly basis. MEDA provides two types of financial assistance, the first one supporting economic transition, and the second covering the social and cultural sphere. Furthermore, MEDA allows financial support for regional projects, which are undertaken by at least two EU member states and two EMP partners.

9. Tunisia concluded the negotiations on a new bilateral agreement in June 1995, Israel in September 1995, and Morocco in November 1995.

10. The agreement with Tunisia already entered into force in 1998, the agreement with both Morocco and Israel in 2000, and the interim agreement with the PLO in 1997. The agreement with Egypt was signed in June 2001 and entered into force in 2004. Lebanon has signed a Euro-Mediterranean Association agreement in June 2002, and an interim agreement has been in force since 2003. The EU's negotiations with Algeria were concluded in December 2001, but the agreement is not yet in force. Syria concluded the negotiations only in 2004. Turkey's economic relations with the EU, on the other hand, are regulated through a customs union agreement of which the last phase entered into force in 1995.

11. Updated information and official figures related to the EMP are available at <http://europa.eu.int/comm/external_relations/euromed>, last accessed February 10, 2005.

12. The Israeli-Palestinian Interim Agreement on the West Bank and the Gaza Strip, commonly called Oslo II, was signed on September 28, 1995 in Washington.

2   Theoretical Framework

1. However, some realist scholars disagree with the orthodox systemic view of neo-realism. For example, Barry Buzan (1991: 96–107) treats the degree of socio-political cohesion as a variable affecting foreign-policy outcome. Other scholars shifted their focus of attention on perceptions (and misperceptions) in foreign-policy making from the mid-1970s onwards (Jervis 1976; Vertzberger 1990).

2. The Oxford Dictionary of Science defines positivism as the "philosophy of Comte, holding that the highest or only form of knowledge is the description of sensory phenomena. Comte held that there were three stages of human belief: the theological, the metaphysical, and finally the Positive, so-called because it confined itself to what is positively known, avoiding all speculation" (Blackburn 1994: 294).

3. During the "Third Debate," however, mainstream IR theory did not take the propositions of critical theory all too serious. One reason was that the critique was not backed up by conceptual elaborations and empirical research. Moreover, at that time, the Soviet Union and the cold war still existed, which apparently spared mainstream IR scholarship the test of theory verification and predictability. Some scholars even argued that the "Third Debate" was actually no debate at all (Kubálková et al. 1998a: 13).

4. In fact, the advent of positivism marked the end of the traditional philosophy of knowledge and cognition. In contrast to previous philosophers, such as Kant and Hegel, positivism did not ask about the conditions of cognition, but rather

defined them through the achievements of science and empirical research. With it, the *subject* of cognition was no longer problematized, and a neat distinction between subject and object was stipulated (Habermas 1994: 88–92).

5. In the words of Martin Hollis (1994: 49), generalizations "are projected forwards for purposes of prediction and backwards for purposes of explanation."

6. However, some constructivist scholars (Wendt 1999; Searle 1995; Dessler 1999) maintain that a subjective (or intersubjective) ontology is compatible with an objective (or positivist) epistemology. Yet in light of our discussion, this position is not fully convincing.

7. The early defenders of pragmatism, however, were still under the spell of positivism (Habermas 1994: 116–143). Pragmatism as used in the present context relies on later developments within this school of thought that includes a departure from positivism.

8. However, the assumption of liberal theory that identities are constant and intrinsic, along with liberalism's negligence of the state-level in its analyses, is rejected.

9. This study will not deal with personal identity, which designates the intrinsic and deeply rooted qualities of an actor's individuality, and which is prior to social interaction.

10. In fact, the concept of the "nation-state" is as fictive as the concept of "nation" itself. The classical "nation-states," such as France and England, were not really constituted by a culturally homogeneous "nation" (Llobera 1993; Anderson 1991). Until the present, true "nation-states" are extremely rare.

11. Factors that potentially trigger a rather peaceful *transformation* of state identities have been identified by different authors (Barnett 1996, 1999; Gross-Stein 1999; Berger 1996; Kowert and Legro 1996; Wendt 1999), although not systematically.

3   Historical Background and Regional Perspective

1. The various agreements notably differed from each other. Unlimited association agreements were signed with Greece (1961) and Turkey (1963), suggesting future EC membership. Limited association agreements were signed with Tunisia and Morocco in 1969, Malta (1970) and Cyprus (1972). Nonpreferential trade agreements were signed with Israel (1964), Lebanon (1965), and Yugoslavia (1970). A preferential agreement (i.e. involving unilateral trade concessions) was signed with Egypt (1972). The second agreement with Israel (1970) involved reciprocal trade concessions, comparable to the agreement signed with Spain in 1970 (Grilli 1993: chapter 5).

2. In this period, cooperation agreements were signed with Israel in 1975; Algeria, Morocco, and Tunisia in 1976; Egypt, Lebanon, Jordan, and Syria in 1977; and Yugoslavia in 1980.

3. In 1979, after four meetings, the Euro-Arab Dialogue was suspended upon request of the League of Arab States. Egypt's return to the Arab League permitted

the reopening of the dialogue in December 1989, followed by a conference in June 1990. In the meantime, the dialogue has once more been suspended.

4. Syria requested a full Israeli withdrawal from the Golan Hights to the June 4, 1967 borders, while Israel insisted on Syria's prior commitment to full normalization of relations, security arrangements, and open borders. It is not clear whether Rabin had in principle agreed to a full withdrawal in exchange for a "full peace" with Syria, as the Syrian chief negotiator in the peace talks with Israel, Walid Al-Moualem (1997), maintains.

5. In the aftermath of the strong earthquake that hit Turkey in August 1999, the international community, and particularly Greece, provided material assistance and support. Turkey reciprocated when an earthquake struck Greece a couple of months later. The "seismic diplomacy" laid the foundations for the improvement of relations between the two countries.

6. Written correspondence with the First Secretary of the EU Delegation to Algeria, June 18, 2001.

7. Written correspondence with the First Secretary of the EU Delegation to Algeria, June 18, 2001.

8. Interview with senior EU officials, April 2001.

9. Interview with senior EU officials, April 2001.

10. Interviews with Israeli Finance Ministry and Foreign Ministry officials, January 2001.

11. Egypt witnessed public protests in 1977, 1981, and 1986; Jordan in 1988; Morocco in the early 1980s and at the end of the 1990s; Tunisia in 1983, 1984, and 1988; and Algeria in 1988. Libya witnessed significant unrest throughout the 1990s, particularly after the UN imposed economic sanctions in 1992 due to the Libyan involvement in international terrorism.

12. In the early 1980s, oil prices rose to approximately U.S.-\$ 40 per barrel, plunged to below 10 U.S.-\$ a barrel from 1982 on, and stabilized around U.S.-\$ 18 at the end of the 1980s (Sela 1998: 218).

13. Before the first multiparty elections were hold, several new electoral codes were passed, which were manipulative and aimed at ensuring the victory of the ruling party FLN (*Front de Libération Nationale*). However, the Islamist FIS won the elections. The army called for the president's resignation, which followed suit, the Constitutional Council headed by General Nezzar took power, and the country was put under martial law (Zoubir 1999c).

4   Israel

1. For an earlier and much shorter version of this chapter see Del Sarto 2003, see also Del Sarto 2006.

2. A minority of secular Zionists, most notably Herzl himself, supported the founding of Israel in Uganda, but during the 1903 Zionist Congress, Palestine became the focus of Zionist aspirations.

3. The most important narratives are the Maccabees' revolt against the Macedonian rulers of Syria, Bar Kochva's revolt against the Romans, and the collective suicide at Massada as expression of resistance against the Romans.

In the 1920 battle of Tel Hai, the Jewish settlement defended itself against Palestinian aggressors.

4. The Maccabees could not resist the Greek rulers in the long run; Bar Kochva actually lost the war against the Romans; and after the collective suicide, Massada fell to the Romans. As for Tel Hai, the Jewish settlers lost the battle.

5. Israel's immigration law (the 1950 "Law of Return" and its 1971 amendment) grants Israeli citizenship to any Jewish immigrant interested in receiving it, as well as to his or her spouse, children, grandchildren and the spouses of the latter. Converts can also receive Israeli citizenship, along with their spouses.

6. The pattern of conflict is commemorated in the official holiday cycle in form of nonchronological historic events. Thus, "Hanukka commemorates the Maccabean revolt against the oppression of the Greeks . . ., Purim revolves around the threat to the Jews of Persia, Passover marks the Jews' liberation from bondage in Egypt, and Israel's Independence Day commemorates the war against Arab forces. Fast days and memorial days further reinforce this emphasis on conflicts: Tish'a be-Av relates to the destruction of the First and Second Temples by the Babylonians and Romans, respectively . . . and the Holocaust and Heroism Remembrance Day commemorates the Nazi atrocities" (Zerubavel 1995: 219).

7. The terms "Jewish state" and "state of the Jews" are often used as synonyms. However, a "state of the Jews" may be secular and democratic, in which the majority of its inhabitants are Jewish. But the concept of a "Jewish state" implies the institutionalization of Jewish religion, and may thus contradict secular and democratic values. Moreover, in a "Jewish state," the definition of the state depends on the religious definition of Jewishness, thus putting religious authority over secular state authority (Evron 1995). Finally, a "Jewish state" entails the preferential treatment of the Jewish collective over non-Jewish citizens (Kimmerling 1993; Smooha 1993). Israel's immigration law that encourages Jewish immigration from all over the world, but does not grant the same rights to non-Jewish Israeli citizens is a concrete case in point.

8. However, some groups among "the Arabs" became Israel's allies, such as the Druze inside the Green Line, who fought on Israel's side and are being drafted into the Israeli Army until present. Yet this does not mean that they are considered as full members of the "we-group."

9. While criticism of Israeli policy sometimes has anti-Semitic undertones, not every criticism of Israel is necessarily anti-Semitic. Generally speaking, a far greater sensitivity to the difference between criticism of Israel's policy (which may or may not be justified) and anti-Semitic arguments would be beneficial to both Israel and its critics.

10. Of course there have always been Jewish communities in Palestine through the ages, but the majority of Jews did not—and still does not—live in this area.

11. According to the Central Bureau of Statistics of Israel (2004, Table 2.1), the breakdown of Israel's average population of 6.748 million according to religion gives the following approximate figures: 76.5% Jewish, 15.9% Muslim, 2.1% Christian (subdivided into 1.7% "Arab Christians" and 0.4% "Other Christians"), and 1.6% Druze. The remaining 3.8% of the average population are not classified by religion. The breakdown according to "population

groups" states that "Jews and others" (including Jews, non-Arab Christians and unclassified) account for 80.7% and the "Arab population" for 19.3% of Israel's total population.

12. An independent commission of inquiry (the so-called Or Commission) subsequently criticized the police's inappropriate use of force in the October riots (*Ha'aretz* August 22, 2001: 3).

13. In a 1988 survey, 74% of the Jewish respondents said that the state should prefer Jews to Arabs, and 43% supported the denial of the right to vote to Israeli Arab citizens. 45% unconditionally supported a state policy encouraging Arab Israelis to leave the country, 37% had reservations, and 23% objected to such a policy (Smooha 1993).

14. Israel's withdrawal from the Sinai Peninsula in the framework of the 1979 peace treaty with Egypt under Begin did not contradict the concept of *Eretz Israel*, since Sinai is not part of "biblical Israel."

15. According to a 1995 survey of 1200 Jewish and Arab Israelis conducted by the University of Haifa, 81% of the Arab respondents supported the option of a bi-national state including full autonomy for Arab Israelis (while 91% of Jewish respondents disagreed). 40% of the Arab respondents agreed with the dominance of an Israeli identity if they could retain secondary identities (95% of the Jewish respondents disagreed). Interestingly, 65% of the Arab respondents agreed with a Jewish democracy, provided that the state gives them limited autonomy and full individual equality. Moreover, 31% of the Arab respondents favored the establishment of a Palestinian state in all of Palestine according to *shari'a* law (Ghanem 1997: 59–61).

16. Secular *Eretz Israel* supporters roughly comprised the *Likud*, the National Union, and *Israel Beiteinu*, a smaller ultra-nationalistic party representing Russian immigrants. Together, they held 27 out of 120 seats in the 15th Knesset. Supporters of *Medinat Israel* comprised Labour/One Israel with 26 seats, *Meretz* with 10 seats, (the now defunct) Center Party and *Shinui* (now in decline) with six seats each, and the two seats of a trade union-affiliated party.

17. *Israel B'Aliyah* merged with the *Likud* in 2003.

18. Interview with a senior official of the EU Delegation to Israel, February 14, 2001.

19. Discussions with Israeli Finance Ministry officials, January 30, 2001.

20. Discussions with Israeli Finance Ministry officials, January 30, 2001.

21. The diagonal cumulation of origin rules among two countries permits the processing of products in the first country, for which materials originating in the second country are used, and vice versa. The final product would still be considered as originating in the country of production and thus enjoy duty-free access to the EU.

22. Discussions with Israeli Foreign Ministry officials, January 31, 2001 and May 30, 2001.

23. Discussions with Israeli Foreign Ministry officials, January 31, 2001, May 30, 2001, and June 13, 2001.

24. Discussion with Israeli Foreign Ministry officials, May 30, 2001, and June 13, 2001.

25. Discussions with Israeli Finance Ministry officials, January 30, 2001.

26. The Foreign Minister portfolio has mostly been occupied by politicians of either the *Likud* or the Labour Party, and rarely of smaller secular parties that split from the latter. The religious parties never held this portfolio. The Arab parties were always excluded from government, and thus never held any portfolio at all.
27. I owe this observation to Sharon Lev.

5   Egypt

1. In the chapter on Egypt, the transcription of Arabic names follows the Egyptian pronunciation, i.e., *Gumhuriya* instead of *Jumhuriya*, *Gamal* instead of *Jamal*, etc. For the names of persons and places, this and the following chapters employ the spelling which is most common in the English-language literature (e.g. Nasser instead of Nasir or Nasr).
2. The name derives from the Egyptian delegation that traveled to Paris to request Egypt's independence at the Versailles conference after World War I.
3. The *Salafi* reformist movement (or *Salafiyya*), which emerged in the late nineteenth century, advocated a purification of Islam from allegedly heretic elements, and called for social justice and the solidarity of the Muslim community of believers. Although the movement was originally sympathetic to modernity, it strictly opposed the extensive influence of the "West" in Muslim countries.
4. Initiated by Britain and the United States, the Baghdad Pact aimed at providing NATO a basis in the Middle East in the context of cold-war politics. Eventually, Iraq was the only Middle Eastern country that entered the Pact.
5. Britain, the United States, the IBDR and, separately, the USSR had offered loans to finance the planned Aswan High Dam, Egypt's largest development project at that time. In July 1956, the Western powers redrew their offer because of Nasser's strong opposition against the planned Baghdad Pact. A week later, Nasser announced that the British-French Suez Canal Company had been nationalized and that revenues from the Canal would serve to finance the High Dam.
6. At present, Egypt's Copts are estimated at between 6 and 10 million in the literature, precise figures are not available. As Ajami (1999: 203) notes, "[t]he demographic weight of the Copts is one of the great riddles of Egypt."
7. Referring to the October 1973 war, the expression *tishreen*—the Arabic name for the months October and November—acquired a positive meaning. While numerous public buildings, streets and places in Egypt are named *tishreen*, a national holiday celebrates the Egyptian "victory" until the present. Similarly, the regime, such as Mubarak's chief political advisor Osama El-Baz (1998), regularly stresses the importance of the October War for Egypt's pride and development.
8. New parties must differ from existing parties, while parties based on region, class, or religion are forbidden. Insufficient difference from existing parties is the most common reason for refusing recognition.
9. In 2001 a military court sentenced Ibrahim to seven years of hard labor on the charges of defaming Egypt, accepting foreign funding without government approval, and embezzling funds. Ibrahim had infuriated the regime with

remarks on the discrimination of the Copts, electoral fraud, and the question of Mubarak's succession (Weaver 2001). The Court of Cassation annulled the verdict on procedural grounds, but a retrial confirmed it at the end of July 2002. Eventually, Said Eddin was released from jail, but he is forbidden to leave the country.

10. Nour, a former *Wafd* member, is accused of having forged signatures. His party *Al-Ghad* was admitted in November 2004 following a court ruling, after the recognition had been denied three times. In the parliamentary elections of November–December 2005, *Al-Ghad* obtained only one seat. In the presidential elections of September 2005, Nour gained 7.6% of the votes, thus coming in second after Mubarak.

11. *Al-hizb at-tagammu' al-watani at-taqaddumi al-wahdi*, or National-Progressive Unionist Party, comprises Nasserists and Marxists, and Left-leaning moderate Islamist (Ramsès 1997).

12. In addition to the Islamists, the Catholic Pope, along with the leader of Egypt's Coptic Church, opposed the provisions on abortion and other gender-related issues.

13. *Hisba*, an ambiguous principle of *shari'a* law from the ninth century permits Muslims to sue if they believe that Islam is being harmed. Following the conviction, Abu Zayd and his wife preferred to leave the country for the Netherlands.

14. It is telling that *Al-Ghad*'s former party secretary, Mona Makram-Ebeid, is a Coptic woman.

15. The main sources of Egypt's foreign aid was first "the West," then the USSR, then the Gulf monarchies (and in particularly Saudi Arabia), and after Camp David, the United States (Dessouki 1991).

16. Egypt's macro-economic indicators considerably improved during the 1990s, following the cancellation of nearly two thirds of Egypt's foreign debts after the 1991 Gulf War. Moreover, IMF-sponsored reforms triggered an investment boom and the repatriation of an estimated U.S.-$ 60 billion in foreign savings of Egyptians. Hence, the World Bank reclassified Egypt as a middle-income developing country with a per capita income of $1,500. However, Egypt continues to be "crowded and poor," as *The Economist* (January 5, 2001) has put it, with unofficial unemployment rates at 20%, poverty, large income gaps, and a scarce education system. Moreover, corruption and economic mismanagement cast doubts on the reliability of official economic data. Thus, it is widely believed that the government figures on Egypt's economic growth in 2001 and 2002 were over-optimistic since they did not consider the global recession of these years (Siddiqi 2000; UNDP 2003).

17. Interview with former Egyptian government official, July 17, 2002.

18. Interview with Egyptian diplomat, September 18, 2002.

19. Interview with Egyptian diplomats, July 17–18, 2002.

20. Egypt became the largest recipient of MEDA funds. EU concessions in agriculture particularly regard Egyptian exports of new potatoes, flowers, peas, beans, and oranges. However, the off-season quota of new potatoes is much higher than Egypt's actual production, so that, paradoxically, Egypt will start cultivating potatoes for exporting them to the EU (*Frankfurter Allgemeine Zeitung* March 21, 2000).

21. Interview with EU officials, February 14, 2001.
22. The strong presence of Egyptian nationals among the *Al-Qaeda* leadership includes one of the primary organizers of the 9/11 attacks, Mohammed Atta, and two top leaders of *Al-Qaeda*, Mohammed Atef and Ayman Al-Zawahiri, an exile leader of the Egyptian *Gihad*.
23. In June 2005, Egypt and Israel signed a long-delayed U.S.-$ 2.5 billion agreement on sales of Egyptian natural gas to Israel (*Ha'aretz* June 30, 2005).
24. Interview with Egyptian diplomat, September 20, 2002.
25. Interview with Egyptian diplomats, September 18, 2002 and July 17, 2002.
26. Interview with Egyptian diplomat, September 20, 2002.
27. In Arabic, the term for "Mediterranean" in the sense of "Mediterranean Sea" is as *al-bahar al-abiyad al-mutawassat* (the "White Middle Sea"), while the adjective "Mediterranean" is usually translated as *mutawassat* ("middle"). These terms do of course not convey the same romantic image as in English or French.
28. Discussion with former Egyptian government official, July 17, 2002; interview with Egyptian diplomats, 18 and September 20, 2002; discussions with Egyptian journalist and several businessmen, throughout October 2000.

6   Morocco

1. When Morocco became a French protectorate in 1912 (parts of the countryside stayed outside of French and Spanish colonial control until 1933), neighboring Algeria had been a French colony for more than eight decades and Tunisia for more than three.
2. The sayings of God in the Qur'an and those of his messenger Mohammed are believed to be the ultimate source of *baraka*. The concept of *baraka* is also embedded in the veneration of saints, which was and remains and important aspect of the *Sufi* tradition of Moroccan Islam.
3. Morocco thus notably differs from the Egyptian case, where the king sided with the British colonialists. This fact deprived the Egyptian king of his legitimacy in the eyes of the population.
4. The Lower House of Representatives, *Majlis an-Nuwab*, comprises 325 representatives that are directly elected for a five-year term. The Upper House, *Majlis al-Mustasharin*, comprises 270 deputies, which are indirectly elected by leaders of regional and municipal councils and professional groups.
5. The word *makhzan* derives from the verb *khazana*, which means to store up goods, money, and supplies, and thus conveys the image of the state as a storage of treasures and benefits.
6. If not indicated otherwise, this and the following translations of the official speeches from the French are the author's translations.
7. Moroccan NGO activists in discussions with the author, Rabat, 4–5 December 2004.
8. In the 2002 elections, the major pro-royal parties lost seats. Thus, the RNI gained 41 seats and the parties that make up the explicitly pro-royal alliance *Wifaq* only 55 (out of a total of 325).

9. In the 1997 elections, the *Istiqlal* won only 10% of parliamentary seats, partly due to the Palace's intervention.

10. The USFP held 60 seats in parliament between 1997 and 2002, and is now represented with 50 seats.

11. Moroccan NGO activists in discussions with the author, Rabat, 4–5 December 2004.

12. *Le Journal / As-Sahifa* reappeared shortly afterwards, whereas the imprisoned editor-in-chief of *Demain*, Ali Mrabet, was only released in 2004.

13. The document was initially available at the Sheikh's website at <http://www.yassineonline.net>, but was then taken off the Internet.

14. Under Hassan II, the mosques were closed except for prayer time, since the Islamists had used them for political propaganda.

15. U.S.–Moroccan relations at least date back to World War II. With the help of the sultan, and later King Mohammed V, American troops landed on the coast of Morocco in November 1942 in order to prevent that Morocco, most of it already controlled by Vichy France, would fall to Nazi Germany. From the mid-1970s, the United States became the most important source of weapon supply for the Moroccan army, followed by France (Pennell 2000: 259–345).

16. The agricultural products of importance to Morocco were covered by the CAP and they were thus granted tariff preferences that reflected the self-sufficiency ratio prevailing in the EC (Grilli 1993: 194–195).

17. According to Lister (1997: 91), Brussels treated the 1984 application "as a joke, much to the mortification of the Moroccans." On Morocco's 1987 application, she remarks that officials in Brussels did not know whether "to laugh or cry."

18. The first financial protocol (1978–1981) granted ECU 130 million in grants and loans, the second protocol (1982–1986) ECU 199 million, the third (1987–1991) ECU 324 million, and the fourth (1992–1995) ECU 472 million (Grilli 1993: 196; Damis 1998: 94).

19. The fisheries dispute concerns the livelihood of some 30,000 people working in fishing and fish processing industries in Spain, Portugal, and the Canary Islands. Under the former agreement, European fishing fleets could catch 82,000 tons of fish in Moroccan territorial waters a year, for which Morocco yearly received U.S.-$ 135 million. Rabat claimed that this agreement was signed before Morocco developed its own fishing industry. In addition, Morocco accused the European fleets of over-fishing (*The Economist* September 9, 1995: 47–48).

20. These provisions take into account the sensitiveness of the respective products for Morocco's economy that will gradually be exposed to EU competition. According to the complex annex to the agreement, trade barriers that are eliminated within 3 years apply to approximately 900 and 300 items respectively. According to Annex 4, approximately 800 items are subject to the elimination of customs duties within 12 years. Annex 6 lists the exceptions to these rules, which apply to approximately 30 items (Commission 1995b).

21. In 1999–2000, Morocco had a population of 28.7 million, a GDP per capita of U.S.-$ 1,180, and an external debt of 48 % of GDP. The unemployment rate was 21.7%, 20% of the population live under the poverty line, and the

illiteracy rate is at 52% of the population (and 80% among rural women). The Human Development Index (HDI) ranks Morocco on place 112 among 174 countries (Commission 2001).

22. Written correspondence with Moroccan foreign ministry official, May 8, 2002.

23. Egypt also claims to be the mentor of the sub-regional Agadir process which involves Morocco, Tunisia, Egypt, and Jordan.

24. Spain and Morocco signed a bilateral agreement in July 2001 on the regulation of legal Moroccan workforce, which also establishes a Spanish-Moroccan commission in charge of setting annual quota for the hiring of Moroccan workers, depending on the demand in Spain. Similarly, the agreement regulates the labor rights of Moroccan workers.

25. According to Moroccan official figures, the area of cannabis cultivation grew from 11,500 hectares in 1986 to 50,000 hectares in 1997 and to 134,000 hectares in 2003 (*The Economist* August 10, 2000: 40; UNODC 2003: 5).

26. Written correspondence with Moroccan foreign ministry official, May 18, 2002.

27. In the meantime, the Ministry of Prevision and Economic Planning has been integrated into the Ministry of Finances and Privatization.

28. Written correspondence with Moroccan foreign ministry official, April 20, 2002.

29. Interestingly, in the French version of the official speeches, the term *espace* is used more often than the term *region*. Designating both "area" and "space," the image conveyed by the term *espace* thus goes beyond territory and geography.

30. In the original French text, Mohammed VI (2001c) stated: "*Pour les Occidentaux, le Maroc, c'est l'Orient, pour les Orientaux, le Maroc, c'est l'Occident. Nous sommes la zone tampon, le sas. Nous sommes un véritable buvard.*"

31. Discussion with Moroccan diplomats and journalists, Paris July 18, 2002 and Brussels, September 19, 2002.

32. Written correspondence with Moroccan foreign ministry official, April 8, 2002.

33. In 1970, the Polisario Front declared the independence of the Democratic Arab Republic of the Sahara, which was admitted to the Organization of African States (OAS) in 1985. As a result, Morocco left the OAS.

34. This moderation has a long history. Mohammed V for instance refused to apply the racial discrimination of the Vichy regime to Moroccan Jews. Yet after his death, and in view of the persisting Arab–Israeli conflict, the situation of Morocco's Jews became more uncertain, and many left to Israel or France. From the late 1970s on, Hassan II adopted a "pro-Jewish" policy, and invited emigrated Moroccan Jews to return (Malka 1978). A few Jewish Moroccans played, and still play, an important political role in Morocco, such as the financial advisor to the king, André Azoulay, or Abraham Serfaty, the former exiled dissident, who was appointed advisor to the state hydrocarbon authority after his return to Morocco in the late 1990s.

35. For instance, in December 2001 the USFP's publication *Al-Ittihad al-Ishtiraki* named the late Palestinian president Yasser Arafat "man of the year."

36. Moroccan diplomats in discussions with the author, Paris July 18, 2002.

37. A similar argument can be made for Michail Gorbatchev's dramatic reform process under the banner of *Glasnost* and *Perestroijka* that eventually led to the end of the Soviet Union—and of his own political career.
38. In 1992, women's groups collected a million signatures for reforming the family code in order to abolish the validity of *shari'a* law regarding marriage, divorce, polygamy, and heritage, which clearly put women at a disadvantage. Some minor changes were made over the years, but due to a large domestic resistance, the reform was on hold until 2003.
39. Moroccan NGO activists in discussions with the author, Rabat, 4–5 December 2004.

Abd al-Nasser, Gamal. 1959. *The Philosophy of the Revolution*. Buffalo, NY: Smith, Keynes & Marshall.

Abdel Nour, Ayman. 2001. "Syrian Views on an Association Agreement with the European Union." *EuroMeSCo Papers*, December 14, 2001.

Académie du Maroc, ed. 1996. *Quel avenir pour le bassin méditerranéen et l'Union Européenne?* Rabat: Académie du Royaume du Maroc.

Adler, Emanuel. 1991. "Cognitive Evolution: A Dynamic Approach to the Study of International Relations and their Progress." In E. Adler and B. Crawford, eds., *Progress in Postwar International Relations*, pp. 43–88. New York: Columbia University Press.

———. 1997a. "Imagined (Security) Communities: Cognitive Regions in International Relations." *Millennium* 26(2): 249–277.

———. 1997b. "Seizing the Middle Ground. Constructivism in World Politics." *European Journal of International Relations* 3(3): 319–363.

Adler, Emanuel, and Beverly Crawford. 2006. "Normative Power: The European Practice of Region Building and the Case of the Euro-Mediterranean Partnership." In E. Adler, F. Bicchi, B. Crawford, and R. Del Sarto, eds., *The Convergence of Civilizations: Constructing a Mediterranean Region*, pp. 3–47. Toronto: University of Toronto Press.

Adler, Emanuel, and Beverly Crawford, eds. 1991. *Progress in Postwar International Relations*. New York: Columbia University Press.

Adler, Emanuel, and Michael N. Barnettt, eds. 1998. *Security Communities*. New York: Cambridge University Press.

Adler, Emanuel, Federica Bicchi, Beverly Crawford, and Raffaella A. Del Sarto, eds. 2006. *The Convergence of Civilizations: Constructing a Mediterranean Region*. Toronto: University of Toronto Press.

Ajami, Fouad. 1979. "The Struggle for Egypt's Soul." *Foreign Policy* 35 (Summer): 3–30.

———. 1992. *The Arab Predicament. Arab Political Thought and Practice since 1967*. Updated edition, Cambridge: Cambridge University Press,.

———. 1999. *The Dream Palace of the Arabs. A Generation's Odyssey*. New York: Vintage Books.

Al-Ali, Nadje. 2000. *Secularism, Gender and the State in the Middle East: The Egyptian Women's Movement*. Cambridge, U.K.: Cambridge University Press.

Alami M'Chichi, Houria, Malika Benradi, Aziz Chaker, Mohamed Mouaqit, Mohamed Said, and Abdel-Ilah Yaakoubd. 2004. *Féminin-Masculin: La marche vers l'égalité au Maroc, 1993–2003*. Rabat: Friedrich Ebert Stiftung-FES Maroc.

Alaoui, Mohamed Ben El Hassan. 1994. *La coopération entre l'Union Européenne et les pays du Maghreb*. Paris: Nathan.

Al-Ashmawy, Muhammmad Said. 1989. *L'Islamisme contre l'Islam*. Paris and Cairo: La Découverte / Al-Fikr.

Al-Fasi, 'Alal. 1954. *The Independence Movements of Arab North Africa*. Translated by Hazem Zaki Nuseibeh, Washington, D.C.: American Council of Learned Societies.

Aliboni, Roberto, and Abdel Monem Said Aly. 2000. "Challenges and Prospects." *Mediterranean Politics* 5(1): 209–224.

Aliboni, Roberto, George Joffé, and Tim Niblock. 1996. *Security Challenges in the Mediterranean Region*. London: Frank Cass.

Al-Jabri, Mohammed 'Abed. 1999a. *Arab-Islamic Philosophy: A Contemporary Critique*. Translated from the French by Aziz Abassi, Austin: The University of Texas, the Center for Middle Eastern Studies.

———. 1999b. "L'ambition du gouvernement Youssoufi: une société démocratique: Entretien avec Mohammed Abed Al-Jabri." *Confluences Méditerranée* 31 (Fall): 133–146.

Al-Moualem, Walid. 1997. "Fresh Light on the Syrian Peace Negotiations." *Journal of Palestine Studies* 26(2): 81–94.

Al-Nahhas, Mona. 2000. "Nasserism's Potential: Untapped." *Al-Ahram Weekly* 503, October 12, 2000.

———. 2004. "Tomorrow Party Today." *Al-Ahram Weekly* 715, November 4, 2004.

Alpher, Joseph. 1995. "Israel: The Challenges of Peace." *Foreign Policy* 101 (Winter): 130–145.

———. 1998. "The Political Role of the European Union in the Arab-Israeli Peace Process: An Israeli Perspective." *The International Spectator* 33(4): 77–86.

Al-Sharkawy, Yussuf. 1997. "Security and Cooperation in the Mediterranean: The Policy of the European Union." *Strategic Papers* 46. Cairo: Al-Ahram Center for Political and Strategic Studies.

Anderson, Benedict. 1991. *Imagined Communities: Reflections on the Origins and Spread of Nationalism*. 2nd edition. London: Verso.

Ansari, Hamied N. 1984. "Sectarian Conflict in Egypt and the Political Expediency of Religion." *Middle East Journal* 38(3): 397–418.

Arad, Ruth, Seev Hirsch, and Alfred Tovias. 1983. *The Economics of Peace-Making: Focus on the Egyptian-Israeli Situation*. London: Macmillan.

Archer, Margaret, et al., eds. 1998. *Critical Realism: Essential Readings*. London and New York: Routledge.

Arian, Asher. 1995. *Security Threatened: Surveying Israeli Opinion on Peace and War*. New York: Cambridge University Press.

Arkoun, Mohamed. 1984. *Critique de la raison Islamique*. Paris: Maisonneuve & Larose.

Aronoff, Myron J. 1993. "The Origins of Israeli Political Culture." In E. Sprinzak and L. Diamond, eds., *Israeli Democracy under Stress*, pp. 47–63. Boulder: Lynne Rienner.

Avineri, Shlomo. 1981. *The Making of Modern Zionism: The Intellectual Origins of the Jewish State.* New York: Basic Books.

———. 1986. "Ideology and Israel's Foreign Policy." *The Jerusalem Quarterly* 37: 3–13.

Avineri, Shlomo, and Werner Weidenfeld. 1999a. "Preface." In S. Avineri and W. Weidenfeld, eds., *Integration and Identity: Challenges to Europe and Israel,* pp. 5–7. Bonn: Europa Union.

Avineri, Shlomo, and Werner Weidenfeld, eds. 1999b. *Integration and Identity: Challenges to Europe and Israel.* Bonn: Europa Union.

Ayubi, Nazih Nassif Michail. 1980a. *Bureaucracy and Politics in Contemporary Egypt.* London: Middle East Centre at St. Anthony College Oxford, and Ithaca Press.

———. 1980b. "The Political Revival of Islam: The Case of Egypt." *International Journal of Middle Eastern Studies* 16(4): 481–499.

Badran, Margot. 2002. "What's in a Name?" *Al-Ahram Weekly* 569, January 17, 2002.

Barak, Ehud. 1996. "Remarks by Foreign Minister Barak to the International Press Institute, 27 March 1996." Jerusalem: Ministry of Foreign Affairs.

Barcelona Declaration Adopted at the Euro-Mediterranean Conference, 27–28 November 1995. Barcelona, November 28, 1995, Final Version.

Barnett, Michael N. 1996. "Identity and Alliances in the Middle East." In P. Katzenstein, ed., *The Culture of National Security: Norms and Identity in World Politics,* pp. 400–447. New York: Columbia University Press.

———. 1999. "Culture, Strategy and Foreign Policy Change: Israel's Road to Oslo." *European Journal of International Relations* 5(1): 5–36.

Barzilai, Vered, and Amnon Barzilai. 2002. "The Discreet Charms of Ariel Sharon." *Ha'aretz Magazine,* English Edition, November 29, 2002: 14–17.

Bayoumi, Gamal. 1998. "L'UE fait preuve de plus de flexibilité: Interview with Gamal Bayoumi." *Al-Ahram Hebdo,* French edition, August 12, 1998.

BBC World. 2002. "The King and the Sheikh's Daughter." *BBC World,* March 28, 2002, 18.30–19.00 GTM.

Beattie, Kirk J. 1994. *Egypt during the Nasser Years: Ideology, Politics, and Civil Society.* Boulder, Co: Westview Press.

Begin, Menachem. 1981a. "Statement by Prime Minister Begin to the Zionist General Council, 23 June 1977." In M. Medzini, ed., 1981, *Israel's Foreign Relations: Selected Documents,* vol. 4–5: 1977–1979, document 6, pp. 9–15. Jerusalem: Ministry of Foreign Affairs.

———. 1981b. "Statement to the Knesset by Prime Minister Begin on His visit to the US, 27 July 1977." In M. Medzini, ed., 1981, *Israel's Foreign Relations: Selected Documents,* vol. 4–5: 1977–1979, document 25, pp. 55–67. Jerusalem: Ministry of Foreign Affairs.

Ben Ami, Shlomo, and Javier Solana. 2000. "Statement by Foreign Minister Shlomo Ben Ami and Javier Solana, EU High Representative for Common Foreign and Security Policy Following their Meeting, 11 December 2000." Jerusalem: Ministry of Foreign Affairs.

Ben Haddou, Ali. 1997. *Les élites du Royaume: Essai sur l'organisation du pouvoir au Maroc.* Paris: L'Harmattan.

Benaïssa, Mohamed. 2000. "Déclaration de Monsieur Mohammed Benaïssa, Ministre des Affaires Étrangères et de la Coopération Internationale, à la MAP en marge de la Conférence Euro-Méditerranéenne à Marseille, le 16/01/2000." Rabat: Ministry of Foreign Affairs.

———. 2001a. "Forum Méditerranéen: Déclaration à la presse, Tangiers le 10 et 11 May 2001." Rabat: Ministry of Foreign Affairs.

———. 2001b. "Synthèse de la Déclaration de Monsieur Mohamed Benaïssa, Ministre des Affaires Étrangères et de la Coopération lors de la Séance Plénière de la 8-ème Session ordinair [sic] du Forum Méditerranéen, Tangier 11/5/2001." Rabat: Ministry of Foreign Affairs.

———. 2002. "Allocution prononcée par M. Mohamed Benaïssa, Ministre des Affaires Étrangères et de la Coopération, Thème: 'Perspectives de la Politique Etrangère du Maroc,' Chatham House, 21/2/2002." Rabat: Ministry of Communication.

Ben-Gurion, David. 1948. "Broadcast to the Nation, May 15, 1948." Jerusalem: Ministry of Foreign Affairs.

———. 1976. "Report to the State Council by Prime Minister and Minister of Defence Ben-Gurion, 22 July 1948." In M. Medzini, ed., 1976, *Israel's Foreign Relations: Selected Documents*, vol. 1–2: 1947–1974, document 16, pp. 153–155. Jerusalem: Ministry of Foreign Affairs.

Benvenisti, Meron. 1996. "Erroneous Mediterranean Port." *Ha'aretz*, March 21, 1996.

Berger, Peter L., and Thomas Luckmann. 1966. *The Social Construction of Reality: A Treatise in the Sociology of Knowledge*. New York: Anchor.

Berger, Thomas U. 1996. "Norms, Identity, and National Security in Germany and Japan." In P. Katzenstein, ed., *The Culture of National Security: Norms and Identity in World Politics*, pp. 317–356. New York: Columbia University Press.

Bhaskar, Roy. 1975. *A Realist Theory of Science*. Leeds: Leeds Books.

———. 1979. *The Possibility of Naturalism: A Philosophical Critique of the Contemporary Human Sciences*. Brighton: Harvester.

Bicchi, Federica. 2004. "L'Unione Europea e la promozione della democrazia." In F. Bicchi, L. Guazzone, and D. Pioppi, eds., *La Questione della Democrazia nel Mondo Arabo: Stati, società e conflitti*, pp. 143–170. Monza: Polimetrica.

Bicchi, Federica, Laura Guazzone, and Daniela Pioppi, eds. 2004. *La Questione della Democrazia nel Mondo Arabo: Stati, società e conflitti*. Monza: Polimetrica.

Bin, Alberto, ed. 1996. *Co-operation and Security in the Mediterranean. Prospects after Barcelona*. Malta: The Mediterranean Academy of Diplomatic Studies.

Biscop, Sven. 2003. *Euro-Mediterranean Security: A Search for Partnership*. Aldershot: Ashgate.

Blackburn, Simon. 1994. *The Oxford Dictionary of Philosophy*. Oxford: Oxford University Press.

Bloom, William. 1990. *Personal Identity, National Identity and International Relations*. Cambridge: Cambridge University Press.

Bourqia, Rahma. 1999. "The Cultural Legacy of Power in Morocco." In R. Bourqia and S. Miller, eds., *In the Shadow of the Sultan: Culture, Power, and Politics in Morocco*, pp. 243–258. Cambridge: Harvard University Press.

Bourqia, Rahma, and Susan Gilson Miller, eds. 1999. *In the Shadow of the Sultan: Culture, Power, and Politics in Morocco*. Cambridge: Harvard University Press.

Brand, Laurie A. 1998. *Women, the State, and Political Liberalization: Middle Eastern and North African Experiences*. New York: Columbia University Press.

Braudel, Fernand. 1972. *The Mediterranean and the Mediterranean World in the Age of Philip II*. English translation of second revised edition. London: William Collins Sons & Co.

Bush, George W. 2002. "President Bush's State of the Union Address to Congress and the Nation." *The New York Times*, January 30, 2002: 22.

Bush, Kenneth D., and E. Fuat Keyman. 1997. "Identity-Based Conflict: Rethinking Security in a Post-Cold War World." *Global Governance* 3(3): 309–328.

Buzan, Barry. 1983. *People, States and Fears: Security Problems in International Relations*. Chapel Hill: University of North Carolina.

———. 1991. *People, States and Fear. An Agenda for International Security Studies in the Post-Cold War Era*. 2nd edition. Boulder: Lynne Rienner.

Buzan, Barry, Ole Waever, and Jaap De Wilde, eds. 1998. *Security: A New Framework for Analysis*. Boulder: Lynne Rienner.

Campbell, David. 1992. *Writing Security: United States Foreign Policy and the Politics of Identity*. Minneapolis: University of Minnesota Press.

Carlsnaes, Walter, Helen Sjursen, and Brian White. eds. 2004. *Contemporary European Foreign Policy*. London: Sage.

Carr, E. H. 1964. *The Twenty Years' Crisis, 1919–1939: An Introduction to the Study of International Relations*. 2nd edition. London: Macmillan.

Central Bureau of Statistics of the State of Israel. 2004. *55th Annual Statistical Abstract of Israel*. Jerusalem: Central Bureau of Statistics.

Chartouny-Dubarry, May. 2000. "Political Transition in the Middle East." *Mediterranean Politics* 5(1): 53–76.

Combs-Schilling, M. Elaine. 1999. "Performing Monarchy, Staging Nation." In R. Bourqia and A. Miller, eds., *In the Shadow of the Sultan: Culture, Power, and Politics in Morocco*, pp. 176–214. Cambridge: Harvard University Press.

Commission (of the European Communities). 1990. *Redirecting the Community's Mediterranean Policy: Proposals for the Period 1992–96*. Communication to the Council, Brussels, June 1, 1990, SEC(90) 812 final.

———. 1992. *Future Relations between the Community and the Maghreb*. Communication from the Commission to the Council, Brussels, April 30, 1992, SEC(92) 401 final.

———. 1993. *Future Relations between the Community and the Middle East*. Brussels, September 1, 1993, COM(93) 375 final.

———. 1994. *Strengthening the Mediterranean Policy of the European Union: Establishing a Euro-Mediterranean Partnership*. Communication from the Commission to the Council and the European Parliament, October 19, 2004, COM(94) 427 final.

———. 1995a. *Strengthening the Mediterranean Policy of the European Union: Proposals for Implementing a Euro-Mediterranean Partnership*. Communication from the Commission to the Council and the European Parliament, March 8, 1995, COM(95) 72 final.

Commission (of the European Communities). 1995b. *Euro-Mediterranean Agreement Establishing an Association between the European Community and their Member States, of the one Part, and the Kingdom of Morocco, of the other Part*, December 12, 1995, COM(95) 740 final.

————. 2000a. *Reinvigorating the Barcelona Process*. Communication from the Commission to the Council and the European Parliament to Prepare the Fourth Meeting of the Euro-Mediterranean Foreign Ministries, Brussels, September 6, 2000, COM(2000) 497 final.

————. 2000b. *The Barcelona Process, Five Years On: 1995–2000*. Luxembourg: Office for Official Publications of the European Communities.

————. 2001. *Maroc: Document de Stratégie 2002–2006 et Programme Indicatif National 2002–2006*. Brussels, December 6, 2001.

————. 2002a. *Egypt: Country Strategy Paper 2002–2006 and National Indicative Programme 2002–2004*. At <europa.eu.int/comm/external_relations/Egypt/ csp/index.htm>, accessed August 5, 2002.

————. 2002b. *Valencia Action Plan Adopted at the Vth Euro-Mediterranean Conference of Ministers for Foreign Affairs*. Valencia, April 23, 2002, final version.

————. 2003. *Wider Europe—Neighbourhood: A New Framework for Relations with our Eastern and Southern Neighbours*. Communication from the Commission to the Council and the European Parliament, Brussels, March 11, 2003, COM(2003) 104 final.

————. 2004. *European Neighbourhood Policy: Strategy Paper*. Communication from the Commission, Brussels, May 12, 2004, COM(2004) 373 final.

Cooper, Mark Neal. 1982. *The Transformation of Egypt*. London: Croom Helms.

Dachs, Gisela, and Joel Peters. 2004. "Israel and Europe, the Troubled Relationship: Between Perceptions and Reality." IEPN Discussion Paper, Tel Aviv: Friedrich Ebert Stiftung.

Dagi, Ihsan D. 1993. "Turkey in the 1990s: Foreign Policy, Human Rights, and the Search for a New Identity." *Mediterranean Quarterly* 4(4): 60–77.

Damis, John. 1998. "Morocco's 1995 Association Agreement with the European Union." *The Journal of North African Studies* 3(4): 91–112.

Daoued, Zakia. 1994. "La conférence du Caire et ses enjeux." *Monde Arabe Maghreb-Machrek* 146: 115–134.

Darwish, Adel. 2001. "A Rebel without a Pause." *Middle East* 314 (July–August): 11–13.

Dawisha, Adeed. 1988a. "Conclusions: Reasons for Resilience." In A. Dawisha and I. W. Zartman, eds., *Beyond Coercion: The Durability of the Arab State*, pp. 276–283. London: Croom Helm and Istituto Affari Internazionali.

————. 1988b. "Arab Regimes: Legitimacy and Foreign Policy." In A. Dawisha and I. W. Zartman, eds., *Beyond Coercion: The Durability of the Arab State*, pp. 260–275. London: Croom Helm and Istituto Affari Internazionali.

Dawisha, Adeed, ed. 1983. *Islam in Foreign Policy*. Cambridge, U.K.: Cambridge University Press.

Dawisha, Adeed, and I. William Zartman, eds. 1988. *Beyond Coercion: The Durability of the Arab State*. London: Croom Helm and Istituto Affari Internazionali.

Deeb, Mary-Jane. 1995. "Socialist People's Libyan Arab Jamahiriya." In D. Long and B. Reich, eds., *The Governments and Politics of the Middle East and North Africa*, 3rd edition, pp. 349–368. Boulder, Co.: Westview Press.

———. 1999. "Political and Economic Developments in Libya in the 1990s." In Y. Zoubir, ed., *North Africa in Transition: State, Society, and Economic Transformation in the 1990s*, pp. 77–89. Gainsville, Fl.: University of Florida Press.

Dekmejian, Richard Hrair. 1971. *Egypt under Nasir: A Study in Political Dynamics*. Albany: State University of New York Press.

Del Sarto, Raffaella A. 1999. "Israeli Identity as Seen through European Eyes. " In S. Avineri and W. Weidenfeld, eds., 1999b, *Integration and Identity: Challenges to Europe and Israel*, pp. 59–79. Bonn: Europa Union.

———. 2003. "Israel's Contested Identity and the Mediterranean." *Mediterranean Politics* 8(1): 27–58.

———. 2004. "Turkey's EU Membership: An Asset for the EU's Policy towards the Mediterranean/Middle East?" In N. Tocci and A. Evin, eds., *Towards Accession Negotiations: Turkey's Domestic and Foreign Policy Challenges Ahead*, pp. 137–156. Florence: European University Institute, RSCAS.

———. 2005. "Setting the (Cultural) Agenda: Concepts, Communities, and Representation in Euro-Mediterranean Relations." In T. Schumacher and M. Pace, eds., *Conceptualising Cultural Dialogue and Social Relations in the Euro-Mediterranean Area*, Mediterranean Politics, special issue, (10)3: 313–330.

———. 2006. "Region-Building, European Union Normative Power, and Contested Identities: The Case of Israel." In E. Adler, F. Bicchi, B. Crawford, and R. Del Sarto, eds., *The Convergence of Civilizations: Constructing a Mediterranean Region*, pp. 296–333. Toronto: University of Toronto Press.

Del Sarto, Raffaella A., and Alfred Tovias. 2001. "Caught between Europe and the Orient: Israel and the EMP." *The International Spectator* (36)4: 61–75.

Del Sarto, Raffaella A., and Tobias Schumacher. 2005. "From EMP to ENP: What's at Stake with the European Neighbourhood Policy towards the Southern Mediterranean?" *European Foreign Affairs Review* 10(1): 17–38.

Denoeux, Guilain. 2000. "The Politics of Morocco's Fight against Corruption." *Middle East Policy* 7(2): 165–189.

Desrues, Thierry. 1999. "Le partnenariat euro-méditerranéen? Une approche illustrée par les cas marocain et tunisien." *Hérodote* 94(3): 94–114.

Desrues, Thierry, and Eduardo Moyano. 2001. "Social Change and Political Transition in Morocco." *Mediterranean Politics* 6(1): 21–47.

Dessler, David. 1999. "Constructivism within a Positivist Social Science." *Review of International Studies* 25(1): 123–137.

Dessouki, Ali E. Hillal. 1991. "The Primacy of Economics: The Foreign Policy of Egypt." In B. Korany and A. E. H. Dessouki, eds., *The Foreign Policy of Arab States: The Challenge of Change*, pp. 156–185. Boulder, Co.: Westview Press.

Deutsch, Karl W., et al. 1957. *Political Community and the North Atlantic Area: International Organization in Light of Historical Experience*. Princeton, N.J.: Princeton University Press.

Di Cara, Stefano. 2001. "The Euro-Mediterranean Partnership: Concept, Structure, Recent Developments." Speech given to the conference *Israel and the*

Euro-Mediterranean Partnership: Experience to Date." Organized by the Delegation of the European Commission to the State of Israel in cooperation with the Swedish Presidency of the EU, Tel Aviv, May 16, 2001.

Don-Yehia, Elizier. 1997. "Religion, Ethnicity and Electoral Reform: The Religious Parties and the 1996 Elections." *Israel Affairs* 4(1): 73–102.

Dowty, Alan et al., eds. 1997. *The Role of Domestic Politics in Israeli Peace-Making.* Jerusalem: Leonard Davis Institute for International Relations, Hebrew University of Jerusalem.

Duchêne, François. 1973. "The European Community and the Uncertainties of Interdependence." In M. Kohnstamm and W. Hager, eds. *A Nation Writ Large? Foreign Policy Problems before the European Communities*, pp. 1–21. London: Macmillan.

Dupret, Baudouin. 2000. "Justice égyptienne, moralité publique et pouvoir politique." *Monde Arabe Maghreb-Machrek* 167: 14–24.

Durkheim, Emile. 1964. *The Division of Labour in Society.* New York: Free Press.

Eban, Abba. 1976a. "Statement to the Security Council by Foreign Minister Eban, 6 June 1967." In M. Medzini, ed., 1976, *Israel's Foreign Relations: Selected Documents*, vol. 1–2: 1947–1974, document 19, pp. 784–792. Jerusalem: Ministry of Foreign Affairs.

———. 1976b. "Statement to the General Assembly by Foreign Minister Eban, 19 June 1967." In M. Medzini, ed., 1976, *Israel's Foreign Relations: Selected Documents*, vol. 1–2: 1947–1974, document 25, pp. 802–818. Jerusalem: Ministry of Foreign Affairs.

Edwards, Geoffrey, and Eric Phillippart. 1997. "The Euro-Mediterranean Partnership: Fragmentation and Reconstruction." *European Foreign Affairs Review* 3(2): 265–489.

Eickelman, Dale F. 2002. "Bin Laden, the Arab 'Street', and the Middle East's Democracy Deficit." *Current History* 100(651): 36–39.

Elazar, Daniel J., and Shmuel Sandler. 1997. "The Battle over Jewishness and Zionism in the Post-Modern Era." *Israel Affairs* 4(1): 1–29.

El-Baz, Osama. 1998. "The Sprit of October." *Al-Ahram Weekly* 398, October 8, 1998.

El-Said, Rifaat. 2000. "Opposition is not about Loud Voices: Interview with Rifaat El-Said," *Al-Ahram Weekly* 500, September 21, 2000.

El-Sayed Said, Mohamed. 2001. "Bothered and Bewildered." *Al-Ahram Weekly* 537, June 7, 2001.

El-Shazly, Fathi. 1996. "Concluding Remarks Delivered by Ambassador Fathi El-Shazly, Assistant Minister of Foreign Affairs, to the First Meeting of Senior Officials Dealing with Political and Security Partnership within the Barcelona Process, March 1996." Cairo: Ministry of Foreign Affairs.

Entelis, John P. 1989. *Culture and Counterculture in Moroccan Politics.* Boulder: Westview Press.

Ergil, Doğu. 2000. "Identity Crises and Political Instability in Turkey." *Journal of International Affairs* 54(1): 43–62.

Essam El-Din, Gamal. 1999. "Normalization on Trial." *Al-Ahram Weekly* 435, June 24, 1999.

———. 2002. "Liberalization vs. Protectionism." *Al-Ahram Weekly* 586, May 16, 2002.

Euro-Mediterranean Parliamentary Forum. 2001. "Final Declaration of the Second Session of the Euro-Mediterranean Parliamentary Forum," Brussels, February 8 and 9, 2001. *Euromed Report* 25, February 9, 2001.

European Council. 1973. "Copenhagen Declaration." *Bulletin of the European Communities*, 12/73, Annex 1.

———. 1980. "Declaration of the European Council on the Middle East." Venice, June 12–13, 1980. *Bulletin of the European Communities* 6/1980.

———. 1994. "Presidency Conclusions of the European Council, 9 and 10 December 1994 in Essen." SN 300/94.

———. 2000. "Common Strategy of the European Council of June 19, 2000 on the Mediterranean Region, 2000/458/CFSP." *Official Journal of the European Communities*, L 183/5.

Evron, Boaz. 1995. *Jewish State or Israeli Nation?* Bloomington: Indiana University Press.

Ezrahi, Yaron. 1993. "Democratic Politics and Culture in Modern Israel: Recent Trends." In E. Sprinzak and L. Diamond, eds., *Israeli Democracy under Stress*, pp. 255–272. Boulder: Lynne Rienner,

Ezzat, Dina. 1998. "Balancing the Barcelona Process." *Al-Ahram Weekly* 380, June 4, 1998.

———. 1999. "For Reconciliation." *Al-Ahram Weekly* 437, July 8, 1999.

———. 2000. "Barcelona Process Survives Hijacking." *Al-Ahram Weekly* 513, December 21, 2000.

Fahmy, Ninette S. 1998. "The Performance of the Muslim Brotherhood in the Egyptian Syndicates: An Alternative Formula for Reform?" *Middle East Journal* 52(4): 551–562.

Fassi Fihri, Taïb. 2002. "Intervention de M. Taib Fassi Fihri, Secrétaire d'État aux Ministère des Affaires Étrangères et de la Coopération à la Conférence Ministérielle Euro-Méditerranéenne (Barcelone V), Valencia 23 avril 2002." Rabat: Ministry of Foreign Affairs.

Fenech, Dominic. 1997. "The Relevance of European Security Structures to the Mediterranean (and Vice Versa)." *Mediterranean Politics* 2(1): 149–176.

Fergany, Nader. 1995. *Egyptians and Politics: Analysis of an Opinion Poll.* Cairo: Al-Mishkat Center for Research

Ferrié, Jean-Noël. 2000. "Les politiques de la morale en Egypte et au Maroc." *Monde Arabe Maghreb-Machrek* 167: 6–13.

Finnemore, Martha. 1996. "Norms, Culture, and World Politics: Insights from Sociology's Institutionalism." *International Organization* 50(2): 325–347.

FMES (Fondation Méditerranéenne d'Etudes Stratégiques), et al., eds. 1997. *Méditerranée: Le pacte à construire.* Collection Strademed no. 3. Paris: Publisud.

Foreign Ministry of Egypt. 1994. "Proposals for Euro-Mediterranean Cooperation in the Framework of the Barcelona Process Presented by the Arab Republic of Egypt." Cairo: Ministry of Foreign Affairs.

———. 2002a. "A Unified Arab Stand in Valencia, Valencia: 22 April 2002." Cairo: Ministry of Foreign Affairs.

———. 2002b. "Statement on Free Trade Area for Arab Mediterranean Countries, Egyptian-Jordanian Initiative, Rabat, 9 May 2001." Cairo: Ministry of Foreign Affairs.

Foreign Ministry of Israel. 1997. "Ministry of Foreign Affair's Response to the Luxembourg Declaration, December 13, 1997." Jerusalem: Ministry of Foreign Affairs.

Friedman, Menachem. 2001. "A People that Dwells Alone." *Ha'aretz*, New Year supplement, September 17, 2001: B9.

Gamblin, Sandrine. ed. 1997. *Contours et détours du politique en Égypte: Les élections législatives de 1995*. Paris: L'Harmattan, and Cairo: CEDEJ.

Garcìa, Soledad, ed. 1993. *European Identity and the Search for Legitimacy*. London: Pinter.

Geertz, Clifford. 1968. *Islam Observed: Religious Development in Morocco and Indonesia*. New Haven: Yale University Press.

Gerges, Fawaz A. 1995. "Egyptian-Israeli Relations Turn Sour." *Foreign Affairs* 47(3): 69–79.

———. 2000. "The End of the Islamist Insurgency in Egypt? Costs and Prospects." *Middle East Journal* 54(4): 592–612.

———. 2002. "What's behind the New Arab Momentum." *The New York Times*, March 15, 2002, 23.

Gershoni, Israel. 1977. *Major Trends in the Evolution of the Egyptian National Self-Image 1900–1945*. Haifa: Haifa University Press.

———. 1981. *The Emergence of Pan-Arabism in Egypt*. Tel Aviv: Shiloah Center for Middle Eastern and African Studies, Tel Aviv University.

Gershoni, Israel, and James P. Jankowski, eds. 1997. *Rethinking Nationalism in the Arab Middle East*. New York: Columbia University Press.

Gertz, Nurith. 1984. "The Few against the Many." *The Jerusalem Quarterly* 30 (Winter): 94–104.

Ghalioun, Burhan. 2000. "Islam, laïcité et modernité: l'exemple des sociétés arabes contemporaines." *Confluences Méditerranée* 33 (Spring): 25–34.

Ghanem, As'ad. 1997. "The Palestinians in Israel, Part of the Problem and not the Solution: Their Status if Peace Comes." In T. Hermann and E. Yuchtman-Yaar, eds., *Israeli Society and the Challenge of Transition to Co-existence*, pp. 55–62. Tel Aviv: Tami Steinmetz Center for Peace Research, Tel Aviv University.

Gillespie, Richard. 2006. "A Political Agenda for Region-Building? The EMP and Democracy Promotion in North Africa." In E. Adler, F. Bicchi, B. Crawford, and R. Del Sarto, eds., *The Convergence of Civilizations? Constructing a Mediterranean Region*, pp. 83–108. Toronto: University of Toronto Press

———. ed. 1996. *Mediterranean Politics*, vol. 2. London: Pinter.

Gilpin, Robert G. 1981. *War and Change in World Politics*. New York: Cambridge University Press.

Goldgeier, James M. 1997. "Psychology and Security." *Security Studies* 6(4): 137–166.

Goldstein, Judith, and Robert O. Keohane. 1993a. "Ideas and Foreign Policy: An Analytical Framework." In J. Goldstein and Keohane, eds., *Ideas and Foreign Policy: Beliefs, Institutions, and Political Change*, pp. 3–30. Ithaca and London: Cornell University Press.

———, eds. 1993b. *Ideas and Foreign Policy: Beliefs, Institutions, and Political Change*. Ithaca and London: Cornell University Press.

Goodman, Russel B., ed. 1995. *Pragmatism: A Contemporary Reader*. New York: Routledge.

Goweili, Ahmad. 1998. "Nous devons mettre les points sur les i avec nos amis européens." Interview with Ahmad Goweili. *Al-Ahram Hebdo*, French edition, August 12, 1998.

Gresh, Alain. 1998. "Turkish-Israeli-Syrian Relations and their Impact on the Middle East." *Middle East Journal* 52(2): 188–203.

Gresh, Alain, and Tariq Ramadan. 2002. *L'Islam en questions: Débat animé et présenté par François Germain-Robin*. 2nd edition. Arles: Babel/Actes Sud.

Grilli, Enzo R. 1993. *The European Community and the Developing Countries*. Cambridge: Cambridge University Press.

Gross-Stein, Janice. 1999. "Ungluing 'Sticky' Identities: Beyond War—and Peace." Paper presented at the conference on *Identities in Transition from War to Peace*, November 30–December 1, 1999, Jerusalem: Hebrew University.

Guazzone, Laura. 1996. "The Evolving Framework of Arab Security Perceptions: The Impact of Cultural Factors." *The International Spectator* 31(4): 63–74.

Haas, Ernst B. 1993. "Nationalism: An Instrumental Social Construction." *Millennium* 22(3): 505–545.

Haas, Peter M. 1989. "Do Regimes Matter? Epistemic Communities and Mediterranean Pollution Control." *International Organization* 43(3): 376–403.

Habermas, Jürgen. 1994. *Erkenntnis und Interesse*. 11th edition. Frankfurt a. M.: Suhrkamp.

Hadash. 2002. "Party Platform, December 2002." At <http://www.hadash.org.il> (in Hebrew and Arabic); accessed March 31, 2005.

Haddadi, Said. 2006. "Securitisation and Democratisation in the Maghreb: Ambiguous Discourses and Fine-tuning Practices for a Security Partnership," in E. Adler, F. Bicchi, B. Crawford, and R. Del Sarto, eds., *The Convergence of Civilizations: Constructing a Mediterranean Region*, pp. 168–190. Toronto: University of Toronto Press.

Halliday, Fred. 2000. *Nation and Religion in the Middle East*. London: Saqi Books.

Hammond, Andrew. 2000. "Egypt Causes Washington Concern." *The Middle East* 300 (April): 15–16.

Hammoudi, Abdellah. 1997. *Master and Disciple. The Cultural Foundations of Moroccan Authoritarianism*. Chicago and London: University of Chicago Press.

Hanafi, Hassan. 1990. "De l'orientalisme à l'occidentalisme." *Peuples Méditerranéens* 50: 115–119.

Hanna, Milad. 1994. *The Seven Pillars of the Egyptian Identity*. Cairo: General Egyptian Book Organization.

———. 1998. "Renovation through Globalization." *Al-Ahram Weekly* 381, June 11, 1998.

Harris, David Zev. 1999. "Party Platforms 1999." *The Jerusalem Post*, Elections Supplement, May 11, 1999: 4.

Harris, George S. 1995. "Republic of Turkey." In D. Long and B. Reich, eds., *The Governments and Politics of the Middle East and North Africa*, 3rd edition, pp. 8–40. Boulder, Co.: Westview Press.

Hassan II. 1993. *La mémoire d'un Roi: Entretien avec Éric Laurent*. Paris: Plon.

Hassan II. 1996. "Discours du Trône 1996." Rabat: Ministry of Communication.
———. 1997a. "Message Royal aux participants au troisième sommet économique et social euro-méditerranéen." Rabat: Ministry of Communication.
———. 1997b. "Sa Majesté offre un dîner en l'honneur du Président Italien Oscar Luigi Scalfaro, 19/3/1997." Rabat: Ministry of Communication.
———. 1998. "Discours du Trône 1998." Rabat: Ministry of Communication.
———. 1999. "Discours du Trône 1999." Rabat: Ministry of Communication.
Hazan, Reuven Y., and Gideon Rahat. 2000. "Representation, Electoral Reform, and Democracy. Theoretical and Empirical Lessons from the 1996 Elections in Israel." *Comparative Political Studies* 33(10): 1310–1336.
Hegasy, Sonja. 1997. *Staat, Öffentlichkeit und Zivilgesellschaft in Marokko: Die Potentiale der sozio-kulturellen Opposition*. Hamburg: Deutsches Orient-Institut.
Heikal, Mohamed H. 1983. *Autumn of Fury: The Assassination of Sadat*. New York: Random House.
———. 1993. *Illusions of Triumph: An Arab View of the Gulf War*. London: Harper Collins.
Heller, Marc. 2000. "Weapons of Mass Destruction and Euro-Mediterranean Politics of Arms Control: An Israeli Perspective." *Mediterranean Politics* 5(1): 158–166.
———. 2004. "The Lesser Middle East Initiative." *International Herald Tribune*, June 11, 2004.
Hermann, Tamar, and Ephraim Yuchtman-Yaar, eds. 1997. *Israeli Society and the Challenge of Transition to Co-existence*. Tel Aviv: Tami Steinmetz Center for Peace Research, Tel Aviv University.
Hinnebusch, Raymond A. 1984. "The Reemergence of the Wafd Party: Glimpses of the Liberal Opposition in Egypt." *International Journal of Middle East Studies* 16(1): 99–121.
Hoffman, Mark. 1991. "Restructuring, Reconstruction, Reinscriptions, Rearticulations: Four Voices in Critical International Theory." *Millennium* 20(2): 169–185.
Hogg, Michael A., and Dominic Abrams. 1988. *Social Identifications: A Social Psychology of Intergroup Relations and Group Processes*. London: Routledge.
Hollis, Martin. 1994. *The Philosophy of Social Science: An Introduction*. Cambridge: Cambridge University Press.
Hollis, Martin, and Steve Smith. 1992. *Explaining and Understanding International Relations*. Oxford: Clarendorf Press.
Horowitz, Dan. 1993. "The Israeli Concept of National Security." N A. Yaniv, ed., *National Security and Democracy in Israel*, pp. 11–53. London: Lynne Rienner.
Hourani, Albert. 1983. *Arabic Thought in the Liberal Age, 1789–1939*. 2nd edition. Cambridge: Cambridge University Press.
Howe, Marvine. 2001. "Fresh Start for Morocco." *Middle East Policy* 8(2): 59–65.
Howeidy, Amira. 1999. "Against Normalization." *Al-Ahram Weekly* 437, July 8, 1999.
Hudson, Michael C. 1977. *Arab Politics: The Search for Legitimacy*. New Haven: Yale University Press.
Huntington, Samuel P. 1996. *The Clash of Civilizations and the Remaking of World Order*. New York: Simon & Schuster.

Husayn, Taha. 1954. *The Future of Culture in Egypt*. Washington: American Council of Learned Societies.

Ibrahim, Saad Eddin. 1993. "Crises, Elites, and Democratization in the Arab World." *Middle East Journal* 47(2): 292–305.

———. 1998. "The Trouble Triangle: Populism, Islam, and Civil Society in the Arab World." *International Political Science Review* 19(4): 373–385.

Ilan, Shahar. 2000. "Second Only to Joseph Caro." *Ha'aretz*, Week's End Supplement, English edition, October 6, 2000: B6–B7.

IMF (International Monetary Fund). 1992. *Direction of Trade Statistics*. Washington: International Monetary Fund.

Inbar, Efraim. 1996. "Contours of Israel's New Strategic Thinking." *Political Science Quarterly* 111(1): 41–64.

Isen, Galip. 1998. "The Politics of Being Mediterranean: What Hope is there for Peace in the Northeastern Mediterranean?" Paper presented to the 3rd Pan-European International Relations Conference and Joint Meeting with the International Studies Association, Vienna, September 16–19, 1998.

Jamaï, Aboubakr. 2001. "Dérive autoritaire du gouvernement marocain." *Le Monde Diplomatique*, January 2001: 8–9.

James, William. 1995. "Pragmatism." In R. Goodman, ed., *Pragmatism: A Contemporary Reader*, pp. 53–75. New York: Routledge.

Jankowski, James P. 1997. "Arab Nationalism in 'Nasserism' and Egyptian State Policy, 1952–1958." In I. Gershoni and J. Jankowski, eds., *Rethinking Nationalism in the Arab Middle East*, pp. 75–66. New York: Columbia University Press.

Jervis, Robert. 1976. *Perception and Misperception in International Politics*. Princeton: Princeton University Press.

Joffé, George. 1996. "Integration or Peripheral Dependence: The Dilemma Facing the South Mediterranean States." In A. Bin, ed., *Co-operation and Security in the Mediterranean: Prospects after Barcelona*, pp. 175–197. Malta: The Mediterranean Academy of Diplomatic Studies.

———. 2001. "EMP Watch, Progress in the Barcelona Process: Report on Public and Private Attitudes towards the Euro-Mediterranean Partnership amongst the 27 Members" *EuroMeSCo Publication*, September 2001.

Julien, Charles-André. 1978. *Le Maroc face aux Impérialismes, 1416–1956*. Paris: Editions Jeune Afrique.

Jünemann, Annette. 2001. "Die EU und der Barcelona-Prozess: Bewertung und Perspektiven." *Integration* 24(1): 42–57.

Kably, Mohamed. 1999. "Legitimacy of State Power and Socioreligious Variations in Medieval Morocco." In R. Bourqia and S. Miller, eds., *In the Shadow of the Sultan: Culture, Power, and Politics in Morocco*, pp. 17–29. Cambridge: Harvard University Press.

Kagan, Robert. 2003. *Of Paradise and Power. America and Europe in the New World Order*. New York: Alfred A. Knopf.

Kamrava, Mehran. 1999. "What Stands between the Palestinians and Democracy." *Middle East Quarterly* 6(2): 3–12.

Karsh, Efraim, and Yezid Sayigh. 1994. "A Co-operative Approach to Arab-Israeli Security." *Survival* 36(1): 114–125.

Kasaba, Reşat, and Sibel Bozdoğan. 2000. "Turkey at a Crossroad." *Journal of International Affairs* 54(1): 1–20.

Katsav, Moshe. 2001. "Nice Guy. Interview with President Moshe Katsav by Amira Segev." *Ha'aretz Magazine*, April 27, 2001: 14–17.

Katzenstein, Peter J. 1996a. "Introduction: Alternative Perspectives on National Security." In P. Katzenstein, ed., *The Culture of National Security: Norms and Identity in World Politics*, pp. 1–32. New York: Columbia University Press.

———, ed. 1996b. *The Culture of National Security: Norms and Identity in World Politics*. New York: Columbia University Press.

Kelman, Herbert C. 1998. "Israel in Transition from Zionism to Post-Zionism." *Annals of the American Academy of Political and Social Science* 555: 46–61.

Keohane, Robert O. 1984. *After Hegemony: Cooperation and Discord in the World Political Economy*. Princeton: Princeton University Press.

———. 1986a. "Realism, Neo-realism and the Study of World Politics." In R. Keohane, ed., *Neorealism and Its Critics*, pp. 1–26. New York: Columbia University Press.

———. 1986b. "Theory of World Politics: Structural Realism and Beyond." In R. Keohane, ed., *Neorealism and Its Critics*, pp. 158–203. New York: Columbia University Press.

———, ed. 1986c. *Neorealism and Its Critics*. New York: Columbia University Press.

Kepel, Gilles. 1993. *Le prophète et pharaon: Aux sources des mouvements islamistes*. Paris: Seuil.

Kerr, Malcolm H. 1971. *The Arab Cold War: Gamal 'Abd al-Nasir and his Rivals*. 3rd edition. London: Royal Institute of International Affairs and Oxford University Press.

Khalidi, Ahmed S. 1996. "The Palestinian's First Excursions into Democracy." *Journal of Palestine Studies* 4(Summer): 20–28.

Khalil, Nevine. 1998. "Cairo's Answer to 'Peace Now.'" *Al-Ahram Weekly* 375, April 30, 1998.

Khallaf, Rania. 1998. "A Long Shadow." *Al-Ahram Weekly* 401, October 29, 1998.

Khene, Djamel Eddine. 1997. "Cross-line Gas Projects Face Daunting Challenges." *Oil and Gas Journal* 95(50): 33–39.

Kienle, Eberhard. 1995. "Arab Unity Schemes Revisited: Interest, Identity, and Policy in Syria and Egypt." *International Journal of Middle Eastern Studies* 27(1): 53–71.

———. 1998a. "Destabilization through Partnership? Euro-Mediterranean Relations after the Barcelona Declaration." *Mediterranean Politics* 3(2): 1–20.

———. 1998b. "More than a Response to Islamism: The Political Deliberalization of Egypt in the 1990s." *Middle East Journal* 52(2): 219–235.

———. 2001. *A Grand Delusion: Democracy and Economic Reform in Egypt*. London: I. B. Tauris.

Kimmerling, Baruch. 1993. "State Building, State Autonomy and the Identity of Society: The Case of the Israeli State." *Journal of Historical Sociology* 6(4): 396–429.

———. 1998. "Between Hegemony and Dormant *Kulturkampf* in Israel." *Israel Affairs* 4(3–4): 49–72.

King, Robert J. 1999. "Regime Type, Economic Reform, and Political Change in Tunisia." In Y. Zoubir, ed., *North Africa in Transition: State, Society, and Economic Transformation in the 1990s*, pp. 61–76. Gainsville, Fl.: University of Florida Press.

Kliot, N. 1989. "Accommodation and Adjustment to Ethnic Demands: The Mediterranean Framework." *The Journal of Ethnic Studies* 17(2): 45–70.

Kodmani-Darwish, Bassama. 1998. "Pulsions et impulsions: l'euro-méditerranée comme enjeu de société." *Politique Étrangère* 1/1998: 35–49.

Kohnstamm, Max, and Winfried Hager, eds. 1973. *A Nation Writ Large? Foreign Policy Problems before the European Communities*. London: Macmillan.

Korany, Bahgat, and Ali E. Hilal Dessouki, eds. 1991. *The Foreign Policy of Arab States: The Challenge of Change*. Boulder, Co.: Westview Press.

Kowert, Paul, and Jeffrey Legro. 1996. "Norms, Identity, and Their Limits: A Theoretical Reprise." In P. Katzenstein, ed., *The Culture of National Security: Norms and Identity in World Politics*, pp. 451–497. New York: Columbia University Press.

Krämer, Gudrun. 1986. *Ägypten unter Mubarak: Identität und nationales Interesse*. Baden-Baden: Nomos.

Krasner, Stephen D. 1982. "Structural Causes and Regime Consequences: Regimes as Intervening Variables." *International Organization* 36(2): 185–205.

———. 1993. "Westphalia and All That." In J. Goldstein and R. Keohane, eds., *Ideas and Foreign Policy: Beliefs, Institutions, and Political Change*, pp. 235–264. Ithaca and London: Cornell University Press.

Kubálková, Vendulka, Nicholas Onuf, and Paul Kowert. 1998a. "Constructing Constructivism." In V. Kubálková, N. Onuf, and P. Kowert, eds., 1998b, *International Relations in a Constructed World*, pp. 3–21. Armonk, N.Y.: M. E. Sharpe.

———, eds. 1998b. *International Relations in a Constructed World*. Armonk, N.Y.: M. E. Sharpe.

Laffan, Brigid. 1996. "The Politics of Identity and Political Order in Europe." *Journal of Common Market Studies* 34(1): 81–102.

Landau, Emily. 2003. *The Middle East Arms Control Process, 1992–95: The Construction of a Strategic Game*. Ph.D. Dissertation. Department of International Relations, Jerusalem: Hebrew University.

Lapid, Yosef. 1989. "The Third Debate: On the Prospects of International Theory in a Post-positivist Era." *International Studies Quarterly* 33(3): 235–254.

———. 1996. "Culture's Ship: Returns and Departures in International Relations Theory." In Y. Lapid and F. Kratochwil, eds., *The Return of Culture and Identity in IR Theory*, pp. 3–20. Boulder, Co.: Lynne Rienner.

Lapid, Yosef, and Friedrich Kratochwil, eds. 1996. *The Return of Culture and Identity in IR Theory*. Boulder, Co.: Lynne Rienner.

Laroui, Abdallah. 1977. *Les origines sociales et culturelles du nationalisme marocain, 1830–1912*. Paris: Maspero.

Layachi, Azzedine. 1999. "Economic Reform and Elusive Political Change in Morocco." In Y. Zoubir, ed., *North Africa in Transition: State, Society, and Economic Transformation in the 1990s*, pp. 43–60. Gainsville, Fl.: University of Florida Press.

Leveau, Rémy. 1985. *Le fellah marocain: Défenseur du trône*. 2nd edition. Paris: Presses de la Fondation Nationale des Sciences Politiques.

———. 1997. "Morocco at the Crossroads." *Mediterranean Politics* 2(2): 95–113.

———. 1998. "Réussir la transition démocratique au Maroc." *Le Monde Diplomatique*, November 1998: 14–15

Levy, David. 2000. "Address by Foreign Minister Levy before the EU-Israel Association Council, 13 June 2000." Jerusalem: Ministry of Foreign Affairs.

Lewis, Bernard. 1998. *The Multiple Identities of the Middle East*. New York: Schocken.

Liel, Alon. 2001. Speech delivered at the conference on "Current European and Israeli Perspectives on the Mediterranean Concept," organized by the EU-Israel Forum, the Interdisciplinary Center Herzliya, and the Van Leer Jerusalem Institute, March 8, 2001, Jerusalem.

Likud. 1999. "Party Platform 1999." At <http://www.likud.org.il/da/default.asp> (in Hebrew), accessed January 24, 2004.

Linklater, Andrew. 1990. "The Problem of Community in International Relations." *Alternatives* 15: 135–153.

———. 1992. "The Question of the Next Stage in International Relations Theory: A Critical-Theoretical Point of View." *Millennium* 21(1): 77–98.

Lister, Marjorie. 1997. *The European Union and the South: Relations with Developing Countries*. London and New York: Routledge.

Llobera, Josep R. 1993. "The Role of the State and the Nation in Europe." In S. Garcìa, ed., *European Identity and the Search for Legitimacy*, pp. 64–80. London: Pinter.

Lombardi, Clark Benner. 1998. "Islamic Law as Source of Constitutional Law in Egypt: The Constitutionalization of the Sharia in a Modern Arab State." *Columbia Journal of Transnational Law* 37(1): 81–124.

Long, David E., and Bernard Reich, eds. 1995. *The Governments and Politics of the Middle East and North Africa*. 3rd edition. Boulder, Co.: Westview Press.

Lübben, Ivesa, and Issam Fawzi. 2000. "Ein neuer islamischer Parteienpluralismus in Ägypten? Hizb al-Wasat, Hizb al-Shari'a and Hizb al-Islah als Fallbeispiele." *Orient* (Hamburg) 41(2): 229–283.

Luciani, Giacomo, ed. 1990. *The Arab State*. London: Routledge.

Luciani, Giacomo, and Ghassan Salamé, eds. 1987. *The Politics of Arab Integration*. London: Croom Helm.

Mafdal. 2005. "Party Platform." At <http://www.mafdal.org.il/?sid=4> (in Hebrew), accessed March 26, 2005.

Maghraoui, Abdeslam. 2001. "Political Authority in Crisis in Mohammed VI's Morocco." *Middle East Report* 218, Spring.

Maher, Ahmed. 2001a. "Statement upon Conclusion of the Euro-Mediterranean Conference: Foreign Minister Maher Rules out Regional Cooperation with Israel, Brussels, 6 November 2001." Cairo: Ministry of Foreign Affairs.

———. 2001b. "Statements by Foreign Minister Ahmed Maher on Meeting with Palestinian High Official, British Ambassador to Egypt, the Upcoming Euro-Mediterranean Meeting in Brussels, Cairo, 29 October 2001." Cairo: Ministry of Foreign Affairs.

Makram-Ebeid, Mona. 2001. "Egypt's 2000 Parliamentary Elections." *Middle East Policy* 8(2): 32–44.

Malka, Victor. 1978. *La mémoire brisée des Juifs du Maroc*. Paris: Editions Entente.

Manicas, Peter. 1998. "A Realist Social Science." In M. Archer et al., eds., *Critical Realism: Essential Readings*, pp. 313–338. London and New York: Routledge.

Manners, Ian. 2002. "Normative Power Europe: A Contradiction in Terms?" *Journal of Common Market Studies* 40(2): 235–258.

Mansour, Abdellatif. 2001. "L'Europe vote Maghreb." *Maroc Hebdo International* 472, July 6, 2001: 4–5.

Maoz, Zeev. 1997. "Regional Security in the Middle East: Past Trends, Present Realities, and Future Challenges." *The Journal of Strategic Studies* 20(1): 1–45.

Marquina, Antonio, and Hans Günter Brauch, eds. 1994. *Confidence Building and Partnership in the Western Mediterranean: Tasks for Preventive Diplomacy and Conflict Avoidance*. UNISCI Papers 1, Madrid: UNISCI.

Martín-Muñoz, Gema. 2000. "Political Reform and Social Change in the Maghreb." *Mediterranean Politics* 5(1): 96–130.

Mednicoff, David M. 1998. "Civil Apathy in the Service of Stability? Cultural Politics in Monarchist Morocco." *Journal of North African Studies* 3(4): 1–27.

Medzini, Meron, ed. 1976–1995. *Israel's Foreign Relations: Selected Documents*. 14 volumes. Jerusalem: Ministry of Foreign Affairs.

Meretz. 2001. "Party Platform." At <http://www.meretz.org.il/HomePage.htm> (in Hebrew), accessed August 13, 2001 (this site no longer exists).

Merlingen, Michael, Cas Mudde, and Ulrich Sedelmeier. 2001. "The Right and the Righteous? European Norms, Domestic Politics and the Sanctions against Austria." *Journal of Common Market Studies* 39(1): 61–79.

Mernissi, Fatima. 1994. *Women and Islam: A Historical and Theological Enquiry*. Translated by Mary Jo Lakeland. 4th edition. Oxford: Blackwell.

Merom, Gil. 1999. "Israel's National Security and the Myth of Exceptionalism." *Political Science Quarterly* 114(3): 409–434.

Ministry of Economic Prevision and Planning of Morocco. 2000. *Plan de Développement 2000–2004*. Rabat: Ministry of Economic Prevision and Planning.

Mohammed VI. 2000a. "Message Royal aux participants au colloque organisé a Rabat à l'occasion de la célébration de la journée nationale de la diplomatie marocaine, Vendredi 28 avril 2000. Rabat: Ministry of Foreign Affairs.

———. 2000b. "Allocution de SM Le Roi lors du dîner offert en son honneur par le Président Italien. Mardi, 11 avril 2000)." Rabat: Ministry of Foreign Affairs.

———. 2000c. "Allocution de S.M. le Roi Mohammed VI lors du dîner offert en l'honneur du Souverain par le Président Jacques Chirac, Lundi 20 mars 2000 au Palais de l'Elysée." Rabat: Ministry of Foreign Affairs.

———. 2000d. "Discours de S. M. le Roi Mohammed VI au dîner de gala offert en son honneur par S. M. le Roi Juan Carlos 1er, Madrid, 18 septembre 2000." Rabat: Ministry of Foreign Affairs.

———. 2001a. "Discours de Sa Majesté Le Roi Mohammed VI à l'occasion du deuxième anniversaire de l'intronisation du Souverain, Tanger, 30/7/2001." Rabat: Ministry of Foreign Affairs.

Mohammed VI. 2001b. Interview with Mohammed VI, *Le Figaro*, September 4, 2001.

———. 2001c. Interview with Mohammed VI, *Paris-Match*, November 1, 2001.

———. 2002. "Discours de Sa Majesté le Roi Mohammed VI à la nation à l'occasion du 27ème anniversaire de la Marche Verte, Rabat, 6 November 2002." Rabat: Ministry of Foreign Affairs.

———. 2003a. "Discours de Sa Majesté le Roi Mohammed VI à l'occasion du 28ème anniversaire de la Marche Verte, Meknes 6 November 2003." Rabat: Ministry of Foreign Affairs

———. 2003b: "Deuxième année législative de la 7ème législature: Code de la Famille, 11/10/03." Rabat: Ministry of Foreign Affairs.

Moheiddin, Khaled. 1995. "Seeking a New Style: Interview with Khaled Moheiddin." *Al-Ahram Weekly* 245, November 2, 1995.

Mohsen-Finan, Khadija. 2002. "The Western Sahara Dispute under UN Pressure." *Mediterranean Politics* 7(2): 1–12.

Moravcsik, Andrew. 1997. "Taking Preferences Seriously: A Liberal Theory of International Politics." *International Organization* 51(4): 513–553.

Morgenthau, Hans Joachim. 1967. *Politics among Nations: The Struggle for Power and Peace*. 4th edition. New York: Alfred A. Knopf.

Morris, Benny. 1999. *Righteous Victims. A History of the Zionist-Arab Conflict, 1881–1999*. New York: Alfred A. Knopf.

Mortimer, Robert A. 1999. "The Arab Maghreb Union: Myth and Reality." In Y. Zoubir, ed., *North Africa in Transition: State, Society, and Economic Transformation in the 1990s*, pp. 177–191. Gainsville, Fl.: University of Florida Press.

Moussa, Amr. 1995. "Statement by H.E. Amr Moussa, Minister of Foreign Affairs of the Arab Republic of Egypt before the Euro-Mediterranean Ministerial Conference, Barcelona, 27 November 1995." Cairo: Ministry of Foreign Affairs.

———. 1997. "Statement by H.E. Amr Moussa, Minister for Foreign Affairs of the Arab Republic of Egypt, before the Second Euro-Mediterranean Conference, Malta, April 1997." Cairo: Ministry of Foreign Affairs.

———. 1998. "Emerging Economies of the Arab World—The Golden Shores of Investment," Luncheon speech by Foreign Minister Amr Moussa at the Euromoney Conference, Cairo, September 15, 1998. Cairo: Ministry of Foreign Affairs.

———. 2000. "Foreign Minister Amr Moussa Praises the Outcome of the Euro-Mediterranean Meeting Underlining the Importance of Arab Participation, Marseilles, 16 November 2000." Cairo: Ministry of Foreign Affairs.

Mubarak, Hosni. 2002a. Interview with Hosni Mubarak. *Yoman*, Weekly News Magazine, Israel TV Channel 1, March 15, 2002, 18 h GTM.

———. 2002b. "Egyptian President Interviewed on Arab Summit Issue." Interview with Hosni Mubarak. *MENA* News Agency (Cairo), March 26, 2002.

Müller, Björn 1993. "Security Concepts: New Challenges and Risks." In A. Marquina and H. G. Brauch, eds., *Confidence Building and Partnership in the Western Mediterranean: Tasks for Preventive Diplomacy and Conflict Avoidance*, pp. 3–49. Madrid: UNISCI.

Munson, Henry Jr. 1993. *Religion and Power in Morocco*. New Haven and London: Yale University Press.

Nafie, Ibrahim. 1999. "A Culture of Cooperation." *Al-Ahram Weekly* 417, February 18, 1999.

Najjar, Fauzi M. 2001. "Book Banning in Contemporary Egypt." *The Muslim World* 92(3–4): 399–424.

NDP (National Democratic Party). 2003. "NDP Principles." At <http://www.ndp.org.eg/aboutus/en/aboutus_2_1.htm>, accessed April 4, 2005.

Netanyahu, Binyamin. 1996. "Address by Prime Minister-elect Netanyahu to *Likud* Meeting, 2 June 1996." Jerusalem: Ministry of Foreign Affairs.

Netanyahu, Binyamin, and Ariel Sharon. 1999. "Reaction by Prime Minister Netanyahu and Foreign Minister Sharon on the EU Statement on Jerusalem, 25 March 1999." Jerusalem: Ministry of Foreign Affairs.

Neumann, Iver B. 1994. "A Region-Building Approach to Northern Europe." *Review of International Studies* 20(1): 53–74.

———. 1996. "Self and Other in International Relations." *European Journal of International Relations* 2(2): 139–174.

Newman, David. 1997. "Conflicting Israeli Peace Discourses." *Peace Review* 9(3): 417–424.

Nicolaidis, Kalypso, and Robert Howse. 2002. " 'This is my EUtopia . . .': Narrative as Power." *Journal of Common Market Studies* 40(4): 767–792.

Norton, Anne. 1988. *Reflections on Political Identity*. Baltimore: Johns Hopkins University Press.

Nye, Joseph S. Jr., and Sean M. Lynn-Jones. 1988. "International Security Studies: A Report of a Conference on the State of the Field." *International Security* 12(4): 5–27.

Ohana, David. 1999. "Israel towards a Mediterranean Identity." In S. Avineri and W. Weidenfeld, eds., *Integration and Identity: Challenges to Europe and Israel*, pp. 81–99. Bonn: Europa Union.

Onuf, Nicholas G. 1989. *World of Our Making: Rules and Rule in Social Theory and International Relations*. Columbia, S.C.: University of South Carolina Press.

Oz, Amos. 1998. *Kol Ha-Tikvot* (All Our Hopes). Jerusalem: Keter.

Parfitt, Trevor. 1997. "Europe's Mediterranean Design: An Analysis of the Euromed Relationship with Special Reference to Egypt." *Third World Quarterly* 18(5): 865–882.

Patten, Chris. 1999a. "Interview with Chris Patten, EU Commissioner for External Relations." *Euromed Special Feature* December 11, 1999.

———. 1999b. "Relations between the EU and Morocco." Speech delivered during the Debate on Morocco in the European Parliament, Brussels, October 1, 1999. Speech/99/139, RAPID database at <http://europa.eu.int>, accessed June 6, 2001.

———. 2000. "The European Union's External Policy and the Mediterranean," Speech delivered at the Egyptian Council for Foreign Relations, Cairo, Egypt, April 1, 2000. At <http://europa.eu.int/comm/external_relations/news/patten/speech_00_116.htm>, accessed May 11, 2001.

Patten, Chris. 2002. Speech of Chris Patten, EU Commission for External Relations, on the Barcelona Process and the Middle East before the European Parliament Plenary, April 24, 2002. At <http://europa.eu.int/comm/external_relations/news/speech/02/178.htm, accessed August 23, 2002.

Peleg, Ilan. 1997. "The Peace Process and Israel's Political Culture." In A. Dowty et al., eds., *The Role of Domestic Politics in Israeli Peace-Making*, pp. 13–24. Jerusalem: Leonard Davis Institute for International Relations, Hebrew University of Jerusalem.

Pennell, C. R. 2000. *Morocco since 1830: A History*. London: C. Hurst & Co.

Peres, Shimon (with Arye Naor). 1993. *The New Middle East*. New York: H. Holt.

Peres, Shimon. 1995. "Address in the Knesset by Foreign Minister Peres Welcoming European Parliamentary Assembly Council President Martinez, 24 January 1993." In M. Medzini, ed., 1995, *Israel's Foreign Relations: Selected Documents*, vol. 13–14: 1992–1994, document 52, pp. 166–168. Jerusalem: Ministry of Foreign Affairs.

Peres, Shimon, Anna Lindh, and Chris Patten. 2001. "Statement Following a Meeting of Foreign Minister Peres with President-in-office of the EU, Swedish Foreign Minister Anna Lindh and EU Commissioner for External Relations Chris Patten, Jerusalem, 13 March 2001." Jerusalem: Ministry of Foreign Affairs.

Peretz, Don, and Gideon Doron. 2000. "Sectarian Politics and the Peace Process: The 1999 Israeli Elections." *Middle East Journal* 54(2): 259–273.

Perlmutter, Amos. 1990. "Israel's Dilemma." *Foreign Affairs* 68(5): 119–132.

Perthes, Volker. 1996. "Security Perceptions and Cooperation in the Middle East: The Political Dimension." *The International Spectator* 31(4): 53–62.

———. 2002. *Geheime Gärten: Die neue arabische Welt*. Berlin: Siedler.

Peters, Joel. 1996. *Pathways to Peace: The Multilateral Arab-Israeli Peace Process*. London: Royal Institute of International Affairs.

Pioppi, Daniela. 2004 : "L'Egitto dell'*infitah*: Quale liberalizzazione?" In F. Bicchi, L. Guazzone, and D. Pioppi, eds., *La Questione della Democrazia nel Mondo Arabo: Stati, società e conflitti*, pp. 271–289. Monza: Polimetrica.

Price, Richard, and Christian Reus-Smit. 1998. "Dangerous Liaisons? Critical International Theory and Constructivism." *European Journal of International Relations* 4(3): 259–294.

Putnam, Hilary. 1995. "The Many Faces of Realism." In R. Goodman, ed., *Pragmatism: A Contemporary Reader*, pp. 163–181. New York: Routledge.

Putnam, Robert D. 1988. "Diplomacy and Domestic Politics: The Logic of Two-Level Games." *International Organization* 42(3): 427–460.

Quine, Willard van Orman. 1963. *From A Logical Point of View: 9 Logico-Philosophical Essays*. 2nd revised edition. New York: Harper Torchbooks.

Rabin, Itzhak. 1976. "Statement to the Knesset by Prime Minister Rabin, 3 June 1974." In M. Medzini, ed., 1976, *Israel's Foreign Relations: Selected Documents*, vol. 1–2: 1947–1974, document 31, pp. 1136–1143. Jerusalem: Ministry of Foreign Affairs.

———. 1995a. "Address by Prime Minister Rabin to the United Nations General Assembly, 24 October 1995." Jerusalem: Ministry of Foreign Affairs.

———. 1995b. "Address by PM Rabin at the National Defense College, 12 August 1993." In M. Medzini, ed., 1995, *Israel's Foreign Relations: Selected Documents*, vol. 13: 1992–1994, document 101, pp. 297–300. Jerusalem: Ministry of Foreign Affairs.

———. 1995c. "Address to the Knesset by Prime Minister Rabin Presenting his Government, 13 July 1992." In M. Medzini, ed., 1995, *Israel's Foreign Relations: Selected Documents*, vol. 13–14: 1992–1994, document 1, pp. 1–9. Jerusalem: Ministry of Foreign Affairs.

Ramsès, Basil. 1997. "Le Tagammu' et les elections." In S. Gamblin, ed., *Contours et détours du politique en Égypte : Les élections législatives de 1995*, pp. 166–195. Paris: L'Harmattan, and Cairo: CEDEJ.

Regelsberger, Elfriede, Philippe de Schoutheete de Tervarent, and Wolfgang Wessels, eds. 1997. *Foreign Policy of the European Union: From EPC to CFSP and beyond*. Boulder, Co.: Lynne Rienner.

Roberson, Barbara A. 1998a: "Islam and Europe. An Enigma or a Myth?" In B. A. Roberson, ed., *The Middle East and Europe: The Power Deficit*, pp. 104–129. London and New York: Routledge.

———, ed. 1998b. *The Middle East and Europe: The Power Deficit*. London and New York: Routledge.

Roque, Maria-Àngels, ed. 1997. *Identidades y conflicto de valores. Diversidad y mutación social en el Mediterráneo*. Barcelona: Institut Català de la Mediterrània d'Estudis y Cooperació.

———. 2004. *La société civile au Maroc: l'émergence de nouveaux acteurs de développement*. Paris: Publisud.

Rosenblum, Doron. 2002. "The Philosophy and Thematics of Janana." *Ha'aretz Magazine*, English edition, January 24, 2002: 5.

Roumani, Ronda. 2004. "New Party Hopes to be Liberal Voice of Egypt." *The Daily Star*, August 20, 2004.

Rubinstein, Amnon. 1980. *Me'Herzl ve'ad Gush Emunim u've'chazara* (From Herzl to Gush Emunim and Back). Tel Aviv: Schocken.

Ruggie, John G. 1993. "Territoriality and Beyond. Problematizing Modernity in International Relations." *International Organization* 47(1): 139–174.

———. 1998. "What Makes the World Hang Together? Neo-Utilitarianism and the Social Constructive Challenge." *International Organization* 52(4): 855–885.

Sachar, Howard M. 1999. *Israel and Europe: An Appraisal in History*. New York: Alfred A. Knopf.

Sadiki, Larbi. 2000. "Popular Uprisings and Arab Democratization." *International Journal of Middle East Studies* 32(1): 71–95.

Said Aly, Abdel Monem. 1996. "The Shattered Consensus: Arab Perceptions of Security." *The International Spectator* 31(4): 23–52.

Said, Abdel Monem. 1999. "Twenty Years of the Peace Dividend." *Al-Ahram Weekly* 421, March 18, 1999.

Said, Edward W. 1995. *Orientalism: Western Conceptions of the Orient*. 2nd edition. London: Penguin Books.

Salamé, Ghassan. 1994a. "Torn between the Atlantic and the Mediterranean: Europe and the Middle East in the Post-Cold War Era." *Middle East Journal* 48(2): 226–249.

Salamé, Ghassan. 1994b. *Democracy without Democrats? The Renewal of Politics in the Muslim World*. London: I. B. Tauris.

Sami, Aziza. 2001. "Tahsin Bashir, the Great Communicator." *Al-Ahram Weekly* 551, September 13, 2001.

Sandler, Shmuel. 1993. *The State of Israel, the Land of Israel: The Statist and Ethnonational Dimensions of Foreign Policy*. London: Greenwood Press.

Sayari, Sabri. 2000. "Turkish Foreign Policy in the Post-Cold War Era. The Challenge of Multi-Regionalism." *Journal of International Affairs* 54(1): 169–182.

Schimmelfennig, Frank. 2001. "The Community Trap: Liberal Norms, Rhetorical Action, and the Eastern Enlargement of the European Union." *International Organization* 55(1): 47–80.

Schumacher, Tobias, and Michelle Pace, eds. 2005. *Conceptualising Cultural Dialogue and Social Relations in the Euro-Mediterranean Area*, Mediterranean Politics, Special Issue (10) November 3, 2005.

Searle, John R. 1995. *The Construction of Social Reality*. London: Penguin Books.

Sela, Avraham. 1998. *The Decline of the Arab-Israeli Conflict: Middle East Politics and the Quest for Regional Order*. Albany: State University of New York Press.

Selim, Mohammed El-Sayed. 1995. "Mediterraneanism: A New Dimension in Egypt's Foreign Policy." *Strategic Papers* 27, Cairo: Al-Ahram Center for Political and Strategic Studies.

———. 1997. "Egypt and the Euro-Mediterranean Partnership: Strategic Choice or Adaptive Mechanism?" *Mediterranean Politics* 2(1): 64–90.

———. 2000. "Towards a New WMD Agenda in the Euro-Mediterranean Partnership: An Arab Perspective." *Mediterranean Politics* 5(1): 133–157.

Sfeir, George N. 1998. "Basic Freedoms in a Fractured Legal Culture: Egypt and the Case of Nasr Hamid Abu Zayd." *Middle East Journal* 52(3): 402–414.

Shamir, Itzhak. 1989. "Interview with Prime Minister Shamir," *The Jerusalem Post*, January 13, 1989.

Shankland, David. 1999. *Islam and Society in Turkey*. Hemingford Grey: The Eothen Press.

Shapiro, Yonathan. 1993. "The Historical Origins of Israeli Democracy." In E. Sprinzak and L. Diamond, eds., *Israeli Democracy under Stress*, pp. 65–80. Boulder: Lynne Rienner.

Sharabi, Hisham. 1988. *Neopatriarchy: A Theory of Distorted Change in Arab Society*. New York: Oxford University Press.

Sharon, Ariel. 1999. "Reaction by FM Sharon to EU Decision, 22 February 1999." Jerusalem: Ministry of Foreign Affairs.

———. 2001. "Sharon Is Sharon Is Sharon," Interview with Ariel Sharon by Ari Shavit. *Ha'aretz Magazine*, English Edition, April 13, 2001: 10–15.

Sharon, Ariel, and Miguel Ángel Moratinos. 1999. "Summary of a Meeting between Foreign Minister Sharon and EU Envoy Moratinos, 29 January 1999." Jerusalem: Ministry of Foreign Affairs.

Shavit, Ya'acov. 1988. "The Mediterranean World and 'Mediterraneanism': The Origins, Meaning, and Application of a Geo-Cultural Notion in Israel." *Mediterranean Historical Review* 3(2): 96–117.

Sheperd, Naomi. 1994. "Ex-Soviet Jews in Israel: Asset, Burden, or Challenge?" *Israel Affairs* 1(2): 245–266.

Sherif, Muzafer. 1966. *In Common Predicament: Social Psychology of Intergroup Conflict and Cooperation*. Boston: Houghton Mifflin.

Shinui. 2005. "Shinui's Principles." At <http://www.shinui.org.il/elections/eng/principles.html>, accessed March 15, 2005.

Shlaim, Avi. 2000. *The Iron Wall: Israel and the Arab World*. London, New York: Allen Lane, The Penguin Press.

Sid-Ahmed, Mohamed. 1999. "Normalization." *Al-Ahram Weekly* 438, July 15, 1999.

———. 2000. "Mediterraneanism and Middle-Easternism." *Al-Ahram Weekly* 508, November 16, 2000.

Siddiqi, Moin A. 2000. "Egypt: Financial Report." *Middle East* 298 (February): 37–39.

Singerman, Diane. 2002. "The Politics of Emergency Rule in Egypt." *Current History* 101(651): 29–35.

Smooha, Sammy. 1993. "Class, Ethnic, and National Cleavages and Democracy in Israel." In E. Sprinzak and L. Diamond, eds., *Israeli Democracy under Stress*, pp. 309–342. Boulder, Co.: Lynne Rienner.

———. 1998. "The Implications of the Transition to Peace for Israeli Society." *The Annals of the American Academy of Political and Social Science* 555 (January): 26–45.

Sobelman, Daniel. 2000. "Denunciation of Israel for Internal Use Only." *Ha'aretz*, March 26, 2000.

Solingen, Etel. 2003. "The Triple Logic of the European-Mediterranean Partnership: Hindsight and Foresight." *International Politics* 40(2): 179–194.

Spiteri, Anna. 1994. "Remote Sensing: The Toll of Integrated Coastal Zone Management. Towards Peace in the Mediterranean." In F. Tanner, ed., *Arms Control, Confidence-Building and Security Cooperation in the Mediterranean, North Africa and the Middle East*, pp. 143–152. Valletta: The Mediterranean Academy of Diplomatic Studies.

Springborn, Robert. 1989. *Mubarak's Egypt: Fragmentation of the Political Order*. Boulder, Co.: Westview Press.

Sprinzak, Ehud. 1997. "The Shaping of the Israeli Right and Its Current Attitudes." In A. Dowty et al., eds., *The Role of Domestic Politics in Israeli Peace-Making*, pp. 35–39. Jerusalem: Leonard Davis Institute for International Relations, Hebrew University of Jerusalem.

Sprinzak, Ehud, and Larry Diamond, eds. 1993. *Israeli Democracy under Stress*. Boulder, Co.: Lynne Rienner.

Stacher, Joshua A. 2001. "A Democracy with Fangs and Claws and its Effects on Egyptian Political Culture." *Arab Studies Quarterly* 23(3): 83–99.

Staloff, Robert. 1988. *Army and Politics in Mubarak's Egypt*. Washington, D.C.: Washington Institute for Near East Policy.

Suleiman, Michael W. 1985. "Socialization to Politics in Morocco: Sex and Regional Factors." *International Journal of Middle East Studies* 17 (August 6, 1985): 313–327.

Sullivan, Denis J., and Sana Abed-Kotob. 1999. *Islam in Contemporary Egypt.* Boulder, Co.: Westview Press.

Tajfel, Henri, ed. 1982. *Social Identity and Intergroup Relations.* Cambridge: Cambridge University Press.

Tamir, Yael. 1999. "The Quest for Identity." In S. Avineri and W. Weidenfeld, eds., *Integration and Identity: Challenges to Europe and Israel*, pp. 9–25. Bonn: Europa Union.

Tanner, Fred, ed. 1994. *Arms Control, Confidence-Building and Security Cooperation in the Mediterranean, North Africa and the Middle East.* Valletta: The Mediterranean Academy of Diplomatic Studies.

Tayfur, Fatih. 2002. "Turkish Perceptions of the Mediterranean." *EuroMeSCo Papers*, March 8, 2002.

Tickner, J. Ann. 1996. "Identity in International Relations Theory: Feminist Perspectives." In Y. Lapid and F. Kratochwil, eds., *The Return of Culture and Identity in IR Theory*, pp. 147–162. Boulder, Co.: Lynne Rienner.

Tocci, Nathalie, and Ahmed Evin, eds., 2004. *Towards Accession Negotiations: Turkey's Domestic and Foreign Policy Challenges Ahead.* Florence: European University Institute, RSCAS.

Tonra, Ben, and Thomas Christiansen, eds. 2004. *Rethinking European Union Foreign Policy.* Manchester: Manchester University Press.

Tovias, Alfred. 1977. *Tariff Preferences in Mediterranean Diplomacy.* London: Macmillan.

———. 1996. "The EU's Mediterranean Policies under Pressure." In R. Gillespie, ed., *Mediterranean Politics*, vol. 2, pp. 9–25. London: Pinter.

———. 1997. "The Economic Impact of the Euro-Mediterranean Free Trade Area on Mediterranean Non-Member Countries." *Mediterranean Politics* 2(1): 113–128.

———. 2006. "Economic Liberalism between Theory and Practice." In E. Adler, F. Bicchi, B. Crawford, and R. Del Sarto, eds., *The Convergence of Civilizations: Constructing a Mediterranean Region*, pp. 191–211. Toronto: University of Toronto Press.

Tozy, Mohamed. 1999. *Monarchie et Islam Politique au Maroc.* Paris: Presses de la Fondation Nationale des Sciences Politiques.

———. 2000a. "Le Nouveau Règne ou nouveau régime: les enjeux de la succession." *Les cahiers de l'Orient* 58(2): 51–66.

———. 2000b. "Où vont les Islamistes?" Interview with Mohamed Tozy. *L'Express*, November 16, 2000.

Ullman, Richard. 1983. "Redefining Security." *International Security* 8(1): 129–153.

UNDP. 2003. *Egypt Human Development Report 2003.* Kalyoub (Egypt): *Al-Ahram* Commercial Press.

———. 2005. *Arab Human Development Report 2004: Towards Freedom in the Arab World.* Amman: National Press.

UNIDIR. 1995. *National Threat Perceptions in the Middle East.* Research paper 37. New York and Geneva: United Nations.

UNODC, and Royaume du Maroc. 2003. *Maroc: Enquête sur le Cannabis 2003*, December, Vienna: UNODC.

Vatikiotis, Panayiotis Jerasimof. 1978. *Nasser and His Generation.* New York: St. Martin's Press.

———. 1998. "Europe and Islam." In T. Veremis and D. Triantaphyllou, eds., *The Southeast European Yearbook, 1997–98,* pp. 5–24. Athens: Hellenic Foundation for European and Foreign Policy.

Veremis, Thanos M., and Dimitrios Triantaphyllou, eds. 1998. *The Southeast European Yearbook, 1997–98.* Athens: Hellenic Foundation for European and Foreign Policy.

Vertzberger, Yaakov. 1990. *The World in Their Minds: Information Processing, Cognition and Perception in Foreign Policy Decisionmaking.* Stanford: Stanford University Press.

Waever, Ole. 1996. "European Security Identities." *Journal of Common Market Studies* 34(1): 103–132.

Walker, R. B. J. 1988. "Genealogy, Geopolitics and Political Community: Richard K. Ashley and the Critical Social Theory on International Relations." *Alternatives* 13(1): 94–144.

Walt, Stephen M. 1991. "The Renaissance of Security Studies." *International Studies Quarterly* 35(2): 211–239.

Waltz, Kenneth N. 1979. *Theory of International Politics.* Reading: Addison-Wesley.

Waterbury, John. 1970. *The Commander of the Faithful: The Moroccan Political Elite, A Study of Segmented Politics.* London: Weidenfeld and Nicholson.

———. 1983. *The Egypt of Nasser and Sadat: The Political Economy of Two Regimes.* Princeton: Princeton University Press.

Weaver, Mary Anne. 2001. "Egypt on Trial." *New York Times Magazine,* June 17, 2001: 46–55.

Weber, Max. 1922. *Gesammelte Aufsätze zur Wissenschaftslehre,* Tübingen: J. C. B. Mohr.

———. 1972. *Wirtschaft und Gesellschaft. Grundriß der verstehenden Soziologie.* 5th revised edition. Tübingen: J. C. B. Mohr.

Weissbrod, Lilly. 1997. "Israeli Identity in Transition." *Israel Affairs* 3(3–4): 47–65.

Weizman, Ezer. 1998. "Interview with Ezer Weizman." *Spectrum* (Monthly Journal of the Israeli Labour Party), June 6, 1998: 10.

Wendt, Alexander. 1992. "Anarchy is What States Make of It: The Social Construction of Power Politics." *International Organization* 46(2): 391–425.

———. 1994. "Collective Identity Formation and the International State." *American Political Science Review* 88(2): 384–396.

———. 1995. "Constructing International Politics." *International Security* 20(1): 71–81.

———. 1999. *Social Theory of International Politics.* Cambridge: Cambridge University Press.

White, Gregory. 2001. *A Comparative Political Economy of Tunisia and Morocco: On the Outside of Europe Looking In.* Albany, NY.: State University of New York Press.

Willis, Michael J. 2000. "Between Alternance and the Makhzen: At-Tawhid wa Al-Islah's Entry into Moroccan Politics." *Journal of North African Studies* 4(3): 45–80.

———. 2004. "Morocco's Islamists and the Legislative Elections of 2002: The Strange Case of the Party That Did Not Want to Win." *Mediterranean Politics* 9(1): 53–81.

Wintle, Michael, ed. 1996. *Culture and Identity in Europe: Perceptions of Divergence and Unity in Past and Present*. Aldershot: Avebury.

Wolfers, Arnold. 1962. *Discord and Collaboration: Essays on International Politics*. Baltimore: Johns Hopkins University Press.

World Bank. 1996. *Growing Faster, Finding Jobs: Choices for Morocco*. Washington, D.C.: World Bank.

Yachad. 2005. "Party Platform." At <www.yachadparty.org.il>, accessed March 30, 2005.

Yaniv, Avner, ed. 1993. *National Security and Democracy in Israel*. London: Lynne Rienner.

Yavuz, Hakan M. 2000. "Cleansing Islam from the Public Sphere." *Journal of International Affairs* 54(1): 21–42.

Youssoufi, Abderrahman. 1998. "8ème assise des barreaux de la Méditerranée, Meknès 25/09/1998." Rabat: Office of the Prime Minister.

———. 1999. "Allocution de M. Abderrahman Youssoufi, Premier Ministre du Royaume du Maroc, prononcée à l'occasion du Colloque Maroc-Europe: un destin commun, Brussels, 21 August 1999." Rabat: Office of the Prime Minister.

———. 2000. "Colloque International organisé par l'Association Marocaine des Anciens Élèves de l'École Polytechnique Française, Casablanca, 19 March 2000." Rabat: Office of the Prime Minister.

———. 2001. "Allocution de M. le Premier Ministre Abdrerrahman Youssoufi à l'occasion de la cérémonie de signature des conventions financières entre le Maroc et l'Union Européenne, Rabat, 14 January 2001." Rabat: Office of the Prime Minister.

Zakariya, Fouad. 1991. *Laïcité ou Islamisme: Les Arabes à l'heure du choix*. Traduit de l'arabe et présenté par Richard Jacquemond. Paris: La Découverte, and Cairo: Al-Fikr.

Zartman, I. William. 1983. "Explaining the Nearly Inexplicable: The Absence of Islam in Moroccan Foreign Policy." In A. Dawisha, ed., *Islam in Foreign Policy*, pp. 97–111. Cambridge, U.K.: Cambridge University Press.

———. 1988. "Opposition as Support for the State." In A. Dawisha and I. W. Zartman, eds., *Beyond Coercion: The Durability of the Arab State*, pp. 61–87. London: Croom Helm and Instituto Affari Internazionali.

Zeghal, Malika. 1996: *Gardiens de l'Islam: Les oulémas d'Al Azhar dans l'Egypte contemporaine*. Paris: Presse de la Fondation Nationale de Sciences Politiques.

Zerubavel, Yael. 1995. *Recovered Roots. Collective Memory and the Making of Israeli National Tradition*. Chicago: University of Chicago Press.

Zoubir, Yahia H. 1999a. "State and Civil Society in Algeria." In Y. Zoubir, ed., *North Africa in Transition: State, Society, and Economic Transformation in the 1990s*, pp. 29–42. Gainsville, Fl.: University of Florida Press.

———. 1999b. "The Geopolitics of the Western Sahara Conflict." In Y. Zoubir, ed., *North Africa in Transition: State, Society, and Economic Transformation in the 1990s*, pp. 195–211. Gainsville, Fl.: University of Florida Press.

———, ed. 1999c. *North Africa in Transition: State, Society, and Economic Transformation in the 1990s*. Gainsville, Fl.: University of Florida Press. University of Florida Press.

Index

(Page numbers in *italics* indicate figures.)

4 + 5 Dialogue, *59*
5 + 5 Dialogue, *59*
9/11, 4, 9, 231–232, 235, 243
   Egypt and, 142, 159, 166, 170
   Euro-Mediterranean relations and
      the EMP since, 71–73
   international relations and,
      17–20, 84
   Israel and, 126–129
   Morocco and, 188, 197, 202,
      205, 210, 216–217
   regional security and, 27–28
   "war on terror" and, 81–82

Abbas, Mahmoud. *See* Abu Mazen
Abu Mazen, 63–64
Abu Zayd, Nasr Hamid, 145,
   149–150, 242
ACRS (Arms Control and Regional
   Security), 60, 137
   See also Madrid peace process
Agadir Declaration, 65, 70, 169,
   197, 203, 206
Agadir Process. *See* Agadir
   Declaration
Ajami, Fouad, 22–23, 62, 75, 78,
   134, 136–138, 143, 145, 151,
   163, 168, 212, 241
AKP, 22, 79
Al-Ahram Weekly, 66, 137, 147, 151,
   155–158, 162–165, 167, 170–171
Alaoui, Mohamed Ben El Hassan.
   See King Mohammed VI

Al-Ashmawy, Mohammed Said, 22,
   148–149
Al-Banna', Hassan, 137, 143
Al-Baz, Osama, 157, 165
Algeria
   CSCM and, 59–60
   EU and, 17, 199
   Morocco and, 181–182, 188, 194,
      203, 206–207, 218
   Oslo peace process and, 62
   political reform and, 19–20,
      67–68, 74, 76, 170
   regional relations, 227,
      235–238, 243
   UMA initiative and, 64–65
Al-Ghad party, 141, 144, 147, 149,
   170–171
Al-Fassi, Abbas, 184, 212, 215
Al-Jabri, Mohammed 'Abed, 145,
   171, 186–188, 213–214, 216
Al-Qaeda, 81, 147, 159
Al-Sadawi, Nawal, 145
Amazigh, 182, 186
   See also Berbers
Anna Lindh Foundation, 17, 71
Arab–Israeli conflict, 10, 14, 20, 62,
   64, 96, 119, 131, 153, 169,
   174, 192, 207–208, 226
Arab–Israeli peace process, 30, 82
   See also Madrid peace process;
      ACRS
   See also Oslo peace process;
      Oslo accords

Arab Mediterranean states
  domestic politics, 73–82
  Islamism and, 75–78
  political liberalization efforts,
    73–75
Arafat, Yasser, 62–63, 75, 77,
  113, 231
Arms Control and Regional Security.
  See ACRS
Ashkenazim, 93, 101–102, 124
Avineri, Shlomo, 92, 94, 97, 101, 118

Baghdad Pact, 133
Baker, James, 207
Barak, Ehud, 63, 99, 104, 119, 121
baraka, 178–179, 189, 243
Barcelona Conference, 9, 60, 107,
  154, 195
Barcelona Process, 1–2, 4, 11,
  14–17, 19, 28, 60, 65–66,
  68–69, 82–83, 105, 107–108,
  111, 113, 117, 124, 155, 172,
  196, 200, 205, 222–224, 227
  See also EMP
Basri, Driss, 182
Bassim, Wafa'a, 157
Bayoumi, Gamal, 158
Begin, Menachem, 90, 94–95, 97
Beilin, Yossi, 121
Belarbi, Aïcha, 198, 201
Benaïssa, Mohamed, 68, 70, 196,
  198–199, 204
Ben-Ami, Shlomo, 119–121
Ben-Barka, Mehdi, 182, 184
Ben-Gurion, David, 89–90
Benikrane, Abdelillah, 209, 214
Berbers, 76, 81, 179, 182–183, 187,
  189
  See also Amazigh
Berlusconi, Silvio, 3, 166
Bloom, William, 24, 44–46, 51
Bourguiba, Habib, 74
Bourqia, Rahma, 178, 182
Bush, George W., 3, 34, 42, 72, 210

Camp David accords, 58, 136–137,
  150, 152, 161, 163–164, 168
Campbell, David, 24, 34, 47
censorship, 78, 145, 170
Chekrouni, Nouzha, 205
Chirac, Jacques, 209, 217
cold war, 3, 10–11, 21, 23, 25, 27,
  29–30, 34, 56, 64, 66, 153,
  191, 236
  Mediterranean politics after,
    59–61
collective identities, 43–45, 53
Common Agricultural Policy (CAP),
  193–194
Common Foreign and Security
  Policy (CFSP), 60
Conference on Security and
  Co-operation in Europe. *See* CSCE
  See also Helsinki Final Act
Conference on Security and
  Co-operation in the
  Mediterranean. *See* CSCM
constructivism, 31, 33–34, 38–41,
  53, 222, 229–230, 237
contested state identities, 48–52
  alleviating factors and, 50, 52
  foreign policy, regional security,
    and, 50–52
  "triggering" developments and,
    49, 52
  variables affecting, 48–50
critical theory, 34, 236
CSCE (Conference on Security and
  Co-operation in Europe), 10,
  21, 56, 59
CSCM (Conference on Security and
  Co-operation in the
  Mediterranean), 59–60
  4 + 5 Dialogue, 59
  5 + 5 Dialogue, 59
Cyprus, 19, 64, 69, 117, 160

Delors, Jacques, 201
De Michelis, Gianni, 59

democratization, 18, 20, 68, 70, 74,
    107, 111–12, 118, 159–161,
    172, 174, 211–214, 227
  See also reform, political
Dessouki, Ali Hillal, 135–137, 150, 152
domestic identity conflicts, 3, 25–27,
    49–52, 54, 87, 102, 114, 126,
    129, 145, 150, 163, 174–175,
    177, 224–225, 227–228, 231
domestic politics
  Arab Mediterranean states, 73–82
  Israel, 78–79
  Turkey, 79–80
Durkheim, Emile, 43–44

Eban, Abba, 90–91
EC (European Community), 10, 13,
    52, 55–59, 66, 105–106, 119,
    152–153, 193–194, 201
  See also EU
economic liberalization, 20, 68, 74,
    79, 135, 137, 166, 170.
  See also infitah policy
Egypt
  domestic reforms, 169–172
  economic policies, 147–148
  EMP and, 161–172
  EU and, 165–167
  independence movement, 132–133
  institutional factors and identity,
    139–142
  as Islamic state, 148–151
  Islamization of, 144–145
  Israel and, 161–165
  launching of EMP and, 153–155
  Mubarak era, 136–138
  Nasser era, 133–134
  pan-Arabism and, 138–139
  "place in the region," 167–169
  politics and, 142–144
  regional relations, 137–139,
    167–169
  relations with Europe, 151–153,
    155–160

  Sadat era, 134–136
  state identity of, 131–151
  umma, qawm, and "Egypt first",
    146–147
"Egypt first", 135, 146–147, 150,
    153, 163, 166
EIB (European Investment Bank),
    12, 18, 58, 197
EMP (Euro-Mediterranean
    Partnership)
  approach to Mediterranean
    security, 10–20
  cold war era, 55–56
  Egypt and, 161–172
  Euro-Mediterranean Association
    Agreements, 16, 67, 70, 108,
    157, 195
  EU and, 66–73: post–9/11, 71–73
  "identity manipulation" and,
    5, 46, 52, 115, 129, 150,
    161, 233
  Israel and, 105–113
  launching of, 107–108
  MEDA (*Mesures
    d'accompagnement*), 16, 18,
    68, 157, 159, 195, 197–199,
    202, 235–236, 242
  MEDA II, 18
  Morocco and, 195–200,
    216–217
  post-cold war era, 59–61
  security region, 2, 13, 25, 31, 40,
    51, 82, 129, 221, 223,
    230–232, 235
  setbacks, 20–23: *See also*
    Barcelona Process
ENP. *See* European Neighbourhood
    Policy
Entelis, John, 177, 179, 183–184,
    186, 189, 191
Eretz Israel, 90, 94, 96–97, 100,
    102–105, 116–117, 123
Erdogan, Recep Tayyip, 79
Essen Declaration, 106, 108

EU (European Union)
  and EMP partners, 66–73:
        post-9/11, 71–73
    Egypt and, 165–167
    ENP, 4, 9, 16, 19, 61, 221, 232
    ESDP, 112, 157
    Israel and, 108–112, 119–123
    Mediterranean policy, 10, 13, 17,
        25, 55–56, 60, 72–73, 109,
        111, 152, 194, 203
    Morocco and, 192–195, 196–200,
        208–210, 216–217
    normative power and the EMP,
        15–17
    See also EC
EU Commission, 10, 17–18, 60, 71,
        111, 159–60, 168, 195, 201
Euro-Arab Dialogue, 57, 59, 237
Euro-Mediterranean Association
        Agreements, 16, 67, 70, 108,
        157, 195
Euro-Mediterranean Partnership.
        See EMP
EuroMeSCo (Euro-Mediterranean
        Study Commission), 17, 65, 109
European Community. *See* EC
European Investment Bank. *See* EIB
European Neighbourhood Policy
        (ENP), 4, 9, 16, 19, 61, 221, 232
European Union. *See* EU
Ezrahi, Yaron, 80, 89

Foda, Farrag, 143, 145
fragmentation, domestic, 9, 22, 33,
        51, 80–83, 191, 228
free trade, 11–12, 16–17, 57, 65, 68,
        70, 105–106, 108, 111, 158,
        193, 195, 197

Gaza, withdrawal from, 61, 94–95,
        99, 104, 127, 161, 225
Ghessous, Azeddine, 193
Gibran, Khalil, 145
Global Mediterranean Policy.
        See GMP

globalization, 2, 11, 23, 81, 117
GMP (Global Mediterranean
        Policy), 57–58, 152
Goweili, Ahmad, 158, 165
Greater Middle East Initiative, 21
Greece, 19, 56, 58, 64, 69, 237–238
Gulf War, 59, 63, 137, 185, 192,
        242

Haidar, Haidar, 145
Hamas, 64, 77
Hammoudi, Abdallah, 178–179,
        181, 213
Hanna, Milad, 168, 171
Hassan II. *See* King Hassan II
Helsinki Final Act, 56
        See also CSCE
Herzl, Theodor, 89
Hizballah, 75, 77
Holocaust, 87–90, 92, 121,
        128, 222
human-rights issues, 11–12, 16–19,
        67–69, 75, 78, 110, 113, 118,
        123, 127, 141, 154, 159, 161,
        171, 181, 189, 199, 209
    See also democratization;
        women's rights
Huntington, Samuel, 3, 19
Husayn, Taha, 167–168
Hussain, 'Adel, 148

Ibrahim, Saad Eddin, 159–160
Ikhwan al-Muslimun. See Muslim
        Brotherhood
infitah policy, 74, 135, 138, 140,
        144, 147–148, 150, 164, 167,
        170, 174
    See also economic liberalization
international law, 12, 15, 110, 127
International Monetary Fund (IMF),
        73, 140, 185, 194
international relations theory
    constructivist approach, 33–34
    contested foundations of, 35–39
    critical theory, 34

culture, identity, and, 34–35
liberal approach, 31–32
liberal constructivism, 222
neo-liberalism, 30–32, 34
positivism, 34–35, 37–40, 53,
    236–237
realism and neo-realism, 29–32, 34
pragmatism, and, 38–39
scientific realism, and, 36–37
Intifada, 3–4, 9, 63–65, 67, 72, 74, 78,
    91, 94–95, 104, 106, 114,
    126–128, 137–138, 151, 161,
    164, 167, 173, 207–208, 210, 225
Iran, 58, 81, 185, 231
Iraq, 3, 21, 58–59, 72, 210, 232, 241
Islamism, 3, 11, 19, 22–23,
    71–72, 75–77, 79, 81, 83, 101,
    142–145, 147–151, 188–192,
    213–217
Israel
    9/11 and, 126–127
    contested state identity of,
        87–105: EMP and,
        114–116
    domestic policies, 78–79
    EMP, and, 105–113
    Eretz Israel, 90, 94, 96–97, 100,
        102–105, 116–117, 123
    EU and, 87, 105, 107, 111, 114,
        117, 119–123, 127, 129
    "Europeanist" foreign policy, 119,
        122
    Holocaust, 87–90, 92, 121, 128,
        222
    Medinat Israel, 96, 99, 103, 122
    Medinat kol ezraheiha, 100
    "place in the region", 116–119
    political parties, 97–99, 100–105
    quest for unity, 123–26
    religion, role of, 97–99
    relations to EU, 119–123
    regional relations, 113–122
    Zionism, 87–89, 91–100, 102–103,
        115, 124, 128, 133–135,
        146–147, 163, 192, 222

Istiqlal, 184, 187, 190–191, 212,
    214–216

Jabotinsky, Zeev, 92
Jettou, Driss, 191
jihad, 77, 149, 208, 211
Jordan
    domestic politics, 74, 77, 80
    EMP and, 65, 70
    EU and, 66–67
    Israel and, 62, 63, 91, 111, 137
Justice and Development Party.
    See PJD

Karim, Khalil 'Abd-el, 148
Katzenstein, Peter, 24, 28, 34, 45
Keohane, Robert, 30–31, 34
Kimmerling, Baruch, 22, 78, 89,
    93–94, 101, 125
King Hassan II, 178, 180–183, 185,
    189, 201, 204–207, 209, 212
King Hussein, 62, 137
King Mohammed V, 179, 181
King Mohammed VI, 70, 74,
    182–183, 190–191, 196,
    199–211, 215–216, 228
Kurds, 19, 23, 64, 78–81

Laffan, Brigid, 50, 124
Labour party (Israel), 88–90, 92–94,
    99, 102–104, 117, 119–122
Lebanon, 63, 65–66, 75, 77–78, 80,
    91, 105, 107, 109, 156
Lebanon War, 95
Levy, David, 119
liberal IR theory, 31–32
    objections to, 32
Libya, 19–20, 56, 59, 62, 64–65, 74,
    76–77, 146, 235, 238
Likud party, 94, 97, 102–104, 117,
    119–121, 123

Madrid peace process, 10, 21,
    59–62, 106–107, 137–138, 153
    See also Arab–Israeli peace process

Maghreb countries, 21, 58, 60,
    65–66, 81, 107, 152–153,
    178, 183, 194, 198, 201,
    204–206, 227
Maher, Ahmed, 155–156
Mahfuz, Naguib, 143, 164
Manners, Ian, 15
Martín-Muñoz, Gema, 75–76, 149,
    182, 185, 187
Mashreq countries, 58, 60, 152
MEDA (*Mesures
    d'accompagnement*), 16, 18, 68,
    157, 159, 195, 197–199, 202,
    235–236, 242
  MEDA II, 18
Mediterranean Action Plan
    (MAP), 56
MENA (Middle East and North
    Africa) conferences, 154
Mernissi, Fatima, 187
Misr al-fattah, 143
Mizrahim, 93, 101–102
Moratinos, Miguel Ángel, 106, 120
Moravcsik, Andrew, 24, 31–32
Morgenthau, Hans, 30
Morocco
  Arab–Israeli conflict and, 192,
      207–208
  cannabis production, 200–201
  consensus, 182–192
  domestic politics, 210–213
  EMP and, 195–200, 216–217
  EU and, 192–95, 196–200,
      208–210, 216–217
  foreign policy, 200–203
  historical background, 178–179
  Islam and, 215–216
  "place in the region", 204–206
  political parties, 186–190
  reform process, 181–182
  regional relations, 206–208
  royalty and identity, 182–183
  state identity of, 177–192
  symbolic politics, 179–181

  tradition vs. modernity, 213–215
  United States and, 210
Moussa, Amr, 67, 70, 138,
    154–158, 169
Mubarak, Gamal, 138
Mubarak, Hosni, 62, 77, 132,
    136–143, 145, 150–151,
    153–155, 159, 162, 165, 168,
    172–173, 225–226, 228
Munson, Henry, 178, 181, 184
Mursi, Mohammed, 170
Muslim Brotherhood (*Ikhwan al-
    Muslimun*), 77, 134, 140–141,
    143–144, 148, 164

Nasser, Gamal 'Abd-el, 131–140,
    143–144, 150, 152, 173–174, 225
Nasserists, 134, 136–138, 140, 144,
    146–148, 163–164, 166, 174
NATO (North Atlantic Treaty
    Organization), 2, 56, 60, 241
National-Democratic Party.
    See NDP
NDP (National-Democratic Party),
    138–142, 144, 149, 163, 168,
    171, 181
neo-liberalism, 30–32, 34
neo-realism, 30–31, 37, 236
Netanyahu, Binyamin, 62–63, 67,
    97, 104, 110, 120–122,
    125–126, 161
Neturei Kharta, 96
NGOs (nongovernmental
    organizations), 68, 109, 123,
    140, 186–187, 197, 217
Non-Proliferation Treaty (NPT), 62,
    137, 155
Nour, Ayman, 141–142, 172

Öcalan, Abdallah, 64
October War, 57, 91, 94,
    135–136, 241
  See also Yom Kippur/October War
Ohana, David, 124

OSCE (Organization for Security and
    Co-operation in Europe), 56
Oslo accords, 18, 60–63, 78, 95,
    104–107, 112, 119, 128, 154,
    156, 164, 174, 236
Oslo peace process. *See* Arab–Israeli
    peace process; Oslo accords
Oz, Amos, 124
Özal, Turgut, 79

Palestine Liberation Organization.
    See PLO
Palestinian Authority (PA), 61, 63,
    67, 72, 75, 77
pan-Arabism, 23, 81, 132–135,
    138–139, 143–144, 146
Peres, Shimon, 71, 83, 104, 106–107,
    116–117, 119–121, 123, 126,
    129, 153, 162–163, 192
Peri, Zohar, 111
PLO (Palestine Liberation
    Organization), 18, 61, 63, 75,
    91, 105, 113, 236
*Parti de la Justice et du
    Développement. See* PJD
Patten, Chris, 11, 16, 61, 72, 196
PJD (*Parti de la Justice et du
    Développement*, Justice and
    Development Party), 188,
    190–191, 209–210, 214, 216
PKK (Kurdistan Workers Party), 64
Polisario Front, 181, 207
    See also Western Sahara
positivism, 34–35, 37–40, 53,
    236–237
Powell, Colin, 210
Prodi, Romano, 17
Putnam, Hilary, 37

qawm, 132–133, 146, 150, 166

Rabin, Itzhak, 59, 62, 78, 89, 91,
    95, 98–99, 104, 106–107,
    115–116, 121, 125, 129, 231

realism, 29–32, 34, 36–39
reform, economic. *See* economic
    liberalization; *infitah* policy
reform, political, 20, 67, 69, 74, 77,
    82, 160, 170–172, 174, 181,
    185, 196, 202, 211, 213–214,
    216, 221, 227, 233
    See also democratization
region-building, EMP and,
    1–4, 9–10, 12–16, 21, 24–26,
    40, 53, 55, 87, 113, 127–129,
    131, 175, 221–222, 226,
    229–233, 235
regional hegemony, 133–134, 138,
    146, 154, 223–224
religious fundamentalism, 11, 25,
    58, 64, 77, 81, 143, 214, 235
Ruggie, John, 33–35, 46

Sadat, Anwar, 132, 134–137,
    139–140, 143, 147, 150, 152,
    163–164, 166–167, 173–174, 225
Sadiki, Larbi, 22, 73, 185
Said, Mohammed El-Sayed, 171
Said, Rif'at, 151
Salafi tradition, 133, 184, 186–187,
    189, 214, 216
Salamé, Ghassam, 58, 74, 81, 138
scientific realism, 36–37
Searle, John, 35–36, 237
security, Mediterranean, 1, 3, 10,
    12, 14–15, 20, 55–56, 59, 61,
    82, 129, 223, 230–131
security region, 2, 13, 25, 31, 40,
    51, 82, 129, 221, 223,
    230–232, 235
Seda, Hafez Abu, 141, 172
Sela, Avraham, 23, 73, 81, 134,
    136–137, 139, 144, 154, 163
Selim, Mohammed El-Sayed, 18, 60,
    66, 152–153, 155, 157–158,
    166, 169
Serfaty, Abraham, 182, 207
Shamir, Itzhak, 91, 104, 106, 122

shariʿa, 135, 138, 143–144,
148–149, 171, 180, 214, 216
sharifian rule, 178, 180, 181
Sharon, Ariel, 63, 67, 79, 90, 97,
104–105, 110, 120–122, 126–127
Shas party, 98, 102–104
Sherif, Muzafer, 44–46, 50
Shinui party, 100, 102
Shoukri, Ibrahim, 168
Six-Day War, 91
socialism, 22, 75–76, 88–89, 124,
133, 135, 139, 143–144,
147–148, 151, 166–167,
173–174, 184, 187–189
Solana, Javier, 120, 196
Southern Mediterranean states
domestic politics, 73–82
relations among, 61–66: outside
EMP, 65–66; within EMP,
61–65
Spain, 19, 56, 58–60, 72, 193–195,
199, 201, 237, 244–245
Springborn, Robert, 136–137,
142–144, 148
state identities
between nations and international
politics, 45–48
collective identities and, 43–45
contested, 48–52
definition of, 42–43
foreign policy, and, 47–48, 50–52
intervening variables, 48–50
functions of, 47–48, *48*
liberal-constructivist approach to,
39–43
regional security, and, 50–52
Suez Canal, 132–133
suicide bombings, 3, 63, 126
See also terrorism
Sunnis, 79–80
Syria
domestic politics, 74–76, 80
Egypt and, 134, 145, 156
EMP and, 17, 19, 65–66
EU and, 68

Israel and, 91, 107, 109
regional relations, 59, 62–66

Tagammuʿ, 142–144, 146–149, 151,
163–164, 166
Tantawi, Sheikh Mohammed
Sayed, 161
terrorism, 3, 221, 231, 233
effects on peace process, 62, 64
Egypt and, 142–143, 147, 159, 166
EMP and, 18–20, 71–72
Islamist movements and, 76–77,
81–82
Israel and, 95, 126–128
Morocco and, 199, 202, 210, 215
war against, 12
See also Al-Qaeda; *Hamas*
Tovias, Alfred, 11, 18, 20, 57–58,
67, 102, 118, 193
Tozy, Mohamed, 178–180, 186,
188–190, 211, 214
Tunisia
domestic politics, 74–76, 80
EC and, 56, 58–60
EMP and, 16
Morocco and, 193, 195, 197
regional relations, 62–66
Turkey
AKP, 22, 79
domestic policies, 79–81, 83
EMP and, 66
EU and, 68–69, 160
Islamism and, 22–23
Israel and, 19, 62–64, 111,
117–118
PKK, 64

UMA (Arab Maghreb Union), 21,
64–65, 203, 206
umma, 133, 146–147, 150, 160, 166
United Nations (UN), 64–65, 91–93,
110, 207
United Nations Environment
Programme (UNEP), 56
United States, 3, 83, 232–233

Egypt and, 137–138, 146–47,
150, 152–153, 160,
166, 173
EU and, 15
foreign policy and, 33, 35
Greater Middle East Initiative
and, 21
Gulf War and, 59
invasion of Iraq, 72–73
Israel and, 87, 97, 106–108, 117,
120, 127
Morocco and, 185, 192, 201,
207, 210
USFP (*Union Socialiste des Forces
Populaires*), 187, 189–191,
212, 215–216

Venice Declaration, 105

Wafd, 132, 143–144, 147–148,
150, 162–164, 166–167,
171
Wali, Yusuf, 164
Waltz, Kenneth, 30, 32
watan, 132, 138
Weber, Max, 38–39
Weidenfeld, Werner, 101, 118
Weissbrod, Lili, 23, 78, 88,
93, 117

Western Sahara, 64–65, 180–181,
188, 206–207, 218, 227
See also Polisario Front
Wendt, Alexander, 26, 33–35,
41–43, 45, 47, 237
WEU (West European Union), 60
WMDs (weapons of mass
destruction), 11–12, 18,
58, 138
women's rights, 144, 149, 182,
187, 214
See also democratization;
human-rights issues
World Bank, 185

Yassine, Abdessalam, 207, 209,
214–215
Yassine, Nadia, 185, 189
Yom Kippur/October War, 57, 91,
94, 105, 135–136
Youssoufi, Abderahman, 74, 187,
201–215, 207–210, 212

Zaghlul, Sa'ad, 132, 137
Zartman, I. William, 23, 138, 140,
182, 184, 186, 192
Zionism, 87–89, 91–94, 96–100,
102–103, 115, 124, 128,
133–135, 146–147, 163, 192, 222